INSIDERS' GUIDE® TO
THE JERSEY SHORE

Help Us Keep This Guide Up to Date

Every effort has been made by the authors, and editors to make this guide as accurate and useful as possible. However, many things can change after a guide is published—establishments close, phone numbers change, hiking trails are rerouted, facilities come under new management, etc.

We would love to hear from you concerning your experiences with this guide and how you feel it could be improved and be kept up to date. While we may not be able to respond to all comments and suggestions, we'll take them to heart, and we'll also make certain to share them with the authors. Please send your comments and suggestions to the following address:

The Globe Pequot Press
Reader Response/Editorial Department
P.O. Box 480
Guilford, CT 06437

Or you may e-mail us at:

editorial@globe-pequot.com

Thanks for your input, and happy travels!

Insiders' Guide®
to the Jersey Shore

By Lillian Africano and Nina Africano

Guilford, Connecticut

An imprint of The Globe Pequot Press

Copyright © 2002 by The Globe Pequot Press

Cover photo credit: Atlantic City Convention & Visitors Authority

Back cover photo credits (from left to right): Andrew Hassard; courtesy Cape May County Tourism; Sea Oaks Golf Club; Atlantic City Convention & Visitors Authority; Lillian Africano

Maps created by Geografx; ©The Globe Pequot Press

Library of Congress Cataloging-in-Publication Data

Africano, Lillian.
Insiders' guide to the Jersey shore / by Lillian Africano and Nina Africano.—1st ed.
p. cm.
Includes index.
ISBN 0-7627-2224-X
1. Atlantic Coast (N.J.)—Guidebooks. 2. New Jersey—Guidebooks. I. Africano, Nina.
II. Title.

F124.A79 A38 2002
917.4904′44—dc21

2002069317

Manufactured in the United States of America
First Edition/First Printing

Contents

Directory of Maps

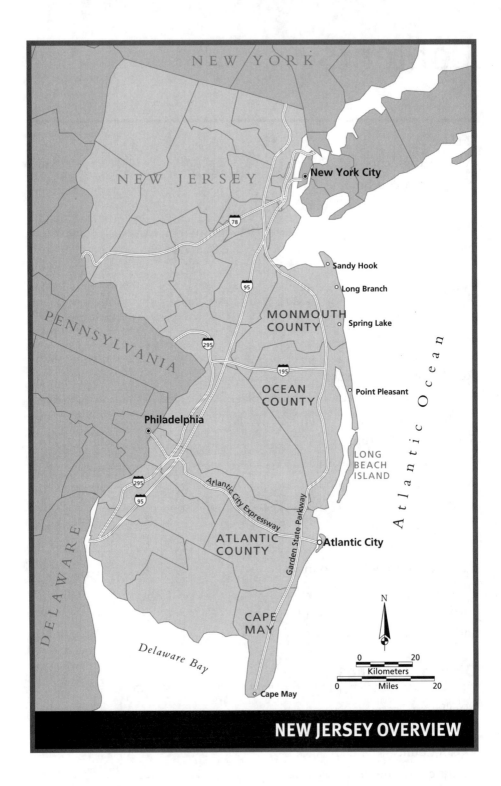

NEW JERSEY OVERVIEW

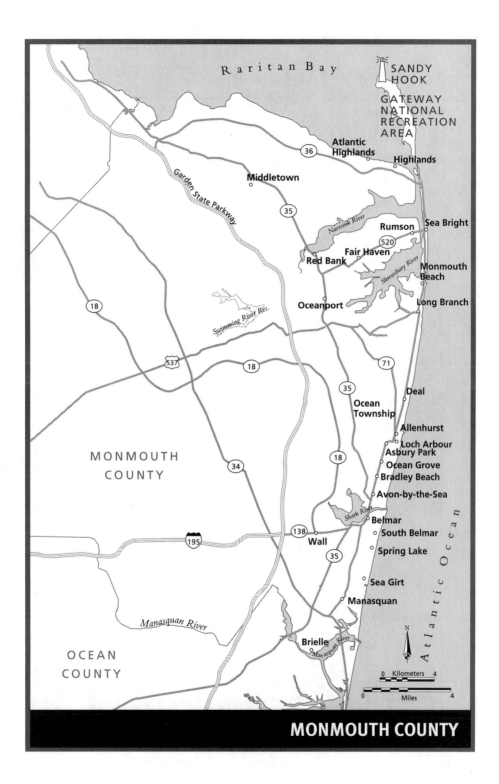

MONMOUTH COUNTY

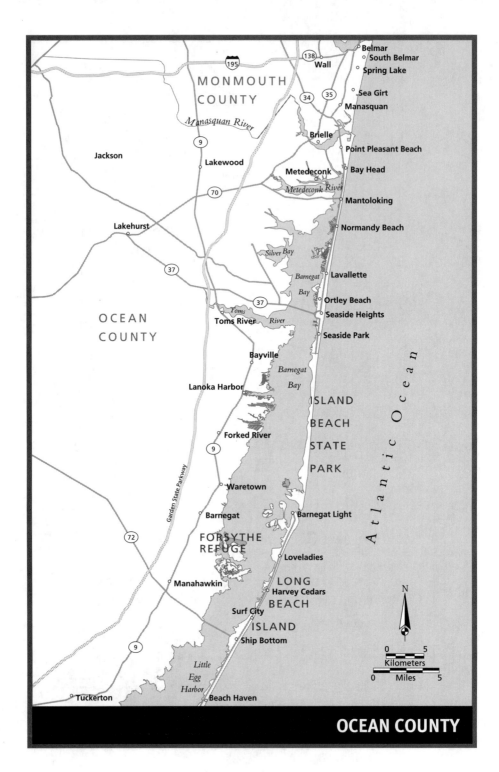

OCEAN COUNTY

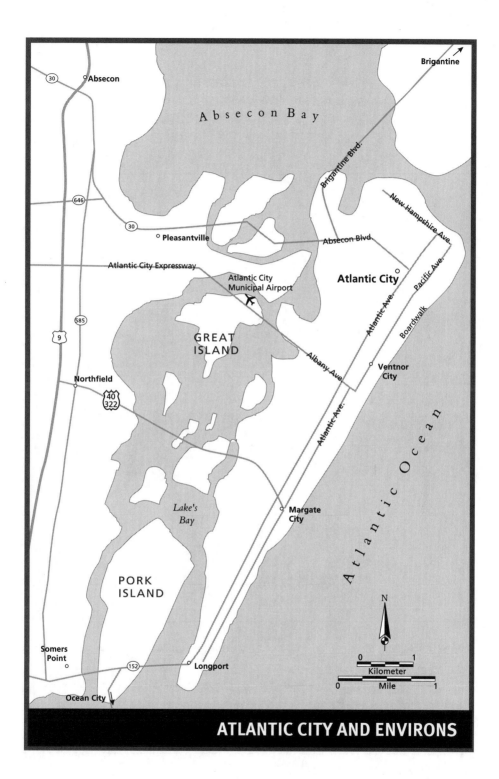

ATLANTIC CITY AND ENVIRONS

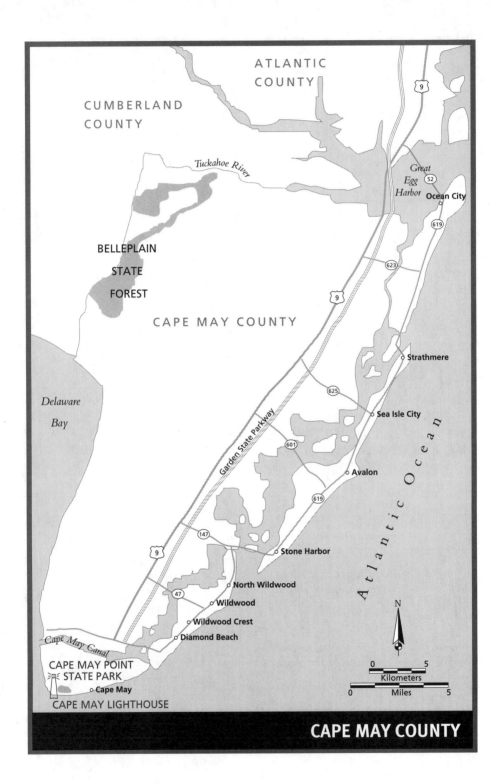

CAPE MAY COUNTY

Preface

The Jersey Shore has been entertaining visitors for more than 300 years, from the Dutch farmers and whalers who came to Cape May's beaches in the early 17th century to the current day-trippers who crowd the Garden State Parkway on summer weekends in search of the ultimate wave or the perfect tan.

With 127 miles of coastline, the Shore (never "The Beach"—that's the Hamptons) offers an infinite variety of pleasures: the quiet serenity of a morning walk on a Bay Head beach; the raucous amusements of the Point Pleasant boardwalk; the spirited camaraderie aboard a Belmar fishing boat—and so much more.

Once upon a time, Shore towns like Long Branch hosted presidents and kings, distinguished actors, financiers, and even a few well-known scoundrels. Artists like Winslow Homer celebrated the rugged natural beauty of the shoreline. Grand hotels dotted the oceanfront, some with hundreds of rooms, splendid pavilions, and magnificent ballrooms. Socialites from New York and Philadelphia played croquet and lawn tennis wearing the latest "casual" fashions from Paris, and gourmands like Diamond Jim Brady feasted on meals that would today feed a family of four. But with the development of ever-faster automobile engines and the growing availability of air travel, vacationers moved on to more exotic destinations, and the grand hotels faded and disappeared.

The Shore towns survived by adapting and reinventing themselves. Today, soaring condominiums and upscale town houses stand on oceanfront blocks once occupied by stately hotels; bed-and-breakfast signs adorn sprawling Victorians that were once summer retreats for wealthy New Yorkers and Philadelphians. Trendy restaurants and chic boutiques lure customers to once-sleepy Main Streets, and young urban professionals fill up the commuter trains and ferries that carry them home to converted carriage houses and former seaside "bungalows."

Today, the pleasures of the Jersey Shore are not just for the privileged few. They're for anyone who believes that there is nothing better than a day at the beach.

For those who have already visited one or two Shore towns, this book will be a companion to further explorations: There are always more surprises farther down (or farther up) the coast. For those who have yet to visit the Shore, this book will serve as a guide to the places and attractions most likely to please.

Acknowledgments

We would like to thank Michael Walker and Karen Wolfe of the New Jersey Commerce & Economic Growth Commission, the South Jersey Cultural Alliance, the Monmouth County Department of Economic Development and Tourism, the Ocean County Department of Public Affairs, the Cape May County Department of Tourism, the Atlantic City Convention & Visitors Authority, the Greater Atlantic City Golf Association, and the many individuals who helped us gather material for this book.

How to Use This Book

The first question we asked ourselves when we began this book was what, exactly, we meant by "the Jersey Shore." We decided to define the Shore as the coastal towns from Sandy Hook south to Cape May. We then realized that our book would break down naturally into counties; for people in Monmouth County, going to the beach in Seaside Heights, say, can be a trip of 30 miles or more. By organizing the book along county lines—Monmouth, Ocean, Atlantic, and Cape May—we could also include restaurants, parks, and activities that are not really on the coast without creating confusion. In some sections—notably the Golf chapter—we will even go well outside these four counties, because we know that golfers are more willing to drive a bit to experience a new course.

It would take a huge tome just to list every restaurant and hotel in our large and populous region, and such a book would be far from helpful. The *Insiders' Guide to the Jersey Shore* is selective, listing the very best the Jersey Shore has to offer. Use this book as if you were calling a friend in the area to ask: "What's a nice place to go for a romantic weekend?" or "Where can we rent a big house for the month of August?" or "What's a good place to go for lobster?" In fact, even if you have friends at the Jersey Shore, consult this guide. That way you can impress them with your local knowledge and savvy recommendations. Who knows? Maybe they'll learn something about the Jersey Shore from you!

Getting Here, Getting Around

By Car
By Bus
By Train
By Sea
By Air

Planes, trains, and automobiles—if you add boats and buses, you'll have pretty well covered the ways to get to the Jersey Shore. In this section, we'll help you figure out what mode of transportation will be most convenient for you.

By Car

No doubt, most people come to the Jersey Shore by car, either solo or packed up with kids, pets, and loads of summer gear. Not only is it the best way to get where you're going, you'll certainly need a car if you plan to stay more than a few days.

From New York City and North Jersey

As we're driving down to the Shore from Manhattan, we always know we're getting close once we leave the industrial odors of the New Jersey Turnpike and get on the Garden State Parkway, a road bordered with trees and wildflowers. While the Turnpike serves the western part of South Jersey, the Garden State Parkway (GSP) is the main artery of the Shore. Its exits are given in mileage markers, so you know exactly how far you have to travel. For example, if you drive from Belmar, exit 98, to Long Beach Island, exit 63, you've gone 35 highway miles.

Heading south, after you come over the Driscoll Bridge at Woodbridge and pass through the Raritan Toll Plaza, the GSP divides into express (left) and local lanes (right). From the express lanes, you can only get off at exit 117, Keyport-Hazlet, and exit 105, Eatontown, until the lanes merge again at exit 99, Asbury Park. We usually roll the dice, choosing according to traffic flow, but it does seem as though more cars get pulled over for speeding in the express lanes.

The Garden State Parkway has frequent 35-cent tolls, especially up north, and to alleviate the bottlenecks they cause, the GSP has begun accepting E-Z Pass. This automatic toll system is used on the N.J. Turnpike and on the bridges and tunnels between New York and New Jersey. Even though E-Z Pass allows Big Brother to monitor your whereabouts, if you wait long enough in the slow lane, you'll give in and get one. Call (800) 333-TOLL or go to www.e-zpassny. com.

From Philadelphia and West

The Atlantic City Expressway connects Philadelphia with Atlantic City (commonly known as A.C.) as well as with the Garden State Parkway, and in good conditions, the trip is only about an hour. To get to the Atlantic City Expressway, get off the Pennsylvania Turnpike at Valley Forge, exit 24, and get on the Schuylkill Expressway (I-76 East). Cross the Walt Whitman Bridge and follow N.J. Highway 42 South to the Atlantic City Expressway.

A word on U.S. Highway 9, which runs parallel to the Garden State south of Toms River: It's what old-timers used to call the "scenic route"—no tolls but plenty of traffic lights.

Traffic

When we feel like driving down to Atlantic City on a summer weekend, we often think of Yogi Berra's remark about Jack

A parasailer's view of Atlantic City. PHOTO: COURTESY OF ATLANTIC CITY CONVENTION & VISITORS AUTHORITY

Dempsey's Restaurant: "Nobody goes there anymore, it's too crowded." Traffic jams have become a daily occurrence, as more people move down to the Shore, adding commuter congestion to traffic caused by summer fun-seekers. The first line of defense is to listen to the traffic reports on news stations such as 880 AM, 1010 AM, or 1130 AM from New York; 101.5 FM and 106.3 FM have New Jersey traffic reports.

One of the traffic hot spots to avoid during rush hours and summer weekend mornings is the N.J. Turnpike exit 11 interchange for the Garden State Parkway. One alternative route from either the Holland or Lincoln Tunnel from Manhattan or from I–278 (Brooklyn and Staten Island) is U.S. Highways 1 and 9. It's a slower road with traffic lights through the Newark area, but on the weekends, it may still save you some time. Another option is to stay on the Turnpike until exit 9 and then take N.J. Highway 18 South, which will take you right to any of the towns between Long Branch and Spring Lake, or let you pick up the Parkway South again either at Eatontown or at Wall. N.J. Highway 18, which runs through New Brunswick, where Rutgers University is located, is one

of the few roads on which traffic is actually lighter in the summertime.

If you take I–278 to the Garden State Parkway/U.S. Highway 9 South exit, you may run into a backup that extends for miles at the off-ramp; skip it. Take the Highway 9 North exit, and follow the Turnpike and Parkway signs until you loop around and get another shot at the Parkway South.

Maps and Directions

Automobile Association of America
(800) 822–9223, T.D.D. (800) 722–4833
www.aaa.com
Local offices:
1200 U.S. Highway 9 South
Cape May Court House
(609) 465–3033
1900 N.J. Highway 70, #300, Lakewood
(732) 918–0500
901 Tilton Road, Northfield
(609) 646–6000
N.J. Highway 35 South and Sunset Avenue,
Ocean Township
(732) 918–0550
864 N.J. Highway 37 West, Toms River
(732) 244–6800

AAA offers members free maps and guide-books as well as towing and roadside assistance (except on the New Jersey Turnpike and Garden State Parkway).

Hagstrom Maps
www.hagstrommap.com

Hagstrom publishes detailed maps of each county, essential for locating garage sales and out-of-the-way places. They're available in drugstores and bookstores.

www.Mapquest.com

At Mapquest, you can plug in your starting point and your destination and print out detailed directions and pertinent map sections.

By Bus

Many commuters take the bus to and from New York, as do carless Manhattanites coming to visit their motorized friends at the Shore. Since Academy bus routes run right along Ocean Avenue from Sea Bright to Asbury Park, just a block from the beach, the bus would seem to be an easy way to get to the beach for the day, but in fact, we rarely see anyone with beach gear on the bus.

Academy Bus Lines
(732) 888–2798, (800) 992–0451
www.academybus.com

Academy offers bus service between New York City's Port Authority Bus Terminal and "Shore Points," as well as Monmouth Park in season. On common commuter routes, service to Wall Street is also available during rush hours. Academy also runs local Shore buses and buses to casinos in Atlantic City.

Greyhound
(800) 231–2222

Greyhound offers bus service to Atlantic City from major cities: New York (Port Authority Terminal, 42nd Street and Eighth Avenue); Philadelphia (13th and Arch Streets); Washington, D.C. (1005 First Street NE); and Baltimore (210 West Fayette Street).

New Jersey Transit
(800) 772–2222 for info on northern routes;
(800) 582–5946 for info on southern routes;
T.D.D. (800) 772–2287 in New Jersey,
(973) 762–5100 out of state
www.njtransit.com

NJ Transit offers bus service as well as train service to Shore points from New York City and Philadelphia. Detailed routes, schedules, and fare information are posted on their Web site.

Atlantic City Jitney
(609) 344–8642

To make it easier for you to spread your money around the various casinos in A.C., the Jitney runs 24/7, 365 days a year, stopping on every corner on Pacific Avenue and in the Marina District.

By Train

Though sociable smoking cars have gone the way of the three-martini lunch, many commuters still prefer taking the train to the bus, as it avoids traffic jams and makes fewer local stops.

New Jersey Transit
(800) 772–2222 for info on northern routes;
(800) 582–5946 for info on southern routes;
T.D.D. (800) 772–2287 in New Jersey,
(973) 762–5100 out of state
www.njtransit.com
For Atlantic City Line info:
(800) AC TRAIN in NJ, (215) 569–3752 in PA

The North Jersey Coast Line connects New York City with Middletown, Red Bank, Monmouth Park Race Track, and all of the Shore towns from Long Branch to Bay Head, with some trains offering express service. The Atlantic City Line connects Philadelphia (30th Street Station) and the Atlantic City Rail Terminal, with free shuttle service to the casinos.

By Sea

Back in the 1670s farmers and early settlers of Monmouth County reached New York by boat, from harbors on the Raritan

When you see the Visitor Welcome Center, you know you'll soon be in Atlantic City. PHOTO: COURTESY OF ATLANTIC CITY CONVENTION & VISITORS AUTHORITY

Bay and the Navesink River. Happily, this delightful means of transportation is enjoying a renaissance, with two companies running high-speed ferries from Highlands and Atlantic Highlands that make the trip to Manhattan in less than an hour. There are even plans for a ferry link to JFK International Airport, which is currently a drive of two to three hours due to the many traffic problems.

New York Fast Ferry
(800) NYF–NYFF
www.nyff.com
New York Fast Ferry is geared mainly to commuters, with service from Highlands to Manhattan's Pier 11, Wall Street, and East 34th Street offered Monday through Friday.

Seastreak America
(800) BOAT RIDE
www.seastreakusa.com
In addition to its commuter schedule, Seastreak offers numerous excursions. For Manhattanites, there are daytrips that include shuttle buses to and from Mon-

mouth Park Race Track or Sandy Hook beaches. Sports fans can cruise from Highlands to Yankee Stadium, Shea Stadium, or West Point football games. Seastreak also offers seasonal excursions, such as fall foliage cruises up the Hudson River, sunset cruises around Manhattan, and trips to Macy's Fourth of July Fireworks on the East River.

Cape May—Lewes Ferry
(800) 64–FERRY
Cape May Terminal
(609) 886–9699
Lewes Terminal
(302) 645–6346
Lewes Ferry provides a wonderful 70-minute respite on your road trip, ferrying cars, buses, and people across the Delaware Bay, between Cape May and Lewes, Delaware. Reservations are advisable, especially in the summer season.

Marinas

If you skipper your own boat, you can really beat the weekend traffic. Check the

Shore-speak

If you're going to get around at the Jersey Shore, you've got to be able to communicate with the natives. So here are few words and phrases that you're likely to hear.

First of all, when you're driving south on the Parkway, you're going "down the Shore." You can't go to the beach until you get to the Shore. When we say "up North," as in: "My cousin lives up North," we mean the northern part of the state, not Canada or points beyond. Summer people from up north are "bennies," which is not exactly an insult, nor a term of endearment. Bennies are blamed for all sorts of problems like traffic, inflated real-estate prices, and litter. You may even hear some locals call bennies "city ginkers," a name that definitely has more of an edge to it. Both names are of uncertain provenance.

On the other hand, if you're from a rural community in South Jersey, you may be a "piney," that is, from the Pine Barrens. Parts of Salem and Cumberland Counties, on the Delaware Bay, are so rural that folks are proud to be called pineys. That area is also called "down Jersey."

If we ask if you'd like to get a pie, we don't mean apple or peach. A "pie" in Shore parlance is a pizza; in some of the older restaurants, you'll see it called a "tomato pie." Similarly, among the Shore's Italian residents, tomato sauce may be referred to as "gravy," a direct translation of the Italian "sugo."

"Fishing and Boating" section of the Outdoor Activities chapter for a listing of marinas. The Shore has a number of great restaurants where you can arrive by boat and park it while you eat.

By Air

With the exception of Atlantic City, perhaps, visitors don't seem to fly to the Jersey Shore. It's more of a load-up-the-station-wagon destination. But folks who do want to fly to the area have two choices:

**Atlantic City International Airport
(609) 645–7895**

A.C. International is only 20 minutes from the Boardwalk and has scheduled flights on Spirit (800–772–7117, www.SpiritAir.com) and USAirways Express (800–428–4322). Spirit recently inaugurated service to Los Angeles, with a stop in Chicago.

**Newark International Airport
(973) 961–6000, (800) 961–7275 for parking info**

In addition to numerous national and international carriers, Newark is a hub for Continental, with flights to dozens of U.S. cities. Construction has recently begun on Terminal C, creating delays. Parking can be a problem, especially during peak travel periods such as Thanksgiving. Newark is 45 miles from Long Branch, 155 miles from Cape May.

Airport Shuttles

**AIRLINK
(800) 772–2222**

AIRLINK connects Newark Airport terminals with NJ Transit buses and trains.

**Olympic Airport Shuttle Express
(800) 822–9797**

Olympic has 18 daily departures from its terminals in Hazlet, Lincroft, and Wall to Newark Airport. It also offers private pickup service.

Royal Airport Shuttle
(609) 748–9777, (800) 824–7767
Though based in South Jersey, Royal serves Newark, Philadelphia, and Atlantic City International Airports as well as New York's JFK and LaGuardia Airports.

State Shuttle
(800) 427–3207
State Shuttle is our latest find, with reasonable rates and good service to Newark from Monmouth County.

Municipal Airports

If you're tooling around in your own Piper Cub, you probably don't need us to tell you where to land it, but that's what we're here for.

Allaire Airport Authority
Wall Township
(732) 938–4800

B & L Aero Club
Marlboro
(732) 591–8438

Bader Field
Atlantic City
(609) 348–4990

Lakewood Airport
Lakewood
(732) 364–0800

Ocean City Municipal Airport
(609) 399–0907

Area Overview

Monmouth County
Ocean County
Atlantic County
Cape May County

The Jersey Shore is many things to many people, with almost as many personalities as it has towns. To singles, it may be the all-night parties of Belmar or Point Pleasant. To families with kids, it's fun in the sun and a trip to the ice-cream parlor in Ocean Grove or Beach Haven. Whatever you're looking for at the Shore, we'll help you find it.

It is sometimes amazing how different two little towns that share the same strip of beach can actually be. History may have had something to do with the different ambiences of our beachfront towns; while some were founded by whalers and fishermen, others, like Ocean Grove and Beach Haven, started out as religious retreats. In this chapter we will give you an idea of what each town is like, starting at Sandy Hook in the north and wending our way south down to Cape May Point.

Monmouth County

When Henry Hudson first explored the coast of New Jersey in 1609, he piloted the *Half Moon* into Sandy Hook Bay, gazed at the Highlands above, and wrote in his log: "a very good land to fall in with, and a pleasant land to see." Upon this discovery, the Dutch laid claim to all the lands in what are now New Jersey and New York. During the 19th and 20th centuries, many Monmouth communities were fancy resorts favored by the elite of New York and Philadelphia. Today, having discovered the wisdom of Hudson's words, many commuters who work in New York or "up North" call the county home. Development here has been intense and not always wise, yet there are still places where condos and town houses don't dominate and where Nature holds her own.

Though the beaches are its primary tourist attraction, Monmouth is still one of New Jersey's important farm belts. And while many farms have been taken over by real-estate developers in recent years, you'll still find vegetable farms in the western part of the county, in Wall Township, Farmingdale, and Howell. There are still fruit orchards in Colts Neck; Delicious Orchards, in fact, is one of the area's most successful businesses.

Commercial fishing, as well as sport fishing, is thriving in Monmouth—as you can readily see by checking out the commercial fishing fleets in Raritan Bay or visiting the Belmar Marina.

And horses are still an important part of local culture. Monmouth Park and Freehold Raceway are located here, as are a number of important breeding farms in the Colts Neck–Freehold area.

Sandy Hook

Long before Giovanni da Verrazano and Henry Hudson explored the waters around Sandy Hook, the Lenni Lenape Indians (also known as the Delaware Indians) visited the beaches to fish, to gather beach plums, and to search for cedar wood to make their canoes.

For the European settlers, it was Sandy Hook's strategic location that made this strip of land so important; from Sandy Hook they could spot any ships trying to enter the Raritan Bay and New York Harbor. During the American Revolution, Sandy Hook was an important stronghold for the British; with help from local Loyalists, they maintained control over the peninsula until after the Battle of Monmouth in 1778. Today the Coast Guard maintains a station here, but Sandy Hook is a place for swimming, fishing, bird-watching, and more; check out the Beaches and Natural World chapters for details.

As Sandy Hook truly offers something for everyone, it attracts just about everyone: singles, families, and gays. And then there are the 5,000 or so folks who show up on busy summer days to enjoy the clothing-optional beach (that would be Gunnison Beach, Area G).

Sea Bright

Flanked on one side by the Atlantic Ocean and on the other by the Shrewsbury and Navesink Rivers, Sea Bright is a mere sandbar of a town, barely two blocks wide. Homeowners in this one-time fishing village can enjoy spectacular sunrises on the ocean from the front deck, and sunsets on the river from the back bedroom. These vistas come at a price, though, as storms of any size will flood the entire town. In fact, you will often see Sea Bright on local TV news, with crews showing the "roiling sea" live from the top of the stone and concrete seawall.

Perhaps it is this feeling of living on the edge that has given Sea Bright its party-town atmosphere, with probably more liquor licenses per square mile than any town in Jersey. Many clubs, like the beachfront Tradewinds, which regularly hosts big-name acts like Hootie and the Blowfish, are open till 2:00 A.M. A word of caution, though: With only one street into and out of town, it's pretty easy for the Sea Bright police to spot drunk drivers.

All this is not to say that Sea Bright is tacky. You'll also find quite a few nice restaurants here, as well as expensive private beach clubs, such as Chapel Hill, that attract well-to-do families from nearby Rumson, Fair Haven, and Navesink year after year. On the Shrewsbury River side, there are at least a half-dozen good-size marinas, leading to quite a bit of boat traffic. All of this summer fun can lead to car traffic jams on Ocean Avenue, especially at dinnertime or whenever the Sea Bright–Rumson drawbridge is open.

Monmouth Beach

In Monmouth Beach, Sea Bright's elegant neighbor to the south, the waterfront is dominated by two posh high-rise condominiums, huge private houses, and the exclusive Monmouth Beach Bath & Tennis Club. Drivers-by also tend to notice the Monmouth Beach Cultural Center, which is in the old Coast Guard tower and holds art exhibits, lectures, and Pilates classes.

Monmouth Beach is popular with the yachting crowd, as it has a good-size marina on the riverside. There are also some nice restaurants, but nothing to attract hoi polloi away from Sea Bright.

Long Branch

While today much of Long Branch is in need of some sprucing-up, this city was once the Monte Carlo of the Jersey Shore. Of course that was a very long time ago, way back in the 1830s when posh gambling parlors and billiard halls first began to attract the fast crowd from New York City.

The healthful sea air and the beaches were also an attraction, though beachgoers back then did not exactly enjoy them as we do today. (Any outfit a lady could have ventured outdoors in would surely have been enough to drown her.) Rather, Long Branch's pristine beaches drew crowds because they were wide enough to stage horse races. Onlookers might have viewed the excitement from one of the huge, oceanfront hotels that dominated the landscape back then.

In the post Civil–War era, Long Branch had its Golden Age; in 1869, President Ullyses S. Grant came to Long Branch for the summer and established a summer White House here, bringing in his wake other people of importance eager to escape Washington, D.C.'s stifling heat.

In 1870, the Monmouth Park Jockey Club was founded, adding the sport of kings to cards and dice, and Long Branch society became a heady mix of government officials and wealthy socialites. Army generals George Meade and Winfield Scott rubbed elbows with the likes of tycoon Jim

Fisk, stage sirens Lily Langtry and Lillian Russell, and Diamond Jim Brady, who was known as much for his gargantuan appetite as for his flashy lifestyle. Artist Winslow Homer celebrated the beauty of Long Branch's coastline in his paintings and chronicled the doings of high society, the noteworthy as well as the notorious, in drawings for *Harper's Weekly*.

Six more presidents followed Grant's lead; Rutherford B. Hayes, James A. Garfield, Chester A. Arthur, Benjamin Harrison, William McKinley, and Woodrow Wilson all spent summers in Long Branch. Garfield, in fact, died in the Elberon section of Long Branch. (There is a plaque marking the spot on Garfield Terrace.) The president was brought here by special train after he was gunned down by an assassin. He died, despite the healthful sea air, and funeral services were held at nearby St. James Chapel on Ocean Avenue, where he had worshipped. Once home to the Long Branch Historical Society, the building is now in serious disrepair. But the memory of those presidents lingers in the names of streets and avenues like Lincoln and Grant.

After presidents stopped visiting, and gambling was outlawed, Long Branch went into decline. The grand wooden hotels deteriorated or burned to the ground. By the 1960s, Long Branch was a place where families from North Jersey, many of them Italian-American, came for the summer. There were also a few gangland-style murders during this period, and notorious mobsters like "Little Pussy" Russo were rumored to frequent the Surf Lounge and Yvonne's Rhapsody-in-Blue Restaurant.

Yvonne's has since been razed to make way for an apartment building, and the Surf Lounge is now home to Max's Hot Dogs, a refugee from the Long Branch Amusement Pier, which mysteriously burned down in 1987. In the past decade this city of 31,000, Monmouth County's largest, has come a long way toward recovering from the recession of the 1970s and early 1980s. But it has changed along the way. Not as lively in the summer as it once was, Long Branch now has a larger year-round population, having attracted former summer people and commuters from "up North" and Manhattan.

The condominiums that have sprung up along Ocean Avenue range from the not-too-expensive to the astronomical; an example of the latter is the high-rise Ocean Cove, where the late Leon Hess had four connected apartments decorated in Hess-station green and white. Though devoid of amusements, the Long Branch promenade was extended to reach the new Ocean Place Conference Resort Hotel. It's all decidedly upscale, but we do miss Criterion Candies.

Deal

In Deal, where unofficial polls note more Jaguars per capita than in any other town in the United States, ostentatious is not an insult, it's a way of life. Most of this wealthy town's summer residents hail from Brooklyn. Many are Sephardic Jews who do not drive on the Sabbath (Saturday) but instead in-line skate or bike over to the Deal Casino, the town's sprawling beach club.

On a summer weekend, you'll often see cars parked and double-parked on a block, a sure sign that there's a huge party going on. Such Shore shindigs are blasts from Deal's elegant past, when Toots Shor entertained the who's who of New York society, giving away party favors from Tiffany's, at his Ocean Avenue villa. That spectacular home, like many of the ornate fantasies that used to make this town a drive-through wonderland, was recently torn down, replaced by a larger new residence.

One of the biggest deals in Deal is the summer sidewalk sale, when chic boutiques such as Steev 19 and the Country Fair on Norwood Avenue offer super bargains on clothes with labels like Giorgio Armani and Katharine Hamnett.

It's a little-known fact, but in the early 1700s, Norwood Avenue was actually a toll road called the Long Branch–Deal Turnpike. Fees collected near the corner of Roseld Avenue were supposedly used to improve roads throughout the county. Unfortunately, the disturbing practice of collecting tolls shows no sign of abating in New Jersey as we wade into the 21st century.

Allenhurst

At the beach in Deal, you're likely to see young women wearing the latest confections to come out of Paris; at the Allenhurst Beach Club, you'll still see moms in old-fashioned skirty one-pieces. But bathing suits are not the only way these towns diverge. Thanks to efforts to preserve its wonderful historic homes, Allenhurst still feels like small-town America, where neighbors remember who used to live in which house.

Shopping on Main Street, you'll find mountain bikes, surfboards, and—oh yes—chocolate decadence cake at Cravings. Allenhurst Beach Club's restaurant is open to the public for dinner or drinks in the bar, which has a huge picture window overlooking the sea; the food is good, too.

Loch Arbour

Whether petty neighbor-versus-neighbor squabbles or just a spirit of independence were the cause, this town—just two blocks long—seceded from Ocean Township in 1957. Grand homes line Edgemont Drive, which looks over Deal Lake to Asbury Park.

Asbury Park

When Bruce Springsteen called his debut album "Greetings from Asbury Park" and put a familiar, gaudy postcard on the cover, it was a statement about his roots, but also an ironic reminder of the city's glory days. Locals and summer people alike remember the excitement of going to Asbury in 1950s and 1960s—the rides, the noise, the cotton candy and frozen custard, skeeball in the arcades, but most of all, the crowds. On a summer evening the mile-long Boardwalk was wall-to-wall people.

Talk of redevelopment of the waterfront has remained just that since early in the 1980s, as reports of bankrupt developers and disappearing funds would periodically make it into the *Asbury Park Press*. Meanwhile, the glorious Art Nouveau carousel at the Casino end of the Boardwalk, where us kids would scramble to get an outside horse so we could grab for the brass ring, was quietly relieved of its valuable vintage horses and sleighs. The city of Asbury Park may have hit bottom a few years ago, when its mayor was arrested for buying cocaine in a sleazy bar called the Tap Room, right across the street from City Hall and the police station.

While tourists deserted Asbury, music clubs like the Stone Pony and the Fast Lane did well, possibly because there was no one to complain about the noise. Now the wonderfully restored Paramount Theater and Convention Hall book big-name bands like the Goo-Goo Dolls every summer.

In addition to rock clubs, quite a few gay clubs have sprung up in the past few years, some respectable places to drink, enjoy music, and socialize, and others a little more notorious. These clubs were the first visible sign of what has become a real change in the area, as affluent gays from "up North" have started buying and renovating homes here and in Ocean Grove. One attraction is that you can buy a lovely old Victorian house for the price of a cramped studio in Manhattan. And Asbury Park is a heck of a lot easier to get to than Fire Island.

While these are second homes for many, some of the gay newcomers are clearly in Asbury Park to stay; there's even a gay bowling league at the Asbury Lanes. In 2001 the first openly gay representative was elected to the City Council. The New Jersey Gay Pride Day event here in June attracts thousands of visitors from New York, Philadelphia, and beyond.

There is also a nascent art scene in Asbury, complete with loft apartments and art galleries springing up beside pawn shops. Although Bruce Springsteen's latest song about Asbury is called "City of Ashes" (it was not about the World Trade Center, although Bruce sang it on the televised benefit for the victims of 9/11), things may finally be looking up in the Boss's "city of ruins."

Ocean Grove

Ocean Grove was founded in 1869 by a group of Methodist ministers as a place to hold summertime religious gatherings called "camp meetings." Members of the National Camp Meeting Association for the Promotion of Holiness arrived the following summer, pitching tents and attending prayer services in the great outdoors.

Shocked by the excesses of drinking, gambling, and loose women in Long Branch, the Association banned alcohol and, later, driving a car on Sunday, a rule that prevailed until 1974. Before that, you had to have a reference letter from a Methodist minister to even buy a house here. (And you thought Manhattan co-op boards were tough!)

The center of life in Ocean Grove is the Great Auditorium, a stunning wooden hall erected in 1894. Here, 10,000 people would assemble to hear famous preachers such as Billy Sunday, Norman Vincent Peale, and Billy Graham. The acoustics in the auditorium are splendid, making it a resonant home for its 4,000-pipe Robert Hope Jones organ. Enrico Caruso opened his pipes here, performing in his first American concert ever. Every summer, such acts as Peter, Paul and Mary, the New Orleans Preservation Hall Jazz Band, and Neil Sedaka appear.

Even in this cynical age, the spirit of the camp meeting endures, and every summer, the tents crop up, sheltering the same families year after year. They rent for $3,000 to $4,000 a season and are harder to get than Giants season tickets, as many are passed down from generation to generation. Sunday services still draw some 3,000 people, but in other ways time has crept up on Ocean Grove.

Hulking SUVs now squeak down its tiny lanes, bringing young families, artsy New York types, and even quite a few gay visitors to this once straitlaced community. Such people are known to openly drink wine on their front porches. They dine at new restaurants like Moonstruck, where the menu is a bit more sophisticated than the old Sampler Inn's liver and onions and macaroni and cheese.

With its colorfully painted gingerbread cottages and its old-time bed-and-breakfasts, Ocean Grove has been called a living museum. The mom and pop grocery sells fresh vegetables out of bins, the drugstore has a real (though restored) soda fountain, and just off Pilgrim Pathway, there will always be Days ice-cream parlor.

Bradley Beach

Bradley Beach has been the destination of choice for generations of middle-class and working-class families from "up North." Fewer seasonal rentals are available than years ago, as many of those summer people from Hudson or Essex County have bought homes here and moved down to the Shore permanently.

Bradley has always welcomed a number of ethnic groups and retains a strong Italian flavor, as seen in Main Street restaurants like Giamano's, Franco's, and La Nonna Piancone's. Locals love a cheap date in Bradley: a pizza and some pasta fagioli at Vic's Tomato Pies, and a movie at the vintage Beach Cinema.

Avon-by-the-Sea

Avon-by-the-Sea is a genteel sort of place with a century-old bathing pavilion and a nice boardwalk. The town took its name from the old Avon Inn, which was built in 1883 and burned down some years ago.

Avon strikes a nice balance, with restaurants and shops on Main Street and big old clapboard colonials on quiet residential streets. It's more upscale than Bradley Beach, but not nearly as expensive as Spring Lake. Once upon a time Avon had a number of guest houses, but these disappeared as real-estate values rose. Four lovely bed-and-breakfast inns still welcome weekenders, though: the Avon Manor Inn, the Inn-to-the-Sea, the Candlewick Inn, and the Cashelmara Bed & Breakfast Inn.

Belmar

Belmar is a big and busy town, where party boats draws thousands of fishermen and party houses draw those just fishing. Belmar Marina, on the Shark River Inlet, is New Jersey's largest commercial marina, and dozens of boats go out every day in search of fluke, bluefish, weakfish, or even sharks. There are also hundreds of slips available for private boats, a launch ramp, a gas station, a bait shop—everything you need for a day at sea.

While fishers troll offshore locales like the Mud Hole and the 28-Mile Wreck, nighttime brings out the pub crawlers, who cast their nets in places like Bar Antic-ipation, D'Jai's, Pat's Tavern, and the Piranha Pub, bringing in mostly other lounge lizards. The nightclub scene in Bel-mar has thrived thanks to the presence of so many 20-somethings, who for years have pooled resources to rent houses here for the summer. At times, things can get a bit rowdy, and the group renters have been blamed for nuisances starting with loud music and escalating to drunkenness, uri-nating in public, even passing out on neighbors' lawns.

Many homeowners in Belmar, envying the peace and the property values in next-door Spring Lake, are fed up with the town's "Animal House" reputation and have succeeded in putting some limits on the group rentals. After all, Belmar has plenty to attract more upscale tourists: big, clean beaches, a mile-long boardwalk, and great seafood restaurants like Ollie Klein's.

One victory for this moral majority was the demolition of Belmar Playland and Reggie's Bar. Of course their disap-pearance probably owed less to the war on vice than it did to the soaring value of oceanfront real estate, as six seashore colo-nials, going for upwards of a million apiece, will soon take their place.

Spring Lake

Spring Lake is one of the loveliest towns on the Jersey Shore, with its wide beaches flanked by grassy dunes. Spring Lake is our favorite walking town, one of the few places at the Shore where you can spend a weekend without getting into your car. The foot-friendly Boardwalk (it's made of recycled plastic) attracts large but well-behaved crowds in the summer. Even when the Boardwalk is busy with exercis-ers, the park that surrounds the lake itself offers a setting with the serenity of a

Pastoral scenes like this one abound in beautiful Spring Lake, one of the Shore's most desirable towns.
PHOTO: ARTHUR AFRICANO

When the beach is crowded, Spring Lake offers a relaxing spot to dip your toes and enjoy a quiet read.
PHOTO: LILLIAN AFRICANO

Japanese print: the wooden footbridge, white swans idling across the water, perhaps a lone fisherman casting a line. A walk along Third Avenue, the town's main street, might yield pleasures of a more commercial variety: a new pair of shoes, perhaps, or some homemade candies from Jean Louise.

Spring Lake was founded more than a century ago when a group of prominent Philadelphians bought farmland to build summer cottages. Some of those early "cottages" are still standing; today they look a lot like mansions. As folks were not very politically correct in the olden days, Spring Lake became known as the "Irish Riviera," and Jews, Italians, and people of color were not particularly welcome.

Perhaps the resident most identifiable with Spring Lake's nickname was Martin Maloney, who spent $8 million building his summer estate, Ballingarry, in the late 19th century. When his daughter died of tuberculosis, Maloney decided to build a church and dedicate it to her namesake saint, St. Catharine. The lakefront church, which took European craftsmen 25 years to complete, bears a striking resemblance to St. Peter's Basilica in Rome.

In those days, when a society matron might sport a fortune in gems at a garden party, out-of-towners would book a room for the season at the palatial oceanfront Essex and Sussex Hotel or the lakefront Warren Hotel. Nowadays, you'll have to settle for one of the many charming bed-and-breakfasts; the Essex and Sussex has been converted to upscale apartments for seniors.

Sea Girt

With its one-mile stretch of unfettered beachfront, Sea Girt does not have much to draw day-trippers except the squawking of the gulls and the rhythmic whoosh of the waves. A good place to enjoy these attractions is the Victorian Sea Girt Lighthouse, where craft shows are held every so often. After drinking in the sea spray, a complete tour of Sea Girt might wind up with a meal at the historic Parker House.

Sea Girt is a lovely (expensive) residential town with a number of elegant oceanfront homes; it's known to Giants fans as the home of retired football coach Bill Parcells. Some fans come to Sea Girt hoping to get a glimpse of the Tuna, but they might have better luck at Monmouth Park when the ponies are running.

Manasquan

Manasquan takes its name from the Lenni Lenape Indians, the first summer visitors here, who called the river "Man-A-Squaw-Hand" or stream of the Island of Squaws. They lived along the river and claimed the exclusive right to hunt and fish here, but somehow things didn't stay that way—the white man knew a good thing when he saw it.

Not so many years ago, the oceanfront bungalows were cheap enough to attract college kids from Rutgers here for the summer. But these days many of those properties are giving way to posh new homes in the $500,000 category.

Young people and surfers are still to be found at Inlet Beach, said to be one of the East Coast's finest surfing areas. There is no boardwalk along the mile of sandy beaches, just a strip of blacktop.

Ocean County

Ocean County is aptly named, as people here have always made their livelihoods and had their fun on the water—fishing, crabbing, whaling, and nowadays, boating, windsurfing, jet-skiing, and what have you. Nearby towns can differ wildly, from don't-park-on-our-streets Mantoloking to stay-all-night Seaside Heights. Real-estate values run the gamut, too, from posh estates worth millions to bungalows smaller than the bass boat parked in the driveway.

Point Pleasant Beach

Point Pleasant Beach is the Jersey Shore in a brash, noisy, fun-seeking mood. By day, the broad beaches can be wall-to-wall blankets, while boardwalk concessions do a brisk trade in such nutritious snacks as frozen custard, chocolate-covered bananas, and waffles with ice cream.

In addition to T-shirts and postcards, the souvenirs that are the rage here are hand-painted, live hermit crabs. This has led to hermit-crab racing, and while it's not exactly cockfighting, there is a strong movement afoot to ban the sale of the crabs.

In the evening, the Boardwalk is lively with groups of parents chatting while little ones enjoy the kiddie rides, and older kids throw away a fortune in quarters at the arcades. Every Wednesday during the summer, Father Alphonse Stephenson conducts the symphony orchestra of St. Peter's by the Sea in free outdoor concerts. There are also weekly fireworks displays.

Later at night, guys with fast cars and Jersey girls with hair teased up to cruising altitude come to Martell's and Jenkinson's on the Boardwalk to hear bands like the Nerds and to see and be seen. It's more pleasant than some music clubs, with open air and boardwalk food on hand.

Even on rainy days, you can't say there's nothing to do in Point Pleasant; for kids, there's Jenkinson's Aquarium, and for adults, there are numerous antiques stores as well as frequent country auctions.

Local tourism began in 1826, when Thomas Cook, owner of a beachfront farm, started a trend by opening his house to boarders. Clark's Landing on the Manasquan River, which had a dance floor, a carousel, and a steam organ, was perhaps the 19th-century version of Jenkinson's. In present-day Point, the White Sands Oceanfront Resort & Spa is at the top end of a range of accommodations that includes bungalows and motels for every budget.

Bay Head

Reminiscent of pre-celebrity Martha's Vineyard, Bay Head is a quiet town of sand dunes and century-old shingle-sided cottages. It almost seems as if time has stood still here, and that's the way Bay Headers like it. Expensive would be a fair description, as oceanfront houses can rent for more than $60,000 for the season. Still, Bay Head has four bed-and-breakfast inns where a warm welcome will not cost your life's savings: Conover's Bay Head Inn, the Bentley Inn, the Bay Head Sands, and the Bay Head Gables.

Price is only one reason *New Jersey Monthly* once described the beach here as the "snootiest" on the Jersey Shore. Many of the 1,300 year-round residents are descended from the borough's founders, and they have a tradition of fighting intrusions. A century ago, when a local utility company began construction to bring a trolley and electricity to Bay Head, the mayor and members of the town council cut down the poles and wires. More recently locals objected when outsiders from Point Pleasant tried to buy Bay Head beach badges.

Summer days in Bay Head are abuzz with activity: regattas at Bay Head Yacht Club, kayaking, diving, fishing, windsurfing, and waterskiing, not to mention tennis and squash.

For those who feel that a vacation without shopping is like a day without sunshine, there are stores selling jewelry, crafts, and antiques. In the center of town is Shoppers Wharf, which was once an outdoor theater; the sloping floors are a reminder of when a high tide might cover the ankles of the moviegoers sitting in the first few rows. Among the shops here is Gull Studios Art Gallery, which displays the work of local artist Robert A. Loder, Jr., who does paintings and sketches of the Jersey Shore, Maine, Chesapeake Bay, and Cape Cod.

Mantoloking

It's hard to believe, but Mantoloking makes Bay Head seem like Coney Island. The type of privacy that the impressive homes here offer costs serious money—well into the millions—enough to give you some idea of why the last census revealed New Jersey to be the most affluent state in the Union.

The beach has no boardwalk, no rest rooms, and no concessions. Parking on the street is not allowed, so if you don't live here, you'll have a ways to walk to get to this beach.

Normandy Beach, Chadwick Beach, and Ocean Beach

These little towns, which are part of Dover Township, along with the nearby metropolis of Toms River, couldn't be more unlike their ritzy neighbors to the north. Skinny one-way streets lined with tiny bungalows are chockablock with people in the summer, deserted in winter. Normandy, though, has some nicer homes on the waterfronts. Whether you're renting or buying, Normandy Beach, Chadwick Beach, and Ocean Beach certainly offer a more affordable summer getaway than other spots on the Jersey Shore.

Lavallette

Founded in 1888, Lavallette is an old-timey family resort, where kids tote candy-colored pails and shovels bought in the old-fashioned five-and-dime. Body boards are the weapon of choice for teens working up to the longboard.

Lavallette's 28-block stretch of beach and boardwalk is a magnet for walkers, both the power kind and those who just meander. There are two piers for crabbing and fishing on the bay side. At low tide, warm, shallow pools offer gentle play areas for youngsters. Concerts at the gazebo on the bay make for a delightful sunset.

Ortley Beach

Ortley Beach is like a bridge between the quiet family atmosphere of Lavallette and the bustling boardwalk happenings of Seaside Heights. Ortley's 20 blocks of ocean beach offer gorgeous views: Seaside Heights and Seaside Park to the south, and beautiful beach vistas to the north, all the way to Asbury Park. At night, Joey Harrison's Surf Club on Ocean Avenue is jumping with dancing and live entertainment.

Seaside Heights

When Great-Uncle Eddie ran a stand in Seaside years ago, he had to teach his nephew Bud a new word—shill. Now, we're not casting aspersions on the honesty of Seaside's games of chance, but *we've* never won any of those Corvettes they raffle off.

If you're a roller-coaster lover, you'll get an honest thrill out of the Jet Star. There may be bigger ones, but as you plunge toward the ocean way below, you'll probably manage a convincing scream.

Daytime is equally busy, with swimming, blanket-hopping, surfing, fishing off the pier, and water play, Seaside-style, at Water Works, home to three water slides, the biggest and best of which is Rainbow Rapids. There's also miniature golf, where many a young Shore duffer has started out.

For a small town, Seaside Heights delivers a big package of amusements and diversions. To us, it's much more fun than mega-theme parks. Seaside attracts singles who come for an evening, and families who return year after year.

Seaside Park

On its lovely wide streets are some spectacular houses and upscale condominiums, surprisingly tranquil for being so close to all the action in Seaside Heights. Of course Seaside Park is fortunate to have a perfect neighbor to the south, the 10-mile-long Island Beach State Park.

Island Beach State Park

Island Beach is an idyllic 10-mile stretch of land at the southern end of the Barnegat Peninsula. We can thank the stock market crash of 1929 for all this natural beauty. A few years earlier, steel magnate Henry Phipps planned to turn the area into a beach resort for his wealthy friends. The crash put an end to those plans, and somehow the area managed to escape development and major change. In 1953, the Phipps estate sold the land to New Jersey, which made it into a state park six years

later. Phipps's home is now the summer residence for the governor, and a lucky few still have cottages within the park.

New Jersey's last important remnant of a barrier island ecosystem, Island Beach has miles of sand dunes and white sandy beaches that are home to the same flora and fauna that thrived here thousands of years ago. Some 300 plant species, including the state's largest expanse of beach heather, grow here. You'll also find migrating songbirds, shorebirds, waterfowl, wading birds, peregrine falcons, and the state's largest osprey colony.

Long Beach Island

Ambling along Long Beach Island's sand dunes on a blustery fall day, after the crowds have gone, the solitary walker enjoys a sense of being face to face with the sea. A hint of wildness still remains, even with all the homes that have been built here.

It's been years since tourism overtook fishing as the island's biggest industry, but islanders never really got the salt out of their blood; fishing, crabbing, and clamming, whether for fun or profit, remain part of what LBI (as it is known) is all about.

Like all seafaring places, Long Beach Island has its share of tall tales of shipwrecks and pirates and buried treasure. The buried treasure bits are fantasy, but there certainly have been an awful lot of shipwrecks off this dangerous bit of coast, especially before Barnegat Lighthouse was built, and it's likely that pirates had a hand in some of them. Local lore has it that Barnegat pirates, or "Mooncussers," as they were called, would lure passing vessels onto the shoals by hanging lanterns on a mule and parading it along the sandbar. Captains trying to hug the coastline would mistake the lights for another ship and, thinking the water was deep enough, run their ships aground, where they would be set upon and robbed.

In more recent times, it was not flickering lanterns but the incredible natural beauty of this 18-mile barrier island that lured folks to Long Beach Island. Once the

N.J. Highway 72 causeway and the Mana-hawkin Bay Bridge connected Long Beach Island to the Garden State Parkway, tourism and home building really took off here.

Once they arrive for the summer, islanders like to leave the mainland behind, so there's plenty here to keep you entertained. There are (obviously) great seafood restaurants, a busy calendar of outdoor activities such as fishing tournaments, and a lively cultural scene, anchored by the Long Beach Foundation in Loveladies and the Surflight Theatre in Beach Haven.

Barnegat Light

At the northern end of Long Beach Island, Barnegat Light is a quiet place, a bit removed from the seasonal hubbub. Here you'll find a number of old Victorian houses and some of the island's nicest beaches. You'll also find fresh tilefish, right off the boats that moor on the Barnegat Bay side, at Viking Village.

After climbing to the top of Barnegat Lighthouse, folks like to know what happened to Barney's big glass eye (its original Fresnel lens); it's in the Barnegat Light Historical Museum, a collection of historic photos and documents kept in an old schoolhouse. Behind the museum are the Edith Duff Gwinn Gardens, the legacy of this local botanist and environmentalist to her hometown.

Barnegat Light has a notorious place in American history. In 1782, during the Revolutionary War, Captain Andrew Steel and 21 patriots slept on the beach after relieving a grounded British ship of its cargo. During the night, they were murdered by a group of Tory sympathizers led by John Bacon. The incident became known as the Long Beach Massacre; there is a plaque honoring Steel and his men in the state park.

Loveladies

Everyone thinks there must be some sexy story behind the name Loveladies. Actually, the town was named after Thomas Lovelady, who came to LBI to hunt ducks, not chase chicks. Much of this very residential town was destroyed by the great

storm of 1962, so you'll see a lot of big, splashy, contemporary houses—on stilts. If these bold, sweeping designs catch your eye, take the popular Seashore Open House Tour, held every August, if only to envy the spectacular ocean views these homes afford.

In Loveladies, the Long Beach Foundation for the Arts and Sciences packs its summer calendar with cultural activities; there are art exhibits and classes on topics from yoga to ocean life.

Harvey Cedars

Gone are the red cedars that once grew here, ditto Harvey's Whaling Station, one of three that once existed on Long Beach Island. (Some of the island's first white settlers were New England whalers, who came here because they could spot their migrating prey from the shore.)

Not much remains of those days except the old Harvey Cedars Hotel, now the Harvey Cedars Bible Conference Center, and the Long Beach Island Fishing Club.

As in Loveladies, you'll see a lot of modern houses on stilts here (it's one way to keep the surf out of your living room). But Harvey Cedars is more accessible to tourists than its neighbor, with more seasonal rentals and more activities for young and old. In addition to swimming, people enjoy beach volleyball, bocce, baseball, and jogging at the track. The playful spirit of Harvey Cedars is expressed in some residents' goofy mailboxes, shaped like mermaids, seagulls, Mickey Mouse, or Snoopy.

By the way, town historians say there was no Mr. Harvey. Rather, the town's name can be traced to a 1751 deed that describes the locality as "a hammock and clump of cedars called Harvest Quarters."

Surf City

Surf City was once known as the Great Swamp (a name not likely to do much for tourism) and later as Long Beach City. However the postal service found that name caused confusion, and in 1899 requested a new one. "Surf City" was the suggestion of a land speculator—a good choice for a community that swells from

1,500 to 150,000 when summer fun-seekers arrive. It's a happening place that does, in fact, attract surfers. Word seems to spread when the waves are just right, usually in the morning or late afternoon. Some of the best surfing at the Shore is here, and in Harvey Cedars, Seaside Heights, and Island Beach State Park. Also popular with surfers is the Ron Jon Surf Shop, one of the many shops and restaurants on Surf City's Long Beach Boulevard.

Moms with young surfers like to keep them in the bay, where the water is calm and shallow. They head for the 16th Street beach, which is also a favorite place to watch the sun set across Barnegat Bay.

Ship Bottom

Ship Bottom got its name back in March of 1817, when Captain Stephen Willets of Tuckerton saved a woman from the wreckage of a ship that had overturned on the shoals. The daring rescue became known as "Ship Bottom," and that was that.

With a year-round population of 2,000, Ship Bottom is another of LBI's cozy little boroughs. As it's the gateway of the island—the first place people come to after they cross the causeway—the beaches can get crowded. However, since there's no boardwalk or flashy entertainment (go to Beach Haven to find that), Ship Bottom is much quieter in the evening, when the sun worshippers go home. You'll see modest homes built in the 1950s and 1960s alongside the more elaborate dwellings put up by recent arrivals. Many of the houses are on stilts—a necessary measure against the damage caused by storm and sea.

When arriving on the island, especially if you're new to the place, stop at the Information Center on Ninth Street in Ship Bottom and grab some of the free handouts: maps, local newspapers, and information on lodging, upcoming events, and beach badges.

Long Beach Township

A number of hamlets on the southern half of Long Beach Island, some just a few blocks long, come under the jurisdiction of Long Beach Township: Brant Beach, Beach Haven Crest, Brighton Beach, Pea-

hala Beach, Beach Haven Park, Haven Beach, the Dunes, Beach Haven Terrace, Beach Haven Gardens, Spray Beach, North Beach Haven, Beach Haven Manor, Holgate, South Beach Haven, and Beach Haven Heights. On the north side of the island, High Bar Harbor, Holly Lagoons, Lighthouse Park South, Loveladies, Loveladies Harbor, and North Beach are also part of Long Beach Township.

Long Beach Township supervises about two-thirds of LBI's beaches and employs one of the country's largest beach patrols, with 350 guards.

Beach Haven

Beach Haven was founded as a Quaker summer meeting place in 1870, and before the century ended, it had an Episcopal church, a Methodist church, a mayor, a post office, and a bustling downtown with general stores, meat markets, ice-cream parlors, and a bakery. Beach Haven still has a small-town charm.

There are diversions for every taste in Beach Haven. The Surflight Theatre stages family favorites like *South Pacific* and *Peter Pan*, and during the summer there are free concerts at Veteran's Bicentennial Park. Beach Haven is also home to Fantasy Island Amusement Park, Thundering Surf Water Park, and Squirt Works. The one-block amusement park, located inland on the Boulevard, is not so large as to be overwhelming, but lively enough to make youngsters feel as if they've had a big outing.

Sailing on the bay is a favorite pastime, but if you have an adventurous nature, you can explore the island by air, thanks to Beach Haven Parasailing.

Atlantic County

To New Yorkers who only know South Jersey from a daytrip to a casino, we say, "Wake up and smell the sea air!" Atlantic City is only *one* of the experiences the southern coast has to offer.

You won't find it on any map, but somewhere in Jersey, there's a Mason-Dixon line, where the in-your-face attitude of the north melts away, and people

Tucker's Island: The Atlantis of the Jersey Shore

If you have a detailed map, you might see a small indication of an island off the southern end of Long Beach Island. This small spot of land is all that's left of a once-thriving community. Tucker's Island was actually once a part of Long Beach Island; the area included Tucker's Beach, Sea Haven, and Short Beach. During the winter of 1800, however, heavy storm tides surged over it and created a channel, now called Beach Haven Inlet, all the way through to Barnegat Bay. Tucker's Island was born.

Originally eight miles long, Tucker's Island at one time had a lighthouse (see "Tuckerton Seaport," in the Lighthouses chapter), a U.S. Life Saving Service Station, homes, and a school. By the turn of the 20th century, though, the shifting tides had whittled the island down to barely a mile. In 1927, the lighthouse collapsed, undermined by erosion. By 1955, the rest of the island was swallowed up as well, though it will sometimes reappear when the tides are right.

The Long Beach Island Museum, located in Beach Haven's original Episcopal church, Holy Innocents, has an area devoted to Tucker's Island with dramatic photos of its demise. People who live on LBI love to fish, sail, and play in the ocean, but they do not forget its destructive power.

become a whole lot more laid-back. They say it's the climate; thanks to the moderating influence of the ocean and Delaware Bay, it's warmer in the winter and less hot in the summer down south, which means they play golf year-round down here. No wonder they're in a good mood.

In Atlantic and Cape May Counties, we'll be focusing on the tourist-magnet towns on the barrier islands, such as Atlantic City and Wildwood, but there are plenty of reasons to venture inland. You don't need to wait for a rainy day to discover the great golf courses, restaurants, historic sites, shopping, amusements, and stunning nature preserves on the mainland.

Brigantine Island

Brigantine Island is just north of Atlantic City, a quick five-minute commute to the Marina District. Motels here attract a family crowd, who come for the fantastic beaches and the boating, and maybe a little blackjack at night.

Weather service statistics say that Brigantine is one of the windiest places in the United States, and over the years, the powerful winds here have led to many shipwrecks, both offshore and at the Brigantine Golf Links. In fact, Brigantine has a fairly modern feel, mainly because many older buildings have been destroyed by various storms.

At the Brigantine Historical Museum, you'll find relics of a colorful history that started when the Lenni Lenape Indians summered on the island. Other exhibits cover the arrival of New England whalers, Captain Kidd and his buried treasure, and naval battles with the British during both the Revolutionary War and the War of 1812.

This is also a place that respects its ocean heritage. North Brigantine, along with some surrounding islets, is a nature preserve. The Marine Mammal Stranding Center here rescues beached whales and dolphins that are lost or injured by passing boats.

Atlantic City

In the early-morning hours, Atlantic City's four miles of Boardwalk are left to the joggers, bikers, and in-line skaters. But soon, hundreds of tour buses begin to arrive, disgorging thousands of folks eager for action. Arriving in waves—senior citizens, Asian businessmen, high rollers in limos—they total 33 million visitors a year. Atlantic City's Convention and Visitors Authority calculates that 25 percent of America's population lives within a day's drive of the City-by-the-Sea.

There are 12 casinos, with more on the drawing board, and each has its theme: the decadence of ancient Rome at Caesars; the American West, complete with computer-controlled gold prospector and a talking buzzard, at Bally's Wild West; the exotic Far East at the Trump Taj Mahal. Inside, the basics are the same: ringing slot machines, spinning wheels, tumbling dice. Some casinos, like Bally's, offer horse racing simulcast from several different tracks at once. Most now offer Pai Gow, the preference of many Asian card players. Though many casinos plug their nickel slots, the stakes seem pretty high to us ink-stained wretches; it's sometimes hard to find a blackjack table where the minimum is less than $10 a hand.

To qualify for perks like free meals, show tickets, and overnight accommodations, you'll have to get a club card at the casino of your choice. The card allows the house to monitor your betting activity, for which you earn points. Gone are the days of a handshake and "take-care-of-my-friend"; it's all in the computer.

Each casino is practically a self-contained city, with shops, beauty salons, barbers, and at least half a dozen different restaurants, from fast-food Chinese that'll get you back on the floor quick, to four-star French. You'll also find the chain theme eateries like Planet Hollywood (Caesars) and the Hard Rock Cafe (Trump Taj Mahal), in addition to the well-known all-you-can-eat buffets.

Part of the whole A.C. experience is taking in a show at one of the casinos. Acts run the gamut from hip to has-been, from hardcore to country, from Tony Bennett to Everclear. Tickets to see performers worth seeing can be tough to get, as the house always sets aside some of the prime seats for preferred customers. Your best bet is always to plan ahead; casinos post their upcoming schedules on their Web sites and advertise in local papers. It's well worth the trouble to secure a good table; the atmosphere is fantastic, more like a large nightclub than a stadium, and you're close enough so that the singer is not just a speck in the distance. Sitting across from your friends seems more sociable, too, and waitresses keep the drinks coming. Even the not-so-great shows will fill up on any given night, as the house will offer free tickets to its club card holders, who will come if only for the two free watery drinks.

If you pine for the good old days when taste and elegance ruled Atlantic City, you might want to check your facts with a visit to the Atlantic City Historical Museum on the Garden Pier. It displays a wealth of photos and relics from the city's palmy days, such as, for instance, the original seven-foot Mr. Peanut. People may have dressed better back then, but A.C. has always been a place where nothing was too outlandish; years ago, they had high-diving horses and human cannonballs. Today, pass by the Steel Pier and you'll hear the blood-curdling screams of people "enjoying" the bungee jump. Ripley's Believe It or Not Museum, with its roulette wheel made entirely of jelly beans, is the rightful heir to the attention-getting stunts of the past.

Few people realize that Atlantic City's best-known event, the Miss America Pageant, actually started out as a publicity stunt devised by the Atlantic City Convention and Publicity Bureau (ACCPB) to attract more tourists to the city in the quiet, but still lovely, autumn season. The first parade of bathing beauties was in 1921, and the pageant has become such a part of the American identity that to some, ogling girls in swimsuits is practically an act of patriotism.

Atlantic City, where picture postcards were first sold, making folks back home wish-they-were-here, also had the first, and possibly the most successful, convention bureau in the country. Organized in 1908, the ACCPB was instrumental in the construction of Atlantic City's magnificent Convention Hall in 1929. Built at a cost of $15 million, the auditorium was the largest in the world without interior pillars, with 120,000 square feet of exhibition space, 33 meeting rooms, and a Grand Ballroom of 23,000 square feet. Even today, few stadiums have as much open floor space.

For decades, Atlantic City was the preferred destination for trade shows, and it looks like a front-runner again with its new $268-million Convention Center, right off the Atlantic City Expressway. The state-of-the-art facility has more than 500,000 contiguous square feet of exhibit space and is connected to the sophisticated new Sheraton Atlantic City Convention Center Hotel. In sharp contrast to the casino hotels with their over-the-top decor, the Sheraton is elegantly restrained, with a neo–Art Deco style, and is also wonderfully quiet. The hotel is the headquarters of the Miss America organization, so you'll see pageant memorabilia displayed throughout the public areas and rooms.

Hundreds of millions of dollars have been spent in recent years on infrastructure to get people into the city quicker, including highway improvements, a new bus terminal, and a tunnel connecting the Expressway to the Marina District.

Even for non-gamblers, Atlantic City has an amazing variety of attractions: Absecon Lighthouse, the Atlantic City Art Center, and the Ocean Life Center in Gardner's Basin. A big hit with locals is the new Sandcastle baseball stadium, home to the minor league Atlantic City Surf. During Beachfest in late June, the four-mile Boardwalk comes alive with a parade, concerts, sporting events, fireworks, and a killer sand-castle-building contest.

For us, a jaunt to A.C. is hardly complete without a stop at the White House Sub Shop for a messy, delicious cheesesteak sandwich with mushrooms and hot peppers. When you're more in the mood for lobster and a Bloody Mary, Dock's Oyster House has been the place to go for more than a century. Before heading home, there's always a quick stop at the

Boardwalk for saltwater taffy, opening up the age-old debate—Fralinger's or James'?

Ventnor City

The name Ventnor will be immediately recognized by any red-blooded American who grew up playing the game for young capitalists: Monopoly. Inventor Charles Darrow took all of the Monopoly property names from the streets of Atlantic City, with the exception of Marvin Gardens, which is in Margate. And true to the game, the corner of Boardwalk and Park Place was a million-dollar location long before Bally's Park Place Casino occupied it, while Baltic and Mediterranean Avenues in Midtown are decidedly less so.

Ventnor is a quiet, well-to-do community, where you'll see many striking old homes. Recently, about 65 beachfront-property owners stymied a $60-million beach replenishment project on the island. It seems their deeds retain riparian rights, although they allow public access to the beach and Boardwalk. However, if more sand is pumped onto the beach, making the high-water line more than 200 feet from their property lines, these homeowners have the right to demand that the city move the Boardwalk out toward the ocean and give the land where it had stood to them. As this would add millions to the cost of the project, things are now at an impasse, which pleases some surfers and environmentalists.

Margate City

It's amazing how far away the hurly-burly of the casinos seems, even though they are just down the road. You know you're in Margate when you see Lucy the Elephant, standing six stories tall, at the beach at Atlantic Avenue. Like many things in Atlantic City, Lucy was built as a publicity stunt, to help sell real estate, and that was back in 1881. Over the years the elephant actually became a tavern, then a rooming house, and later suffered storm and fire damage.

Thanks to the Save Lucy Committee, the elephant has been refurbished and even has its own Webcam. The Lucy beach, as locals call it, is a great place to meet friends, with the I Love Lucy Beach Grille next door.

Cape May County

To many Philadelphians, Cape May County *is* the Jersey Shore. But even on this small peninsula, each town differs noticeably from its neighbor, from family-friendly Ocean City to sedate Stone Harbor to raucous Wildwood. Maybe it's the nature of the coastal barrier islands, maybe it's the traffic on a summer weekend, but folks really seem to stick with their usual destination. We'll try to shake you out of that habit, because there's a lot to discover, even if you've been coming to the Shore for 20 years and think you know it well.

Ocean City

Ocean City calls itself "America's Greatest Family Resort," and clearly tens of thousands of families agree, as they return year after year. This emphasis on wholesome summer fun has been part of Ocean City since it was founded in 1879 by Methodist ministers, who laid down two laws: no commerce on the Sabbath and no alcohol. Nature, too, made Ocean City perfect for families; an offshore sandbar creates waves that roll gently in to shore.

Amusements at the Boardwalk, like the 140-foot Ferris wheel and the 18,000-square-foot, water-spraying playground, keep kids happy (if wet). But with no bars and no other nightlife, Ocean City works hard to keep folks of all ages from getting bored with all sorts of organized sports like tennis, softball, basketball, and a Jersey Shore classic, shuffleboard. There are lots of special events, too, including two that are unique to Ocean City: the annual Baby Parade, and the Night in Venice, when boat owners decorate their vessels in hopes of winning a prize.

The town tries to make it easy for you to stay here, too; the Ocean City Guest and Apartment House Association will search for something that fits your budget and schedule, whether it's an oceanfront house, an apartment, or just a clean motel.

With a year-round population of 17,000 and a summer influx of about 150,000, the biggest problem on this eight-mile-long island is its sheer popularity. Lately, residents complain of "duplex fever," a disease that sees developers buying up older homes to build two much larger new houses in place of each old one.

Sea Isle City

Originally called Ludlam Beach after Charles Ludlam, who bought the island in 1692, Sea Isle City is a resort that tries hard to be eco-friendly. The Environmental Commission of Sea Isle City has "graduated" more than 21,000 from its guided Beachcomber Walks, which educate adults and children about sand dunes, tides, shore birds, and the endangered diamondback terrapins.

From June until the end of July, female terrapins leave the marshes and cross a busy street in Sea Isle to reach higher ground, where they lay their eggs. To create public awareness and to save the turtles from being run over by cars, Sea Isle has adopted Sara the Turtle as its official mascot. There's an annual festival named after Sara to raise funds for the Sea Isle City Environmental Commission and the Wetlands Institute in Stone Harbor.

Of course, saving the turtles doesn't mean that folks in town have given up fishing. Party boats go out after bluefish, while crabbers dot the bay. You can buy live lobsters right off the boat in the afternoon. Surf-casting competitions offer cash prizes to whoever lands the biggest bluefish, weakfish, striped bass, kingfish, or what have you.

On the whole, Sea Isle is similar to Ocean City, but it is not and has never been dry. During Prohibition, the Coast Guard was kept busy chasing bootleggers around the island. These rumrunners were not Sea Isle's first outlaws, however; muzzle-loading pistols have been found in the sand dunes, left by pirates who hid in the inlets, waiting to plunder unsuspecting ships.

Avalon

Avalon was the name of the legendary island paradise where King Arthur went when he died, and Charles Bond, who bought the entire island in 1722 for $380, obviously thought he'd died and gone to heaven.

Avalon's glorious white sand beaches are not merely a tourist attraction, though; they're part of an ecosystem that's the focus of a determined preservation effort. Thanks to this effort, many of the native plants first seen by European settlers in 1722, like Compass grass, still thrive. This deep-rooted American dune grass anchors the sand dunes, even through hurricane-force winds. Local residents learned the value of the plant after a storm devastated the Shore in 1962; homes and property sheltered by wide beaches and high, healthy sand dunes survived. You're supposed to keep out of the dunes, as foot traffic can kill the grass.

One more reason to stay out of the sand dunes is that poison ivy grows there, too; though not kind to barefooted people, it also prevents erosion. Early settlers found holly trees along the secondary dunes; they are still here, along with fragrant honeysuckle from Japan, and native bayberry that feeds the birds, rabbits, and mice.

For visitors, Avalon offers a low-key place to enjoy the ocean. For locals, summer activities center around the Avalon Yacht Club, one of the Shore's finest. Avalon has some restaurants and a small boardwalk, but it's a far cry from the wilds of Wildwood. Though some condominiums have been built here, Avalon seems destined to remain unspoiled, as the World Wildlife Fund owns nearly a thousand acres of virgin marshland here.

Stone Harbor

In Stone Harbor, at the south end of Seven Mile Beach, ecological awareness is even more extensive than at the north end of the beach, in Avalon. Here, the Wetlands Institute has preserved 6,000 acres of marshlands, along with the thousands of birds, butterflies, and other creatures that call them home. This living laboratory is also a hands-on classroom for children, who take "mud walks" to learn about native plants and animals. In "Wetlandia," there are games and exhibits to reinforce the lessons learned from wading through the mud. Adults can explore this environmental wonderland in other ways: getting up close on a kayak trip, walking the gardens, or photographing the salt marsh trail.

A natural companion to the Wetlands Institute is the Stone Harbor Bird Sanctuary, which is registered as a national landmark by the National Park Service. The sanctuary began when various ornithological groups noted that a tract of virgin land between 111th Street and 117th Street attracted a variety of shore birds. They petitioned the mayor and council to preserve the area, and Stone Harbor Bird Sanctuary was created, the only municipal heronry in the United States. On its 21 acres birders can spot such species as the American egret, the snowy egret, the Louisiana heron, the green heron, and the glossy ibis. The best time to bird-watch is at dawn in late July to early August, when thousand of birds are still nesting.

As for human nests, Stone Harbor's cost well into the millions of dollars. (Word is that Oprah bought a place here.) You'll still see some magnificent Victorian houses on First Avenue and 85th Street and on the bay at 92nd Street. The imposing Villa Maria by the Sea was built at a cost of $250,000 in 1937; it houses 225 sisters of the Immaculate Heart of Mary.

Stone Harbor has a greater number of year-rounders than some of the other towns on the coast. It's not hard to figure out why: If you lived in this gorgeous sanctuary, would you ever want to leave?

Wildwood

Back when Elvis was king, and American cars sported big, useless tail fins, Wildwood was one of the Shore's top family resorts, a neon-light paradise of boardwalk amusements, turquoise and white motels, and lively nightspots where rising stars like Frankie Avalon and Tony Bennett crooned.

In most places, the eye-grabbing architecture of the 1950s and 1960s, called "populux" or "googie," with its space-age imagery, tropical colors, and exaggerated, angular elements, faded into oblivion. In Wildwood, though, the wacky structures of those Happy Days are here again, thanks in part to the efforts of the Doo-Wop Preservation League, which has drawn attention to some 220 buildings of the era in Wildwood.

These days, the mom-and-pop motels are freshly painted in turquoise, orange, and pink, while inside, Naugahyde, chrome, and Formica are rampant. At Big Ernie's Fabulous '50s diner, the 1959 Seeburg jukebox still plays records for a dime. Newer businesses like Restaurant Maureen jibe with older ones; its two-story neon martini glass, complete with olive, is the work of an architecture student. The Starlux Motel, a boutique property with a pool and Jacuzzi, features Jetson-style chairs in the lobby and such 1950s' touches as lava lamps and Swanson TV dinners. Even chains like Subway and Pizza Hut have followed suit, altering their facades to fit in.

Trolley tours of these flamboyant relics are given during the summer season. Tours start at the Doo-Wop Preservation League's headquarters, but even without a formal tour, it's not hard to pick out such fine specimens as the Waikiki, with its thatched-roof entryway, or the five-story pagoda-like Singapore Motel. At the Memory Motel, a neon electric guitar illuminates a mural of stars from the 1950s and 1960s.

Wildwood's two-mile Boardwalk is still going strong, with five amusement piers and 100 rides (more than Disneyland). The 140-foot-tall Ferris wheel and the Great White wooden roller coaster are the highest on the East Coast. Three water parks feature waterfalls, raft rides, tube floats, water guns for soaking, and even a 1,000-gallon dumping bucket that periodically douses those playing below.

For those who like their getaways active, there are tennis, beach volleyball, parasailing, helicopter rides, fishing aboard local party boats, bike rentals, and miniature golf.

The island does have quieter attractions, too. The free beaches, with their silky, smooth sand, get wider every year, unlike the rest of the Shore's. (All the sand that washes away has to go somewhere.)

In North Wildwood, the Hereford Inlet Lighthouse is a serene spot to watch a sunset. For a bit of local history, there are the George F. Boyer Historical Museum, the Wildwood Crest Historical Museum, and the Doo-Wop Museum. At Garfield Avenue and the Boardwalk, art lovers can contemplate "The Whaling Wall," a 220-foot-long seascape mural painted by renowned environmental artist Wyland.

Cape May

Cape May, the stately Victorian lady that is Wildwood's neighbor, is as far removed from neon lights and plastic palms as it is possible to be. Locals insist Cape May is the nation's first seaside resort. While residents of Long Branch could lay an equally convincing claim to that honor, Cape May has managed to retain its period character and charm, and Long Branch has not.

Cape May and West Cape May sit on an island that's known as Cape Island. Henry Hudson may have sailed by, but it was Cornelius Jacobsen Mey who explored the island in 1621 and named it "Cape Mey." Cape May's first European settlers were Quakers who chose the spot as a base for whaling.

The first visitors from Philadelphia came in 1766 to escape the heat of their city, to bathe in the sea, and to stroll the sandy beaches. When local innkeepers started running advertisements in the Philadelphia papers, they generated a rush, resulting in a shortage of accommodations. By the mid-18th century, Cape May had big hotels that could house hundreds of guests, music pavilions, and ballrooms; it soon became known as "Queen of the Seaside Resorts."

The list of distinguished visitors grew; it included Presidents Pierce, Arthur, Buchanan, Grant, and Harrison. Before Lincoln became president, he and his wife checked into The Madison House. By 1850, 3,000 people a day were visiting

Cape May. But in the period before the Civil War, when tensions ran high between North and South, the resort's popularity slumped. Northerners feared traveling "south" (if the Mason-Dixon line were straight, instead of dipping down into Pennsylvania, Cape May would be south of it); Southerners feared traveling north because of the abolitionist movement.

Some accounts of the period speak of Harriet Tubman and a Cape Island connection; the 1850 census does show that the abolitionist lived and worked in an island hotel at the time. There are rumors of various homes with secret rooms and long tunnels, and though these are difficult to document, it seems fairly certain that the Underground Railroad did indeed run through the island.

Hotel building continued, and such opulent properties as The Mount Vernon went up in 1853. This magnificent four-story establishment could accommodate 3,500 guests and seat 2,500 for dinner. Unfortunately it burned down in one of the several disastrous 19th-century fires that destroyed entire sections of Cape May. Today, two of the mammoth old hotels remain: the Inn of Cape May and Congress Hall, both 100 years old and relatively unchanged, their exteriors painted in the original colors of white and yellow, respectively.

In the aftermath of its great fires, Cape May's distinctive architecture took shape. From the 1860s to the 1880s, a building boom produced the wealth of Victorian-style homes that are Cape May's major asset today. Top architects created hundreds of buildings, representing every major style of the Victorian era. Lavishly ornamented with latticework, scrolls, and frets, houses were painted in a rainbow of colors to make every detail stand out.

Today Cape May boasts the greatest concentration of Victoriana in the country, some 600 beautifully restored structures. It has been designated a National Historic Landmark, the only city in the United States to achieve this status.

Cape May also has the distinction of being "The Birding Migration Capital of North America." In spring and fall, the birding areas can attract 75,000 to 80,000 visitors a day.

Cape May stands out among Shore communities for its brilliant use of all its resources and for the successful marketing

A carriage ride through Cape May is a good way to get into the spirit of this thoroughly Victorian town.
PHOTO: COURTESY OF CAPE MAY COUNTY TOURISM

of the town as a year-round destination. In fact, the so-called fall "shoulder season" is often busier here than the summer months. Tours are given daily, some on foot and some by trolley; these offer visitors a pleasant and informative peek into the past.

During the summer, Cape May offers a full schedule of events, including a six-week music festival, open-air concerts, winery tours and tastings, culinary classes, and kids' programs featuring jugglers, puppeteers, and storytellers. But social and cultural activities don't stop in September; Cape May engages visitors year-round with such events as Victorian Week in October, Thanksgiving Holiday Tours in November, and Christmas Candlelight Tours in December. It helps, of course, that Cape May's climate is milder than that of the northern Shore communities; its latitude is not much removed from that of Washington, D.C.

Cape May's beaches are not its strongest suit—those in neighboring towns are much nicer—but you won't mind because there is so much to do here. We'll give you detailed descriptions of places to go and things to do in the Attractions chapter. For now, we'll just tell you that Cape May has a wonderful selection of bed-and-breakfast inns and restaurants to suit every taste (the town likes to call itself the restaurant capital of the state).

Cape May Point

Cape May Point is a tiny community with a year-round population of 280. It's connected to Cape May by Sunset Boulevard, at the end of which you'll find the hull of a concrete ship called the *Atlantus*. Because steel was scarce during World War I, the government experimented with concrete and in 1918 built the *Atlantus*, a 3,000-ton freighter used as a coal steamer. The vessel was the Edsel of the high seas, far too bulky and heavy, slow and impractical. Decommissioned after the war, the ship was sold to a private ferry company. During a storm in 1926, the *Atlantus* broke loose and ran aground, where it remains, now a state historic site.

At Cape May Point you'll also find the Higbee Beach Wildlife Management Area, a 600-acre preserve of beach, meadows, ponds, and holly and scrub oak forests. Swimming is not allowed, but you can hunt, fish, and bird-watch. If you're interested in sea life, you'll see lots of horseshoe crabs in early summer, when they come up on the beach to lay their eggs.

Higbee Beach was once known as Diamond Beach for the "Cape May diamonds" that wash up here and at Sunset Beach. Pieces of almost pure quartz, ground smooth by weather and sand, they can be faceted and polished to resemble real gems. Most are colorless, others have a yellow or amber-brown hue, and they vary from pea-size to walnut-size. You can buy jewelry made from Cape May diamonds in local boutiques or create your own.

Cape May Point State Park, with its 19th-century lighthouse, was once part of the U.S. Coastal Defense network, so if you walk the beach today, you may (depending on the tide) be able to see remnants of the bunker and gun emplacement. Of course, these days it's not enemy ships that we're on the lookout for, it's the thousands of migratory birds that pass through here in the spring and fall. Legions of bird-watchers come from all over the country to take in the colorful spectacle and make use of the various bird-watching vantage points in the area; the Cape May Bird Observatory is almost next door.

Cape May Point has no restaurants and no hotels, but you can rent a cottage or bungalow if the solitude of this idyllic spot is to your taste. There are only three licensed businesses in the borough: the general store, which is seasonal; the Audubon Society, which sells books, photos, T-shirts, and the like; and the Italian-ice vendor, who has been selling his confections on the beach for 35 years. As there is no home delivery, all mail must be picked up at the post office. "It's a kind of social event," says one resident of the daily postal pickup. It's also the reason why there was no actual population count here during the last census (census forms must be sent to a street address).

Pirates and Brigands

Looking at Cape May today, it's hard to believe that at one time this staid Victorian village was the hub of pirate activity in South Jersey. Like all good pirate tales, especially those involving buried treasure, Cape May's certainly have a hefty dose of fiction padding the scanty facts. Some historians, for example, say that pirates actually had little treasure to bury, being given to drunkenness and carousing and generally living beyond their means. But who cares? It's fun to imagine that a treasure chest may be only a plastic shovelful of sand away.

Though pirates ranged the entire Shore, they seem to have been especially fond of Ocean City and Cape May. Ocean City, it is said, was much frequented by pirates, who docked their ships here to make repairs and replenish their stores. Supposedly the place was so popular with brigands that honest ships hesitated to approach. A guard barracks and garrison were established in 1723, which did curtail pirate activity.

Legend has it that Captain Kidd docked in the port of Ocean City before he was arrested and sent back to England, where he was tried and hanged. Many believed he was able to bury treasure around Ocean City before the authorities took him.

In its early days, Cape May served as a small port and a base of operations for the whaling industry. It was also popular as a provisioning stop for ships sailing eastward, through the Spanish Main to Europe. As port traffic increased, so did pirate interest. Given that the area was primarily swamp and marshlands, it afforded many natural hiding places among the marshy reeds. As unsuspecting captains guided their heavily laden vessels through the Delaware Bay, the pirates would pounce and plunder.

Captain Stede Bonnet, the "Gentleman Pirate," was a popular fellow around Cape May, thanks to his impeccable manners (he was born to an upper-class English family) and his habit of buying drinks for one and all, then tipping generously. It's said that the colonial governor of New Jersey offered Bonnet a full pardon, but the pirate declined, graciously, saying that he could not offer any assurances that he would give up his chosen career. So Bonnet continued to raid and rob until he was hanged in the Caribbean in 1721.

Captain Howell Davis, the "Jester Pirate," reportedly met his end at the hands of the British Navy off the coast of Cape May. And Captain Bartholomew Roberts supposedly lost a fortune in looted gold when one of his barques was sunk while he was attempting to run a blockade in Delaware Bay.

In case you didn't know that piracy was an equal-opportunity career choice, we offer the story of Anne Bonny and Mary Read. Anne, it seems, was a troubled child, born of an illicit union between her father and the household maid. Anne's marriage to James Bonny was equally unhappy, and brief. But she did catch the eye of pirate "Calico" Jack Rackham, who took her on as a member of his crew, and probably much more.

Dressing in men's clothing, Anne proved to be skillful with pistol and cutlass. While she was busy helping Jack pillage a merchant ship, one of its crew members—a Mary Read (who also liked to dress in men's clothing)—caught Anne's eye. Anne persuaded Jack to spare Mary's life, and the three went into business together.

Mary set up shop in Cape May, acting as a fence for whatever Jack and Anne could plunder. When the British colonial authorities caught on, they burned Mary's shop and issued arrest warrants for the trio. They fled, but after a bloody battle with

British ships in the Delaware Bay, they surrendered, were tried in England, and were found guilty of piracy. Jack was hanged, but Anne and Mary received stays of execution. Mary soon died of fever, but Anne mysteriously disappeared.

It is widely believed that Anne Bonny took on the new name of Mary Pritchard and began a new life in Cape May. The "proof" for this assumption is that when Mary Pritchard died in 1751, at the age of 64, her personal possessions included family heirlooms and documents relating to the Bonny family.

Though we have indicated a certain skepticism about buried treasure, we pass on the following rumors, just in case you're interested in searching for those elusive doubloons. Believers insist that Blackbeard, Captain Kidd, and Stede Bonnet buried some of their loot around Cape May. Some accounts even specify that Higbee's Beach is where Blackbeard stashed some of his gold. Stede Bonnet's treasure is supposed to be buried along the Delaware Bay. Though we've never found any, we have read that gold coins have washed ashore from time to time.

Natural World

Monmouth County
Ocean County
Atlantic County
Cape May County

We all know that the Jersey Shore has fabulous beaches, but what may come as a surprise to some of you bennies (see "Shore-speak," in the Getting Here, Getting Around chapter) is how much open space the Garden State preserves. Though New Jersey is the nation's most densely populated state, its Division of State Parks and Forestry administers some 325,000 acres of land, with more than 90 parks, forests, and natural areas.

Some of these open spaces are devoted more to wildlife than to people, like the 42,000-acre Edwin B. Forsythe National Wildlife Refuge, the Stone Harbor Bird Sanctuary, and of course, the Pine Barrens.

The Pine Barrens is an ecosystem that is unique in the world. Its 1.1-million acres, which sprawl across eight counties, comprise the largest tract of open space east of the Mississippi, about one-fifth of the size of the entire state. The pygmy pines that grow here barely reach 10 feet high, and the sandy soil drains off the rain that falls, leading to dry conditions and frequent forest fires. Nevertheless, many rare species thrive in this environment, like the bog asphodel, found nowhere else on the planet.

People thrive in the Shore's many parks, too. You'll find facilities for swimming, boating, fishing, hunting, canoeing, horseback riding, hiking, picnicking, camping, or just observing the wildlife.

There are no admission fees for the parks in this chapter, although some may have a nominal parking fee in summer. When no hours are listed, the parks are open daily from about 7:30 A.M. to dusk.

Monmouth County

Allaire State Park
Highway 524, Wall Township
(732) 938–2371

Though most visitors come to the park to see the 19th-century iron-making town of Allaire Village (see Attractions), there is more to do here. The 3,000-acre park is also a habitat for more than 200 species of wildflowers, trees, birds, and other wildlife, which makes it a pretty place to spend a few hours, especially in spring or fall. You can fish or canoe in the Manasquan River, which winds through the park. You can hike or ride mountain bikes or horses on the many trails. In winter, the park is a good place for cross-country skiing. There's also a playground for kids, and picnic tables where you can enjoy an outdoor lunch (bring your own or buy something from the food concession). More than 40 programs and events take place at Allaire Village each year; call (732) 938-2253 for the annual calendar, which includes living-history programs, antiques shows, arts and craft shows, and flea markets. The camping facilities are described in the Camping section of the Outdoor Activities chapter. The park is open year-round, with varying hours: from Memorial Day through Labor Day, from 8:00 A.M. to 8:00 P.M.; in spring and fall, from 8:00 A.M. to 6:00 P.M.; in winter, from 8:00 A.M. to 4:30 P.M.

Bayshore Waterfront Park
Port Monmouth Road, Port Monmouth
(732) 787–3033

With beach frontage on the Raritan Bay, this 145-acre park is a place where you can fish or launch a small boat. The Monmouth Cove Marina, which is part of the park, is a year-round boat facility with slips and rack storage. Call (732) 495-9440 for marina information.

Clayton Park
Emley's Hill Road, Upper Freehold
(609) 259–5794

You'll find farm fields, meadows, and woodlands in this 417-acre park. There are six miles of trails, so you can hike, bicycle, and ride your horse.

Deep Cut Gardens
352 Red Hill Road, Middletown
(732) 671–6050

Deep Cut Gardens, like a number of places in New Jersey, has a shady past. The scenic 54-acre tract was bought in 1925 by mob boss Vito Genovese, head of the Genovese crime family. Genovese, who lived in Atlantic Highlands, spared no expense in creating a veritable Eden, complete with Italian statuary and a model of Mount Vesuvius. He built stone walls, and on the hillside, he created an Italianate rock garden, an English boxwood garden, and ornamental pools. When he was charged with murder a few years later, Genovese fled to Italy and abandoned the property. The house burned down two weeks later. In New Jersey, these things happen. The next owner, Mrs. Marjorie Wihtol, bequeathed half the property to the Monmouth County Park System, which later acquired another 20 acres with state Green Acres funds. The horticultural park, which has commanding views of Atlantic Highlands and New York Harbor on a clear day, opened to the public in 1978; 13 more acres were added in 1990.

Plan to spend some time exploring the gardens. You'll see exotic trees and shrubs, daffodils in early spring, a riot of tulips and magnolias and rhododendrons in May, and roses during the summer. You may also see tree trunks covered with PVC piping to protect them from the deer. (The county's smaller garden, the Lambertus C. Bobbick Memorial Rose Garden in Thompson Park, was lost to deer. You'll find more exotics, including gorgeous orchids, in the greenhouse. There is also a gift shop and an extensive horticultural library. The garden is open daily year-round from 8:00 A.M. to 8:00 P.M.; the main building is open until 4:00 P.M.

Insiders' Tip

Enjoy the Shore's wildlife whenever you can, but protect the environment by observing some basic rules. Leave only footprints, take only pictures. Follow the trails and don't disturb the fragile habitats beside them.

Dorbrook Recreation Area
Highway 537, Colts Neck
(732) 542–1642

This 510-acre park has been developed for recreational activities such as tennis, basketball, softball, soccer, rugby, lacrosse, flag football, horseshoes, swimming, and model airplane flying. There is also a paved trail for walking, jogging, in-line skating, and biking.

East Freehold Park
Kozloski Road, Freehold
(732) 780–1021

This 81-acre park hosts a number of animal shows and special events each year. The Central Jersey Horse Club, the 4-H Association, and Los Alamos (dressage) hold equestrian events here every year. Call (732) 842–4000 for the current schedule. The annual Monmouth County Fair is held here every July; it's a five-day event that draws upwards of 100,000 visitors.

Fisherman's Cove Conservation Area
Third Avenue, Manasquan
(732) 922–3868, (732) 842–4000
www.monmouthcountyparks.com

This 52-acre site, the last undeveloped property on the Manasquan Inlet, was taken over by the Monmouth County Park System in 1995. It's a swell place to fish and watch birds.

A Word about Weather

New Jersey is 166 miles long, so there is a marked difference in climate between the mountains in the north and the southern shores of Cape May. Folks have always come down the Shore to enjoy the more moderate temperatures here, cooler in the summer and warmer in the winter. We all know how lovely the sea breeze is, but few people understand why the hotter it gets, the cooler the ocean breeze seems. Here's the explanation: When the land is warmed by the sun, the heated air rises, allowing cooler air at the ocean surface to spread inland. Sea breezes can be felt several miles inland.

Gateway National Recreation Area
Sandy Hook Unit
Off N.J. Highway 36
(732) 872–5900, (732) 872–5970

To most people, Sandy Hook is a beach peninsula that marks the northern tip of the Jersey Shore. It is, in fact, a 1,665-acre barrier peninsula that shelters the entrance to Raritan Bay and New York Harbor. It was created by accumulations of sediment moved by the longshore current. This narrow six-mile strip is a national park that includes six miles of beachfront and six miles of bayfront, as well as salt marshes, dunes, a maritime forest, and a habitat for migratory birds.

In this park you'll also find Sandy Hook Lighthouse, the Spermaceti Cove Life Saving Service Station, and Fort Hancock. The fort's guns have been dismantled, but you can still see the batteries and bunkers amid the sand dunes and sea grass.

Most of Sandy Hook's visitors come for the beaches, but there are so many other things to do here, including hiking, fishing, windsurfing, bird-watching, and ranger-guided tours. Pick up a map and activity information at the visitor center when you enter. The holly forest, the largest and oldest on the East Coast, is a wildlife sanctuary; some trees are said to be a century and a half old, but because of the salt air, they are much smaller than trees growing in gentler environments.

The nearby wooden boardwalk will take you to the salt marsh on Sandy Hook Bay. Watch for ospreys and other birds from the observation deck. The Audubon Society of New Jersey (www.njaudubon.org) has a center at Fort Hancock (in the park); it offers tours and programs throughout the summer season and into the fall.

Our favorite time to visit Sandy Hook is fall—after the summer crowds and the admissions-takers have departed. In September and often through October, temperatures (air and water) are still balmy, and the beaches are as peaceful and quiet as those on any island paradise. The visitor center is open daily from 10:00 A.M. to 5:00 P.M; the grounds are open every day.

Hartshorne Woods Park
Navesink Avenue, Locust (Middletown)
(732) 872–0336

A magnet for mountain bikers, joggers, walkers, and equestrians, the park has 736 acres, including three miles of paved paths closed to vehicular traffic in the Rocky Point section. The park's location in a posh residential area makes it especially appealing. The Rocky Point section was once a military installation and part of the Atlantic Coast Defense System. It fronts the Navesink River, so you can fish there. In winter, bring your cross-country skis and have a good time. There are group cabins available, by reservation. The park is open dawn to dusk.

Henry Hudson Trail
Aberdeen to Atlantic Highlands
(732) 842-4000

Walkers, cyclists, and in-line skaters use these nine miles of paved trail parallel to N.J. Highway 36, on what was once a railroad right-of-way.

Holmdel Park
Longstreet Road, Holmdel
(732) 946-9562, (732) 842-4000

The 343-acre Holmdel Park is one of the county system's most-used facilities. At the front is historic Longstreet Farm, a living-history site where employees in period dress milk cows, tend chickens, and do farm chores as they were done in past centuries. (See the Living-History Farms and Historic Villages chapter for more on Longstreet.) In good weather, you can fish for trout, bass, catfish, and bluegill. You can hike the eight miles of trails that take you through beech, hickory, oak, tulip, spruce, and pine trees. Enjoy the hillside arboretum, where you'll see flowering crabapple and cherry trees, rhododendrons, and shade trees.

In winter, bring ice skates, cross-country skis, or a sled (there's a sledding hill). Warm up later in the shelter building.

Huber Woods Park
25 Brown's Dock Road (off Navesink River Road), Locust (Middletown)
(732) 872-2670

Located in a gorgeous estate area (not far from Bon Jovi's French chateau), this 258-acre park lets you enjoy land-baron privileges without the investment. The fabulous view of the Navesink River is a start. Walk the Nature Loop, a short, easy path that takes you through stands of mountain laurel and pink azalea; in fall, you can keep an eye out for migrating birds and butterflies. The park's trails, for hiking, biking, or horseback riding, take you across meadows or through woods that are home to foxes, chipmunks, woodpeckers, and great horned owls.

Manasquan Reservoir
311 Windeler Road, Howell Township
(732) 919-0996

Bring your fishing pole and try for largemouth bass, smallmouth bass, hybrid striped bass, tiger muskie, panfish, bullhead catfish, or trout. If you don't own a boat, rent one (kayaks available, too) and spend a peaceful day relaxing on the water. The boating season is March through November. See the park rangers for boat rentals, boat passes, fishing rules, and other regulations. Walk the five-mile perimeter trail at this splendid 1,354-acre site built by the New Jersey Water Authority and managed by the county parks system. You'll see an abundance of wildlife in the 1,200 acres of woods and wetlands, including birds and waterfowl. In the winter, you can ice-skate, ice-boat, or ice-fish here. And just about anytime, you can enjoy a panoramic view of the reservoir from the visitor center lounge.

Manasquan Stream Valley
Howell
(732) 919-0996, (732) 842-4000

Almost 700 acres here have been acquired by the county and are now preserved as open space in their natural state. There's access to the river for canoes and kayaks from a parking lot on Squankum-Yellowbrook Road in Howell.

Mount Mitchell Scenic Overlook
Scenic Drive, Atlantic Highlands

Rising hundreds of feet above sea level, this small park has a million-dollar view of Sandy Hook and the New York skyline. Bring your lunch, park your car, and be dazzled. After the World Trade Center tragedy, crowds gathered here to gaze at the sadly altered skyline.

Seven Presidents Oceanfront Park
Ocean Avenue at Joline Avenue (N.J. Highway 36), Long Branch
(732) 229-7025

Named after the seven U.S. presidents who vacationed in Long Branch between 1869 and 1921, this park is a great place to sun, swim, fish, and surf. It's especially nice in the off-season, when the crowds have gone and you can listen to the gulls and the waves. There's a boat launch for small craft, a pavilion with a snack bar (seasonal), and an activity center with programs run by the county parks system. The park is open daily from 8:00 A.M. to dusk. You'll pay an admission and parking fee only during the summer season. An added bonus from spring till October: a short walk from the park is Strollo's Italian Ice stand.

Shark River Park
1101 Schoolhouse Road, Neptune
(732) 922–3868

Acquired in 1961, this was the county system's first park, occupying land on either side of the Shark River, in Neptune and Wall Townships. With almost 600 acres, the park invites you either to relax or play. You can fish or hike. If it's winter, you can get out the skates and cross-country skis. Or you can do nothing but take in the fresh air and the beauty of the river, sandy hills, and forest.

Tatum Park
Red Hill Road and Holland Road, Middletown
(732) 671–9283

Rolling hills, open fields, woods crisscrossed with four miles of trails that wind through tulip trees and red and chestnut oaks—that begins to describe this 368-acre park. You won't get bored with this landscape, for it changes in color every season. Most visitors hike, bike, ride horses, or ski, but you can just bring the kids to the playground near the Red Hill Activity Center at the edge of the woods and watch them have a workout. There are picnic tables and two activity centers (Holland and Red Hill) that offer many programs for adults and children.

Thompson Park
805 Newman Springs Road, Lincroft
(732) 842–4000

The Monmouth County Park System's administrative and program registration offices are located in this 665-acre former horse farm, so there is always something interesting going on here. There are classes in everything from astronomy to nature photography, summer adventure programs for young people, and outdoor programs for every age group. If you don't

like too much structure, take a nature walk or fish for bass, bluegill, and perch at the lake in the western part of the park. There used to be a beautiful memorial rose garden here, but the burgeoning deer population decided the prize-winning blooms smelled and looked good enough to eat. And they were.

Turkey Swamp Park
Georgia Road, Freehold Township
(732) 462–7286

A prime attraction of this thousand-acre park is the 17-acre lake, where you can boat or fish for bass, catfish, and bluegills, either from the shore or from canoes and rowboats (these can be rented in summer). In winter, ice-skate on the lake. If you walk the four miles of trails, you'll come across forests of pitch pine and oak trees—and possibly some wet areas because of the swamps and bogs. The park has an archery range and playgrounds. If you're planning a big outdoors get-together, you can reserve a picnic shelter for your group. You can camp here, too, but more about that in the Outdoor Activities chapter.

Ocean County

A. Paul King County Park
N.J. Highway 72 and U.S. Highway 9,
Stafford Township
(609) 296–5606

Here's a pleasant summer alternative to ocean beaches that charge badge fees, especially when you have company. Swim from the protected sandy beach (open from mid-June through August), fish, toss horseshoes, or take the kids to enjoy the brightly colored playground.

Barnegat Lighthouse State Park
Broadway and the Bay, Barnegat Light
609) 494–2016

Once you've appreciated the view from the lighthouse—a panorama of Island Beach, Barnegat Bay, and Long Beach Island—you can explore the natural beauty of this 32-acre site on the northern tip of Long Beach Island. Follow a short

Nor'easters

Coastal winter storms, called nor'easters because the wind comes from that direction, are most common between October and April. Historically, nor'easters have been a bigger threat to the Jersey Shore's beach towns than hurricanes, causing major flooding, power outages, beach erosion, and millions of dollars worth of property damage. Fortunately, within recent memory there have only been a few really big nor'easters, with gale-force winds and super-high tides.

During the early part of the 20th century, nor'easters changed the very geography of the Shore. For example, during the winter of 1916, a storm virtually destroyed a 10-block section of Longport on Absecon Island, then washed the debris, including the land on which it stood, on to the northern section of Ocean City. In effect, the Great Egg Harbor Inlet separating Atlantic City from Ocean City moved north. This phenomenon has happened elsewhere, affecting virtually every inlet along the coast during the past two centuries.

In February 1920, the Shore (like the rest of the state) was hit with 17 inches of snow and sleet. On Long Beach Island, storm-driven seas opened up a new inlet between Holgate and Tuckers Beach; it became known as the Beach Haven Inlet. To the north, entire streets vanished as the Barnegat Inlet continued its movement south.

One storm that many residents still remember (with a shudder) is the Great Atlantic Storm of 1962. That March storm devastated the Jersey Shore, causing $130 million in damage, and killed 40 people. More than 4,000 buildings were demolished, and boardwalks all along the Shore were splintered and tossed around like so many toothpicks. The storm surges rolled over Long Beach Island, opening up five new ocean-to-bay inlets, in effect breaking the island into smaller pieces.

We remember the nor'easter of December 1992, when winds of over 90 miles an hour pounded the Shore from Sea Bright down to Atlantic City, tearing up boardwalks and toppling power lines. Residents were evacuated from some flooded towns. What saved the Shore from a repeat of 1962 was that this storm waned after the first day—unlike the earlier nor'easter, which maintained its intensity for three days.

self-guided trail through one of the state's last remaining maritime forests, dominated by black cherry, eastern red cedar, and American holly. The forest is an important resting and feeding area for migrating birds; spring and fall is the time to see them. In addition you can observe shorebirds and ducks, black-crowned night herons, snowy egrets, brown pelicans, and harlequin ducks.

If you like saltwater fishing, use the bulkhead along the picnic area to try your luck with striped bass, bluefish, weakfish, summer flounder, tautog, winter flounder, and black bass. The park is included as a maritime site on the New Jersey Coastal Heritage Trail and is open from dawn to dusk. The lighthouse is open daily throughout the summer and on weekends in the spring and fall. The lighthouse also is open some evenings during the summer (see the Lighthouses chapter for details).

The New Jersey Coastal Heritage Trail

The New Jersey Coastal Heritage Trail route was established in 1988 "to provide for public appreciation, education, understanding, and enjoyment" of the significant natural and cultural sites associated with the state's coastal area.

The Coastal Heritage Trail is divided into five regions linked by a common heritage of life on the Jersey Shore and the Raritan and Delaware Bays. The trail extends along coastal New Jersey—from Perth Amboy to Cape May on the Atlantic Coast—and west along the Delaware Bay from Cape May to the Delaware Memorial Bridge at Deepwater, New Jersey. Designed for automobile touring, the route covers nearly 200 miles. Along the way you'll pass through cranberry bogs, salt hay meadows, and fishing villages. You can explore forts, lighthouses, historical mansions and hotels; see boardwalks and amusements; or learn about glassmaking and ironworks.

If you'd like to make all or part of this trip, visit the trail's Web page for a listing of destinations, with site descriptions of each region. It's www.nps.gov/neje.

Bass River State Forest
762 State Road, New Gretna
(609) 296–1114

There is so much to see and do in this wonderful place. You can hike the Batona Trail (see "The Pine Barrens," page 38), or walk the trail in the Absegami Natural Area, where Atlantic white cedars share the canopy with magnolias and red maples. Swim, boat (electric motors only), or canoe in beautiful Lake Absegami. You may trap or hunt in the park, subject to regulations. Bring your mountain bike or your horse, if you have one.

In the West Pine Plains Natural Area, you'll find the rare ecosystem known as the Pygmy Forest; here the pine and oak trees reach a height of only 4 feet. This area also supports the endangered broom crowberry as well as some rare species of moths. The park is open daily from 9:00 A.M. to sunset.

Beaver Dam Creek County Park
Bridge Avenue, Point Pleasant

It's not a big place, just 40 acres, but you can take a stroll along the boardwalk through tidal wetlands, have a picnic, or

watch the kids enjoy the playgrounds and playing fields. The park is open from dawn to dusk.

Berkeley Island County Park
Brennan Concourse, Berkeley Township

This park is another of the nice alternatives to the ocean beaches, with protected bay bathing and a nice sandy beach. Situated on a scenic peninsula jutting out into the calm waters of Barnegat Bay, it also offers a swell view of the bay. Bring a beach chair and spend the day as the locals do, swimming, sunning, or crabbing from the 100-foot pier. The park has a small boat launch and is open from dawn to dusk.

Cattus Island County Park
1170 Cattus Island Boulevard, Toms River
(732) 270–6960, (877) OCPARKS
www.oceancountygov.com/county/parks

Unspoiled and environmentally sensitive, this park encompasses almost 500 acres and has miles of trails, many with scenic vistas of Silver Bay. Stroll the boardwalk through wetlands, or try your luck at fishing or crabbing. At the Cooper Environmental Center, you'll see snake and reptile displays along with other environment-related exhibits. The center offers a Junior Naturalist Program, which involves youngsters in various hands-on activities.

Colliers Mills Wildlife Management Area
Toms River Road (Highway 571) and High Bridge Road, Jackson
(609) 259–2132

If you love rugged outdoor activity, you'll find happiness at this 12,369-acre area. Bring your mountain bike or your horse—or your canoe or kayak. If you're traveling light you can hike the unmarked trails or look for birds. If you hunt, you'll find shotgun, archery, and rifle ranges here, along with a dog-training area. You may hunt for small game, deer, turkey, and waterfowl.

Double Trouble State Park
Pinewald-Keswick Road (Highway 618), Bayville
(732) 341–6662

First it was a sawmill, then a cranberry farm and packing plant; the former company town of Double Trouble reflects typical Pinelands industries, past and present. Today Double Trouble Village, which is part of the state park, includes active cranberry bogs leased to the New Jersey Devil Cranberry Company and 14 original historic structures from the late 19th century through the early 20th century: a general store, a schoolhouse, and cottages. The sawmill was restored in 1995, and the restoration of the cranberry sorting and packing house was completed in 1996.

The park encompasses more than 5,000 acres of Pine Barrens habitats. You can fish or canoe on Cedar Creek, which provides pure water for the cranberries and the wildlife. Look for otters, beavers, bluebirds, and deer. There are trails for hiking, biking, horseback riding, or nature walks. Hunting is allowed here, too; check with the ranger for rules. The park is on the New Jersey Coastal Heritage Trail; it is open from dawn to dusk.

E. B. Leone Conservation Area
Silver Bay, off Hooper Avenue, Toms River
(732) 270–6960

Insiders' Tip

When you hike in wooded areas, be aware of ticks. Wear a hat and long-sleeved shirt for protection. Choose loose-fitting, light-colored clothing so that you can see ticks more easily. To lessen the likelihood of ticks getting inside your clothing, tuck your pants into your socks or boots and your shirt into your pants. Avoid heavy vegetation and stay on trails. Check yourself often. It takes ticks hours to attach, so if you're alert, you can pull them off before they do.

Join the park department's pontoon boat tour to visit these 45 acres of pristine wetlands on the northern shore of Silver Bay. Call for schedule information.

Eno's Pond County Park
330 East Lacey Road, Forked River

Once upon a time, back in colonial days, Eno's Pond was a source of ice for the hotel that was located here. The hotel is long gone, but there's a nice observation deck overlooking the pond. As this park is adjacent to the Forsythe Refuge, there's a rustic foot trail that begins at Eno's, loops through a half mile of the refuge, and ends at Eno's. Your journey will take you through a variety of upland and freshwater wetland habitats. In addition to the observation decks, there's also a wildlife observation blind. After you look for

The Pine Barrens

The New Jersey Pine Barrens—1.1 million acres that sprawl over eight counties, about one-fifth of the entire state—is the largest tract of open space east of the Mississippi. The Pine Barrens, also known as the Pinelands, is designated as a biosphere reserve by the United Nations; the Nature Conservancy, recognizing its environmental importance, named it a "Last Great Place." You'll find many rare and interesting plants in the Pinelands. The federally protected swamp pink lily grows here; in fact, the Pine Barrens has two-thirds of the known specimens left in the country. The exotic lady slipper orchid thrives down south, along with pitcher plants, sundews, and curly grass fern. The bog asphodel grows nowhere else in the world.

Thirty-nine animal species considered threatened with extinction in New Jersey, such as the barred owl and northern pine snake, are found in the Pine Barrens. Look out for the Pine Barrens tree frog, an endangered species about one and one-half inches long that makes its home here.

Clearly the Pine Barrens are not barren at all. The Dutch settlers gave the area this name because they could not grow their traditional crops here because of the high pH of the soil. Only a few agricultural crops thrive here, namely cranberries and blueberries. (See the Farms and Wineries chapter for more on these.)

In addition to its alkalinity, the Pine Barrens' sandy soil creates a unique climate here. On clear nights, solar radiation absorbed during the day is quickly radiated back into space, resulting in surprisingly low minimum temperatures. For example, Atlantic City's airport, which is surrounded by sandy soil, can be 15 to 20 degrees cooler than the Atlantic City Marina on the bay, even though these two areas are separated by only about 13 miles.

Canoeing on the Batsto River is a good way to explore the Pine Barrens. PHOTO: LILLIAN AFRICANO

It rains less in the Pine Barrens than it does up north, and the porous soil here absorbs precipitation quickly, leaving the surface quite dry. These drier conditions create a wider range of temperatures during the day—and make the area vulnerable to forest fires. Fires are actually part of the life cycle of the Pine Barrens; for example, the pygmy pine cones open and germinate after a fire.

Many of the parks listed in this chapter lie at least partly within the Pine Barrens: Allaire, Bass River, Double Trouble, Ocean County Park, Wells Mills, and Wharton State Forest. Though the parks preserve wildlife habitats, there are plenty of ways for the entire family to enjoy nature in the Pine Barrens: hiking, boating, swimming—and that's just a start.

You'll find some of the Pinelands' most scenic vistas along the Forked River Mountains. Drive north on Highway 539 from Barnegat. Take a guided hike with either the Forked River Mountain Coalition or the Ocean County Parks Department and you'll see pristine ponds, meandering sugar-sand trails, and breathtaking woods.

The Batona Trail wanders through the heart of the Pinelands, so it's a fine way to get acquainted with this teeming-with-life preserve. Though this is a 50-mile wilderness trail, it is not difficult to walk, and there's no need to tackle the whole thing. Pick up a map from the Wharton State Forest visitor center and ask the ranger's advice on choosing a section you can handle. The trail, which is maintained by the Batona Hiking Club and the New Jersey Park Service, is well marked with pink blazes and presents no hardships, save for some rolling hills and wet areas. It runs near Batsto Village and connects Wharton State Forest, Lebanon State Forest, and the Bass River State Forest. It crosses streams and passes through forested areas that were once home to prosperous towns like Four Mile, Butler, Martha, and Washington. If you're alert, you may see some of the unique plant life found only in the Pine Barrens, as well as orchids, great horned owls, hummingbirds, and great blue herons. This walk is especially inspiring in fall or spring. Horses, bikes, motorcycles, and ATVs are not permitted on the trail.

shorebirds and other wildlife, adjourn to the picnic area. Eno's Pond Park is on the New Jersey Coastal Heritage Trail.

Florence T. Allen Conservation Area
Along Mill Creek, Berkeley Township

This 45-acre conservation area of cedar swamp and uplands borders Mill Creek; the wetlands protect the creek as it flows into the Toms River.

Forest Resource Education Center
370 Veterans Highway, Jackson
(732) 928–0987
www.state.nj.us/dep/forestry

Don't you wish you had a classroom like this when you were in school? Where you could learn all about trees—outdoors? Run by the New Jersey Forest Service, the center has 400 acres near the headwaters of the Toms River; the "school" features the ABC Arboretum, the New Jersey Forestry Learning Deck, and the Forest Tree Nursery. Call if you'd like to schedule a tour or learn about the center's special events.

Forked River Mountain Wildlife
Management Area
Jones Road, off Highway 532,
Lacey Township
(609) 259–2132

Take in the scenery from one of the highest elevations in the Pine Barrens. These mountains are typical of the mixed pine-oak habitats you'll find in South Jersey. The waterfront boardwalk and the gazebo make for nice photographic props.

Gull Island County Park and Conservation Area
Broadway, Point Pleasant Beach

Most of this 48-acre parcel is an island conservation area, but you can fish the Manasquan River just across from the site. Though it's small, this park is a pleasant spot for bird-watching or relaxing with a picnic lunch on a bench. The area is open from dawn to dusk.

Island Beach State Park
N.J. Highway 35, Seaside Park
(732) 793–0506
www.state.nj.us/dep/forestry/parknj/divhome

Island Beach State Park, with more than 3,000 acres of ocean- and bayfront land, is both a nature preserve and a place for people to enjoy. This 10-mile strip of barrier island must look much as it did a century ago, the bleached-white driftwood dotting the beaches, and the red cedar, beach plum, and American holly trees thriving in the sandy soil.

If you want to swim, there are pavilions with lockers, showers, and rest rooms in the center of the park. Though there are also food concessions, you may bring your own food and picnic; you're even allowed to barbecue, providing your fire is at least 50 feet east of the dunes. You can also surf, fish, or scuba dive at Island Beach.

Take a nature hike on your own or, if it's summer, join a guided tour with a park naturalist; these are given twice a day. If you're a bird-watcher, then you know that Island Beach, like Sandy Hook, Cape May, and so many other Shore areas, is on the Atlantic Flyway. So in spring and fall

you'll see lots of resting migratory birds.

On summer Sundays, you can take canoe or kayak tours of Sedge Island. During these three-hour trips, you'll paddle through pristine wetlands and see the largest osprey colony in the state, along with other bird species. The park will furnish equipment, though you may bring your own canoe or kayak. You'll also need to bring drinking water, snacks, bug spray, sunblock, a hat, and water shoes (not flip-flops). Children between 8 and 13 must be accompanied by two adults. The tours are free, but reservations are necessary; call (732) 793–0506 or (732) 793–1698.

If you're a boater, then Tice's Shoals is where you'll go. Just leave your craft at the dock and simply walk to the beautiful Atlantic for a dip in the ocean. Tice's Shoals (also known as "Cocktail Cove") is not one of those well-kept secrets, however. On a nice day you're likely to see scores of boats bobbing on the water while their owners sunbathe or lunch on board, picnic on the beach, ride their jet skis, swim in the ocean, and just generally have a good time. Though you've no doubt heard about the costly maintenance that boats require, their owners get a little financial break here: they get into the park free. (Entry fees to the park are by the carload, so walkers and bikers also enter free.) It's open from dawn to dusk.

Jacques Cousteau National Estuarine Research Reserve at Mullica River–Great Bay
800 Great Bay Boulevard, Tuckerton
(732) 932–6555, ext. 521, (609) 294–3746
www.marine.rutgers.edu/cool

At this research facility, which encompasses more than 115,000 acres of aquatic and forested habitat, the JCNERR collects information about the ocean, using remotely controlled instruments, and relays it to a Web site. The reserve's Coastal Learning Center offers interactive educational programs. Visit the Web site to learn more about these programs.

Lake Shenandoah County Park
N.J. Highway 88 (Ocean Avenue), Lakewood
(732) 363–9678

A beautiful 100-acre lake surrounded by majestic pine and oak trees—who could ask for more tranquil surroundings to fish trout-stocked waters? There are large piers, on-site boat rentals, and a bait-and-tackle shop, for your convenience. If fishing isn't your pleasure, there are trails for hiking and biking, too. The park is open from dawn to dusk.

Metedeconk River County Conservation Area
Lakewood and Brick Townships

This 318-acre greenway was acquired by the county freeholders to preserve the wetlands along the north and south branches of the Metedeconk River. It includes the Forge Pond Conservation Area. Canoe, fish, and watch for birds, any time between dawn and dusk.

Mill Creek County Park
Mill Creek Road and Chelsea Avenue, Berkeley Township

Mill Creek County Park is located in Berkeley Township between Pine Beach and Ocean Gate. Cedar-chip trails, the Mill Creek and the Toms River beyond, and three playgrounds make this a scenic and inviting park. It's the perfect spot for a family picnic under the pavilion or at one of several secluded picnic tables. The 14-acre park also has basketball courts, a conservation area, and a nature trail.

Ocean County Park
N.J. Highway 88 (Ocean Avenue), Lakewood
(732) 506–9090

Formerly part of the summer estate of financier John D. Rockefeller, this park is the flagship of the county system. As befits a property from the days when Lakewood was an upscale resort, the park abounds with mature white pine, hemlock, and other specimen trees that were imported by Rockefeller from all over the country. Today, these 323 acres are available for everyone's enjoyment. Swim in the large clear lake, fish, hike or bike the trails, have a picnic, or play on the open fields. There's even a driving range. If you'd like to throw a big family picnic on land that a Rockefeller once called his own, you can—but reserve early. In winter, the park becomes a magical wonderland, so bring your cross-country skis. The park is open from dawn to dusk.

River Front Landing County Park
Water Street, Toms River (Dover Township)

Located on the water in downtown Toms River, this tiny park is a popular lunch-break spot among people who work in the area. A sandwich tastes better when it comes with a scenic river view.

Robert Miller Airpark
Highway 530, Berkeley

Once a year, in July, this park becomes a star: 4-H Clubs, vendors, entertainers, exhibitors, and crowds of visitors gather here for the really big Ocean County Fair (call 732-349-1227 for information). The rest of the year, locals walk or bike the trails, frolic in the playground, and feast in the picnic area; there's an independently managed airport here, too.

Sister Mary Grace Arboretum and Historic Gardens
Georgian Court College, Lakewood
(732) 364–2200, ext. 345
www.georgian.edu/arboretum/index.html

Do you need a good excuse to visit what was once the home of railroad tycoon Jay Gould? Here are four: the classically designed gardens that were part of this glamorous estate. There's an Italian garden, a sunken garden, a formal garden, and a serene Japanese garden. You'll see exotic plants as well as some native to the Pine Barrens.

Stanley H. "Tip" Seaman County Park
Lakeside Drive, Tuckerton
(609) 296–5606

Located on the banks of Lake Pohatcong, just across from Tuckerton Seaport, "Tip" is a hometown favorite. Site of the Barnegat Bay Decoy Museum, the park is probably best known for the two-day annual Ocean County Decoy and Gunning Show, which draws exhibitors and visitors from all over the East Coast; it's been named as one of the top 100 events in North America. You can fish at the park (there's a small boat launch), view the many varieties of waterfowl that gather here from fall to spring, walk the fitness trail, or relax with a picnic. The park is open from dawn to dusk.

Wells Mills Country Park and Nature Center
905 Wells Mills Road (Highway 532), Waretown
(609) 971–3085

Get acquainted with the ecology of the Pine Barrens: the 32-acre freshwater lake, streams, bogs, swamps, uplands—and the rare and interesting vegetation that's unique to each habitat. In this one 900-acre park, you'll find pine-oak forests and Atlantic white cedar swamps, freshwater bogs, and maple gum swamps. After looking up to the soaring cedars, cast your eyes closer to the ground and you'll see pitcher plants, sundew, and sphagnum moss, to name just a few of the resident plants.

Experience the park with a picnic under the pines. Bring your binoculars along for bird-watching. Hike the 16 miles of trails; paddle a canoe on the lake. View the exhibits at the three-story Nature Center. If you like formal activities, the park offers plenty—including Jersey Devil hunts (organized walks accompanied by spooky tales).

Atlantic County

Edwin B. Forsythe National Wildlife Refuge
Great Creek Road, Oceanville
(609) 652–1655

If shorebirds are your passion, you'll want to visit this remarkable wildlife refuge. Most of the 40,000 acres here are tidal salt meadow and marsh interspersed with shallow cover and bays. These provide resting and feeding habitats for shorebirds, while the marsh vegetation provides food and cover for many varieties of wildlife. Another 3,000-plus acres of the refuge are woodlands, which provide a home for songbirds, woodcocks, white-tailed deer, box turtles, and other creatures.

The Forsythe is a birder's paradise any time of year, but especially during the spring and fall migration, when thousands and thousands of ducks, geese, wading birds, and shorebirds arrive. On any given day, you might see snow geese from Canada, peregrine falcons and bald eagles, or shorebirds from Tierra del Fuego or Arctic Canada.

To protect the refuge from foot traffic, visitors' primary access is by car; you can drive an eight-mile trail guided by a brochure (pick one up at the information office) that lists points of interest. There are areas where you may walk; you may also climb the three observation towers, all equipped with spotting scopes. And thanks to a quirky bit of geography, amid all this nature you'll have a terrific view of the resort towers of Atlantic City looming on the southeastern horizon. The refuge is open daily from sunrise to sunset. The information office is open daily from 8:00 A.M. to 4:00 P.M.

Estell Manor Park—Atlantic County Parks
109 N.J. Highway 50, Mays Landing
(609) 645–5960, (609) 625–1897

This 1,700-acre park is bordered by Great Egg Harbor/South River to the east and by N.J. Highway 50 to the west. It's the Atlantic County Park System's most popular park, and the parks division headquarters. The land, which was once occupied by Native Americans, was later owned by the Estell family. During the 19th century it was the site of a glassworks; during World War I it held a munitions plant. Now reclaimed by the forest, the park is home to many animals and plants, including bald eagles, otters, red foxes, beavers, yellow-bellied sapsuckers, swamp pink, and spatulate-leaf sundew. You can get maps and brochures at the Warren E. Fox Nature Center, which also houses animals and environmental displays. A number of educational and recreational programs are also held at the center. You can canoe or kayak off the floating dock on Stephen's Creek or at South River; boats may be launched from the north end of the park. There's fishing off the dock and on the river, too. There are grills and picnic tables as well as pavilions you can reserve for large family outings or other special events. There's a 2.2-mile multiuse loop road that's good for walking, jogging, biking, or exercising (there are exercise stations within the loop). Be careful, however, since cars also use the road. Recreation facilities include volleyball courts (sand), a soccer field, and a softball field (equipment on loan in the Nature Center). During Nature Center hours, you may also borrow bikes and helmets, Frisbees, jump ropes, and horseshoes. Most of the park trails convert to cross-country ski trails when it snows. The park is open from 8:00 A.M. to 4:00 P.M. from Monday through Friday and from 10:00 A.M. to 4:00 P.M. on weekends and holidays.

Marine Mammal Stranding Center and Sea Life Museum
3625 Brigantine Boulevard, Brigantine
(609) 266–0538

When a humpback whale gets beached or a dolphin gets lost, the rescue workers of the Stranding Center are on the spot, ready to do whatever is needed. Since the center was established in 1978, they've made about 2,000 rescues. One of the tiniest creatures rescued was a 2½-ounce loggerhead turtle hatchling. "He was so tiny, we had to weigh him on a postage scale," said a staffer. The turtle did well and was eventually released. One of the biggest mammals the center handled was a 66-ton finback whale, which was, unfortunately, dead on arrival.

You can see whatever mammals are currently being cared for at the center, if they're not too sick. You also can tour the museum, which has photos of some of the spectacular rescues, as well as a giant tank housing all kinds of creatures that live in New Jersey waters. The museum also has life-size replicas of game fish, sea turtles, and other marine mammals. During the summer, it's open Tuesday through Sunday from 10:00 A.M. to 4:00 P.M.; from Labor Day to Christmas, it's open Saturday and Sunday from 11:00 A.M. to 3:00 P.M.; after Christmas, it's Sunday only, from 11:00 A.M. to 3:00 P.M. In the off-season, it's a good idea to call ahead.

Wharton State Forest
Batsto Station: Highway 542, eight miles east of Hammonton

Atsion Station: Highway 206, eight miles north of Hammonton
(609) 561–0024, (609) 561–3262, (609) 268–0444

If, like most people, you come to Wharton to visit Batsto Village, allow some time to savor the natural beauty of this magnificent place. It's the largest single tract of land within the New Jersey State Park System, extending into Atlantic, Burlington, and Camden Counties, and it can be enjoyed in so many ways.

You can swim in Atsion Lake (there's a bathhouse), canoe on your choice of rivers—Mullica, Batsto, Wading, and Oswego—hike the Batona Trail, fish, hunt, mountain bike, ride your horse, or hike the marked nature trails.

If you're interested in the rare plants of the Pine Barrens, the free leaflet "Plant Life of Wharton State Forest" will help you search. Perhaps you'll come across the rare bog asphodel. If it's birds you want to see, look for bald eagles, red-tailed hawks, ospreys, great blue herons, or spotted owls, to name just a few. And as for other woodland creatures, Wharton is also home to beavers, river otters, foxes, and deer. There are extensive camping facilities in Wharton, and we'll describe them in the Camping section of the Outdoor Activities chapter.

Cape May County

Belleplain State Forest
Highway 550, Woodbine
(609) 861–2404

At this sprawling 15,811-acre forest, you'll find seasonal activities to suit every preference. In warm weather, you can swim in Lake Nummy, which has a bathhouse and floating dock, canoe (rentals available), or boat (electric motors only). Fishing, trapping, and hunting are allowed; check with the park ranger for regulations. In winter, there are all kinds of fun options, including ice-fishing, snowmobiling, and cross-country skiing. And of course, you can always hike the trails through forests of pine, oak, and Atlantic white cedar. There are extensive camping facilities (see the Outdoor Activities chapter).

The World Series of Birding

Every year, legions of birders gather at the southern tip of the state to participate in the New Jersey Audubon Society's World Series of Birding. The challenge? Count as many bird species as you can during a designated 24-hour period. The field of play? The entire state, but teams must check in at the finish line in Cape May Point State Park before the end of the 24-hour period. For more information on this and many other birding get-togethers throughout the state, call (609) 884–2730 or visit www.njaudubon.org.

Cape May Bird Observatory
East Lake Drive, Cape May Point
(609) 884–2736

Founded in 1975 by the New Jersey Audubon Society, the Cape May Observatory holds daily walks and events. In spring and fall, it's one of the best places in the country to observe migrating birds. Hundreds of birders come to watch the birds at rest, at play, and in flight. Excitement mounts with the sightings of eagles, osprey, and other rare or endangered species. To find out about recent sightings, call the birding hotline, (609) 861–2736.

Birds are not the only wildlife that can be observed here. More than 100 species of butterflies flutter around these wetlands, and in early October, you can see hundreds of migrating monarchs.

Cape May Point State Park
Lighthouse Road, Cape May Point
(609) 884–2159

Cape May Point State Park is known for stellar bird-watching and for its lighthouse. Several blazed trails will lead you to ponds, coastal dunes, and marsh and forest habitats; there you can view birds and other wildlife from observation platforms. There are many bird-watching vantage points in the area; the Cape May Bird Observatory is close by (see above), and from mid-September through October, on Saturdays and Sundays, the Audubon Society demonstrates hawk-banding there.

We've discussed the park's other major attraction, the 157-foot lighthouse, in the Lighthouses chapter. It is still an aid to navigation, and if you climb to the top, you can see the scenic Cape May peninsula. For lighthouse information, call (609) 884–5404.

Once this area was part of the U.S. Coastal Defense network, so if you walk the beach, you may, depending on the tide, be able to see remnants of the bunker and gun emplacement. There's an environmental center that houses a classroom for interpretive programs and a museum on the area's natural and historic features. If you'd like to picnic at this pleasing location, there are tables and shelters. You can also hike the nature trails or surf fish here for weakfish, bluefish, flounder, tautog, and striped bass.

Located on the southern tip of New Jersey, Cape May Point State Park is a key site on the New Jersey Coastal Heritage Trail (see the Close-up on page 36). The park is open daily from dawn to dusk. The museum is open during the summer season from 8:00 A.M. to 8:00 P.M.; in the off-season, it is open Wednesday through Sunday from 8:00 A.M. to 3:15 P.M.

Corson's Inlet State Park
Ocean City and Upper Township
Cape May County
(609) 861–2404

This park of uncommon beauty is one of the last undeveloped tracts of land along New Jersey's oceanfront. Rich in wildlife, it's a place where hundreds of species live and breed. The sand dunes serve as a protected nesting site for the endangered piping plover, the least tern, and black

In spring and fall, armies of birders gather at Cape May Point to watch migrating birds. PHOTO: COURTESY OF CAPE MAY COUNTY TOURISM

skimmers. Other shorebirds and water-fowl, such as the American oystercatcher, can also be observed here.

Understandably the park is a popular spot for saltwater fishing, crabbing, boat-ing, sunbathing, and hiking. There are boat ramps and catamaran storage. You can explore the park, which is on the New Jersey Coastal Heritage Trail, on your own or take an interpretive tour. The park is open from dawn to dusk.

Leaming's Run Gardens and Colonial Farm
1845 U.S. Highway 9 North, Swainton
(609) 465–5871
www.leamingsrun.com

Leaming's Run is the largest annual gar-den in the United States; it's actually a series of 25 separate theme gardens along a walking path. There's a colonial garden, an English garden, and a garden of differ-ent flowers that share the same color, to name just a few.

The gardens are informal and inviting, as befits the labor of love this has been for Jack Aprill and his wife, Emily. Everything here has been started from seed and planted in the ground. Feeding and weed control are accomplished naturally, with grass clippings and spent blooms, rather than with fertilizers and chemicals. If you bring children with you, they will appreci-ate the sign that says: YOU MAY WALK ON THE GRASS. This lets them know they can relax amid the beauty around them.

The 30-acre property is not only beau-tiful, it's historic. The house in which Jack and Emily live was built by Thomas Leam-ing in 1706. It's one of the oldest houses in Cape May County—and is also the last remaining whaler's home in the state. After you walk through the gardens, you'll come upon a small cabin. This is a repro-duction of the temporary house that the Thomas Leaming family used while their permanent house was being built. The cabin now serves as a small museum show-ing what life was like for the original owner. Next to the cabin is a small farm that would have been typical in the early 1700s. Along with the vegetable garden, you'll see a poultry exhibit representing the birds that were brought to the United States by settlers from various countries: there are Swedish chickens, English chickens, Polish chickens, and more—16 varieties in all.

In August of each year, Leaming's Run Gardens become a haven for hummingbirds migrating south to Central America; there are so many birds, the place has been called the hummingbird capital of the East Coast. In October, if you're lucky, you may also see migrating monarch butterflies. Leaming's Run Gardens and the Cooperage (gift shop) are open May 15 to October 20, from 9:30 A.M. to 5:00 P.M. daily.

The Wetlands Institute
1075 Stone Harbor Boulevard, Stone Harbor
(609) 368–1211

In the wetlands, where the land meets the sea, nature maintains a unique balance. Left undisturbed, wetlands provide views of uncommon beauty—and the opportunity to learn more about life at the Shore. Here you'll see terrapins plodding through the salt-marsh grasses, shorebirds swooping down to pluck dinner from a tidal creek, crabs scuttling along the water's edge.

Situated on 6,000 acres of coastal marshlands, the Wetlands Institute offers many educational programs and tours. The main building is an attractive cedar-shingle structure with an observation deck, auditorium, gift shop, and a hands-on children's museum. A nearby building houses an aquarium, a salt-marsh exhibit, and a touch tank containing some of the creatures found in the back bays. In the summer, you can watch a 25-minute film called *The Secrets of the Salt Marsh* and then go out on a docent-led tour of the marsh.

Insiders' Tip
You'll find some gorgeous photos of the Pine Barrens on the Internet at these addresses:

www.mikebaker.com
www.georgian.edu/
pinebarrens
www.hoganphoto.com

In winter, you can watch the same film on video—and take yourself on a tour, with the assistance of the pamphlet available at the front desk of the main building. You can climb the observation deck for a bird's-eye view of the wetlands.

In summer, there's a camp program for children, run by the institute's education department. In winter, schoolchildren have the opportunity to visit and to learn about life in this area. In September, the institute sponsors its biggest fundraising event, the "Wings 'n' Water" Festival, which features the work of nationally acclaimed decoy carvers, and paintings of wildlife and the sea; guided beach and marsh tours are given, too. The institute is open May 15 to October 15 from 9:30 A.M. to 4:30 P.M. Monday through Saturday, and from 10:00 A.M. to 4:00 P.M. on Sunday. From October 16 to May 14, the institute is closed on Sunday and Monday, but the other hours remain the same.

Beaches

Monmouth County
Ocean County
Atlantic County
Cape May County

Whether you're a surfer, a sunbather, or a dedicated swimmer, New Jersey has a beach for you. Thanks to a beach replenishment program by the Army Corps of Engineers, many of the Shore's 127 miles of beaches are wider than they have been in decades. In general, the ocean is cleaner than it was a generation ago, too. And thanks to an extensive monitoring system—New Jersey was the first state to mandate testing for disease-causing bacteria and viruses along ocean beaches—bathing in the ocean here is as safe as human effort can make it.

Since beaches are the Shore's major attraction, we have devoted a separate chapter to them, providing basic information on fees, bathhouses, rest rooms, lifeguards (during the summer season), and the availability of food. Since beach fees are subject to change—as are rules governing surfing, usually allowed only in designated areas, and picnicking—we suggest that you call the information numbers listed before visiting a beach for the first time.

Each of the Shore towns we've covered in this book has at least one beach open to the general public. Almost all charge a daily entrance fee, but also sell beach badges that are good for the whole season. Some offer weekly badges as well. Almost all Shore communities offer free or discounted beach badges to seniors (defined as persons either 62 or 65 and older) and disabled persons. According to a recent ruling by New Jersey's attorney general, children under 12 must be admitted to beaches free; some towns offer discounted admission to young people between the ages of 13 and 17 or 18, too.

Many Shore municipalities operate beach clubs that offer seasonal memberships. Some clubs are generally only open to town residents (and their guests); some clubs may sell memberships to residents of other towns when they're not fully subscribed. There are also many private beach clubs that sell memberships to anyone willing to pay the annual fees, which often run into the thousands, but many have long waiting lists.

In theory, there really are no "private" beaches anymore—the law permits free access to the ocean and the beach. However, many towns have not entirely caught on to this democratic notion and restrict beach access by issuing parking tickets and fines for fishing, surfing, or swimming without a lifeguard present.

At the beaches we've listed here, you can expect to find lifeguards and rest rooms. Many have bathhouses or cabanas, which may be available on a daily or seasonal basis. Most have a snack bar, but also allow you to bring coolers for picnicking. Most beaches do not allow fishing or surfing side by side with bathers, but many allow fishing off piers or jetties, and surfing in the late afternoon (after the crowds leave) or early in the morning. (For more on surfing, see the Close-up later in this chapter.) As in other chapters, we'll start with Sandy Hook and work our way south to Cape May.

Monmouth County

Gateway National Recreation Area
Sandy Hook
(732) 872–5970
Free, parking fee in summer

During the summer season, Sandy Hook can get very crowded; not only is it popular with Jersey natives, it also offers an attractive "day at the beach" for Manhattanites who'd rather take a delightful 40-minute ferry ride here than subways and buses to New York beaches.

Sandy Hook's seven miles of beachfront and bayfront, salt marshes, nature trails, and dunes offer plenty of opportunities for outdoor sports and activities. A 200-plus-year-old lighthouse and vestiges of old fortifications provide visitors with places to explore. (You'll find more about these in the Natural World, Lighthouses, and Attractions chapters.)

Surf casters park at Area F, which is exclusively for fishing and hiking. Fishermen also like the calm waters of Horseshoe Cove on the bay side, especially in the late afternoon. There's a small parking area across the road that they share with windsurfers, who set out here and across from South Beach (Area C). All the major bathing areas have rest rooms, snack bars, and showers, but pick up a map at the visitors center, between areas B and E, just to get the lay of the land.

Plenty of sunblock goes on at Area South Gunnison Beach, closest to Area E—it's clothing optional. We like Area D because it's home to the Seagull's Nest, a good place to grab a burger, listen to music (live on weekends), and watch the sun set across the water while listening to a recording of Kate Smith singing "God Bless America." It's cheesy for sure, but lately folks have gotten downright choked up.

Surfers are battling to save Big Cove from being destroyed by proposed beach replenishment. After recent sand pumping ruined the surf breaks in Sea Bright and Long Branch, Big Cove is the last public beach worth surfing north of Belmar.

Parking permits for cars are $10 daily, $50 for the summer season. Before Memorial Day and after Labor Day, parking is free.

Sea Bright
(732) 842–0214, (732) 842–0099
$5.00 daily, $75.00 season

There is no food concession at Sea Bright beach—it doesn't need one. There are at least a dozen restaurants and pubs within easy walking distance—selling pizza, deli, Chinese, fish and chips—you name it. If you're too lazy to detach yourself from your sand chair, don't sweat it; place an order with your cell phone, give your location, and many of the local entrepreneurs will deliver your order to the beach. Save your strength for parading up and down the beach like the locals do, running into friends who belong to the eight expensive private clubs. Sea Bright has showers and changing rooms and attracts large weekend crowds from "up North," so parking and traffic are the biggest problems, especially when Sandy Hook fills to capacity. Sea Bright allows surfing on unguarded Anchorage Beach.

Season parking passes are $75.00; parking is $5.00 per day at the municipal beach parking lot. There is limited metered parking along Ocean Avenue, very limited free parking on local streets, and don't imagine you can get away with parking all day in the little lot by the supermarket.

Monmouth Beach
(732) 229–2204
$5.00 daily, $40.00 season

Much quieter than Sea Bright, Monmouth Beach attracts a mostly family

A Word about Sharks and Other Pesky Critters

We would love to tell you that you can swim the ocean waters off New Jersey with nary a thought of sharks—but that, dear readers, would be a fib. Instead, we'd like to put the shark issue in perspective. There have been shark sightings as long as people have been swimming off New Jersey's shores. In his best-selling book *Close to Shore, A True Story of Terror in the Age of Innocence,* New Jersey writer Michael Capuzzo tells a real-life *Jaws* story of terrifying attacks—possibly by a single great white shark—that claimed the lives of four people. All this happened in 1916, and there was another shark attack in 1960. But the story resonates with every shark sighting—and there are some virtually every summer. In fact, the numerous reports in the summer of 2001 had some area experts invoking the theory that these attacks return after a 44-year cycle. Another theory advanced was that the sharks faded away because of the shortage of striped bass—and that they recently returned because of the abundance of dolphins, a new food source. In any event, Shore lifeguards are generally vigilant and will issue warnings if they hear or see any potential danger. Of course, it's always wise to be aware of your surroundings, especially when venturing far from shore.

Jellyfish like the same kind of water you do—gentle and warm—so you'll likely see a lot of them in August and September. The clear ones are slimy but generally harmless; the purple ones sting, and so do the ones with the curly red manes, so be careful, especially if you might be allergic.

Calico crabs will bite if you step on them, but not instantly, so move away quickly if you think there might be a living creature underfoot.

crowd of borough residents, who secure their bathhouses early. The large beach is not too crowded and allows surfing. There is a snack bar and a swimming pool, which is the center of seaside social life here. Parking is $3.00 daily.

Long Branch—Seven Presidents Oceanfront Park
Atlantic Avenue South to Joline Avenue, Long Branch
(732) 229-0924
$5.00 daily, $42.00 season

Operated by Monmouth County Park System, this 38-acre oceanfront park has wide, clean beaches, a playground and an activity center, beach volleyball, and a boat launch. There is a snack bar, but you can also walk to the Windmill, one of a local chain that sells great hot dogs, chargrilled burgers, and fried mushrooms.

Next door to the Windmill is Strollo's Italian Ice stand, our favorite. The new Boardwalk to the south draws joggers, bikers, and strollers from all over. The Atlantic Avenue beach draws surfers and singles. Daily parking costs $4.00, seasonal parking, $40.00.

Long Branch—West End
Broadway south to Brighton Avenue, Long Branch
(732) 222-0400, (732) 571-6545
$5.00 daily, $35.00 season

There are snack bars at this municipal beach, but there are other eateries, too, so you can conduct a great hot dog taste test: Max's on Matilda Terrace vs. the original Windmill on Ocean Avenue near Brighton. In fact, the Brighton Avenue end of the beach is convenient to a number of shops and restaurants, including

Sea Shells at the Seashore

Who can resist picking up the pretty shells that wash up on Shore beaches? We have more than 75 varieties, including our own state shell, the knobbed whelk, which resembles a snail shell. Some varieties don't turn up very often, while others are fairly common: the Atlantic jack-knife clam, the Atlantic oyster drill, the Atlantic surf clam, the blue mussel, the channeled whelk, the coquina, the eastern oyster, the Northern moon snail, and the Northern quahog.

Larger clamshells make good soap or trinket dishes; the smaller ones look attractive when grouped in an aquarium along with sea glass.

If you're planning to keep your shells, wash them in a half-and-half solution of water and bleach. If you find a starfish and want to preserve that, soak it overnight in 70-percent alcohol, then dry on a paper towel or in the sun. To preserve a sand dollar, soak in fresh water, repeat until the water is clear; then soak briefly in a mild water-and-bleach solution, rinse in fresh water, and let dry. To whiten your sand dollar, put it in the sun; to preserve it, paint it with a half-and-half solution of water and white glue.

If you don't find any shells that strike your fancy, try the souvenir shops on the bigger boardwalks; you may find some special ones for sale. If you're in Ocean City, visit the Discovery Seashell Museum at 2717 Asbury Avenue; you'll see rarities from all over the world, as well as some more common varieties that you can buy (also see the Attractions chapter).

---

the Circle Freeze ice-cream parlor. The West End beach has always attracted a mix of families and singles. Many enjoy walking or jogging on the pedestrian road and the Boardwalk. There is street and metered parking along Ocean Avenue and some side streets.

Deal
(732) 531–1454
$5.00 weekdays, $6.00 weekends/holidays, $75.00 season

Inlanders come to Deal to enjoy the higher class of sand, so this municipal beach does get crowded on weekends and holidays. But it adjoins the much larger Deal Casino beach, so there's room to spread out a bit. (The Deal Casino is a municipally run beach club open to town residents.) The Phillips Avenue beach has bathhouses, a snack bar, a deck, and a volleyball net; surf-

ing and fishing are allowed on the adjoining beach. Bathhouses ($155) always sell out well before the season starts. There's free parking in the adjoining lot.

Allenhurst
(732) 731–2700
$5.00 daily

Season badges ($120 for residents, $230 for nonresidents) can be purchased only through membership in the borough's beach club, which has a saltwater pool and two wading pools. Memberships sell out well in advance of the season, since most people return year after year. Members also pay a locker or cabana fee, which runs from $560 to $2,346. Allenhurst Beach Club has an excellent restaurant and bar that is open to the public in the evening; it has a nice ocean view. There's free parking in the lot adjoining the beach and on nearby streets.

Loch Arbour
(732) 531–4740
$5.00 daily, $80.00 season

Loch Arbour is a tiny town, and its municipal beach is only one block long, so it really only attracts locals and families from Interlaken and Ocean Township. The beach has a snack bar, outdoor showers, and for fun, a beach volleyball net. There is very limited parking on nearby streets.

Asbury Park
(732) 502–4526
$3.00 weekdays, $4.00 weekends/holidays, $20.00 season

The beaches in Asbury have been replenished, but alas, the summer crowds have not. Asbury's once-bustling Boardwalk is still devoid of the concessions and amusements that used to attract throngs, and so you'll mostly find locals spreading out their blankets and taking up just as much space as they like. The Casino Carousel is now an in-line skating rink, and there are concerts at the bandshell at Howard Johnson's. In recent years Asbury has begun to attract a bit of a singles crowd. Parking is not a problem, as lots were built to accommodate the huge crowds of years gone by, and ample metered parking is also available.

Ocean Grove (Neptune Township)
(732) 531–9283, (732) 988–5533
www.oceangrove.org
$5.50 daily, $10.00 for a Saturday–Sunday pass, $27.50 for a weekly pass, $60.00 for a season pass

Since Ocean Grove was founded by Methodist ministers and is still home to an annual Camp Meeting, the beach does not open until 12:30 P.M. (after church) on Sundays. The 480-foot pier and four jetties are popular with fishers of every age and denomination, while the Boardwalk appeals to walkers and joggers. There is no snack bar, but that will force you to explore the restaurants and quaint shops on Main Street. There are showers and the beach is spacious and low-key, but parking on Ocean Grove's narrow lanes is difficult at best. Spaces are available but scarce.

Insiders' Tip
Many towns offer reduced prices on seasonal beach badges when they are purchased early in the year.

Bradley Beach
(732) 776–2998
$6.00 daily, $50.00 season

Bradley Beach attracts many seasonal renters and families, so the sand can get quite crowded, even during the week. The mile-long Boardwalk has miniature golf, a playground, and a bandstand gazebo where concerts fill the air with music four nights a week during the summer. There are beach concession stands as well as restaurants on Ocean Avenue. Surfers are welcome on the Third Avenue beach. There's free but limited street parking.

Avon-by-the-Sea
(732) 502–4508
www.avon-by-the-sea.com
$5.75 daily, $60.00 season

No mini golf on this Boardwalk—Avon is a place to bring your beach book and read until you're sunburned. Showers are located at several spots along the beach, and the Beach Pavilion at Washington Avenue has shops, rest rooms, and beachfront dining. The long jetty at the south end of the beach is a popular fishing spot. Parking is free but scarce; look either in the municipal lot at East End Avenue or along Ocean Avenue.

Belmar
(732) 681–1176
www.belmar.com
$5.50 daily, $40.00 season

This is where the action is—if that's what you're looking for. Throngs of tattooed 20-somethings cruise up and down Belmar's 21-block-long Boardwalk, looking for snacks, drinks, souvenirs, and each other. There are kayak rentals on the Boardwalk and volleyball courts on the beach (but you must supply the net). Families with small children cluster around the playgrounds at Fourth, Eighth, 10th, and 16th Avenues, and at a smaller beach on L Street along the Shark River Inlet, which is free and close to Maclearie Park. The area between 16th and 18th Avenues draws large numbers of surfers. There is metered parking along Ocean Avenue and free parking on side streets.

Spring Lake
(732) 449–8005, (732) 449–0577
$6.00 daily, $73.00 season

Spring Lake's inviting beach and uncommercialized Boardwalk are popular with families and guests from the borough's bed-and-breakfast inns. The two pavilions—one at Ludlow Avenue, the other at Atlantic Avenue—have second-floor porches that offer sweeping ocean views; they also offer concession stands, rest rooms, and showers. Locals tend to cluster near the south pavilion, which has a pool and is open only to residents of Spring Lake and their guests. Parking is free on Ocean Avenue.

Sea Girt
(732) 449–7079, (732) 449–0577
$6.00 daily, $60.00 season

A little out of the way for day-trippers, Sea Girt has a quiet Boardwalk that lets you take in the natural beauty here. A bathhouse and rest rooms are located in the Pavilion at Beacon Boulevard, so named for the Sea Girt Lighthouse located there (see the Lighthouse chapter). The bathhouse fee is $12 weekdays, $15 weekends/holidays. The season bathhouse fee of $600 includes five season badges. With outdoor tables, the snack bar is more like an outdoor cafe, and picnicking is discouraged. Surfing is allowed on the Philadelphia Boulevard beach; kayaking is permitted at North Beach during the week and on Trenton Beach on weekends. There's free street parking but it's limited, so you'll want to arrive early.

Manasquan
(732) 223–2514, (732) 223–1221
www.manasquan-nj.com
$5.00 daily, $47.00 season

Manasquan Beach is on the "A" list for fishers, surfers, and teens. Fishermen jockey for position on the big jetty that buttresses the northern side of the Manasquan Inlet. There is also a fishing area at Inlet Beach, which is one of the best-known surfing beaches on the East Coast, attracting longboarders from all over the country. Traditionally, Manasquan's beach bungalows have attracted groups of college kids, and Recreation Beach caters to active types who play volleyball, whiffle ball, and other games there. But Manasquan is not just for the young; Elks Beach is the only fully wheelchair-accessible beach at the Shore, with handicapped parking, a wooden access ramp to the beach, and several large beach wheelchairs that can be taken right down to the water's edge. Manasquan has four parking lots, at Second, Third, Fourth, and Pompano Avenues; even so, it can be tough to find a spot. Parking fees are $3.00 on weekdays, $8.00 on weekends, and $45.00 for the season. You can also walk to the beach from the train station.

Ocean County

Point Pleasant Beach—Jenkinson's
(732) 892–0600
$5.00 weekdays, $6.00 weekends/holidays,
$70.00 season

Jenkinson's one-mile beach, from the southern shore of the Manasquan Inlet to Trenton Avenue, draws large crowds because of the boardwalk pleasures it offers: the aquarium and amusements for the kids, arcades for the joystick crowd, and food and drink of all kinds for all kinds. At night, Jenkinson's live music attracts crowds as well. A word about surfing at Point Pleasant: don't. The predominant shore break produces waves that break right onto the beach, unpleasant for body surfers, too. There's metered street parking as well as parking for a fee in nearby lots.

Point Pleasant Beach is busy all summer long—volleyball by day and free family entertainment at night.
PHOTO: COURTESY OF OCEAN COUNTY PUBLIC AFFAIRS

Bay Head
(732) 892–4179
$5.00 daily, $55.00 season (two-badge minimum purchase)

The beach and the sand dunes at Bay Head are beautiful, and the Bay Head Improvement Association strictly enforces the rules to keep it that way: No food or drinks are allowed on the beach. You can, however, sit down and eat your snack on one of the eight beach platforms on East Avenue. The beach has no snack bar, no rest rooms, and no bathhouses. Children under 12 must be accompanied by an adult. There's free street parking.

Mantoloking
(732) 899–6600
Season only, $8.00

Lifeguards? No. Bathhouses? No. Rest rooms? No. Snack Bar? No. You're not even allowed to bring your own food or drinks except for nonalcoholic drinks in non-disposable containers. Wooden walkways over the dunes at 10th Street and between Downer Avenue and Mathis Place provide access to Mantoloking's lovely, undeveloped beaches. The limited parking and lack of facilities tend to discourage people from coming here, though, unless they have homes nearby. Some (marked) beaches are so private, they're not even open to badge holders. The beaches from Herbert Street south to Albertson are operated by the Mantoloking Beach Association; the beach along Downer Avenue is operated by the South Mantoloking Beach Association. These are also unguarded and have neither rest rooms nor showers. There's free street parking, but with a two-hour limit.

Ortley Beach (Dover Township)
(732) 793–3890
$4.00 weekdays, $5.00 weekends/holidays, $25.00 weekly, $30.00 season

The small Boardwalk is for sitting and strolling—there are no concessions, and no food or drinks are permitted. Such is not the case, however, at the south end of the Boardwalk, where Joey Harrison's Surf Club has an outdoor bar and live music. Watercraft rentals are available on both the ocean and bay, but surfing is prohibited. There's free parking in a lot.

Surfing at the Jersey Shore

Surfboards first began appearing at the Jersey Shore way back in the 1940s, but the sport really took off here in the 1960s, when long-haired kids discovered the pleasures of the longboard, which include communing with nature while catching a few waves.

The first surf shops opened up here at that time, too; before that, would-be surfers had to make their own boards or find one on the West Coast. That was Ron DiMenna's situation when he decided to open up a surf shack on Long Beach Island in 1961; his Ship Bottom store, Ron Jon Surf Shop, is now world-famous, with locations in Florida and California. The Ship Bottom shop is now a four-floor emporium carrying everything you could possibly need for surfing or the beach.

Now, the eternal debate: Where are the best surf breaks (places where offshore sandbars create long, smooth waves)? Ask any surfer, and you'll encounter evasive maneuvers. "They change all the time," hedges Ron Fernicola, owner of Spellbinders Surf N' Sport in Allenhurst. One spot that has changed, and not for the better, is northern Monmouth County. Back in the day, surfers and hippies flocked to North Long Branch, West End, and Sea Bright. Now, according to Fernicola, "the beach replenishment completely destroyed the surf breaks there. It's a desert. Nobody goes there anymore."

Actually, most of the shore's best surf breaks are pretty well known. Manasquan Inlet, at the southern end of Monmouth County, is one of the best-known surf breaks on the East Coast and gets crowded in summer, as does Belmar. Farther north, the Darlington Road beach in Deal is now an open secret, since the Surfrider Foundation sued the town for the right to surf there. (Now surfing is allowed, but swimming is not on this unguarded beach. Bathers have to bring along some sort of decoy board to avoid getting a summons.)

In Ocean County, Seaside Heights and Island Beach State Park are reliable spots. On Long Beach Island, Harvey Cedars and Holyoke Street Beach in Beach Haven get mentioned. Down south, Brigantine's South Jetty, Ocean City, and the 37th Street beach in Sea Isle City are local favorites.

We've already noted that most towns restrict surfing between 9:00 A.M. and 5:00 P.M. in the summer; the good news is that the best time to surf is either early in the morning or late in the afternoon, when the wind tends to come in from offshore. Of course, local hardcores love it once the summer crowds have gone. Donning wet suits (a must, as water temperatures get down to 40 degrees) they surf right through the winter, especially after a storm has passed.

Surf Shops

Heritage Surf & Sports
3700 Landis Avenue, Sea Isle City
(609) 263–3033
744 West Avenue, Ocean City
(609) 398–6390
9223 Ventnor Avenue, Margate
(609) 823–3331

Inlet Outlet
146 Main Street, Manasquan
(732) 223–5842

Ron Jon Surf Shop
Ninth and Central Avenues, Ship Bottom,
Long Beach Island
(609) 494–8844

Spellbinders Surf N' Sport
318 Main Street, Allenhurst
(732) 531–SURF, surf report: (732) 531–1028

Surfing the Web

Surfrider Foundation USA
www.surfrider.org
Surfrider is a national organization that campaigns for surfers' rights and environmental causes.

Eastern Surfing Association
(800) 937–4733
www.surfesa.org
The Eastern Surfing Association, the largest amateur surfing organization in the world, holds surfing contests and stumps for clean water. Its Web site has links to california.earth.911, which regularly posts water-quality reports for many areas of the country, including the Jersey Shore. Other links are to live Webcams at Monmouth Beach, Point Pleasant, and Sea Isle City, as well as to Surfline.com

Surfline.com
This is a complete surfers' site, with live Webcams at Belmar, Manasquan, and Cape May, and daily reports on Long Beach Island and Ocean City, which give water temperature, weather, and tides, in addition to the skinny on the surf.

Lavallette
(732) 793–7477
$5.00 daily, $25.00 weekly, $30.00 season
Though the beach has no snack bar and no rest rooms, there are restaurants nearby. This beach is especially beautiful; an offshore sandbar creates shallows pools at low tide that make perfect play areas for youngsters. Flat-walkers love it, too, as do kids with body boards. There's free street parking, but a $7.00 annual permit is required at the nearby municipal lots.

Seaside Heights
(732) 793–9100, (800) SEASHOR
Free Wednesdays and Thursdays; $3.00 Mondays, Tuesdays, and Fridays; $5.00 weekends/holidays; $35.00 season
What is there on the Boardwalk in Seaside? Rides, junk food, and games of chance or dubious skill. Fishers like to take their chances on the Casino Pier, where rods and tackles can be rented. Umbrellas, rafts, and lounge chairs can be rented at Ocean Terrace, ditto showers and lockers. Anyone who's ever basked on the beach has seen small airplanes dragging advertising banners; in Seaside, every day brings a new sand-castle billboard, created by sand sculptors. Surfers drift over to the north end of Seaside, where the offshore sandbar creates a "beach break," a place where waves roll a nice distance into the shore. On Wednesday nights in summer there are fireworks displays, and on summer Thursdays, beach parties with entertainment. Metered parking is $1.00 per hour; the charge at nearby lots ranges from $3.00 to $20.00 per day. There's free parking along Bay Boulevard a few blocks away.

Seaside Park
(732) 830–2100
$6.00 daily, $17.00 weekly, $32.00 season
The northern end of the Boardwalk here has some vendors and amusements, but things get quieter as you head south. There is a concession stand on Ocean Avenue with rest rooms, bathhouses, and showers. Surf fishing is allowed in designated areas. There's metered parking along Ocean Avenue.

Island Beach State Park
(732) 793–0506
Free, parking fee in summer
Get here early; the gates close as soon as the parking areas are full. You can enjoy this 10-mile stretch of protected dunes and beaches in so many ways: swim, fish, hike the nature trails, take a canoe or kayak tour (free on Thursday), snorkel, or

About the "Other" Shore—the Bayshore Beaches

Lesser known than New Jersey's ocean beaches are the state's small bayshore beaches, where locals sometimes retreat when summer visitors crowd the Shore. In Monmouth County, for example, the bayshore beaches stretch along the entire eastern edge, from Highlands west to the Cliffwood Beach section of Aberdeen, some 27 miles on the Sandy Hook and Raritan Bays. You can enjoy a broad range of water activities here, including swimming, windsurfing, and fishing. These beaches are free and some are even guarded. For information on Monmouth County bay beaches, call Highlands (732) 872–1959, Keansburg (732) 787–0215, Middletown (732) 615–2260, Union Beach (732) 264–2277.

In Ocean County, bay beaches offer their own brand of fun, whether it's water-skiing, crabbing, sailing, or boating. For information on these beaches, call Barnegat Township (609) 698–0080, Berkeley Township (732) 269–4456, Manahawkin (609) 597–1000, Shelter Cove (732) 341–1000, Bayville (732) 506–990.

In Atlantic County, the bay beaches have special family appeal. Margate has a guarded beach with shallow waters; for more information, call (609) 822–2605. Somers Point has several bay beaches offering bathhouses, fishing, picnicking, and rafting; for more information, call (609) 927–5253.

In Cape May County's Lower Township, you'll find a fine bay beach where you can swim, picnic, and fish; for more information, call (609) 886–2005. And just around the tip of New Jersey, Cape May Point's bay beach is a prime location for searching out those Cape May diamonds (actually sea-polished quartz). You can swim and fish there, too. For more information, call (609) 884–8468.

---

watch for birds. Pavilions with lockers, showers, and rest rooms are located in the center of the park. There are snack bars, but many people bring a picnic (no alcohol); you're even allowed to barbecue, as long as you keep the fire at least 50 feet east of the sand dunes.

Surfing is allowed here, though strong currents make it a place for experts, rather than beginners. Scuba diving is also allowed, but you must be certified, and you must follow park rules and procedures; you can get details on these from one of the rangers. Fishing is terrific, either surf casting for fluke or going for striped bass off the jetty.

The parking fee is $6.00 per car on weekdays, $7.00 on weekends/holidays. There's free parking before Memorial Day and after Labor Day.

Long Beach Island

Long Beach Island (or LBI, as regulars call it) is four miles out at sea and 21 miles long north to south. You can swim just about anywhere; we've listed some of its better-known beaches. A word about picnicking: It's generally not allowed on these beaches, but if you bring along a small sandwich and consume it discreetly and without leaving any litter behind, you should be okay. Another word, this about surfing: Except where there are designated surfing beaches, it is not allowed; however, the rule is generally enforced only when lifeguards are on duty (generally between 10:00 A.M. and 5:00 P.M.) during the summer season.

Barnegat Light
(609) 494-9196, (800) 292-6372
$3.00 weekdays, $4.00 weekends/holidays, $25.00 season

Some of the best beaches on Long Beach Island are found here—along with Old Barney, the 165-foot red and white lighthouse that served honorably during World War II as a lookout station for German submarines. (See the Lighthouses chapter.) There are rest rooms at 10th Street and Bayview Avenue, and also at Barnegat Light State Park. There are no snack bars, and food is not allowed on the beach. The boat ramp at the end of 10th Street is pretty popular with pleasure craft and with the crabbers. Daily passes to the boat ramp are $11; a season pass is $75. There is free street parking.

Long Beach Township
(609) 361-1200
$5.00 daily, $10.00 weekly, $20.00 season

The township accounts for about two-thirds of the island's beach area. It encompasses: Loveladies, North Beach, Brant Beach, Beach Haven Crest, Brighton Beach, Peahala Park, Beach Haven Park, Haven Beach, The Dunes, Beach Haven Terrace, Beach Haven Gardens, Spray Beach, North Beach Haven, South Beach Haven, Holgate, and Beach Haven Inlet.

The Long Beach Township beach patrol is one of the largest in the country, with more than 350 guards. It operates a number of programs, including a scuba search-and-rescue team. Rest rooms are located at Bayview Park, 68th Street, Brant Beach, Holgate, and Harbour South in Loveladies. Holgate, at the southernmost end of Long Beach Island, is home to the Edwin Forsythe National Wildlife Refuge, a 2½-mile stretch of barrier beach that's a haven for nesting birds. There is street parking throughout the area.

Harvey Cedars
(609) 494-7211, (609) 494-2843, (609) 494-6405
$5.00, $10.00 weekly, $22.00 season

The Hudson Avenue surfing beach is one of the best-known at the Shore, and

> ## Insiders' Tip
> The best times to hunt for shells are after summer storms and at low tide.

Harvey Cedars is so surfer friendly, it even sponsors a surfing contest. There are many other summer events, too, like the "Anything Floats" race. The beach also has volleyball nets, a bocce court, a baseball field, a playground, and a track. There are rest rooms at 77th Street and at the bay beach. Parking spaces can be found on side streets and at the bayfront park and recreation center.

Surf City
(609) 494-3064, (800) 292-6372
$5.00 daily, $12.00 weekly, $23.00 season

The surfing in Surf City is between North First and North Third Streets. This popular family resort also has a fine fishing beach that runs between North 23rd and North 25th Streets. There are no bathhouses, and the public rest rooms are in the municipal building on North Ninth Street. Parking is along Long Beach Boulevard and on designated side streets.

Ship Bottom
(609) 494-1614, (609) 494-2171, (800) 292-6372
$4.00 weekdays, $5.00 weekends/holidays, $12.00 weekly, $22.00 season

As this is the gateway to Long Beach Island, the first beach you come to off the N.J. Highway 72 causeway, it does get crowded. But many feel the great beaches and excellent surf are worth sharing a little. There is no snack bar, but there are nearby places to grab a bite. There are rest rooms in Borough Hall at 17th Avenue and Long Beach Boulevard, and near the boat ramp, between 10th and 11th Streets. There's daily parking on bayside streets and at the plaza between 18th and 22nd Streets;

hourly parking is permitted on side streets off the ocean.

Beach Haven
(609) 492–0111, (800) 292–6372
$5.00 daily, $10.00 weekly, $20.00 season

Beach Haven is devoted to summer pleasures—walking along the beach, getting an ice cream at the Show Place, cooling off at the Thundering Surf Waterslide. There are rest rooms at the oceanfront deck, but no concession stand; no matter, there are plenty of places to find something to eat. Families with youngsters like the toddler beach on the bay at Taylor Street, which is also rest room–equipped. The surfing beach at Holyoke Street, south of the jetty, draws longboarders from all over. There's free street parking in designated areas.

Atlantic County

Brigantine
(609) 266–7600
$5.00 daily, $10.00 weekly, $15.00 season

There are three surfing beaches in Brigantine: Tenth Street South, Twelfth Street North, and South Jetty, which gets the nod as the best. There are no beach rest rooms or snack bars, but there are restaurants nearby. If the weather is less than perfect, the kids might enjoy learning how dolphins, sea turtles, and whales are cared for at the Marine Mammal Stranding Center's Sea Life Museum (see the Natural World chapter). There's free street parking, and lots at 16th, 27th, and 36th Avenues charge $10 daily.

Atlantic City
(609) 449–7130, (609) 347–5300, (888) 228–6877
Free

After you lose all your dough in the casino, it's nice to know that you can still catch a few rays—the beaches in A.C. are free. The beaches in front of some hotels—notably the Hilton—are especially nice; chair and umbrella rentals are conveniently located here. With the vast array of fat-filled foods available on the Boardwalk, you might want to pack a roll of Tums. Surfing is allowed after hours, and

at Delaware Avenue. There is both free and metered street parking; many casino garages charge $2.00.

Ventnor
(609) 823–7948
$5.00 weekly, $10.00 season

Though neighboring Atlantic City beaches are free, Ventnor fans say the sand here is softer and whiter—and less crowded. There are rest rooms, but no snack bar, so you'll have to rely on nearby restaurants. Surfing is allowed on the Cornwall Avenue beach. There's both free and metered street parking.

Margate
(609) 822–2605, (609) 822–0424
$3.50 weekly, $10.00 season

If you bring youngsters to this beach, park yourself near Lucy the Elephant and watch their eyes pop. (See the Attractions chapter for more on Lucy.) You can even have lunch at the I Love Lucy Grill. The beach is lovely here, but the portable potty is a definite minus. Surfing is allowed at Brunswick Avenue, north of the fishing pier, and between Thurlow and Osborne Avenues. There is free street parking.

Longport
(609) 823–2731
$5.00 weekly, $15.00 season

This small (1¼-mile), quiet beach is a great place to get away from it all; the bonus is a spectacular view of the Atlantic City skyline, six miles away. The beach has no rest rooms or snack bars. Surfing is allowed at the 12th, 22nd, 32nd, and Pelham Street beaches. There's very limited street parking.

Cape May County

Ocean City
(609) 391–0240, (609) 391–6111, (800) BEACH NJ
www.oceancity-nj.com
$3.00 daily, $6.00 weekly, $16.00 season

The busy Boardwalk here offers many places to find lunch, and many rides on which to lose it, so if you're after some rollicking family-style fun (without alcohol),

Families are drawn to Ocean City's brand of good, clean (without alcohol) fun, its beaches, and its attraction-filled Boardwalk. PHOTO: LILLIAN AFRICANO

you've come to the right place. Surfers find their fun at the beach between First and Third Avenues. There's metered street parking as well as nearby lots.

Sea Isle City
(609) 263–4461, (609) 263–8687, (609) 263–TOUR
$4.00 daily, $8.00 weekly, $15.00 season

On Wednesdays, beach admission is free; on Tuesday and Thursday mornings at 10:00 A.M., there are free, guided Beachcomber Walks at the 29th Street beach. The walks educate children and adults about the endangered diamondback terrapins that nest in Sea Isle. There are rest rooms and a snack bar and amusements at the Arcade. Surfing is allowed at seven beaches: 33rd, 37th, 42nd, 48th, 52nd, 63rd, and 74th Streets; the 37th Street beach is said to be the best. There is both free and metered street parking.

Avalon
(609) 967–3936, (609) 967–5928
www.avalonbeach.com
$4.00 daily, $8.00 weekly, $17.00 season

This family-friendly beach in an upscale community is a nice compromise between the ultra-quiet beaches with no facilities whatsoever and those that are totally commercial. There is a half-mile-long Boardwalk and a small arcade, rest rooms, and a snack bar. You'll find surfers at 9th Street, between 10th and 11th, at 30th Street, and at 15th Street when the wind is out of the south. There's free street parking and a lot at 29th Street.

Stone Harbor
(609) 368–6101
www.stoneharborbeach.com
$3.00 daily, $8.00 weekly, $15.00 season

Like its neighbor Avalon, Stone Harbor is a family-friendly beach in a (very) upscale community. The beach is guarded; there are rest rooms but no boardwalk or commercial amusements. It's quiet here and everyone likes it that way. Surfing is allowed at 81st, 110th, and 122nd Streets. There's metered street parking.

Avalon Beach is beloved by families and surfers. PHOTO: COURTESY OF CAPE MAY COUNTY TOURISM

The Wildwoods
(800) WWBYSEA
www.wildwoodsnj.com
Free

While towns farther north watch storms erode their beaches year after year, Wildwood's huge beaches keep getting bigger and bigger. Good thing too—plenty of blanket space is needed to accommodate everyone who comes to enjoy a day of sun and an evening on the bustling Boardwalk, which has five amusement piers and more than 100 rides. The beaches are guarded, and you'll find bathhouses, rest rooms, and food concessions. For thrills, try the Great White roller coaster—or ride the great waves at the north end of Anglesea Beach in North Wildwood. If an uncommercialized beach is more your speed, then head for Wildwood Crest. In addition to metered street parking, there are parking lots on Ocean Avenue.

Cape May
(609) 884–5508, (609) 884–9525, (800)
227–2207
$4.00 daily, $11.00 weekly, $17.00 season

The beach in Cape May is downright scrawny compared to its well-endowed neighbor, Wildwood, but people here like it just the same. To escape the crowds that cluster near the food concessions, go to the far end of the beach. Surfing is allowed at the Brighton Avenue beach, near Cape May State Park; at Colonial Beach; and at the beach between Jefferson and Queen Streets. There's metered street parking.

Cape May Point
(609) 884–8468
$5.00 daily, $10.00 weekly, $15.00 season

If you like an uncrowded, natural environment, this is the beach for you, though you won't find much in the way of facilities. A general store and an Italian-ice vendor can be found in town. There's free street parking.

Outdoor Activities

Some of us are content to stick with sunbathing as our primary outdoor activity. But for those who like to see and go and do, the Shore is an open invitation to get out and smell the fresh air.

You may already have guessed that fishing is a big thing here. After all, we do have a conveniently located ocean. Boating is also huge, with or without fishing. We'll identify marinas where you can dock your boat, rent one for the day, or just buy a ticket and let someone who knows what he's doing take you out to sea. At or near the Shore, you'll also find dozens of lakes and streams where you can canoe, kayak, and fish.

There is also plenty to do on dry land. Biking used to be just something kids did to get around when they were too young to drive. Now, mountain bikes can tackle some pretty rugged terrain, and it seems the tougher it gets, the more off-road bikers like it. You'll find a number of parks and open spaces at the Shore where you can follow a trail through the woods or carve your own.

Camping is also a popular way to spend time outdoors, especially on the Southern Shore. Since some areas in Monmouth County, like Colts Neck, are well-known horse country, we've added a word about horseback riding in the area. To top off this compendium of outdoor adventures, we've noted a few places where you can take a joyride in an airplane, learn to fly one, or even jump out of one. Compared to skydiving, parasailing (also available in these parts) seems downright tame.

Fishing and Boating

Many Shore folk make a living at sea, but for the casual fisherman, there's no better way to unwind at the end of the day than by casting a line into the surf and seeing if dinner comes out on the end of it. The fishing at the Shore is excellent. Fishers fish off jetties and beaches, or off the big party boats that dock in the big marinas. You'll also find large charter boats that go after big, deep-sea game fish. Freshwater fishing is also popular, and we'll help you find one of the public streams, lakes, reservoirs, and rivers in your area. So go fish!

Fish Species at the Shore

The most common ocean fish at the Shore are bluefish, weakfish, blackfish, fluke, and striped bass. Bluefish are the most common of all Shore species. You'll find blues along the beaches, in deep ocean water, in the bays and tidal rivers. While many party boats run day and night trips to fish for them, local fishers often catch them off piers, bridges, jetties, and even just by surf casting off the beaches. If you want to feel like an ace, chase these fish; it's not uncommon to come home with a dozen or more. And if you want to feel as if you've had to work for your catch, rest assured that blues will fight.

Blues usually arrive in late spring and stay around well into October. They may be as small as a pound or two or as big as 20 pounds. Most of the larger fish are caught in the fall, when you'll see local fishers grabbing them off the beaches.

Diving birds are a sure sign that there are bluefish in the area. If you have your own boat, check out the fishing at Sandy Hook, at Shrewsbury Rocks, and at Barnegat Light.

Weakfish, also known as sea trout, are among the Shore's tastier fish. Generally found in rivers and bays, they tend to run in schools. Look for a concentration of birds to help you locate them. Weakfish weigh between a few pounds up to about 10 pounds. They arrive in early summer and stay till mid-September. Good spots to fish for them are Delaware Bay, Sandy Hook Bay, and areas of Barnegat Bay. The best time to try for weakfish is at dusk and in the evening. Try to choose an area that isn't heavily trafficked, as the fish scare easily.

Blackfish, also called tautog, like cold water, so you'll usually find them in the early spring and late fall. As blackfish aren't so easy to catch, it's best to put yourself in the hands of an experienced charter captain who knows where to find them (wrecks and rock piles). Bring plenty of rigs when chasing blackfish, as you'll be fishing in areas where you're likely to snag often.

A big striped bass is the catch that will make any surf fisher's day. Thanks to the state's conservation measures, striped bass are abundant again. They can weigh as much as 50 pounds or more (cows); this makes them very popular with anglers. Catch them along the beaches, bays, and tidal rivers. Popular party boat and charter areas for stripers are Leonardo, Atlantic Highlands, Shark River/Belmar, Brielle/Point Pleasant, Barnegat Light, and Cape May. If you have your own boat, try the Sandy Hook area, Shrewsbury Rocks, Manasquan Inlet jetty, along rock jetties on Long Beach Island, Island Beach State Park, Barnegat Inlet, and Cape May.

Fluke are also among our ocean's tastier offerings. They are flat fish, like flounder, and similarly light in taste. You'll find them between June and August (best month is June), along the beaches, bays, and tidal rivers. They can weigh between two and ten pounds, the lower weights being the most common. Many party boats specialize in fluke. Popular areas are the Sandy Hook Bay; off the shores of Elberon, Deal, and Spring Lake; Point Pleasant; Barnegat Bay and close to local beaches in Point Pleasant and Barnegat Light; Delaware Bay and close to local beaches in Cape May.

Freshwater Fishing

The New Jersey Division of Fish and Wildlife stocks more than 200 waters, principally with trout (brook, brown, and rainbow), but also with northern pike, tiger and "true" muskellunge, walleye, hybrid-striped bass, and channel catfish.

Anyone age 16 and older must have a valid license to fish the fresh waters of New Jersey with a handline, rod and line, or longbow and arrow. This includes privately owned lakes and other waters. You can get a license from most county or municipal clerks. You can also purchase a license over the Internet and from sporting goods stores that are designated agents. If you've lived in New Jersey for at least six months (or if you're a resident on active duty in the armed forces), you can get a resident license. No license is required if you're under 16 years of age. If you're fishing for trout, you will need a trout stamp affixed to your license.

Blind residents and resident veterans with service-connected disabilities can obtain free licenses from the Division of Fish and Wildlife. Seniors between the ages of 65 and 69 are eligible for discounted licenses; seniors age 70 and over do not need a license and may instead use their drivers' licenses for identification.

For general information on freshwater fishing, call the New Jersey Department of Fisheries and Wildlife at (609) 292–2965.

Monmouth County
Allentown Pond, Allentown

35 acres, car top launch, no boat ramp, electric outboards only

Assunpink Lake, Roosevelt

225 acres, car top launch, boat ramp, electric outboards only

Deal Lake, Asbury Park

158 acres, car top launch, boat ramp, outboards allowed

Echo Lake, Southard

6 acres, car top launch, no boat ramp, electric outboards only

Englishtown Mill Pond, Englishtown

6 acres, car top launch, no boat ramp, no outboards allowed

Garveys Pond, Navesink (Middletown)

2 acres, no car top launch, no boat ramp, no outboards allowed

Hamilton Fire Company Pond, Neptune

2 acres, no car top launch, no boat ramp, no outboards allowed

Holmdel Park Pond, Holmdel

l5 acres, no car top launch, no boat ramp, no outboards allowed

Kesslers Pond, Allenwood

3 acres, car top launch, no boat ramp, electric outboards only

Lake Como, Spring Lake

30 acres, no car top launch, no boat ramp, no outboards allowed

Lefferts Lake, Matawan

69 acres, car top launch, no boat ramp, no outboards allowed

Macs Pond, Manasquan

2 acres, no car top launch, no boat ramp, no outboards allowed

Manasquan Reservoir, Howell Township

720 acres, car top launch, boat ramp, electric outboards only. All boats are required to have a permit, issued (for a fee) at the Manasquan River Boat Ramp (732–842–4000).

Millhurst Mills Lake, Millhurst

22 acres, no car top launch, no boat ramp, no outboards allowed

Mohawk Pond, Red Bank

2 acres, no car top launch, no boat ramp, no outboards allowed

Poricy Pond, Red Bank

16 acres, no car top launch, no boat ramp, no outboards allowed

Rising Sun Lake, Roosevelt

38 acres, car top launch, boat ramp, electric outboards only

Shadow Lake, Red Bank

88 acres, no car top launch, no boat ramp, no outboards allowed

Shark River Park Pond, Glendola

3 acres, no car top launch, no boat ramp, no outboards allowed

Silver Lake, Belmar

15 acres, no car top launch, no boat ramp, no outboards allowed

Spring Lake, Spring Lake

16 acres, car top launch, no boat ramp, no outboards allowed

Stone Tavern Lake, Roosevelt

52 acres, car top launch, boat ramp, electric outboards only

Takanassee Lake, Long Branch

14 acres, car top launch, no boat ramp, no outboards allowed

Thompson Park Lake, Lincroft

22 acres, car top launch, boat ramp, electric outboards only

Topenemus Lake, Freehold

21 acres, car top launch, no boat ramp, no outboards allowed

Turkey Swamp Park Pond, Freehold

20 acres, no car top launch, no boat ramp, no outboards allowed

Fishing is a year-round sport in Ocean City. PHOTO: COURTESY OF OCEAN COUNTY PUBLIC AFFAIRS

Ocean County

Bauer Pond, Keswick Grove
10 acres, car top launch, no boat ramp, electric outboards only

Butterfly Bogs Pond, Vanhiseville
18 acres, no car top launch, no boat ramp, electric outboards only

Colliers Mill Pond, Colliers Mills
17 acres, car top launch, no boat ramp, electric outboards only

Deerhead Lake, Forked River
37 acres, no car top launch, no boat ramp, no outboards allowed

Enno Lake, Bennetts Mill
46 acres, car top launch, boat ramp, electric outboards only

Forge Pond, Bricktown
45 acres, car top launch, boat ramp, outboards allowed

Goose Pond, Woodmansie
10 acres, no car top launch, no boat ramp, no outboards allowed

Horicon Lake, Lakehurst
50 acres, no car top launch, no boat ramp, no outboards allowed

Kennedy Pond, Colliers Mills
11 acres, car top launch, no boat ramp, electric outboards only

Lake Barnegat, Forked River
50 acres, no car top launch, no boat ramp, no outboards allowed

Lake Carasaljo, Lakewood
67 acres, no car top launch, no boat ramp, no outboards allowed

Lake Fishigan, Lakewood
6 acres, no car top launch, no boat ramp, no outboards allowed

Lake Manahawkin, Manahawkin
70 acres, car top launch, no boat ramp, no outboards allowed

Lake Manetta, Lakewood
18 acres, no car top launch, no boat ramp, no outboards allowed

Lake of the Lilies, Point Pleasant Beach
20 acres, no car top launch, no boat ramp, no outboards allowed

Lower Shannoc Pond, Colliers Mills
8 acres, car top launch, no boat ramp, electric outboards only

Manahawkin Impoundment #1, Manahawkin
45 acres, no car top launch, no boat ramp, electric outboards only

Manahawkin Impoundment #2, Manahawkin
35 acres, no car top launch, no boat ramp, electric outboards only

Mill Pond, Double Trouble Park
20 acres, no car top launch, no boat ramp, no outboards allowed

Oakford Lake, New Egypt
35 acres, car top launch, no boat ramp, outboards allowed

Pohatcong Lake, Tuckerton
33 acres, no car top launch, no boat ramp, no outboards allowed

---

Insiders' Tip
If you intend to fish on the jetties, be extra careful. Conditions tend to be very slippery; many anglers use jetty spikes.

Prospertown Lake, Hornerstown

80 acres, car top launch, no boat ramp, no outboards allowed

Shenandoah Lake, Lakewood

50 acres, car top launch, boat ramp, electric outboards only

Stafford Forge Main Line, Stafford Forge

73 acres, car top launch, no boat ramp, electric outboards only

Stafford Forge Pond #1, Stafford Forge

48 acres, car top launch, no boat ramp, electric outboards only

Stafford Forge Pond #2, Stafford Forge

22 acres, car top launch, no boat ramp, electric outboards only

Stafford Forge Reservoir, Stafford Forge

68 acres, car top launch, no boat ramp, electric outboards only

Success Lake, Colliers Mills

40 acres, car top launch, no boat ramp, electric outboards only

Turn Mill Pond, Colliers Mills

100 acres, car top launch, boat ramp, electric outboards only

Wells Mill Lake, Waretown

34 acres, car top launch, no boat ramp, electric outboards only

Whitesbog Pond, Whitesbog

53 acres, car top launch, no boat ramp, electric outboards only

Atlantic County

Bargaintown Pond, Bargaintown

18 acres, no car top launch, no boat ramp, electric outboards only

Birch Grove Park Ponds, Northfield

30 acres, no car top launch, no boat ramp, no outboards allowed

Corbin City Impoundment #1, Corbin City

104 acres, car top launch, no boat ramp, electric outboards only

Corbin City Impoundment #2, Corbin City

243 acres, car top launch, no boat ramp, electric outboards only

Corbin City Impoundment #3, Corbin City

284 acres, car top launch, no boat ramp, electric outboards only

Egg Harbor City Lake, Egg Harbor

30 acres, no car top launch, no boat ramp, no outboards allowed

Hammonton Lake, Hammonton

75 acres, car top launch, no boat ramp, no outboards allowed

Heritage Park Pond, Absecon

6 acres, no car top launch, no boat ramp, no outboards allowed

Lenape Lake, Mays Landing

350 acres, car top launch, boat ramp, outboard motors limited to 10 horsepower maximum

Makepeace Lake, Hammonton

300 acres, car top launch, no boat ramp, electric outboards only

Crabbing

Crabbing is a popular Shore activity, especially in the upper section of Barnegat Bay and in Little Egg Harbor. Blue crabs are abundant all along the Jersey Coast, in tidal creeks and rivers and in shallow, saltwater bays, from the Hudson River to Delaware Bay. Although most crabbers use small boats, you can also do well on piers, banks, and bridges that border tidal waters.

Use traps or line baited with any fresh fish. You don't need fancy equipment; all you need is a six-ounce sinker, a large hook, and about 20 feet of sturdy cord tied to a stick. If you want to run more than one line, just secure the sticks on land. When chasing the soft crabs, some folks just wade into shallow water and use a scoop net to scoop the little fellows from around bulkheads and bridge pilings.

Before you cook your crabs, make sure they're alive. Discard any that aren't moving. Rinse in fresh water. Then you can simply drop the live crabs into a large pot of boiling water flavored with your favorite herbs or with a commercial seasoning and cook for eight to 10 minutes. The shells will be bright red when they're done.

After you've cooled the crabs, use a knife and/or a nutcracker to remove the meat from the claws and the two thin-shelled sections on either side of the body. Promptly refrigerate what you don't eat—and use within a day or so.

Maple Lake, Estelle Manor

35 acres, car top launch, no boat ramp, no outboards allowed

Mill Pond, Port Republic

32 acres, car top launch, no boat ramp, electric outboards only

Cape May County
Cape May Park Ponds, Cape May Court House

11 acres, no car top launch, no boat ramp, no outboards allowed

Dennisville Lake, Dennisville

50 acres, car top launch, no boat ramp, no outboards allowed

East Creek Pond, Eldora

62 acres, car top launch, no boat ramp, electric outboards only

Lake Nummy, Woodbine

26 acres, car top launch, no boat ramp, electric outboards only

Tuckahoe Impoundment #1, Middletown

42 acres, car top launch, no boat ramp, electric outboards only

Tuckahoe Impoundment #2, Middletown

220 acres, car top launch, no boat ramp, electric outboards only

Tuckahoe Impoundment #3, Middletown

75 acres, car top launch, no boat ramp, electric outboards only

Tuckahoe Lake, Middletown

10 acres, car top launch, no boat ramp, electric outboards only

West Pond, Cape May Court House

3 acres, no car top launch, no boat ramp, no outboards allowed

Charter Fishing and Party Boats

If you don't own your own boat, the easiest way to experience a day on the briny deep is to hook up with one of the many party boats that go out of the big marinas. If you bring your own crowd, you can even charter your own boat.

Monmouth County

Atlantic Highlands Municipal Marina
Atlantic Highlands
(732) 291–1670

Belmar Marina
Belmar
(732) 681–2266

Bogan's Basin Deep Sea Fishing Marina
Brielle
(732) 528–8377

Brielle Marine Basin
Brielle
(732) 528–6200

Hoffman's Marina
Brielle
(732) 528–6160

Leonardo State Marina
Leonardo
(732) 291–1333

Ocean County

15th Street Marina
Barnegat Light
(609) 494–6611

Bayview Marina
Barnegat Light
(609) 494–7450

Big Bill II Charter Fishing
Forked River
(215) 785–2567

Black Whale II and Black Whale III
Barnegat Light
(609) 492–0333

Carolyn Ann III
Waretown
(609) 693–4281

Cock Robin
Point Pleasant Beach
(732) 892–5083

Connie Claire Charter Fishing
Barnegat Light
(609) 494–6787

Crystal Point Yacht Club
Point Pleasant
(732) 892–2300

Dauntless Broadway Basin
Point Pleasant Beach
(732) 892–4298

Doris Mae IV
Barnegat Light
(609) 494–1692, (609) 494–7468

Fleet King Charter Fishing
Forked River
(609) 693–3321

Fish Trap Charter Fishing
Beach Haven
(609) 492–1046

Four Aces II Charter Fishing
Barnegat Light
(201) 891–2551 (day), (201) 891–4820 (night)

Jersey Devil
Barnegat Light
(609) 294–2090

Lighthouse Marina
Barnegat Light
(609) 494–2305

Mimi VI
Point Pleasant Beach
(732) 370–8019

Miss Barnegat Light
Barnegat Light
(609) 494–2094

Miss LBI
Barnegat Light
(609) 361–2250

Miss Michelle III
Point Pleasant Beach
(732) 899–4984

Norma K III
Ken's Landing, Point Pleasant Beach
(732) 899–8868

Purple Jet Sport Fishing
Point Pleasant Beach
(732) 701–1960

Queen Mary
Point Pleasant Beach
(732) 899–3766

Sea Gypsy
Beach Haven
(609) 492–2843

The Shark
Barnegat Light
(800) 437–4275

Super Chic
Barnegat Light
(609) 296–1685

Tampa VII
Ken's Landing, Point Pleasant Beach
(888) 31–TAMPA

White Star IV
Barnegat Light
(609) 494–1462

Atlantic County

Angler's Choice Sportfishing Charter Service
Northfield
(609) 272–2244

Duke O'Fluke Party Fishing Boat
Somers Point
(609) 822–2272

Historic Gardner's Basin
Atlantic City
(609) 348–2880

Kammerman's Atlantic City Marina
Atlantic City
(609) 348–8414

Senator Frank S. Farley State Marina
Atlantic City
(609) 441–8482, (800) 876–4386

Cape May County

Adventurer II
Wildwood
(609) 729–7777

Avalon Anchorage
Avalon
(609) 967–3592

Insiders' Tip

A good place to look for up-to-date fishing information is www.newjerseyvisitors network.com; click on the "NJ Fishing" link.

Captain Cramer
Stone Harbor
(609) 368–9803

Captain Robbins
Sea Isle City
(609) 263–2020

Gallant Lady
Cape May
(609) 884–7754

Higbee's Marina
Fortescue
(856) 447–4157

Laura Marie III
Ocean City
(609) 653–9164

Miss Avalon II
Avalon
(609) 967–7455

Miss Chris Fleet
Cape May
(609) 884–3939
Moran's Dockside
Avalon
(609) 368–1321

North Star Fleet
Ocean City
(609) 399–7588

Porgy III
Cape May
(609) 465–3840

Royal Flush
Wildwood
(609) 522–1395

Sea Hunt
Cape May
(609) 884–0909

Sea Raiders Deep Sea Fishing
Wildwood
(609) 522–1032

Sea Star Fleet
Cape May
(609) 884–3421

Starfish
Sea Isle City
(609) 263–3800

Starlight
Wildwood Crest
(609) 729–7776

Smuggler's Cove
Stone Harbor
(609) 368–1700

Boat Trips

Most of the boat trips included here are seasonal, but some companies operate in the off-season, with reduced schedules. If you wish to take a trip in the off-season, call ahead or check the appropriate Web site.

Price Code

The ratings here are for adult tickets. Virtually all operators offer senior discounts and half-price tickets for children. Very young children (the age varies with different companies) sail free. Many of these cruise companies also offer discount coupons, either on their Web sites or in various free area newspapers. Dinner cruises, of course, cost more than a simple sightseeing cruise or eco-cruise.

$ . . . . under $20
$$ . . . . $20 to $40
$$$ . . . . $40 to $60
$$$$ . . . . over $60

Atlantic City Cruises $
New Hampshire Avenue, Atlantic City
(609) 347–7600
www.Atlanticcitycruises.com

Take your choice of the cruises aboard the *Cruisin' 1*—they're all fun. The one-hour Morning Skyline trip is a seagoing guided tour of Atlantic City. The two-hour Marine Mammal Adventure, with an onboard naturalist, takes you out to sea in search of whales, dolphins, or whatever marine life happens to be around. The hour-long Harbor Tour is a cruise through the harbors and marinas of Brigantine and Atlantic City, and the Sunset Cruise combines beautiful vistas with a spectacular sunset. The dual-deck ship carries 150 people; there's a full-service bar, and snacks are available. You can get souvenir photos or rent binoculars if you forgot your own. During the summer, there are four cruises a day, plus a moonlight dance cruise on Thursday night. In the spring and fall (through late October), there's a reduced cruise schedule; call ahead for information.

Barnegat Sail Charters $$–$$$
Cedar Creek Marina
100 Harbor Inn Road, Bayville
(732) 269–1351

This company offers cruises of varying lengths (including a sunset cruise) in the Barnegat Bay. The shorter cruises (about 2½ hours) depart twice daily, as do the half-day cruises. Snacks and beverages are served.

Bay Cruiser Excursions $
Wheelhouse Marina
267 24th Avenue, Seaside Park
(732) 793–3296
www.wheelhousemarina.com

In addition to exploring Barnegat Bay in a 35-foot covered boat, passengers learn about the bay's ecosystems by getting out of the boat, walking around in the shallow water, and seeing what forms of life they can spot. The morning cruise runs an hour and 15 minutes, while the afternoon cruise goes for two hours; sunset cruises are offered during July and August.

Cape May Whale Watch $–$$
1286 Wilson Drive, Cape May
(609) 898–0055, (888) 531–0055
www.capemaywhalewatch.com

The Cape May Whale Watch offers seagoing safaris on a 75-foot catamaran. Passengers are instructed on how to spot and identify dolphins, whales, and birds. With luck you'll see some of the "regulars" named by the crew: Tippy and Nubby, the bottlenose dolphins, and Slammer, the humpback whale. If for some reason you don't see any marine life on your cruise, you'll get another trip free. There are morning and afternoon cruises.

Cape May Whale Watcher $–$$
Second Avenue and Wilson Drive, Cape May
(609) 884–5445, (800) 786–5445
www.capemaywhalewatcher.com

Here's another Cape May company offering whale- and dolphin-watching cruises. Cape May Whale Watcher's vessel is larger than Cape May Whale Watch's; in fact, at 100 feet and with a capacity of 290 passengers, it's the largest in South Jersey. You have a choice of two- or three-hour trips, both departing three times daily. As with the other whale watches in town, if you don't see marine life, you get another cruise free. Lighthouse cruises and fireworks cruises are also offered.

Captain Schumann's $$
4500 Park Boulevard, Wildwood
(609) 522–2919, (800) 246–9425

Captain Schumann will take you out to look for whales and other sea creatures or to simply enjoy the sunset. The cruises aboard the Big Blue, a converted World War II PT boat, run about 2½ hours and depart three times a day from July through Labor Day.

Delta Lady $
Wildwood Marina
Rio Grande and Susquehanna Avenues, Wildwood
(609) 522–1919
www.deltalady.com

The *Delta Lady* offers several narrated tours aboard an 1850s-style riverboat. These cruises include the inland waterways of Cape May, Cape May Canal, area bird and wildlife sanctuaries, commercial fishing fleets, and the U.S. Coast Guard base. The Wildlife and Nature Cruise offers passengers opportunities to photograph rare and endangered species along these waterways. There are also sunset cruises with dinner and music, sing-along cruises, and even a breakfast cruise with Captain Kidd, with the Captain regaling passengers with tales of derring-do during the pirate days. This is a dual-deck ship with a full-service bar and snack bar.

River Belle $
Broadway Basin
47 Broadway, Point Pleasant Beach
(732) 528–6620

River Queen $
Bogan's Basin
800 Ashley Avenue, Brielle
(732) 892–3377

Nicely executed replicas of Mississippi riverboats, complete with mahogany decks, these two vessels cruise the inland waters of the Manasquan and Metedeconk Rivers, the Point Pleasant Canal, and Barnegat Bay. Dinner, lunch, and brunch cruises, as well as mystery cruises, pizza-and-fireworks cruises, and Fourth of July and New Year's Eve galas are offered.

River Lady $–$$
1 Robbins Parkway, Toms River
(732) 349–8664
www.riverlady.com

The *River Lady*, a Mississippi-style paddle wheeler, offers numerous cruises from May to September. You can take a lunch cruise and learn about the Toms River and Barnegat Bay while you dine. Other options include: an early-bird dinner cruise and a dinner-and-dancing excursion.

Riverboat Services/*The Great Ga-Zee-Boat*
Weston's Marina
Park Road, Monmouth Beach
(732) 780–4217
www.riverboatservices.com

So you want to party with 30 or 40 of your closest friends and you want to do it on the water. You can charter *The Great Ga-Zee-Boat* and cruise the Shrewsbury and Navesink Rivers. The boat's name comes from the octagonal cabin, which resembles a Victorian gazebo. It sails from the Oceanport Marina on River Street (call or check the Web site for directions), and as you cruise you'll spot the splendid mansions of the rich and very rich on the Shore. You may also spot a dolphin. A private cruise for up to 48 guests is $420 for two hours. You can arrange to have music and all kinds of catered food and beverages (for additional fees).

Silver Bullet Speedboat Rides $–$$
Wildwood Marina
Rio Grande and Susquehanna Avenues, Wildwood
(609) 522–6060

Lovers of speed can take their dolphin- and whale-watching cruises aboard the *Silver Bullet*, a 70-footer billed as "The World's Largest and Fastest Speedboat." The narrated cruises depart three times daily in season; refreshments are available on board.

Salt Marsh Safari $
Miss Chris Marina, Shellenger's Landing
Second Avenue and Wilson Drive, Cape May
(609) 884–3100
www.skimmer.com

Explore the coastal salt marsh of Cape May aboard the *Skimmer*, a covered boat that carries up to 41 passengers. During a narrated tour through calm inland waters, you'll learn about the area's natural history and its bird, fish, and plant life. Along the way you may meet ospreys, laughing gulls, herons, and diamondback terrapin. Cruises go out three times daily in summer.

Yankee Schooner $-$
Dolphin Cove
Ocean Highway Dock, Cape May
(609) 884–1919

If you'd rather be a deckhand than a passenger, the captain of the *Yankee Schooner* will let you help set the sails, coil the halyards, and even try your hand at the helm. Otherwise, just relax and enjoy the breeze as you cruise harbor, intercoastal, or ocean waters. Cheese and crackers and soft drinks are served during the three-hour ocean cruise; you may bring your own wine or beer. The ship sails daily from mid-May until late September.

SeaStreak America, Inc. $$–$$$$
(800) BOAT RIDE
www.seastreakusa.com

Though the SeaStreak vessels are primarily commuter ferries running between Highlands and Atlantic Highlands in New Jersey and New York City (Wall Street, East 34th Street, and Brooklyn), we like to take their excursions. Especially popular is the July 4 trip to New York Harbor and the Macy's fireworks display. Other fun options include: sunset cruises, fall foliage cruises, Santa cruises, cruises to watch the Yankees and Mets play, and more. The baseball cruises include upper-tier reserved stadium seats, as well as round-trip boat transportation. The line's 82-foot catamarans are modern and fast (with cruising speeds of 38 knots) and offer full bar and snack service.

Marinas

There are literally hundreds of marinas at the Jersey Shore. We're sure you can find one that's convenient for you. Here is a list of the marinas operated by the state. For information on private marinas, visit www.mpcnetwork.com or www. mpconline.com. Private marinas are also listed in local telephone directories and in the free *Boaters Directory,* available at Shore boat and fishing shops.

Forked River State Marina
311 South Main Street, Forked River
(609) 693–5045

Forked River State Marina is located on U.S. Highway 9, a few miles from exit 74 of the Garden State Parkway. By water, the marina is a leisurely 15-minute ride to the "BB" Buoy, Barnegat Bay, and the Intracoastal Waterway. Barnegat Inlet and the Atlantic Ocean are easily accessible.

The marina has 125 berths (maximum length, 50 feet; draft, 6 feet). Water, electricity, and cable TV and telephone hookups are available dockside. Other facilities include a laundry, showers and rest rooms, and a holding tank pumpout. Bait and tackle, gas and diesel fuel, ice, a ship store, a restaurant, and repair facilities are nearby.

Leonardo State Marina
102 Concord Avenue, Leonardo
(732) 291–1333

Leonardo State Marina is four blocks off N.J. Highway 36 in Leonardo. By water, it

In pleasant weather, you'll see fleets of boats at Shore marinas like this one, the Senator Frank S. Farley State Marina. PHOTO: COURTESY OF ATLANTIC CITY CONVENTION & VISITORS AUTHORITY

is due southwest of Sandy Hook and is the closest marina to the Sandy Hook Bay entrance. Its proximity to the east of the Earle Naval Pier makes it easily identifiable as you enter the bay from either New York Bay or the Atlantic Ocean.

The marina has 179 berths (maximum length, 45 feet; draft, 6 feet). Water, electricity, and telephone hookups are available at dockside. The marina also offers charter/head boats, a launch ramp, winter wet storage, gas and diesel fuel, holding tank pumpout, ice, bait and tackle, a luncheonette, and shower/sanitary facilities.

Senator Frank S. Farley State Marina
600 Huron Avenue, Atlantic City
(609) 441–8482

Situated on Clam Creek, the marina is a short distance from the Atlantic Ocean via Absecon Inlet or the Intracoastal Waterway. From exit 40 of the Garden State Parkway, it is a 15-minute drive on N.J. Highway 30 to Farley Marina, which is located directly across Huron Avenue from Trump's Marina Hotel Casino.

The marina has 640 berths (maximum length, 300 feet; draft, 12 feet). Facilities include water, electricity, cable TV hookups, and telephone hookups. Ice, a laundry, shower/sanitary facilities, a restaurant, a lounge, a luncheonette, bait and tackle, charter boats, a ship store, gas and diesel fuel, and holding tank pumpout are available on-site.

Biking

Biking is the way to get to the top of the heap in Jersey. Just ask our former governor, Christy Whitman, an avid sportswoman and now head of the EPA. One of her favorite events while head of the Garden State was her annual Tour of the Shore on her Cannondale mountain bike. She pedaled on the Henry Hudson Trail, through Atlantic Highlands and Navesink, and past Hartshorne Woods, covering some hilly terrain that had some of her cycling companions grumbling and saying

Insiders' Tip

When riding on roads, a few basic rules will keep you safe and on the right side of the law. Observe the same traffic laws as car drivers (stop at traffic lights, stop signs, etc.) and use hand signals. Stay on the right-hand side of the road except when you're making a left turn from a left lane. Your bike must have a bell or horn and a red rear reflector. Bike helmets are mandatory for children under 14, and a good idea for anyone with brain matter to protect.

they thought the Shore was supposed to be flat.

Well, if it's flat you're looking for, head east and turn before you hit the water. Riding on the boardwalks or oceanfront roads, smelling the salt air, watching the seagulls, and hearing the whoosh of the breakers is one of the great Shore pleasures, and the going is easy enough for kids, grandmas, and everyone in between—except, of course, when the wind kicks up on your way home. There are boardwalks in many Shore towns from Long Branch to Wildwood, and most allow bikes in the off-peak hours—early in the morning and later in the day.

If you've already perused the Natural World chapter of this book, you will have noticed that many of the state and county parks listed have bike trails, and we're not going to repeat them all here, but rather highlight a few from each county. In northern Monmouth County, you will find the kind of hilly terrain that makes life interesting for mountain bikers at Hartshorne Woods and nearby Huber Woods. Farther south the terrain is flatter, but open spaces like Wharton State Forest let you get up close and personal with the preserved natural areas of the Pine Barrens. On the Barnegat Peninsula, Island Beach State Park attracts both folks who go there to bike and those who bike just to get there.

Monmouth County

Allaire State Park
Highway 524 (West Atlantic Avenue),
Wall Township
(732) 938-2371

The terrain at this 3,068-acre park is flat to slightly hilly. Get a map of the trails from the park office. There's a 7½ mile loop that crosses over a dirt road and swings down by the Manasquan River, and a three-mile loop that begins near the antique Pine Creek Railroad and crosses over Highway 524. The surface on the park's two loops is sand, dirt, and gravel, with some very sandy parts, though nothing as difficult as the deep "sugar sand" of Wharton State Forest. Horses are permitted on the trails, and their hooves tend to churn up the middle, so many bikers find themselves keeping to the sides, looking for firmer footing. (The surface can actually be at its best when winter freezes it hard.) To avoid paying the entrance fee charged for parking when you come to tour historic Allaire Village (see the Living-History Farms and Historic Villages chapter), pass up the main entrance; instead continue for another mile and a half, and take the first right turn after the golf course onto Hospital Road. Go another mile and a quarter or so, pass the first parking lot and continue to the larger lot, which is on your right.

Edgar Felix Bikeway
Wall to Manasquan
(732) 449-8444

This seven-mile route runs from Hospital Road in Wall (not far from Allaire, off Highway 524) to Manasquan, following an abandoned railroad right-of-way, which has been paved, so the going is pretty flat and easy. Like the Henry Hudson Trail, this is a popular multiuse trail, so be careful. The bonus here is that you can explore the beach town of Manasquan and surrounding areas.

Gateway National Recreation Area
Sandy Hook Unit
Off N.J. Highway 36, east of Highlands, north of Sea Bright
(732) 872-5970, (732) 872-0115
www.nps.gov/gate

There's a lot to explore on Sandy Hook's 11 miles, and biking is a great way to cover some ground. Paved roads lead to the beach parking lots, the Revolutionary War-era lighthouse, Fort Hancock's abandoned battlements, and other points of interest, but be careful of loose sand on the roads and gull-smashed clam shells in many parking lots. If you cycle into the park, you can dodge the summer parking fee for cars. Leave your car at the Rocky Point section of Hartshorne Woods, if you don't mind a nice uphill trek at the end of the day. If you're lucky enough to be around after the summer season is over, you'll have a delightful and easy ride with little competition from other bikers or automobiles. Stop at the Spermaceti Cove visitors center for a map and other park information. As you make your way through the park, look for birds, take in the holly forest, and just generally enjoy the dramatic surroundings: the Twin Lights rising high above you on one side, the New York skyline on the other. If you decide to linger, you can swim, picnic, fish, or take a guided tour.

Hartshorne Woods Park
Navesink Avenue, Middletown
(732) 842-4000

Any day with a hint of sunshine will bring SUVs loaded with mountain bikes to this 736-acre park in the posh Navesink River area. It has miles of hilly terrain, which can challenge even the fittest off-roaders—but the deer seem to like it fine. There are two main access areas, with

Avenue in North Middletown. The trail wends its way through Belford, Port Monmouth, Keansburg, Union Beach, and Keyport, so you'll have to watch out for cars at street crossings, not to mention the joggers and walkers who also enjoy this trail. On the plus side, however, you have the option of meandering off the trail and pedaling to nearby beaches or stopping for a snack. The trail is flat and well maintained by the Monmouth County Parks System and by the surrounding communities. The elevated railbed provides some scenic moments, with bridges crossing the tidal wetlands, and even the odd glimpse of the Raritan Bay.

Huber Woods Park
25 Brown's Dock Road (off Navesink River Road), Locust (Middletown)
(732) 872-2670

From the hilltop near the Environmental Center of this 250-acre park, you'll get a perspective of the Navesink River that homeowners on Navesink River Road (like rocker Jon Bon Jovi) paid millions to enjoy. Most of the six miles of trails are graded easy or moderate, with only the Many Log Run getting the black diamond. It's a pretty ride through these woods and gentle hills on trails that are mostly hard-packed, though some bikers complain that horseback riders can leave trails rutted. You can also ride to nearby Hartshorne Woods by taking the Claypit Run to the end at Locust Point Road. Make a left turn onto this busy street (County Road 8A), a quick right over the Locust Avenue bridge, and then a right turn at the five-way intersection onto Navesink Avenue to get to the Buttermilk Valley trailhead; a hard right at that intersection will put you on Hartshorne Road, the back way to enter the Laurel Ridge Trail.

parking, portable toilets, and trail maps: the Buttermilk Valley Trailhead on Navesink Avenue, and the Rocky Point Trailhead off Portland Road, behind Twin Lights. At Rocky Point, which fronts on the Navesink and Shrewsbury Rivers, moderate-difficulty loops explore abandoned military fortifications and connect to the difficult Grand Tour, six miles of primitive trail through the Monmouth Hills section. You'll be rewarded for your pain, though, with scenic picnic spots that overlook the Navesink River. In the more benign-sounding Buttermilk Valley section, bikers with average skills head for Laurel Ridge Trail, which runs about 2½ miles and is mostly made up of fire roads.

Henry Hudson Trail
Aberdeen to Atlantic Highlands, north of N.J. Highway 36
(732) 842-4000

The Henry Hudson Trail is a nine-mile stretch of abandoned railroad bed that has been partially paved, with sections of packed dirt and gravel. The east end of the trail can be accessed from the parking lot at 5 N.J. Highway 36 West in Leonardo (Middletown), just west of Avenue D. Additional off-street parking is available near the intersection of Clark Street/Gerard Avenue and Lloyd Road/Broadway at the Aberdeen-Hazlet border; off Spruce Street in Union Beach; and at MacMahon Park, off Atlantic

Manasquan Reservoir
311 Windeler Road, Howell Township
(732) 919-0996

The Manasquan Reservoir is more than just a source of drinking water, it's a wildlife habitat and a recreation area for southern Monmouth County. Boating

Long Beach Island Road Riding

In this chapter, we've focused on parks and trails set aside for biking, but of course, you can bike anywhere at the Shore—to get from here to there, or just to get out in the fresh air. One place where biking is both a practical means of locomotion and something to do on a nice day is Long Beach Island. From the tip of Barnegat Light down to Holgate, LBI is about 18 miles, as the crow flies. But crows miss a lot—beautiful beaches, swell houses, and the Show Place Ice Cream Parlor in Beach Haven (although the birds may be quite familiar with Old Barney and Forsythe National Wildlife Refuge in Holgate). If your goal is to make a complete circuit of the island, the ideal time is certainly fall. But for summmer folk on LBI, biking is often the best way to get from beach to beach, skimming by traffic on broad, well-maintained shoulders and avoiding parking hassles.

and fishing are popular activities here, as is bird-watching. Circling the park perimeter is an easy five-mile ride beginning near the main park entrance (look for the sign before the tollbooth). The main trail is cinder/dirt. If yours is a biking family, this is a nice place to spend the day.

Ocean Avenue—Pedestrian Road
Brighton Avenue to South Bath Avenue, West End (Long Branch)

Back in the day, when we were trying out our first two-wheelers here, we called this the "Green Road." It's no longer green, but cars are still kept off this section of Ocean Avenue from Brighton Avenue to South Bath, where you can connect to Long Branch's Boardwalk. The Boardwalk extends north to Seven Presidents Park, making for a nice, long, oceanfront outing.

Ocean County

Cattus Island County Park
1170 Cattus Island Boulevard, Toms River
(732) 270–6960, (877) OC PARKS
www.oceancountygov.com/county/parks

Cattus Island is really a peninsula that extends out into Barnegat Bay (while Barnegat Peninsula is really an island). The park encompasses 500 acres of salt

marsh and wetlands and is one of the Shore's wonderful nature preserves. At the Cooper Environmental Center, named after the family that did much to preserve this beautiful site, you can learn about the area, past and present; if you're interested, there are nature walks, boat trips, and other programs. Unfortunately, bikes are limited to the dirt fire road that runs the length of the park, out to Silver Bay; the ride is brief (only two miles) but lovely.

Island Beach State Park
N.J. Highway 35, Seaside Park
(732) 793–0506
www.state.nj.us/dep/forestry/parknj/divhome

A bike ride is the perfect way to experience this slender barrier beach and idyllic park situated between the Atlantic Ocean and Barnegat Bay. As the park is a sanctuary for birds including the osprey (the park is the state's largest osprey colony) and even the occasional piping plover, access to some areas is restricted. Ride the two-lane road that passes right through the park and then hit the five-mile bike path; it's 16 miles total, out and back, with easy, flat terrain the whole way. You may want to stop for a swim—there are showers and changing rooms. As with Sandy Hook, arriving by bike is a great way to avoid the entrance fee—and to make sure that you make it into

Cyclists enjoy a fall ride through Cattus Island County Park. PHOTO: COURTESY OF OCEAN COUNTY PUBLIC AFFAIRS

the park on peak summer weekends when the parking places get taken quickly.

Wells Mills County Park
Wells Mills Road (Highway 532), Waretown
(609) 971-3085

At 900 acres, Wells Mills is the largest park in the Ocean County Park System. It's a typical Pinelands environment of streams, bogs, swamps, and uplands. The observation deck in the nature center, which also serves as the park office, is a fine place to view the beauty of the Pinelands ecosystem; it also features exhibits relating to "piney" tradition and culture. You can also pick up a map noting the trails where mountain bikes are allowed (some of the park's 16 miles of trails are off-limits to bikers). The terrain is fairly flat and not overly challenging.

Atlantic and Cape May Counties

Belleplain State Forest
Highway 550, Woodbine
(609) 861-2404

This 11,000-acre preserve in upper Cape May County is not only an inviting place to explore on your bike, it's one of the state's major camping destinations, with some 200 tent sites spread over 100 acres, as well as canoeing and fishing on Lake Nummy. The terrain is pretty flat, and if you start out near the park station off Highway 347, your first impression of the 20-some miles of trails may be that they're wide and a little blah. But the track soon becomes narrow and winding, with many fallen logs, large and small, to negotiate. In the northwest area of Belleplain, there's a hillier section, but you'll be sharing space with dirt bikes and quads. Locals also cut their own trails through the woods, but do their best to cover their tracks to keep the dirt bikes out. A triathlon is held at this park in June. There are no stores here, so BYO H_2O.

Estell Manor Park
109 N.J. Highway 50, Mays Landing
(609) 645-5960, (609) 625-1897

When cycling the multiuse loop road in this 1,700-acre park, do be careful, because cars also use it. The paved road is

Cape May Road Riding

Bike riding is a marvelous way to explore the Victorian charms of Cape May; you can cover more ground than just by walking, but you have more time to savor the passing views than you do when driving in a car. In fact, many of the hotels and bed-and-breakfasts in town provide guests with free loaner bikes, so that they can explore the oceanfront promenade and the quaint streets lined with historic inns.

If you're not staying in town, you can park at Cape May State Park and start your exploration of Cape Island at the Cape May Point Lighthouse. If summer traffic jams the Lafayette Street access to Cape May from the Garden State Parkway, consider parking at Historic Cold Spring Village, about a mile north of Cape May on U.S. Highway 9 (735 Seashore Road), and then pedaling across the somewhat less congested Seashore Road bridge into town.

If you didn't bring your own wheels, you can rent something spiffy at Cape Island Bicycles, at the corner of Beach and Howard Streets (609–889–8300, CapeBike@Bell Atlantic.net). They have a variety of types of bicycles and cycling equipment, including tandems, child trailers, and even electric bikes for the lazy. Rental packages include locks, maps, and helmets.

just over two miles, an easy introduction to Atlantic County Park System's most popular green space. Stop at the Warren E. Fox Nature Center to pick up maps and brochures; you can even borrow a bike here if you leave your driver's license. For off-road bikers, 13 miles of mostly flat trails await, passing through various Pinelands habitats. The ground is not overly sandy, but it can be quite wet. After your ride, you can canoe, kayak, fish, toss a Frisbee, pitch some horseshoes, play volleyball or softball, or just enjoy the scenic beauty of the park, which is home to a wide diversity of plants and animals. You can adjourn to one of the observation booths (camouflage netting is available) to spy for bald eagles, otters, red foxes, beavers, and other park residents.

Linwood Bikeway
Off Wabash Avenue, Linwood

Right in the center of Linwood, a town on the mainland just west of Margate, connected to Absecon Island by the Highway 563 bridge, is the Linwood Bikeway. It's a flat, 4½-mile asphalt multiuse trail that's a great, family-friendly place to tool around.

Wharton State Forest
Batsto Station
Highway 542, eight miles east of Hammonton
(609) 561–0024, (609) 561–3262
Atsion Recreation Area
Highway 206, Atsion, eight miles north of Hammonton
(609) 268–0444

Wharton State Forest covers more than 110,000 acres in the heart of the Pine Barrens, an amazing natural preserve where bald eagles, osprey, great horned owls, herons, and wild turkeys are just a few of the species that you may encounter. With 500 miles of unpaved roads for biking and horseback riding, it would seem to be a cyclist's heaven, but there is one problem: the sugar sand. Stick to the beaten paths or you may find yourself ankle-deep in soft, rutted sand that sucks your tires down like quicksand. It's also easy to get lost here. You can pick up a map at either of the two park stations, at Batsto Village,

Canoeing is a fun way to explore the state parks. PHOTO: LILLIAN AND NINA AFRICANO

Insiders' Tip

If you're a mountain biker, you will be using the county and state parks systems. Many of the trails in these parks are multiuse; some are open to mountain bikes, others are not, so it's a good idea to pick up the free maps at the various parks.

and at Atsion Recreation Area, and get some advice on your choice of route. From Atsion, you could set out on Quaker Bridge Road and follow the Mullica and Batsto Rivers to Batsto. At Batsto, you'll cross the river on a paved road and head back to Quaker Bridge, where you can retrace your route back to Atsion. This 22-mile trek is flat but sandy, so you will have to work for your pleasure here. Starting out from Batsto, it's about a 12½-mile out-and-back on the Batsto-Washington Road to the Godfrey Bridge Campsite on Jenkins Road. Be sure to take along water and snacks, as there are no places nearby to stop.

Biking Clubs

Being part of a club can make biking even more fun. You can find out about upcoming events and competitions or just find companionable people to ride with.

Atlantic Bicycle Club
Allenwood
(732) 291–2664
www.atlanticbicycleclub.org
This is an organization for serious riders, with an emphasis on racing.

Insiders' Tip

At the Shore, unpaved roads are likely to be sandy, especially down south. To avoid digging into soft sand, keep your weight over the saddle and off the handlebars.

BMX

Veterans Memorial Park
Egg Harbor Township
(609) 609–8550

BMX promotes physical fitness through biking, safe riding, and sportsmanship.

Central Jersey BMX
2449 U.S. Highway 9 North, Howell
(732) 863–1010

Though the focus of this organization is on competition, it also supports biking for recreation and exercise.

Jersey Shore Touring Society
Red Bank
(732) 747–8206

This is a bicycle advocacy group, with a focus on social riding and recreation.

Camping

If your idea of paradise involves the open air and a starry sky above, you'll find no shortage of places to pitch your tent or park your camper at the Shore.

State Parks

The New Jersey state parks, which we've discussed in the Natural World chapter, have hundreds of campsites, with a variety of accommodations. Policies at the parks are uniform, and fees are gentle, starting at under a dollar per person for a group campsite to $100 for a group cabin that can accommodate up to 30 people. For individual campers, fees for a site start at $10 and rise to $20 for a shelter or a yurt (a circular tent built on a wooden frame); there is a two-night minimum for the yurts. Some parks have tent areas, some have cabins or yurts, but all the parks offer certain basics such as toilets and showers.

The state parks at or near the Shore that have camping facilities are Allaire, Bass River, Belleplain, and Wharton. All have campsites for tents and/or trailers for up to six people; there are no trailer hookups. They also have group campsites; these are designated for organized groups (a minimum of seven people, with the maximum determined by the size of the facility).

Allaire State Park
Highway 524, Wall Township
(732) 938–2371

At Allaire and Belleplain, you'll find yurts with wood floors, decks, and plexiglass skylights. Each yurt has a wooden door that locks, window screens and flaps, and two double-deck bunks that sleep up to four people. Cooking facilities, water, and rest rooms are within walking distance.

Bass River State Forest
762 Stage Road, New Gretna
(609) 296–1114

Bass River and Wharton (see next page) have lean-tos, which are enclosed structures that have four walls and a wood-burning stove, as well as cabins with fireplaces or wood-burning stoves, kitchens, and bathrooms. The cabins have running water and electricity, furnished

Insiders' Tip

If you're really into bicycles, check out the vintage machines at the Metz Bicycle Museum in Freehold. See the Attractions chapter for a detailed description.

New Jersey State Park Camping Rules

If you camp in a state park, you will need to follow a few basic rules.

- Fires are permitted only in stoves, fireplaces, fire rings, or in approved camp stoves (provided by the camper). Fires may be prohibited if there is a threat of forest fire. Firewood is not provided at campsites, lean-tos, or shelters, but it can be purchased at some areas. Firewood is provided at cabins.
- Pets are not permitted in campground facilities.
- You may not possess or discharge any firearm, pellet gun, bow and arrow, slingshot, or other weapon capable of injuring people or wildlife. Target practice is prohibited.
- No more than two vehicles (including trailers) may be parked at a camping facility. Additional vehicles may be parked in a location designated by the superintendent. More than two vehicles may be parked at group campsites and group cabins subject to approval of the superintendent.
- No alcohol is permitted in the campground facility.
- You must take all your trash with you when you leave.
- Visitors are allowed at camping facilities between 8:00 A.M. and 8:00 P.M. All visitors must pay day-use parking fees, if applicable. The number of visitors may be restricted due to limited facility capacities.
- Water, electric, and sewer hookups are not provided for trailers at campsites.
- Check-out time is noon at all campsites. Check-out time is indicated on permits issued for lean-tos, shelters, and cabins.
- To reserve a campsite, lean-to, camp shelter or cabin, you must be 18 or older. A group campsite or cabin must be occupied by a minimum of one adult supervisor, age 18 or older, for each nine campers who are under 18 years of age in the group.
- Total initial length of stay allowed is 14 consecutive nights. Additional stays may be granted in intervals of not more than seven nights, provided the applicant has vacated the camping facilities for at least seven nights between each occupancy.

living rooms, and bedrooms with bunk beds. You'll have to bring your own bed linens, towels, and cooking utensils.

Belleplain State Forest
Highway 550, Woodbine
(609) 861-2404

In addition to the facilities noted in the introduction, Belleplain has group cabins, which are basically the same as the regular cabins except that they can accommodate 28 to 30 people.

Wharton State Forest
Batsto Station, eight miles east of
Hammonton
(609) 561-0024

With lean-tos and cabins (see Bass River State Forest, page 81), as well as campsites for tents and trailers, Wharton has a number of different options for outdoorspeople. You'll also find wilderness campsites in the forest; these can be reached by backpacking, boating, canoeing, or on horseback.

Other Campgrounds

Whenever possible, we've listed campgrounds that are a short (15 minutes or less) drive to the beach. When there are limited options—in Monmouth County, for example—we've included campgrounds that are convenient to other attractions and offer some recreational possibilities (like fishing). Most of these private campgrounds require a minimum stay of two or three nights. When pets are allowed, they generally must be kept on a leash; if this is an issue, check with the campground before you make a reservation. Unless otherwise noted, the daily base rate we list is for no-frills tent camping; when the rate mentions "children," it means children under the age of 18. If your stay is for an extended period—a week or longer—the rate drops.

Monmouth County
Pine Cone Campground
340 Georgia Road, Freehold
(732) 462–2230

There are 127 sites in this 35-acre campground that's near Six Flags Great Adventure, the Monmouth Battlefield, Freehold Raceway, and the Englishtown Flea Market. Amenities include dumping stations, electric/sewer/water hookups, fire rings, flush toilets, hot water, showers, ice, laundry facilities, grocery shopping, and a snack bar. Kids will entertain themselves at the playground, grown-ups at the 78-foot pool, the tennis court, or the recreation hall. Pine Cone offers many planned weekend activities, including live entertainment, movies, dances, and country-western jamborees. The campground is open from mid-April to mid-October, and the base rate is $27 for two people (with water and electricity).

Turkey Swamp Park Campgrounds
66 Nomoco Road, Freehold
(732) 462–7286
www.monmouthcountyparks.com

As we've mentioned in the Natural World chapter, Turkey Swamp is a big (1,400 acres) county park with lots of open play areas and plenty of outdoor activities for young and old—including boating, fishing, and swimming. Each of the 64 sites has a dumping station, an electric/water hookup (it's recommended that you have 100 feet of hose to reach your site), a fire ring, a picnic table, and a lantern holder. There's a centrally located comfort station with flush toilets and showers, as well as laundry and vending facilities that sell ice and firewood. There are no stores on-site, but you can shop for food, drugstore items, and hardware about 10 minutes away.

You may fish or boat, but not swim, on the lake in Turkey Swamp Park. The group camping area has a swimming pool (not available on Monday or Tuesday). Your campground permit will entitle you to use all the beach and other recreational options at Seven Presidents Oceanfront Park in Long Branch, about a 40-minute drive away. Pets are allowed, but they must be kept on a leash, and you must clean up their waste. No alcohol is allowed. The season here is from mid-March through November, and the base price is $23.

Ocean County
Albocondo Campground
1480 Whitesville Road, Toms River
(732) 349–4079

Nestled in a scenic setting on the northern branch of the Toms River is this 65-acre campground with 192 sites. If the Shore's Indian history inspires you to camp in a teepee, you can do that here; if you require more than basic shelter, you can rent a cabin. There are dumping stations, electric/sewer/water hookups, flush toilets, hot water, showers, ice, grocery shopping, picnic tables, and a snack bar. In addition to a playground, there are swimming pools, a game room, a nine-hole chip 'n' putt course, a recreation room, and hayrides in the fall. You can boat on the river, but no motors are allowed; canoe and paddleboat rentals are available. Pets are allowed. The campground is open from mid-April through September. The base rate for two adults is $22.

Atlantic City North Family Campground
Stage Road, Tuckerton
(609) 296–9163

This sandy 30-acre campground located between Long Beach Island and Atlantic City (free shuttle to Atlantic City with a two-night stay) has 153 wooded sites; trailer rentals are available. It has dumping stations, electric/sewer/water hookups, fire rings, flush toilets, hot water, ice, laundry facilities, showers, grocery shopping, and a snack bar. Pets are allowed. During the summer, there's a recreation director and an activities program that includes badminton, volleyball, and horseshoes. On your own, you can swim in the pool, relax in the whirlpool, or play a round of mini golf. Campers get free beach badges for Long Beach Island. The campground is open year-round; the base rate for two people is $28.

Brookeville Campgrounds
224 Jones Road, Barnegat
(609) 698–3134

You'll find 100 campsites on this 30-acre site, which is just minutes from Long Beach Island and Seaside Park. There are dumping stations, electric/sewer/water hookups, fire rings, flush toilets, hot water, showers, ice, and trailer rentals. Though the campground is not large, there is a game room, a camp store, and a playground. Brookeville is open from May through September. The base rate for a family of four is $20.

Long Beach Island Trailer Park
19 West Harding Avenue, Beach Haven
(609) 492–9151

This lovely 10-acre property offers 140 RV sites (no tents) located at the beach, adjacent to a mobile home park. It has electric/sewer/water hookups and flush toilets. Groceries, hot water, ice, laundry facilities, and showers are nearby, and so are places to boat, fish, or swim. Pets are allowed. The trailer park is open year-round. The base rate here is for trailers; it's $36 for four people.

Scrubbie Pines Family Campground
30 N.J. Highway 72, Barnegat
(609) 698–5684, (800) 590–2879
www.scrubbiepines.com

Just seven miles west of Long Beach Island,

this 14-acre campground has 107 sites; cabin rentals are available. There are dumping stations, electric/water hookups, fire rings, flush toilets, hot water, showers, ice, laundry facilities, grocery shopping, picnic tables, and a playground. Pets are allowed. Though the campground is on the small side, it does have an adult pool, a kiddie pool, an inviting playground, and a new mini-golf course. The season runs from April through October, and the base rate is $22 for two adults.

Sea Pirate Campground
154 U.S. Highway 9 North, West Creek
(609) 296–7400
www.seapiratecamp.com/

Sea Pirate is a family campground located eight miles from the ocean beaches of Long Beach Island and about a half-hour drive north of Atlantic City. It has 250 wooded sites on 300 acres. You can camp in a tent, a cabin, or a trailer (rentals available). The campground has dumping stations, electric/sewer/water hookups, cable TV, fire rings, flush toilets, hot water, ice, laundry facilities, showers, on-site grocery shopping, and a snack bar. If you camp on one of the secluded tent sites, you can still choose to have cable TV, as well as electricity and water.

There are creeks for crabbing, a pool for swimming, a pond stocked for fishing, and a basketball court to practice those free throws. For kids, there's a playground as well as an extensive program of organized activities. Pets are allowed. The campground is open from May through September. The base rate is $28 for two adults and two children.

Surf and Stream Campground
1801 Ridgeway Road, Toms River
(732) 349–8919
www.surfnstream.com

Surf and Stream is an inviting wooded property that's convenient to Seaside Heights and Six Flags Great Adventure. It has 225 open and wooded campsites on 20 acres; trailer and cabin rentals are available. The facility has dumping stations, electric/sewer/water hookups, fire rings, flush toilets, hot water, showers, ice, laundry facilities, grocery shopping, and a snack bar. For relaxation, there's a swimming pool (and a kiddie pool), a playground, and a game room. In spring and fall, the campground offers hayrides; during the summer season, there's a calendar of activities. The campground is open year-round. The base rate is $25 for two people.

Atlantic County

Blueberry Hill Campground
283 Clarks Landing Road/Highway 624, Port Republic
(609) 652–1644, (800) 732–2036

This 30-acre campground has 180 sites and is just 13 miles from Atlantic City; for a fee, it provides transportation to the casinos. The Forsythe National Wildlife Refuge is nearby, as is the Towne of Historic Smithville. The facility has dumping stations, electric/sewer/water hookups, fire rings, flush toilets, hot water, showers, ice, laundry facilities, picnic tables, and a snack bar. Trailer rentals are available; so is cable television, for a fee. The Olympic-size pool here is quite appealing; there's a kiddie pool, too, as well as a spacious clubhouse, a playground, and a whirlpool spa. Pets are allowed. The campground is open from February until mid-December, and the base rate is $24 for two people.

Buena Vista Camping Park
775 Harding Highway, N.J. Highways 40 and 54, Buena
(856) 697–2004

If you like to camp surrounded by amusements, this 175-acre park with 700 shaded open sites might be for you. Located between Philadelphia and Atlantic City (about 30 minutes from Atlantic City), Buena Vista has the basics: dumping stations, electric/water hookups, fire rings, flush toilets, showers, ice, laundry facilities, picnic tables, and grocery shopping. You can rent a trailer or a cabin.

To while away a balmy day, you might swim in the Olympic-size pool (there's a kiddie pool, too), play on the gigantic water slide, fish in the spring-fed lake, or relax on the beach surrounding the lake.

During the warm months, there's an outdoor movie theater, where you and your kids can reminisce about the old drive-in days. Kids like the petting zoo and the kiddie rides; for adults, there's an antique auto museum and a country store. The campground is open year-round, and pets are allowed; the base rate is $28 to $32 for a family of four.

Indian Branch Park Campground
2021 Skip Morgan Drive, Highway 322, Hammonton
(609) 561–4719, (800) 974–CAMP

If you're seeking a family-oriented spot with a Christian atmosphere, you might like this 100-acre lakeside campground. It has 214 shaded sites, some located on the lake. There is swimming in the lake, which is surrounded by sandy beaches, and boating as well (electric motors only). You can rent canoes or paddle boats, fish on the river, or hike the nature trail. In addition to a clubhouse, the campground has a sports field and shuffleboard courts; horseshoes and volleyball equipment are also available. The facility has dumping stations, electric/sewer/water hookups, fire rings, flush toilets, hot water, showers, picnic tables, grocery shopping, and laundry facilities. Pets are allowed, but alcohol is not. The season runs from May through September, and the base rate is $18 for two adults.

Pleasant Valley Campground
60 South River Road, Estell Manor
(609) 625–1238

Located in the heart of the Pinelands, Pleasant Valley is a mile south of Mays Landing, and a 20-minute ride to Atlantic City's casinos and to Ocean City's beaches. It has 250 large wooded sites set on 79 acres; you can camp in a tent or go for the luxury of a two-room air-conditioned cottage with cable television and everything supplied except linens.

The campground has dumping stations, electric/sewer/water hookups, fire rings, flush toilets, hot water, showers, ice, picnic tables, laundry facilities, and a playground. Surrounded as you are by Nature, you can commune with the deer, squirrels, chipmunks, and birds that live on this property. Or, you might go for the man-made pleasures: the swimming pool or kiddie pool, the whirlpool spa, the pool tables or video games in the recreation pavilion. If outdoor sports are your preference, you'll find plenty of opportunities on the athletic field and during the planned activities. Pets are allowed. The campground is open from mid-April until mid-October, and the base rate for a family of four is $27.

Shady Pines Campground
443 South Sixth Avenue, Absecon
(609) 652–1516

This 11-acre campground with 140 shaded sites and trailer rentals is just six miles from Atlantic City. Batsto Village and the Towne of Historic Smithville are also nearby. Shady Pines has dumping stations, electric/sewer/water hookups, fire rings, flush toilets, hot water, showers, ice, laundry facilities, and picnic tables. There's a swimming pool, a playground, and a clubhouse. Pets are allowed. Economy rental cars are available. Shady Pines is open from March through October; the base rate is $29 for four people.

Sleepy Hollow Family Campground
132 Bevis Mill Road, Egg Harbor Township
(609) 927–1969, (800) 272–1969

Sleepy Hollow is the closest campground to Ocean City; Atlantic City is 12 miles away. The campground has 151 sites on 73 acres; trailer rentals are available. There are dumping stations, electric/sewer/water hookups, fire rings, flush toilets, hot water, showers, ice, and a snack bar. Recreational options include a swimming lake, a playground, and a small animal farm for the kids. In season, the campground runs hayrides. Pets are allowed. The season runs from May to mid-October, and the base price is $25 for two adults and up to four children.

Winding River Campground
6752 Weymouth Road, Mays Landing
(609) 625–3191

Winding River Campground is a 25-minute ride to Atlantic City and ocean beaches. It has 132 wooded sites on 34 acres; trailer and cabin rentals are available. The facility has dumping stations, electric/sewer/water hookups, fire rings, flush toilets, hot water, ice, showers, grocery shopping, and laundry facilities.

Since it's located on Egg Harbor River, you can rent a canoe, kayak, or tube and spend a day on the scenic river that does indeed wind; there's a ramp for those who bring their own boats. For recreation on dry land, you'll find a clubhouse, a playground, a heated pool, and equipment for badminton, horseshoes, and the like. On weekends, the campground offers planned activities. Pets are allowed. Winding River is open from late April until mid-October; the base rate is $22 for two adults.

Cape May County

Beachcomber Camping Resort
462 Seashore Road, Cape May
(609) 886–6035, (800) 233–0150
www.beachcombercamp.com

Located just four miles from Cape May and four miles from the Wildwood Boardwalk, Beachcomber is one of the Southern Shore's newer (and bigger) campgrounds, with 530 sites set on more than 100 acres. Of course, it has all the basics: dump stations, electric/sewer/water hookups, fire rings, flush toilets, hot water, ice, laundry facilities, grocery shopping, and a snack bar. If you prefer to camp in comfort, you can rent a lakefront cabin or a trailer. In addition to two spring-fed lakes with sandy beaches, the resort has three adult pools and three kiddie pools, a clubhouse, a playground, six shuffleboard courts—and lots of planned activities. You can rent a canoe, kayak, or paddleboat and go out on one of the lakes to fish or just hang out. The season runs from mid-April until mid-October, and the base rate is $33 for a family of two adults and two children.

Cape Island Campground
709 U.S. Highway 9, Cape May
(609) 884–5777, (800) 437–7443
www.capeisland.com

If you'd like to sample some of Cape May's attractions without using a car, base yourself at this campground, which is located across the road from Historic Cold Spring Village and the Cape May Seashore Lines train depot. The train makes four trips daily from Cape May Court House, across the Cape May Canal, and into the city of Cape May, stopping directly across from the campground. There are 455 sites set on 175 acres. The basics are here: dumping stations, electric/sewer/water hookups, fire rings, flush toilets, hot water, showers, ice, laundry facilities, a snack bar, a recreational pavilion, and playgrounds. When you're not busy exploring Cape May or riding the nearby Lewes Ferry, you can wander through the acres of forests and fields, swim in one of the two pools (there's a kiddie pool, too), or play tennis, mini golf, or shuffleboard. In the evening, watch a movie or try your hand at bingo. In the fall, the campground runs hayrides. It's open from May through September, and the base rate is $36 for two adults and two children.

Depot Travel Park
800 Broadway, West Cape May
(609) 884–2533

This small—nine acres—travel park has just 100 grassy sites, but it's located 10 blocks from Victorian Cape May, and that makes it a good choice if you don't want to do a lot of driving. The campground has dumping stations, electric/sewer/water hookups, flush toilets, hot water, showers, ice, picnic tables, and grocery shopping. Trailer rentals are available. There is a playground for kids, but the point of camping here is to be very close to the beaches, Boardwalk, local restaurants, and other Cape May attractions. Pets are allowed. The season runs from mid-May through September, and the base rate is $23 (with water and electricity) for two adults and two children.

North Wildwood Camping Resort
240 West Shellbay Avenue, Cape May
Court House
(609) 465–4440, (800) 752–4882
www.nwcamp.com

This campground is the closest to Wildwood's free beaches and to Stone Harbor; it's also just 10 minutes north of Cape May. You'll find 260 sites on 30 wooded acres. The resort also offers log cabins with water, electricity, air-conditioning, refrigerators, covered porches, and optional linen service, but no bathrooms or kitchens. On-site facilities include dumping stations, electric/sewer/water hookups, fire rings, flush toilets, hot water, showers, ice, laundry facilities, picnic tables, and grocery shopping.

For recreation, you have an Olympic-size swimming pool, a playground, a clubhouse, a tennis court, a paintball field, and a calendar of planned activities. The season is from April through October, and the base rate is $26 for two adults and two children.

Ocean View Resort Campground
255 U.S. Highway 9, Ocean View
(609) 624–1675
www.ovresort.com

Located just a quarter mile north of Sea Isle Boulevard and midway between Wildwood and Atlantic City, this 180-acre campground has 1,175 shaded sites; for camping with comforts, you can rent an air-conditioned trailer or cabin. There are dumping stations, electric/sewer/water hookups, fire rings, picnic tables, flush toilets, hot water, showers, ice, three laundry facilities, two snack bars, picnic tables, and playgrounds. Though the ocean beaches are close by, there are pleasures to be had here, too. You can take a pedal boat onto the spring-fed lake or relax on the white sandy beach. There's more: Ocean View has an Olympic-size pool, a kiddie pool, a stocked fishing pond, tennis courts, a basketball court, mini golf, a well-equipped game room—and plenty of planned activities, both day and night. The season is from mid-April to mid-September, and the base rate for a family of four is $35.50 (includes sewer, water, electricity, and cable TV).

Seashore Campsites
720 Seashore Road, Cape May
(609) 884–4010
www.seashorecampsites.com

This 89-acre campground is just five minutes from the beach at Cape May. It has 600 sites, dumping stations, electric/sewer/water hookups, fire pits, flush toilets, hot water, showers, ice, laundry facilities, picnic tables, and grocery shopping. When you're not exploring Cape May, you can sample the on-site recreation options. These include a lake with a sandy beach, a heated swimming pool, a kiddie pool, a tennis court (lighted), shuffleboard, and a mini-golf course. In season, the campground has an activities director and days full of things to do. Pets are allowed. The season is from mid-April through October, and the base rate is $29 for two adults and two children.

Whippoorwill Campground
810 South Shore Road, Marmora
(609) 390–3458, (800) 424–8275
www.whippoorwill.com

Ocean City's beaches are just three miles away from this campground, which offers resort accommodations in a wooded setting. (Atlantic City is 20 miles away.) There are 288 sites on 28 acres; cabin rentals are available. The facility has dumping stations, electric/sewer/water hookups, fire rings, flush toilets, hot water, showers, ice, laundry facilities, a snack bar, and a playground. In addition to an Olympic-size pool, Whippoorwill has tennis courts, a video arcade, and planned activities. The season is from April through October, and the base rate is $37 for two people (includes water, sewer, and electricity).

Horseback Riding

The Shore offers many opportunities for riding. We've already mentioned (in the Natural World chapter) the state, county, and national parks that have mixed-use trails open to riders. To refresh your memory, a few of these are Allaire, Bass River, Belleplain, Double Trouble, Island Beach, Monmouth Battlefield, Wharton, and Batsto Village. Horses also are allowed on trails in Hartshorne Woods, Huber Woods, Tatum Park (in Middletown), Thompson Park (Lincroft), Shark River Park, Turkey Swamp Park, and the Dorbrook Recreation Area in Colts Neck; riders may also use the Henry Hudson Trail.

You may be surprised to learn that Monmouth County is home to the largest number of horses of any county in the state; it has 19,000 acres devoted to equine activity. Here are a few area stables that offer trail rides as well as riding instruction and training.

Monmouth County

Circle A Riding Academy
116 Herbertsville Road, Howell
(732) 938–2004

What's neat about the Circle A is that it offers guided horseback riding through scenic Allaire Park, one of our favorite places. Even if you're a rank beginner, they'll find a horse for you here; however, children must be at least seven years old. You can ride any day of the week, year-round; in summer, the hours are from 9:00 A.M. to 6:00 P.M.; the rest of the year it's open from 9:00 A.M. to 4:00 P.M.

Huber Woods
Brown's Dock Road, Locust (Middletown)
(732) 872–2928

The Monmouth County Park System offers good programs for children and young adults at the Equestrian Center in Huber Woods, especially summer equestrian camps. You can also contact the park system for information on this and other programs at its main number, (732) 842–4000.

Tall Oaks Farm
151 Oak Glen Road, Howell
(732) 938–5445

Tall Oaks does not run trail rides, but it does offer lessons for adults and children. It has two lighted outdoor arenas and two lighted indoor arenas.

Horseback riding is easy at the Triple R Ranch in Cape May Court House. PHOTO: LILLIAN AND NINA AFRICANO

Ocean County

Lakewood Riding Center
436 Cross Street, Lakewood
(732) 367–6222
Ride by the day or become a regular at this Ocean County stable.

Cape May County

Triple R Ranch
210 Stagecoach Road, Cape May Court House
(609) 465–4673
The Triple R Ranch caters to novices and kids, so the horses are docile, and the one-hour trail ride is scenic, but easy, meandering through some pretty woods and ending around a man-made lake. This is a ride you can take with your kids (ages 10 and up); they have pony rides for younger children. If the ride's a hit, you can have your child's next birthday party here. We liked the horses and the friendly staff here. Rides are offered daily, year-round, at designated times; call ahead.

Insiders' Tip

For more on horse happenings, check www.NewJerseyHorse.com.

Horse Shows

Many horse shows are held throughout the year at various horse farms and private stables. You'll also find horse shows at various 4-H events, including the county fairs, which we've listed in the Annual Events and Festivals chapter. The two facilities listed below host many prestigious shows.

East Freehold Showgrounds
Kozloski Road, East Freehold
(732) 842–4000

If you're a fan of animal shows, you'll find plenty at these show grounds, which are rented for various occasions from the Monmouth County Park System. Among the groups that hold their shows here are the Central Jersey Horse Club, the 4-H Association, and Los Alamos (dressage); there are jumper shows here, too. Call for a schedule.

Horse Park of New Jersey at Stone Tavern
Highway 524, Allentown
(609) 259–0170
www.horseparkofnewjersey.com

This 147-acre show facility was purchased by the New Jersey Department of Environmental Protection with Green Acres funds. With the cooperation of the New Jersey Department of Agriculture, it has been developed into a world-class equine exhibition facility. The first important event of international interest to be held here was the National Hunter Pony Finals. Equine events (some multiday affairs) are scheduled most weekends and many weekdays from March through November. Food vendors are on-site during show days. Check the Web site for a current calendar.

Extreme Activities

If you have a taste for more adventuresome activities, a few options on the Jersey Shore include flying in a small plane, skydiving, and parasailing. We'll give you the information you need, and then you're on your own.

Airplane Rides

Explore the Shore from above, on your own or with a friend. Several airports in the area offer airplane rides as well as lessons, if that's your pleasure. What's fun is that you can pick the route (within reason), so you can fly over your favorite Shore town, lighthouse, beach, or other landmarks. Depending on the plane and the number of people on board, a one-hour ride will cost under $150; price is usually figured in one-tenth of an hour increments. Airplane rides are a year-round activity, but you should call ahead to make a reservation.

Del Rosso's Blue Baron Biplanes
Old Bridge Airport, Hanger C-12,
Pension Road, Englishtown
(732) 792–1189

Garrett Flight Center
Allaire Airport
1717 N.J. Highway 34, Wall Township
(732) 938–9333

Robert J. Miller County Airpark
Highway 530, Toms River
(732) 797–1077

Skydiving

We have never jumped from an airplane, though a member of our family has, much to our extreme dismay. For those who enjoy such things, we offer the following information.

Skydive Jersey Shore
Allaire Airport
1717 N.J. Highway 34, Wall Township
(732) 938–9002, (877) 444–JUMP

You must be at least 18 years old to skydive here, and the normal weight limit is 220 pounds (but the decision is made on a case-by-case basis). Tandem skydiving, which is the most popular approach, costs $215, and a video proving you did the deed is $95. If once is not enough, you can take the Accelerated Free Fall (AFF) program and work toward becoming a licensed skydiver. The office hours are

Monday from 10:00 A.M. to sunset, Wednesday through Friday from 10:00 A.M. to sunset, and Saturday and Sunday from 8:00 A.M. to sunset. Skydive Jersey Shore is closed during the winter months.

Parasailing

If you like your views of the Atlantic Ocean from the sky, you can soar above your pals below, held aloft by a parachute pulled by a boat. You take off from the deck of the boat and land about 10 minutes later, either on the boat or in the water—your choice. You can climb as high as you like—well, from about 300 to 500 feet, anyway. Some places will let you fly with a pal. We've done it a couple of times, had our picture taken to prove it. And now we don't need to do it again.

Believe it or not, you can take kids as young as two on these rides; there's generally a weight limit of about 300 pounds. If you and a friend together weigh less than that, you can take the ride in tandem. The trip will cost about $50 per person.

Though the boats operate with some regularity during the season (generally from Memorial Day through Labor Day), you do need a reservation, so call ahead. As there aren't that many options, we've listed the operators in alphabetical order, instead of by county.

Atlantic Parasail
1025 Ocean Drive Highway, Wildwood Crest
(609) 522–1869

Beach Haven Watersports
2702 Long Beach Boulevard, Beach Haven
(609) 492–0375

Ocean City Parasail
232 Bay Avenue, Ocean City
(609) 399–3559

Point Pleasant Parasail
Canyon River Club
407 Channel Drive, Point Pleasant
(732) 701–1006
www.pointpleasantparasail.com

Sea Isle City Parasail
Sunset Pier
86th Street and the bay, Sea Isle City
(609) 263–5555

The dogleg right 16th around a pond at Sea Oaks Golf Club. PHOTO: SEA OAKS GOLF CLUB

Golf

Monmouth County

Ocean County

Atlantic and Cape May Counties

Road Trip

There's no better way to enjoy a summer day at the Jersey Shore than with a round of golf followed by a dip in the pool. Shore courses run the gamut from nine-hole municipal courses to exclusive clubs with fees that run into the six figures, but we've listed only courses that are open to the public. Most of the courses that are included here are actually semi-private, meaning that they offer various types of memberships as well as daily fee access. Shore courses tend to be busy, especially on weekends and all summer, so always call ahead for a tee time. Many are closed for tournaments on Mondays or Tuesdays as well. With prices being what they are, most courses take credit cards, so we've noted the exceptions.

To give you an idea of what the course is like at a glance, we've given the total length as well as the slope and USGA rating from the back tees. (A higher rating and slope mean the course is more difficult.) We've also included the name of the course architect and the year the course was built, which can reveal a lot about a course's character.

Greens fees can vary from month to month, from weekday to weekend, even from hour to hour, with premium rates charged for prime weekend morning tee times, and discounts or "twilight" rates for times later in the afternoon. It would be impossible to list all of your options here, so inquire when you call the course to reserve.

Monmouth County

With two courses, Howell Park and Hominy Hill, that regularly rate among the country's best public tracks, the six facilities operated by Monmouth County may be the best reason to live here. Bel-Aire, Charleston Springs, Shark River, and Pine Brook are also county-run. Nonresidents as well as residents may purchase golf ID cards in order to make advance tee-time reservations on the Fairway System (732–758–8383). The card must be bought in person at one of the county courses, and residents need two forms of identification showing residency. Bel-Aire and Shark River are open all year, weather permitting, while the others are open from March 15 to December 23.

At Monmouth County's courses, greens fees are under $25 on the weekend and carts are $29, while at some of the semi-private clubs you can expect to pay closer to $100 per person with a cart for a prime tee time.

Bel-Aire Golf Club
N.J. Highway 34 at Allaire Road, Allenwood
(732) 449–6024
par 60, 3,623 yards; par 27, 1,350 yards
1964, Mort Hansen

Since being taken over by the county, Bel-Aire has seen some improvements, like the elimination of its one heinous Astro-turf green. In addition to its executive 18, Bel-Aire has a nine-hole par 3 course and a driving range for irons, making it ideal for beginners of all ages. Though county-run, Bel-Aire is strictly walk-on.

Charleston Springs
101 Woodville Road (Highway 527 South), Millstone Township
(732) 409–7227, (732) 758–8383
North Course: par 72, 7,018 yards
rating 73.1, slope 125
1998, Mark Mungeam
South Course: par 72, 6,953 yards
2001, Mark Mungeam

In Millstone, farms and woods are giving way to upscale housing developments, and Charleston Springs is right in the middle of this transformation. The North Course is links-inspired, with lots of tall fescue, and though it is surrounded by woods, there are only a few places where the trees really come into play. The greens are lovely to look at and groomed to be fast. The easiest county course to reserve a tee time or even walk on, Charleston Springs also has women-friendly lengths in the 5,100-yard range from the front. The new South Course is a more traditional, parkland-style layout, but it also incorporates native grasses.

Colonial Terrace Golf Club
1005 Wickapecko Drive, Wanamassa
(732) 775–3636
par 35, 2,704 yards
1925

Colonial Terrace's senior specials and easy walking make it popular among retirees. The antiquated nine-holer gives Jerseyans a little taste of Texas, with hardpan fairways that let a well-skulled worm-burner go on forever. The small greens can be equally hard, so if you want to score at Colonial Terrace, you'll have to learn to hit a 60-yard chip-and-run instead of a nice, high pitch.

Colts Neck Golf Club
50 Flock Road, Colts Neck
(732) 303–9330
www.coltsneckgolfclub.com
par 71, 6,236 yards
rating 70.0, slope 126
2000, Cornish, Silva, and Mungeam

The gently rolling hills on Colts Neck's front nine recall the site's old dairy farm, with some tall fescue and Scottish-style bunkers added. The back nine is tighter and more tree-lined. The hole golfers love to hate is 16, a 233-yard par 3 that's all carry over a lake.

Cream Ridge Golf Club
181 Highway 539 South, Cream Ridge
(609) 259–2849, (800) 345–4957
par 71, 6,491 yards
rating 71.8, slope 124
1958, Frank Miscoski

At Cream Ridge, golf is a family business; Bill Miscoski manages the course built by his dad, Frank. The signature 18th hole, a double-dogleg par 5 with water, keeps 'em coming back for more. Electric carts are mandatory on weekends until 2:00 P.M.

Cruz Farm Country Club
55 Birdsall Road, Farmingdale
(732) 938–3378
par 70, 5,062 yards
rating 64.3, slope 114
1979, Evaristo Cruz

If you speak Portuguese, you might be able to sweet-talk the Portuguese staff at Cruz Farm into giving you a tee time; otherwise, things are first-come, first-served, and cash or check only. The course grew from nine holes built by the owner of a successful construction firm for himself and his guests. The grounds also have an extensive picnic area and a soccer field, making it popular for company outings. The course has some funky holes, but the low-key atmosphere makes Cruz Farm enjoyable.

Gambler Ridge Golf Club
Burlington Path Road, Cream Ridge
(609) 758–3588, (800) 427–8463
www.gamblerridge.com
par 71, 6,370 yards
rating 70.2, slope 119
1985, Nickelson and Rockhill

Once a potato farm, Gambler Ridge is fairly flat and open, but with water coming into play on a number of holes, it's challenging enough for the average duffer. Reasonably priced and well kept, Gambler Ridge is popular even if the design is less than spectacular. Electric carts are mandatory on weekend mornings.

Hominy Hill Golf Course
92 Mercer Road, Colts Neck
(732) 462–9222, (732) 758–8383
par 72, 7,049 yards
rating 74.2, slope 131
1964, Robert Trent Jones

There are no gimmes at Hominy Hill, where all 12 of the par 4's are doglegs, many long and uphill. Many a match can turn at the 535-yard 14th, where long hitters can carry the ball far enough to benefit from the downslope; your approach to the green, whether on your second or third (or fourth), will have to be good enough to carry a creek and make it uphill to a shallow green that slopes nastily from back to front. Good luck getting a tee time—you'll need it.

Howell Park Golf Course
Preventorium Road, Farmingdale
(732) 938–4771, (732) 758–8383
par 72, 6,916 yards
rating 73.4, slope 128
1972, Frank Duane

Built on a former dairy farm along the Manasquan River, Howell is consistently one of the top-rated public courses in the country, with a layout that presents a great mix of shots. Its large, sloping greens are well-served by soft spikes, keeping their quickness even through the heavy play. Howell's vaunted bent-grass fairways, on the other hand, can get pretty scarred by mid-season.

Knob Hill Golf Club
350 N.J. Highway 33 West, Manalapan
(732) 792–8118
par 70, 6,513 yards
rating 72.0, slope 126
1998, Mark McCumber

Home of a 2001 SBC Futures Tour event, Knob Hill proves that a great test of golf doesn't need killer yardage. Case in point: the 386-yard eighth hole, a dogleg that hops across water twice. Hit good shots and the hole seems easy, otherwise...The 510-yard par 5 14th gives players a great look, with a fairway split by a bunker into the upper level on the right and a lower level on the left.

Old Orchard Country Club
54 Monmouth Road (N.J. Highway 71 South), Eatontown
(732) 542–7666
par 72, 6,624 yards
rating 71.8, slope 121
1928, A. W. Tillinghast

Old golf courses are like old friends, and walking 18 at Old Orchard is like a stroll

Water guards the front of the green on the par 5 seventh hole at Knob Hill, one of Monmouth County's premier semi-private clubs. PHOTO: ARTHUR AFRICANO

down memory lane. Golfers old and young remember seven, a 480-yard par 5 with an island green. Another favorite is 13, a 360-yard dogleg right that demands two shots across a creek. In the fall, apple trees from the Old Orchard provide free snacks.

Pebble Creek Golf Course
40 Highway 537 East, Colts Neck
(732) 303–9090
par 71, 6,265 yards
rating 69.3, slope 116
1996, Hal Purdy

A popular spot for golf outings, Pebble Creek can get quite crowded with slow-moving groups. Several holes impinge on each other and this can create delays. A couple of doglegs around two lakes, the 585-yard par 5 14th and the 344-yard par 4 16th, felt awkward to us, but maybe it's a matter of taste.

Pine Brook Golf Course
1 Covered Bridge Boulevard, Englishtown
(732) 536–7272
par 61, 4,168 yards
rating 58.1, slope 90

This executive course was donated to the county by Hovnanian Enterprises, builders of the surrounding Covered Bridge development. Flat, with some scattered water, Pine Brook is a great place to get your iron play on target, with 12 par 3's, five par 4's, and one par 5. Fanatical friends have been known to warm up here early in the morning before a big match.

Shark River Golf Course
320 Old Corlies Avenue, Neptune
(732) 922–4141, (732) 758–8383
par 71, 6,180 yards
rating 68.9, slope 112
1920, Joseph "Scotty" l'Anson

This flat, old-style layout has narrow fairways, venerable old trees, and small greens decorated with numerous pot bunkers. Even by modern standards of length, the ninth hole, a 586-yard double-dogleg par 5 is a test; of course, it's the No. 1 hole at Shark River.

Spring Meadow Golf Course
4181 Atlantic Avenue (Highway 524 West), Farmingdale
(732) 449–0806
par 72, 6,224 yards
rating 70.4, slope 125
1920s

Adjoining Allaire State Park, Spring Meadow is very hilly and woodsy, and can be a challenge to walk, so if you're not a hiker, take a cart. A branch of the Manasquan River meanders through the course, coming into play on five holes. The course has five par 5's and five par 3's, and from the red tees, four long par 4's also become par 5's, making the course a par 76 for women, with nine (!) par 5's. Spring Meadow does not have reserved tee times, and in the summer, golfers will

Insiders' Tip

Golf in Monmouth County can get pricey, but many courses offer discounts for late afternoons or weekdays.

start lining up as early as 10:00 P.M. on Friday and Saturday nights, sleeping in their cars to be among the first groups to get out. It's usually easier to play in the afternoon.

Sun Eagles at Fort Monmouth (Military)
Building 2067, Fort Monmouth
(732) 532–4307
par 72, 6,385 yards
rating 70.7, slope 121
1926, A. W. Tillinghast
Military

Like other military base courses, Sun Eagles is open only to active-duty military personnel, 20-year retirees, civilian fort employees GS 9 or above in rank, and their guests. The course is said to be typical Tillinghast, with small undulating greens surrounded by plenty of bunkers. Byron Nelson claimed his first pro victory here in 1935, when he was the assistant pro at Ridgewood Country Club.

Twin Brook Golf Center
1251 Jumping Brook Road, Tinton Falls
(732) 922–1600
par 27, 1,305 yards
1992, Harry Harsin

This nine-holer with well-kept greens and fairways is a great place to practice your iron play and your short game. It also has a two-level driving range, miniature golf, and a snack bar.

Ocean County

Even though Ocean County has fewer courses than Monmouth, it seems a little less difficult to get a tee time here. Maybe folks in this county just prefer boating and fishing.

At the Ocean County course at Atlantis, weekend greens fees are $24 for residents and $42 for nonresidents, with discounts for seniors and students; at Pine Barrens, top rates are over $125.

Bay Lea Golf Course
1536 Bay Avenue, Toms River
(732) 349–0566
par 72, 6,677 yards
rating 71.3, slope 122
1969, Hal Purdy

This open layout presents you with fairly generous-sized targets, i.e., fairways and greens—so why do you keep staring at the water hazards? The toughest hole is the last, a 505-yard par 5 with a lake to clear. Rates are dirt cheap for Dover Township residents with an ID card, and so the course is usually pretty busy.

Cedar Creek Golf Course
Bill Zimmermann Jr. Way, Bayville
par 72, 6,325 yards
rating 70.5, slope 120
1980, Nicholas Phsias

Accuracy is key at this scenic course locals like to call the "Jewel in the Pines." The front nine is flat, but the back is surprisingly hilly for this area of Ocean County. The elevated 14th tee provides a lovely vista of the course's three large lakes. Watch out for the 12th, a long (441 yards) par 4 with water down the right side that comes into play for longer hitters.

Eagle Ridge Golf Club
2 Augusta Boulevard, Lakewood
(732) 901–4900
www.eagleridgegolf.com
par 71, 6,607 yards
rating 71.8, slope 132
1999, Ault, Clark & Associates

Built on a former gravel pit, Eagle Ridge takes advantage of considerable elevation changes to pose a variety of challenges. The 520-yard par 5 fifth is the course's signature hole, and even though the fairway slopes downhill off the tee, not many players can consider going for the green in two, as water guards the front of the green.

Lakewood Country Club
45 Country Club Drive, Lakewood
(732) 364–8899
par 71, 6,248 yards
rating 70.7, slope 118
1892, Willie Dunn

Lakewood is a historic course in need of a little TLC, with bunkers and small, undulating greens that seem to have shrunk over the years. Located in New Jersey's Pine Barrens, the course is short and wooded, fairly flat on the front side with some elevated tees and greens on the back.

Ocean Acres Country Club
925 Buccaneer Lane, Manahawkin
(609) 597–9393
www.allforeclub.com
par 72, 6,563 yards
rating 70.8, slope 124
1960s

They're used to summer people at Ocean Acres, as it's the closest track to the Long Beach Island causeway. The opening holes are fairly open, but on the back nine, fairways become narrower and more tree-lined. Stop in the clubhouse to enjoy the great view of the lake and watch other golfers put balls in the water on number 10, a terrific 183-yard par 3 to an island green.

Ocean County at Atlantis
Country Club Boulevard, Tuckerton
(609) 296–2444
par 72, 6,848 yards
rating 73.6, slope 134
1962, George Fazio

While conditions at Atlantis can vary, its Fazio pedigree is impeccable. The 200-yard par 3 sixth hole over a lake is memorable. Next, Fazio taunts you with a 517-yard par 5 that demands a little guesswork from the tee. Be advised: Go too long and straight off the tee, and you could end up in the woods.

Ocean County at Forge Pond
Chambers Bridge Road, Brick
(732) 920–8899
par 60, 3,916 yards
rating 59.4, slope 98
1990, Hal Purdy

What's your hurry, sonny? Forge Pond always seems busy, and playing here, you may realize just how many adult communities have sprung up in this part of Ocean County. Tight and short, with small greens, Forge Pond is a test of accuracy and discipline. Can you actually learn to keep the driver in the bag, or better yet in the car, even when the longest hole is only 340 yards?

Pine Barrens Golf Club
540 South Hope Chapel Road, Jackson
(877) 746–3227
www.PineBarrensGolf.com, www.EmpireGolf
USA.com
par 72, 7,118 yards
rating 74.2, slope 132
1999, Eric Bergstol

When Pine Barrens unveiled the vast sandy waste areas that line its wide fairways, it was hailed as "a more playable Pine Valley," but more to the point, it's a course that you can actually play. The short par 4 seventh hole with a river of sand left of the fairway has attracted much attention; it's just 303 yards to reach the huge green, but the approach (or drive, heavy hitters?) must carry about 30 yards of scrub. With five sets of tees, you can bite off as much as you can chew.

Pine Ridge Golf Course (Military)
Lakehurst Naval Base, Lakehurst
(732) 323–7483
par 36, 3,073 yards
1957, U.S. Navy

If you're not in the service and you have no idea what a D.O.D. civilian is (Department of Defense), you're probably not eligible to get out on this wide-open, playable nine-holer popular with retired career military types. Lakehurst, of course, is historically known for the Hindenburg, which exploded in flames on May 6, 1937, killing 36 passengers.

> ## Insiders' Tip
> Golfers like to play around, and the downside of joining a club is that you are committed to playing one course. The All-Fore Club solves this dilemma by offering privileges at four area clubs—Ocean Acres CC, Buena Vista CC, Pinelands GC in nearby Winslow, and Cohanzick CC in Fairton—for around $1,500 a year. Call one of the clubs or go to www.allforeclub.com for more information.

Atlantic and Cape May Counties

Golf in Atlantic and Cape May Counties has a history going back more than a hundred years, and courses like Donald Ross's Bay Course at Seaview Marriott Resort and Brigantine Golf Links let players get back to the roots of the game. In recent years, high-end daily fee courses such as Blue Heron Pines, Sand Barrens, and Sea Oaks have opened, offering visitors the experience of being a member for a day. But that's not the whole story. There are also quite a few nine-hole courses, well known to locals, that don't have much snob appeal, but provide surprisingly good tests of golf skill at reasonable prices.

In high season, it'll run you $25 to walk nine at the Pines at Clermont, while a ride and eighteen at posh layouts like

Seaview or Twisted Dune will ring in at over $125.

If you're around in the off-season, the world is your oyster, as the climate in South Jersey is noticeably milder than up north, and most courses are open all winter. There are also many ways to get a bargain, even at the top-of-the-line courses.

Avalon Golf Club
1510 U.S. Highway 9 North, Cape May Court House
(609) 465–GOLF
par 71, 6,325 yards
rating 70.7, slope 122
1971, Bob Hendricks

The bay breezes can keep you cool or get you steamed up on this scenic, tree-lined course with eight natural lakes. The prevailing wind adds spice to the difficult par 4 sixth, a 408-yard dogleg right. After a 230-yard drive to make the corner, you'll still have a long shot to a green guarded in front by bunkers and back and left by water. The 166-yard par 3 17th is a hole where you have to pick the right club and hit the right shot; from the elevated tee, you hit over a lake to a bulkheaded green with bunkers left, right, and rear, and out of bounds beyond.

B. L. England Golf Course
U.S. Highway 9 South, Beesley's Point
(609) 390–0472
par 34, 2,478 yards
1961, Atlantic City Electric Co.

B. L. England fits a little of this and that into its short nine: trees, meadow, water hazards. The great condition of its greens and fairways make it a pleasure.

Blue Heron Pines Golf Club
550 West Country Club Drive (Highway 563 Tilton Road), Cologne
(609) 965–1800, (888) 4STAR–GOLF
www.blueheronpines.com
West Course: par 72, 6,810 yards
rating 73.0, slope 136
1993, Stephen Kay
East Course: par 72, 7,221 yards
rating 74.8, slope 135
2000, Steve Smyers

Since it opened, Blue Heron Pines has been winning awards for its challenging use of marsh and waste areas and setting the standard for high-end daily fee courses in South Jersey. Example: The shortest way to carry the huge cross bunker that looms from the seventh tee is down the right, but the left side of the fairway affords a much better angle into the green. The new East Course across the street offers a strong contrast in style, a sort of obstacle-links design with many elevated tees and greens and dozens of deep, gaping bunkers surrounding the fairways as well as the greens. Bring your sand wedge and your game.

Brigantine Golf Links
Roosevelt Boulevard at the bay, Brigantine
(609) 266–1388, (800) 698–1388
par 72, 6,570 yards
rating 71.9, slope 123
1927, John Van Kleek

So Scottish are the links at Brigantine that in the old days, players would warm up for the British Open here, practicing the bump-and-run and other shots demanded by the windy conditions. As any Scotsman knows, the golfer who floats short irons up into the crosswind is likely to lose the bet. Recent renovations include a new clubhouse and much improved turf and bunkers.

Buena Vista Country Club
U.S. Highway 40 and Country Club Lane, Buena
(609) 697–3733
www.allforeclub.com
par 72, 6,869 yards
rating 71.8, slope 127
1957, William Gordon

Some locals consider Buena Vista (or Byew-nuh, as they call it down here) the best public course in South Jersey. The fairways are narrow and tree-lined, with a generous helping of sand thrown in. The back nine starts with a bang or a sputter, with a 500-yard par 5 that doglegs left around an enormous bunker. You'll have to fly your approach over more sand to reach the sloping, elevated green.

Cape May National Golf Club
U.S. Highway 9 North at Florence Avenue, Cape May
(609) 884–1563
par 71, 6,592 yards
rating 72.9, slope 136
1991, Carl Litten and Robert Mullock

Located in Cape May's famous migrating bird flyway, Cape May National has its own 50-acre bird sanctuary and enjoys a lovely natural setting of grasslands, woodlands, and lakes. Birdies of the golf variety may be harder to come by, though, as this beauty has teeth. The 200-yard par 3 third is all carry over a protected natural area to a difficult, high-pitched green. Then there's the famous 550-yard par 5, whose tricky putting surface is well protected by water and sand-pit bunkers. Wild Turkey, anyone?

Frog Rock Golf Club (formerly Hammonton CC)
420 Boyer Avenue, Hammonton
(609) 561–5504
par 70, 6,019 yards
1970s, Rocky Colaserdo

Recently expanded from 12 holes to 18, Frog Rock Hammonton is fairly tight and hilly. The original 12 holes were built by a local farmer, and the course is a bit chopped up in design. Busy and inexpensive, the condition of the course is questionable, especially the fairways. There are no reserved tee times.

Green Tree Golf Course
1030 Somers Point–Mays Landing Road, Egg Harbor Township
(609) 267–8440
par 70, 5,709 yards
rating 66.6, slope 110
1968, Horace Smith

Owned by Atlantic County, Green Tree is inexpensive for residents and therefore sees a lot of rounds. Even so, the course is usually in pretty good shape. It plays easy in spite of the water holes on the back, as the length is very manageable.

Hamilton Trails
620 Harbor Road, Mays Landing
(609) 641–6824
par 35, 3,265 yards
1983, Bill Sholtko

This flat, nine-hole course is a quick walk, perfect for those anxious to get back to the casino. If you try, you can find some trees and water to get into, and the large greens are pretty quick and protected by sand. The conditions are variable. There are no reserved tee times.

Harbor Pines Country Club
3071 Ocean Heights Avenue, Egg Harbor Township
(609) 927–0006
par 72, 6,827 yards
rating 72.3, slope 129
1996, Stephen Kay

Wide fairways, huge greens, and immaculate conditioning characterize this upscale track. Even the rough is short and tidy at Harbor Pines, which makes for an enjoyable day for the average player. There are 17 acres of ponds here, and they come into play on a number of holes, like the 215-yard par 3 eighth hole, where a cool dip awaits your slice. On the 460-yard par 4 ninth, rated the No. 1 hole, you'll have to keep the ball on the crowned fairway to avoid the water on the left and the trees on the right.

Latona Golf & Country Club
Oak and Cumberland Roads, Buena
(609) 692–8149
par 35, 3,150 yards
1963, Garret Renn

Latona is a legitimate nine-hole course, with two par 5's that are almost 500 yards. The greens are its source of pride though, maintained in excellent condition that conceals subtle breaks. Play is on a walk-up basis.

Mays Landing Country Club
Cates Road at McKee Avenue, McKee City
(609) 641–4411
www.mayslandinggolf.com
par 72, 6,624 yards
rating 71.8, slope 123
1962, Leo Fraser

Leo Fraser, past president of the PGA, designed Mays Landing with the goal of introducing more players to the game by providing a challenging golf course at an affordable price. His son Jim carries on this tradition, keeping this picturesque course in South Jersey's Pinelands in great condition. Though pine trees line the fairways, the landing areas are not skimpy, making the course fair for high and low handicappers alike. Mays Landing is known for its demanding par 3's, the toughest of which is the 15th, which plays every inch of 220 yards with trouble in every direction.

McCullough's Emerald Golf Links
3016 Ocean Heights Avenue, Egg Harbor Township
(609) 926–4014
par 71, 6,547 yards
2002, Stephen Kay

Slated to open in July 2002, Emerald Golf Links is a salute to the great links courses of Scotland and Ireland. Working from memory and aerial photos, Stephen Kay has re-created the fairway contours, greens, and bunkers of some of the great holes at St. Andrews, Troon, Gleneagles, and Carnoustie. Although it is not right on the ocean, as the original links are, the sandy soil of this area lends itself beautifully to this style of course.

Ocean City Golf Course
Bay Avenue at 26th Street, Ocean City
(609) 399–1315
par 37, 1,750 yards
1962

Ocean City's family atmosphere pervades this busy municipal 12-hole layout, which consists of 11 par 3's ranging from 70 to 180 yards and one 230-yard par 4. The first tee is about a 3-wood away from Ocean City Municipal Airport, convenient for Cessna-flying hackers.

The Pines at Clermont
358 Kings Highway, Clermont
(609) 624–0100
par 31, 2,085 yards
1999, Steve Malikowski and Vince Orlando

This challenging executive nine has a couple of bona fide par 4's, tree-lined fairways, and water on several of the par 3's. A new course, it is in excellent condition and is a great place to hone your iron play.

Pomona Golf & Country Club
Moss Mill Road at Odessa Avenue, Pomona
(609) 965–3232
par 34, 2,426 yards
1940s

This executive nine with six woodland holes and three open-meadow holes across the street has an interesting his-

Insiders' Tip

If you're around after Labor Day, you'll save a lot of money with the "Passport to South Jersey Golf," a coupon booklet of off-season discounts at 42 golf courses in the South Jersey and Philadelphia area. For details, call (609) 645-3621.

tory. Originally called Apex, the course was built by Sara Spencer Washington, an African-American cosmetics merchant from Atlantic City who founded the chain of Apex Schools of Scientific Beauty Culture. She owned Apex hair salons and manufactured 75 different cosmetics and hair-care products under the Apex label. Madame Washington, as she was called, envisioned the golf course as the center of a vacation colony. The real-estate venture did not materialize, but the course remained a place that black golfers could play hassle-free.

Ponderlodge Golf Course
7 Shawmount Avenue, Villas
(609) 886–8065
par 71, 6,184 yards
rating 69.9, slope 120
1977, Tony Funari

The long, tree-lined drive to the entrance of this former estate, once owned by Schmidt's Brewery, is an indication of things to come for the golfer. Water is also a factor on a number of holes on this scenic track, but if you keep the ball in play, you'll be fine, as most of the par 4's are of a very manageable length.

Sand Barrens Golf Club
1765 U.S. Highway 9 North, Swainton
(609) 465–3555
North and West Nines: par 72, 7,092 yards
rating 73.2, slope 135
South Nine: par 36, 3,386 yards
1997, Michael Hurdzan and Dana Fry

Don't imagine that Sand Barrens is just a cute name; not one of its 27 holes lacks a bunker. In fact, vast waste areas line one side of almost every fairway. Add some pines and oaks and you'll soon realize that you'd better keep the ball in the fairway. In addition to enormous bunkers, Sand Barrens boasts gargantuan greens; on the second hole on the North Course, for instance, the green is 86 yards deep and 55,000 square feet in area. But with five sets of tees rated according to handicap, you should be able to find a length that makes the course manageable.

Insiders' Tip
Wildwood Golf & Country Club is a vintage links right on the bay in Cape May Court House. It's private, but welcomes members of other clubs in the Philly area. Have your club pro call David Smolsky at (609) 465-7823 to set you up.

Sea Oaks Golf Club
Highway 539 at Sea Oaks Drive, Little Egg Harbor Township
(609) 296–2656
par 72, 6,950 yards
rating 72.4, slope 129
2000, Ray Hearn

Sandy soil and pine trees are natural assets to a golf course, and Sea Oaks adds magnificent views of the ocean, Atlantic City, and Long Beach Island. Ray Hearn's reticulated bunkers are a distinctive feature not soon forgotten if you've had to extract your ball from their grassy fingers. The signature hole is the 16th, a Z-shaped par 5 that goes 540 yards to a green surrounded on three sides by water. Take advantage of the 55,000-square-foot, 18-hole putting course, either to improve your stroke or just to drink beer and bet.

Seaview Marriott Resort
401 South New York Road (U.S. Highway 9 South), Absecon
(609) 652–1800, (800) 932–8000
www.SeaviewGolf.com
Bay Course: par 71, 6,247 yards
rating 70.7, slope 122
1913, Donald Ross
Pines Course: par 71, 6,731 yards
rating 71.7, slope 128
1929, Toomey and Flynn

Donald Ross's Bay Course, a windswept links whose undulating greens crouch behind waiting bunkers, captivated golfers for the better part of the 20th century, and continues to do so in the 21st. Among those smitten are the stars of the Ladies Professional Golf Association, who return every year for the ShopRite Classic. The Pines Course provides a fantastic contrast; while the Bay Course is wide open, the Pines is carved into the woodlands, with narrow fairways and well-protected landing areas. Seaview also offers first-rate practice facilities and the Nick Faldo Golf Academy. The fabulous Jazz Age hotel recently added an Elizabeth Arden Red Door Spa to its amenities, perfect for when golfing leaves you in need of a massage.

Shore Gate Golf Club
35 School House Lane, Ocean View
(609) 624–TEES
www.shoregategolfclub.com
par 72, 7,200 yards
2002, Fream and Dale

Scheduled to open for summer 2002, Shore Gate is the work of the California team of Fream and Dale and combines elements of both links and parkland design to create a visually striking layout. Shore Gate's 245 acres embrace woods, wetlands, and rolling sand dunes to create varied challenges, with water coming into play on seven holes.

Twisted Dune Golf Club
2101 Ocean Heights Avenue, Egg Harbor Township
(609) 653–8019
www.EmpireGolfUSA.com
par 72, 7,336 yards
2001, Archie Struthers

Privacy is the buzzword at Twisted Dune, where two-million cubic yards of earth have been moved to transform the flat terrain into a golf links where mounds of heather and tall grass insulate one hole from another. Director of Golf Tom McCarthy promises no more than 100 to 125 rounds a day, with tee times spaced at 12 to 15 minutes apart, allowing plenty of time for purists who prefer walking.

Road Trip

Living or vacationing at the Shore needn't tie you down to local courses. After all, most golfers are willing to travel an hour or more to play, and we offer here a selection of courses that are definitely worth the trip. In fact, Pine Hill and Scotland Run are easy stopovers en route between Philly and the Atlantic City area. One note: These are all newer courses and in the high-end daily fee category.

The Architect's Golf Club
700 Strykers Road, Lopatcong
(908) 213–3080
www.thearchitectsclub.com
par 71, 6,863 yards
rating 73.3, slope 130
2001, Stephen Kay with Ron Whitten

Working with *Golf Digest*'s Ron Whitten, Stephen Kay has created an 18-hole trip through the history of golf-course design, with holes inspired by great architects from Old Tom Morris to Robert Trent Jones. These are not cheesy replicas of famous holes, but a subtler form of flattery that springs from a real understanding of each man's style. The 9th hole is a doff of the cap to Donald Ross, and Kay has managed to point this 447-yard, uphill par 4 into the prevailing wind.

Crystal Springs Golf & Spa Resort
105-137 Wheatsworth Road, Hamburg
(973) 827–5996
www.crystalgolfresort.com

Ballyowen Golf Club: par 72, 7,032 yards
rating 73.6, slope 131
1998, Roger Rulewich

Black Bear Golf Club: par 72, 6,673 yards
rating 72.2, slope 130
1996, Jack Kurlander and David Glenz

Crystal Springs Golf Club: par 72,
6,816 yards
rating 74.1, slope 137
1991, Robert Von Hagge

The Spa: par 31, 2,305 yards
1987, Robert Trent Jones

Wild Turkey Golf Club: par 71, 7,233 yards
2001, Roger Rulewich

Near Mountain Creek Ski Resort (formerly Great Gorge), Crystal Springs boasts 81 holes of golf, with two tracks, Ballyowen and Crystal Springs, that are considered among the top public courses in the state. You can make the drive for just a round, but you'll need a few days to sample all the area has to offer. Ballyowen conjures up an Irish links, with great swaths of untamed fescue, while Crystal Springs challenges players to keep the ball in the fairway with many moguls and steep drop-offs. Black Bear is the home of the renowned David Glenz Golf Academy, said pro being the 1998 PGA Instructor of the Year.

Hawk Pointe
294 N.J. Highway 31 South, Washington
(908) 689–1870, (877) 322–4295
par 72, 6,907 yards
rating 73.4, slope 133
2000, Kelly Blake Moran

Hawks are indeed to be seen in this wonderful, woodsy setting along with, we hope, birdies of another kind. Moran's design is straightforward, with generous fairways that roll across 220 acres of this former farm, but stray from the paths of righteousness and you'll find tall grass, rocks, trees, and bogey-men.

New Jersey National
579 Allen Road, Basking Ridge
(908) 781–2575
www.njngolfclub.com
par 72, 7,056 yards
rating 73.6, slope 133
1997, Roy Case

New Jersey National is blessed with many natural advantages, with 266 acres of rolling woodlands that allow for many changes in elevation and strategically tree-lined holes. Some bad weather in recent years made for less than perfect conditions, which tends to irk when paying boutique prices. Don't start adding up your score until after the 17th, a narrow, uphill 396-yard par 4 that demands a 180- to 220-yard carry over wetlands.

Pine Hill Golf Club
500 West Branch Avenue, Pine Hill
(856) 453–3100, (877) 450–8866
www.golfpinehill.com
par 70, 6,969 yards
rating 74.2, slope 140
2000, Tom Fazio

When describing this golf experience among the towering pines and oaks, we run out of superlatives: immaculate greenskeeping, fabulous shot values, superb putting surfaces, magnificent natural scenery, plus great views of Philadelphia. Unlike most other golf courses, Pine Hill is actually busier during the week than on weekends, so try for a Saturday or Sunday.

Avoid the numerous bunkers on the sixth hole of Royce Brook's West Course. PHOTO: COURTESY OF SMITH O'KEEFE AND ASSOCIATES

Royce Brook
201 Hamilton Road, Hillsborough
(888) 434–FORE
www.roycebrook.com
West Course: par 72, 7,158 yards
rating 73.9, slope 132
1998, Steve Smyers
East Course: par 72, 6,983 yards
rating 73.4, slope 131
1998, Steve Smyers

Just a few miles off busy I-78, Royce Brook is a busy exec's heaven. On a flat, windy site, Steve Smyers has drawn inspiration from two of the game's masters for his designs. The East Course evokes Donald Ross's crowned greens and shallow, grass-faced bunkers, while the tougher West Course's deep, sculpted bunkers are a nod to Alistair MacKenzie. The Academy of Golf at Royce Brook offers instruction in the Mike Adams LAWs of Golf teaching method.

Scotland Run
U.S. Highway 322 and Fries Mill Road,
Williamstown
(856) 863–3737
www.scotlandrun.com
par 71, 6,819 yards
rating 73.3, slope 134
1999, Stephen Kay

On the site of an old sand quarry, Stephen Kay has created a unique golf experience. While the front nine meanders through pine woods, the back opens onto the former quarry site, with tee boxes perched above vast sandy waste areas, some so deep that ladders are built in to allow duffers to reach their errant shots. You can play the ball out of these pits, but you're certainly better off in the fairway.

Attractions

For kids, teens, and the young at heart, there's never any doubt about what to do on a beautiful summer evening at the Shore—the Boardwalk is where the action is! We've devoted a special section to the Shore boardwalks' raucous charms, but there are a few other area amusement parks to take note of, too. Keansburg and Six Flags Great Adventure are described here, and you'll find special places for the very young, like Storybook Land, listed in the Kidstuff chapter.

Of course, the Jersey Shore isn't all honky-tonk. Since some of our towns are well over 300 years old, we've got more than our share of historic houses—and one of them is even haunted! Other historic sites include forts, war memorials, and cemeteries. Living-history farms and historic villages are covered in a separate chapter.

If you like things a little more fast-paced, you'll find horse racing at Monmouth Park and Freehold Raceway and car racing at Wall Stadium and New Egypt Speedway. Speaking of cars, you may have noticed that New Jerseyans love theirs, and you'll find a number of museums here showcasing all manner of vehicles: trains, planes, boats, bicycles, fire engines, and even the infamous *Hindenburg*. There are other museums as well, with exhibits on everything from local flora and fauna to Atlantic City memorabilia.

The new game in town is minor league baseball. The Lakewood Blue Claws and the Atlantic City Surf have become instant fan favorites, thanks in part to reasonable ticket prices and the low-key atmosphere at the games.

Some of the attractions we've included here aren't within the borders of the Shore counties, but we have listed them here (rather than in the Daytrips chapter) because they're within easy reach. For example, Wheaton Village is in Cumberland County, but it's not that far from Atlantic City or Cape May County.

If you don't find what you're looking for in this chapter, check out the Natural World, Living-History Farms and Historic Villages, Farms and Wineries, Annual Events and Festivals, Kidstuff, Daytrips, and Arts and Culture chapters for additional ideas for things to see and do.

Price Code

$	under $5
$$	$5 to $10
$$$	$10 to $20
$$$$	over $20

Monmouth County

Amusement Parks and Racetracks

Freehold Raceway   Free
U.S. Highway 9 and N.J. Highway 33, Freehold
(732) 462–3800

The Shore has had harness racing ever since the days when swells from New York and Philadelphia stayed at the grand hotels and entertained themselves with all forms of gambling. Today Freehold Raceway offers the only daytime harness racing in the country, with post time at 12:30 P.M. or 1:00 P.M., depending on the time of year.

Two major races take place here: the Cane Pace (held over Labor Day weekend) has a $350,000 purse and is the first leg of harness racing's Triple Crown. In October, the James B. Dancer Memorial Race offers a $300,000 purse. The raceway is open 10 months a year, from August through Memorial Day; call for post times.

Keansburg Amusement Park and Runaway Rapids Waterpark $$–$$$
275 Beachway, Keansburg
(732) 495–1400, (800) 805–4FUN
www.KeansburgAmusementPark.com

If you have distant but fond memories of Palisades Amusement Park up North (long gone now, with only towering condominiums in its place), you may well enjoy an evening amid Keansburg's nicely old-fashioned amusements. The rides are classics: the same kind of roller coaster and Ferris wheel you might have begged Mom to ride when you were a kid. You won't find the latest electronic gadgetry here, but you will find plenty to do among the 40 rides, games of chance, arcades, and food concessions. And the prices are gentler than those at the glitzy newfangled parks. Other attractions here are a 2,500-foot fishing pier and a free bayshore beach.

The Runaway Rapids Waterpark is state of the art, with tropical landscaping, a lazy river feature, a spa pool, and a huge interactive kids' area. The amusement park is open during the summer from 10:00 A.M. until midnight, with limited openings in October. The water park opens at 10:00 A.M. daily for most of June, all of July and August, and in early September. Call for closing hours. Admission is $18.95 for three hours.

Monmouth Park Racetrack $
175 Oceanport Avenue, Oceanport
(732) 222–5100
www.monmouthpark.com

Even if you're not devoted to the Sport of Kings, you might choose to while away a summer afternoon at Monmouth Park, which is undoubtedly one of the prettiest racetracks in the country. It's beautifully landscaped, the clubhouse is a pleasant place to have lunch, and there is plenty of parking. The racing season here runs from late May until early September.

The Monmouth Park Jockey Club dates back to 1870; in its heyday, the racetrack attracted the rich and influential, including President Ulysses S. Grant. Though the park no longer has that kind of luster, and offtrack betting has reduced the once-enormous crowds, attendance at

the important races is still high. The biggest of these is the Haskell, named for the late Amory Lawrence Haskell, who, back in the 1940s, lobbied for an amendment to the state constitution that would legalize pari-mutuel betting on horses. When the amendment passed, Haskell was appointed president and chairman of the Monmouth Park Jockey Club in 1945. He died in 1966. Haskell Day (in August) is one of the biggest non-football sporting events in the state; top horses race for the richest invitational prize in the country.

To attract visitors, Monmouth Park offers a number of family-type attractions. The oldest of these is the Dawn Patrol, an early-morning two-hour tour (from 7:00 to 9:00 A.M.) that offers you an insider's look at a day in the life of a thoroughbred racehorse. It includes a tram ride through the stable area to the starting gate, and then to the jockeys' room, where you can see the colorful silks. In addition to complimentary juice, coffee, and doughnuts, there are little gifts for the youngsters on the tour. If you bring carrots, you may be allowed to feed them to the horses. The tour is free, but reservations are necessary; call (732) 919–3500. Park in the valet lot, then walk up the ramp to the Patio Terrace.

On Sundays during the racing season McDonald's sponsors Family Fun Day, with free pony rides, clowns, music, and more.

After the racing season, the *Asbury Park Press* holds its annual garage sale in the racetrack's parking lot. This is a huge event, with hundreds of vendors, some professional, some just plain folks who want to clean out their garages and attics. Tens of thousands of customers show up during the course of the day, but traffic and crowds are kept moving in an orderly fashion by local police.

New Egypt Speedway $$$
720 Highway 539, New Egypt
(609) 758–1900

If you like watching stock cars race around at frightening speeds, you won't be disappointed at this .4-mile clay track. Modified cars, sportsman cars, and street stocks race Saturday nights from April to

October, with some mid-week special events. There's a supervised playground on the premises.

Wall Stadium
N.J. Highway 34 and Hurley Pond Road, Wall
(732) 681–6400
www.wallstadium.com
On Saturday nights from April through September, you can hear the roar of engines for miles around. As the top stock-car racing track in the Central Jersey Shore area, Wall draws crowds of enthusiastic fans to watch the action. The raceway also features such crowd-pleasers as Monster Truck and Demolition Derby events. The gates open at 5:00 P.M., and the first qualifying heat race starts at 5:45 P.M.

Historic Sites

Allen House $
Sycamore Avenue and N.J. Highway 35 South, Shrewsbury
(732) 462–1466
In colonial America, the tavern was at least as popular as the church as a community gathering place. Given the excellent location of Josiah Halstead's tavern, The Blue Ball (known today as Allen House), at the crossroads of two highways, it was a real hot spot. We know that because in 1755, Halstead's excise taxes were the highest among all the tavern keepers in the area.

Not only was The Blue Ball popular among locals, it was also a meeting place for the Monmouth County Circuit Court, the Library Company, and the vestry for Christ Church, across the street.

A decade or so later, however, Halstead fell on hard times, and later ended up in debtor's prison. The property changed hands several times and was used as a medical office and pharmacy, a dry-goods store, a private residence, tearooms, and antiques shop. Today it stands as a fine example of an 18th-century tavern—and a testament to the importance of tavern life in colonial times.

The Monmouth County Historical Association operates summer excavation camps for 12- to 15-year-olds on the grounds. The object is to learn more about the people who lived and worked here—and to teach youngsters in a hands-on way about history and archaeology. To date, more than 21,000 objects have been found, including bottles, lamp glass, flower pots, buttons, cups, and pistol flints.

Like the other houses that are cared for by the historical association, Allen House is open from May through September, Tuesday and Thursday from 1:00 to 4:00 P.M., and Saturday from 10:00 A.M. to 4:00 P.M.

Centennial Cottage $
Central Avenue and McClintock Street, Ocean Grove
(732) 775–0035
Originally home to the Fels family of Philadelphia, this authentic Ocean Grove seashore house has been completely restored and furnished in the style of the 1870s.

Though owned by the Ocean Grove Camp Meeting Association, Centennial Cottage is operated by the Historical Society of Ocean Grove, whose members serve as hostesses. The cottage is open Monday through Saturday in July and August, from 10:00 A.M. to noon and from 2:00 to 4:00 P.M. Special tours are available by appointment.

Christ Church   Free
380 Sycamore Avenue, Shrewsbury
(732) 741–2220
Located across the street from historic Allen House, this Episcopal Church was founded in 1702. It was designed in the federal style; a clock tower with a narthex (vestibule) was added in 1874. What's especially interesting is that this church is the only one in the United States that retains its original gilt crown—signifying its royal beginnings—atop the spire. The church has a number of historical artifacts, including a rare Bible; a Bishop's chair carved from a churchyard oak; the parish's royal charter, granted in 1738; and pieces of the communion service given to the church by Queen Anne in 1708. Sunday services are at 8:00 A.M. and 10:00 A.M. Call the parish office to arrange a tour.

The Christ Church   Free
King's Highway and Church Street, Middletown
(732) 671-2524

Middletown's Christ Church congregation, part of the Church of England, has existed since the 1680s. In 1705, the congregation was deeded the land of the Middletown Village blockhouse and county court by a former justice of the court. In 1744, a church was built on the blockhouse foundation. The present church building was constructed in 1836, again using the old foundation. If you'd like to visit, call for an appointment or attend a Sunday service at 8:00 A.M. or 10:00 A.M.

Covenhoven House $
150 West Main Street, Freehold
(732) 462-1466

After Dutch farmer William Covenhoven came into a large inheritance, he built a house in 1752 to reflect his newfound wealth and social position. Combining elements of English Georgian style and traditional Dutch features, the house was more highly styled than homes generally found in the area at the time.

Though it's sometimes referred to as the headquarters of British General Henry Clinton, the general occupied it only for a brief period, just before the Battle of Monmouth. Covenhoven House was restored and opened to the public by the Monmouth County Historical Association. The interior design and furnishings are based on a 1790 inventory taken after William Covenhoven's death. The furnishings are authentic reproductions of Covenhoven's own, which were plundered or destroyed by Clinton's troops. The house is open May through September on Tuesday, Thursday, and Sunday from 1:00 to 4:00 P.M., and on Saturday from 10:00 A.M. to 4:00 P.M.

Fort Hancock at Sandy Hook   Free
Gateway National Recreation Area, Sandy Hook
(732) 872-5970

The attractions of Sandy Hook are discussed at length in the Natural World chapter, but this is just a reminder that when you don't want to spend the day swimming or bird-watching, you might want to visit a site that has played an important role in harbor defense and navigation since 1764, when the Sandy Hook Lighthouse was built.

Fort Hancock was the last of the forts built to protect the shipping channels into New York in the late 19th century. It played an important role in America's coastal defense during both world wars. During World War II, Fort Hancock was a major staging area for troops shipping out to Europe, and the headquarters for the defense of New York Harbor, with huge gun emplacements and a mortar battery. Though the guns were dismantled after the war, you can still see the batteries and bunkers amid the sand dunes and sea grass.

Fort Hancock was active until 1974, when its Cold War-era Nike Ajax missiles were made obsolete by intercontinental ballistic missiles. It's open from 9:00 A.M. to 5:00 P.M. on weekdays, and from noon to 5:00 P.M. on weekends.

The Holmes-Hendrickson House $
62 Longstreet Road, Holmdel
(732) 462-1466

The house gets its name from the two families who lived here during the 1700s. It was built in 1754 and was designed to resemble an English-style Georgian house from the outside, but the sloping roof and the interior room arrangement reflect the builder's Dutch heritage.

What's unique about the house is that it is, except for necessary repairs, virtually in original condition. It was never lived in during the 20th century, so it has never had electricity, plumbing, or a heating system.

Like Monmouth County's other historic homes, this one had its Revolutionary War moments, which your tour guide will no doubt recount. You may hear that Monmouth County farms were frequently raided by both the British and the colonists. On February 8, 1782, a British raiding party came ashore at Sandy Hook and ended up at this farm. They not only took captives (for ransom), they also stole a ham and wrapped it in the lady of the house's best silk dress. Fortunately, a couple of the farmer's relatives, who had hidden during the raid, went to Captain John Schanck for help; they all gave chase, routed the raiding party, and rescued the hostages. We don't know what happened to the ham.

The house is open May through September on Tuesday, Thursday, and Saturday from 1:00 to 4:00 P.M., and on Sunday from 10:00 A.M. to 4:00 P.M.

Marlpit Hall $
137 Kings Highway, Middletown
(732) 462–1466

Travel back to 1756, when this Georgian-style house was a showplace, home to one of the area's wealthiest families, the Taylors. The family's wealth is reflected in the spacious rooms (not to mention a dining room that was used just for dining) and the imposing furniture made by the area's finest craftsmen—pieces like New Jersey Queen Anne–style chairs and a fine grandfather clock.

As Edward Taylor, a landowner and slaveholder, was also a British loyalist, you'll see paintings of George II and Queen Caroline prominently displayed. As the guide at the house will explain, Taylor spent most of the war under house arrest—because of his habit of tattling about the American positions to his son, who was with the British militia.

Compare the more spacious part of the home to the earlier one-room section of the house that was built in the late 17th century by James Grover Jr. This section reflects a time when families did not enjoy much privacy, sharing limited space for all the activities of life.

After an ambitious eight-year, $800,000 restoration undertaken by the Monmouth County Historical Association, Marlpit Hall is finally open to the public May through September on Tuesday, Thursday, and Saturday from 1:00 to 4:00 P.M., and on Sunday from 10:00 A.M. to 4:00 P.M.

New Jersey Vietnam Veterans Memorial/
Education Center   Free
Adjacent to the PNC Bank Arts Center,
Garden State Parkway, exit 116, Holmdel
(732) 335–0033, (800) 648–VETS
www.njvvmf.org

This memorial was a long time coming. It began with the visit by four Vietnam vet-erans to Washington in 1982 and ended in 1995 with the dedication of this open-air pavilion honoring New Jersey residents who died or are MIA as a result of the Vietnam conflict.

For those who are too young to remember the conflict, there's an educational center, where school groups often visit. Visiting schoolchildren sometimes take rubbings from the names of their hometown heroes. You can visit the memorial anytime, since it is outdoors; the center is open Tuesday through Saturday from 10:00 A.M. to 4:00 P.M.

Museums and Libraries

Guggenheim Memorial Library   Free
Monmouth University, 400 Cedar Avenue,
West Long Branch
(732) 571–3400

This magnificent structure is familiar to moviegoers as Daddy Warbucks's mansion in *Annie*. Listed on the National Register of Historic Sites, it was once the summer residence of mining magnate Murray Guggenheim and his wife, Leonie; it was designed to emulate Versailles' Petit Trianon. It now serves as the University's library and is open to the public; call for hours.

The Metz Bicycle Museum $
54 West Main Street, Freehold
(732) 462–7363

Do you like old stuff? David Metz does. He's been collecting antique bicycles for some 50 years, and now he has a collection of hundreds that's one of the finest in the world. Among his special bikes: high-wheel tricycles, boneshakers, quadricycles, and even a lamplighter, an eight-foot-high number that was used by the men who lit the street lamps. There's more: antique children's riding toys, kitchen gadgets (more than 100 antique mousetraps!), farm tools, and antique cars—including a 1915 Metz (no relation). The museum is open Wednesday and Saturday from 12:30 to 4:30 P.M. Group visits can also be arranged by appointment.

Monmouth County Historical Association
Museum $

**70 Court Street, Freehold
(732) 462–1466**

In addition to an abundance of artifacts and documents, the museum has a fine collection of furnishings, paintings, and objects from the colonial era. One of the highlights is Emmanuel G. Leutze's painting *Washington at Monmouth*. You may recall Leutze's most famous painting, *Washington Crossing the Delaware*, which hangs in the Metropolitan Museum of Art in New York (a fine copy hangs in the Trenton Museum).

In the Battle of Monmouth exhibit, you'll find the story of the battle, as well as firearms, snuffboxes, drinking horns, and cartridge belts. Browse on your own or take a guided tour to learn about Monmouth County's early history; the life of colonial children is presented in the Discovery Room.

If you suspect that you might have ancestors in Monmouth County—or if you'd just like to peek at colonial lives—look through the genealogy resources, which include original deeds, letters, and accounts. The museum is open Tuesday through Saturday from 10:00 A.M. to 4:00 P.M., and Sunday from 1:00 to 4:00 P.M. The library is open Wednesday through Saturday from 10:00 A.M. to 4:00 P.M.

The association also oversees tours and special exhibits at four of the county's historic homes: Covenhoven House, also in Freehold; the Holmes-Hendrickson House in Holmdel; Marlpit Hall in Middletown, and the Allen House in Shrewsbury.

**Monmouth Museum $
Brookdale Community College, Newman
Springs Road, Lincroft
(732) 747–2266
www.monmouthmuseum.com**

The Monmouth Museum is a center for education and culture, as well as a showplace for changing exhibits and programs. At some exhibitions, you'll learn about local history, flora, and fauna. Others allow you to watch animated prehistoric beasts. During the holiday season, visitors enjoy Beatrix Potter characters, trains, and festive trees.

In the Becker Children's Wing, school-age youngsters will find a comfortable, hands-on learning environment. The WonderWing, an interactive place for fun and play for youngsters age six and under, features a pirate ship, a whale slide, and water play in an under-the-sea setting. The museum is open Tuesday through Saturday from 10:00 A.M. to 4:30 P.M., and Sunday from 1:00 to 5:00 P.M. Call for Becker Wing and WonderWing hours.

**National Guard Militia Museum of New Jersey
Free
Sea Girt Avenue, Sea Girt
(732) 974–5966**

Given the uncertainties we live with now, the wars of generations past seem to hold a special interest. In addition to artifacts and memorabilia relating to the contributions made by New Jersey's National Guard, this museum includes items from many wars. There's a MASH exhibit from the Korean War; a restored Civil War–era submarine; military vehicles; and a collection of World War II photographs you're not likely to see anywhere else. They were taken by army photographer Al Meserlin, a Sea Girt resident who captured some of the war's memorable moments in black and white. The photos depict heroes—like General Dwight D. Eisenhower and General George S. Patton Jr. shaking hands—and villains—like Major Wilhelm Oxenius, General Gustav Jodl, and Admiral Hans Georg Von Friedburg signing Germany's surrender in France.

The museum is open from 10:00 A.M. to 3:00 P.M. Tuesday and Thursday; it is also open every weekend in the summer and the last weekend of the month in the off-season.

**Ocean Grove Historical Society
50 Pitman Road, Ocean Grove
(732) 774–1869**

Founded by Methodists as a camp meeting ground in 1869, present-day Ocean Grove is a living Victorian museum. The historical society operates the Centennial Cottage (listed on page 108), sponsors special events, and gives walking tours of the town.

The Shore's Haunted House

The Shoal Harbor Museum, located at 119 Port Monmouth Road in Port Monmouth, (732–787–1807), was described by *U.S. News & World Report* as "one of the three most haunted houses in America." Local lore has it that during the American Revolution, the "Spy House," as it is known, was an inn frequented by British officers and sailors; when they came ashore, their ships would be attacked by patriots in whale-boats. Though there's no documentation for this story, it's a good one, as is the tale that pirates, in particular a bloodthirsty fellow called Captain Morgan, frequented the Spy House.

The house, which has four sections dating from different periods, started out as a one-room cabin built by Thomas Whitlock in 1663. It was sold to Daniel Seabrook, founder of the farming family that would make a fortune in frozen foods under the Seabrook Farms label. The house stayed in the Seabrook family for several genera-tions, then passed to the Reverend William Wilson. You would think that the pres-ence of a cleric would have cleared whatever negative energy was lurking here, but there are stories about more than 30 ghosts and over 70 sightings. One of the ghosts reported to haunt the place is that of Thomas Whitlock, the house's first owner.

The museum is not devoted to the supernatural, however, but to the heritage of the Bayshore: the history of commercial fishing, the farms of the early settlers, and the tools they used. Though there are only a couple of original pieces of furniture, the collection of 18th-century tools used by area farmers and fishermen is substantial.

On the grounds you'll find shaded picnic benches, antique farm equipment, anchors, and stockades—a reminder of the days when working on Sunday or spitting in public could earn you a few hours of public disgrace. Behind the house is a beach with sweeping views of Sandy Hook Bay and New York Harbor. The museum is open Saturday and Sunday from 2:00 to 4:00 P.M.

To find out more about ghosts and haunted places in New Jersey, consult Lynda Lee Mackin's book *Ghosts of the Garden State*. In it, she explains that our state's long and sometimes violent history—more than 100 Revolutionary War battles were fought here—has yielded a bumper crop of spirits and apparitions. The book includes some 50 tales of hauntings and strange doings, some in such mundane set-tings as the Garden State Parkway!

Squan Village Historical Society/Bailey-Reed House   Free
105 South Street, Manasquan
(732) 223–6770

The Bailey-Reed House, one of the oldest in southern Monmouth County, is a museum and the society headquarters. The earliest section of the house, the kitchen, was built in the late 18th century and is now equipped much as it would have been at the time. The other rooms show the house as it was during the 19th century. The house is open the second Sunday of each month from 1:00 to 4:00 P.M. and by appointment. Along with a tour, the house offers a new themed exhibit each month. One month, for example, the exhibt was a display of some "treasures" that might have been found in Grandma's old trunk.

Steamboat Dock Museum $
American Legion Drive, Keyport
(732) 264–2102

Located as it is on an inlet of Raritan Bay (and named for its key-shaped harbor), Keyport developed into an important shipping center, particularly for food-stuffs, back in the 19th century. It also became a steamboat-building center and, later, in the 20th century, a center for building amphibious planes.

The museum, which is located in a building previously occupied by the Keans-burg Steamboat Company, is dedicated to these facets of the town's history—and to the oystering and commercial fishing that have been a constant part of Keyport's cul-ture. If you're intrigued by the romance of the old steamboats, you might like to know that *The River Queen*, one of the boats General Ulysses S. Grant used during the Civil War, was built in Keyport. If you like unusual seafood, you might be interested to learn about the Chingarora oyster found in Keyport waters and about the oystermen who bring such delicacies to your table. The museum is open May through September, Sunday from 1:00 to 4:00 P.M., and Monday from 10:00 A.M. to noon.

Village Inn   Free
2 Water Street, Englishtown
(732) 462–4947

This historic tavern/inn, which served as a stage stop, courtroom, and church, was fre-quented by Revolutionary War militia. It's now a museum and a meeting place for the Battleground Historical Society. Though volunteer staff is limited, it may be possible, if you call ahead, to arrange a tour.

Woodrow Wilson Hall   Free
Monmouth University, Norwood Avenue,
West Long Branch
(732) 571–3476

Along with the nearby Guggenheim Man-sion, Woodrow Wilson Hall was one of the locations for the 1980 film *Annie*. Now the administrative headquarters of Monmouth University, this 130-room former mansion was once Shadow Lawn,

the private residence of Hubert T. Parson, the late president of the Woolworth Com-pany. It was built in 1930 on the founda-tions of President Woodrow Wilson's Summer White House and takes up a full chapter in James Maher's *Twilight of Splen-dor*, a book about the five most opulent private houses built in this country between the first World War and the Depression.

It's open for tours Monday through Friday from 10:00 A.M. to 3:00 P.M.; candle-light tours are given on several evenings during the year. Call ahead for tour hours.

Other Attractions

The Horse Park of New Jersey
Highway 524, Allentown
(609) 259–0170

This 147-acre facility was the state's first major horse show grounds. It's now the site of such events as the Garden State Horse and Carriage Show, the Middlesex County Horse Show, and the New Jersey All-Breed Horse Show. The shows gener-ally take place from March through November; call for schedule information.

Ocean County

Amusement Parks and Racetracks

Blackbeard's Cave
136 U.S. Highway 9, Bayville
(732) 286–4414
www.blackbeardscave.com

The Shore has many family recreation facilities like this, where the amusements are varied and where everyone can find a game or activity to enjoy. Your choices are miniature golf, a driving range, batting cages, archery, water games, bumper boats, and go-carts. Starting in mid to late March, you can play here daily from 10:00 A.M. to midnight; the hours are reduced in fall, and the facility closes in November.

Fantasy Island Amusement Park
320 West Seventh Avenue, Beach Haven
(609) 492–4000
www.fantasyislandpark.com

Fantasy Island is one of the Shore's nicest old-fashioned amusement parks. It's a manageable size (one block) and clean, and it features traditional rides like the giant Ferris wheel, the Tilt-a-Whirl, and a beautiful carousel with vintage horses. There are games and refreshments and an ice-cream parlor, too. There isn't a general admission fee; charges are per game or per ride. The park is open daily May through September from 5:00 to 11:00 P.M. or midnight.

Six Flags Great Adventure, Wild Safari, and Hurricane Harbor $$$$
Highway 537, Jackson
(732) 928–1821
www.sixflags.com

America's largest (225 acres) seasonal theme park has more rides than any other park, more than 100. There are dozens of kiddie rides, including mini coasters and race cars. And if you enjoy screaming your head off, you won't be disappointed with the dozen or so that will certainly get your adrenaline pumping. Try the Medusa, the world's first floorless roller coaster. If that doesn't do the trick, the Nitro will; it's a coaster that blasts off to 230 feet, with a 215-foot dive at speeds approaching 80 miles per hour.

For adventure of a gentler sort, try the drive-through Wild Safari, which is home to more than 1,200 freely roaming animals. As you make the 4½-mile drive, you'll see more than 50 species of animals, including tigers (Siberian and Bengal), ele-phants, giraffes, white rhinos, lions, baboons, and many other creatures you'd never expect to encounter in New Jersey.

The newest addition to the park complex is Hurricane Harbor, which features a million-gallon wave pool, a river with rapids and waterfalls, and lots of water slides and chutes. The setting is lushly landscaped, with a tropical theme. If you want to play in water in a man-made setting, this one's clean and appealing.

Six Flags is open daily from 10:00 A.M. to 10:00 P.M. in summer, with reduced hours in spring and fall. They're closed in winter. Hurricane Harbor has the same schedule, but closes at 8:00 P.M.

Thundering Surf Water Slide $$$
Taylor and Bay Avenues, Beach Haven
(609) 492–0869

If the day is very hot and your family is not in the mood for this town's Fantasy Island Amusement Park, cool them off with water rides and interactive "squirt works" water play.

Museums and Libraries

Colonel Charles Waterhouse Historical Museum   Free
17 Washington Street, Toms River
(732) 818–9040
www.usmcartist.com

The walls of this museum are hung with paintings that speak vividly of America's history and of wars past. Colonel Waterhouse, a Marine Corps artist-in-residence, does painstakingly researched paintings that span U.S. history from Revolutionary times to the present. In addition to a revolving display of the artist's paintings in the main area, the museum also exhibits his sculptures and a collection of American illustrations. The museum is open from noon to 4:00 P.M. on weekdays; call for additional hours.

Long Beach Island Historical Society Museum
Engleside and Beach Avenues, Beach Haven
(609) 492–0700

Families have fun getting wet under the giant spilling bucket at Six Flags Hurricane Harbor in Jackson Township. PHOTO: COURTESY OF OCEAN COUNTY PUBLIC AFFAIRS

If you'd like to learn more about LBI's history and see artifacts of days gone by, visit this museum, located in Beach Haven's original Holy Innocents Church. You'll find relics from the island's hunting and fishing days and mementos of Tucker's Island, which was reclaimed by the sea and which lives in memory today as a kind of Shore Atlantis. The society also offers walking tours, lectures, and historical programs. There is no admission fee but the museum charges for various events. Call for an appointment.

Navy Lakehurst Historical Society   Free
Highway 547, Lakehurst
(732) 818–7520
www.nlhs.com

There are still a few locals who remember seeing the *Hindenburg* pass overhead on May 17, 1937, on its way to Lakehurst, where a crowd of reporters and onlookers were waiting. Before it could be moored,

this, the largest zeppelin ever built—it held 6.7 cubic feet of hydrogen gas—exploded into flames, and 35 of its 97 passengers were killed.

With such a gruesome past, it's not hard to imagine why historic Hangar One, built in 1921, is said to be haunted. Lakehurst was, in fact, the center for Lighter-Than-Air (LTA) aeronautics in the United States. The first blimp that came to Lakehurst, the *Shenandoah*, arrived in 1924 and perished in turbulence a year later. The *Los Angeles* was a German-built airship acquired as compensation after World War I. When another airship, the USS *Akron*, was lost off Barnegat Light, the tragedy shook public confidence. Still, bigger and better airships followed; the *Hindenburg* and the *Graf Zeppelin* made headlines with their transatlantic flights. The *Graf Zeppelin* logged more than a million miles, including a round-the-world flight that began and ended at Lakehurst. Rigid airship development pretty much

Red Bank, the Hippest City in New Jersey

Rather than single out any one area, we decided to treat the entire town of Red Bank as one big attraction, because it is such a fun place to explore. Though Red Bank considers itself New Jersey's hippest community, it has a funky small-town charm, including an authentic main street (Broad Street) that moviegoers may recognize from the movie *Chasing Amy*.

Add a pleasant riverfront, an eclectic downtown shopping area, a thriving antiques mart, art galleries, an old-fashioned movie house that shows interesting films, a good collection of clubs, restaurants, and coffeehouses—and you have a pretty good explanation for Red Bank's appeal.

Red Bank began as a port settlement in the 1600s, and for more than a century, its boats carried produce and goods to markets in New York. Now the riverfront is a place to sail, kayak, fish, or just hang out and smell the freshly cut grass in Marine Park.

Among antique lovers, Red Bank is known for good prices and selection; there are dozens of dealers in the three buildings of the Antique Center on West Front Street. The Clearview Cinema on White Street shows movies that rarely make it to the big multiplex theaters.

An added bonus for celebrity watchers: Jon Bon Jovi and Bruce Springsteen live nearby and can often be seen in Red Bank restaurants and night spots. Red Bank's resident celebrity is Kevin Smith, director of *Clerks, Mall Rats, Chasing Amy, Dogma*, and *Jay and Silent Bob Strike Back*. Smith's quirky shop, Jay & Silent Bob's Secret Stash, is loaded with comic books and reproductions of movie props.

Red Bank hosts many special events throughout the year, including concerts on the riverfront; "Cruisin' with the Oldies," a vintage car event; and, on July 3, a spectacular fireworks display by the Grucci brothers, the same company that does the big Macy's fireworks on July 4 in New York City. For more information on doings in Red Bank, call (888) HIP–TOWN or visit www.redbank.com.

went up in smoke that May day when the words *"Hindenburg"* and "disaster" were forever joined in history books. In any event, the winds of World War II accelerated the development of airplanes.

Today the museum keeps 40 years of unique aeronautic history alive with exhibits such as a replica of the *Hindenburg* gondola, built for the disaster movie of the same name. Free tours of the site, including the *Hindenburg* crash site, the memorials, the blimp hangars, and other artifacts, are given the second Saturday of each month. Crowds flock to Lakehurst in June for special airshows by the Navy's Blue Angels, a team of six jet fighters that fly in incredibly tight formations and perform unbelievably dangerous stunts. If you're intent on seeing the Blue Angels, arrive early—the Navy closes the gates after the lot reaches its capacity of 60,000 cars (and it does). You can also scout out a nearby viewing location such as the Lakehurst Diner, at the corner of Center Street and N.J. Highway 70.

Ocean County Historical Museum $
26 Hadley Avenue, Toms River
(732) 341–1880
www.oceancountyhistory.org

Like other historical museums in our area, this one, the 1820 Pierson Sculthorpe

House, offers an inside peek at Shore life when it was simpler and harder. Kids may chortle at the one-room schoolhouse, heated by a potbelly stove, the only light being the lamps that hung on the windows. Adults may wince at a kitchen that evokes the days when everything revolved around the coal stove, where water had to be heated, and laundry was a full-day (usually Monday) project, with everything done by hand.

There's a poignant exhibit relating to the lighter-than-air crafts that were once thought to be the wave of the future—a future that ended abruptly with the horrifying crash of the *Hindenburg* in Lakehurst. The oldest exhibits are Native American artifacts dating from 10,000 B.C. to A.D. 1700. Civil War buffs will find memorabilia from that war here, as well as from the American Revolution.

The Ocean County Historical Society runs some terrific hands-on educational programs for school groups. On Thursday, there's a "Laundry Day"; on Tuesday, kids learn how butter is made; on Wednesday, there's a program on Lenni Lenape Indian lore. The museum is open Tuesday and Thursday from 1:00 to 3:00 P.M., and Saturday from 10:00 A.M. to 4:00 P.M.

Point Pleasant Historical Society Museum
Free
Point Pleasant Borough Hall, 416 New Jersey Avenue, Point Pleasant
(732) 892–3091
www.pointpleasanthistory.com
The museum has a large collection of photographs, maps, and local memorabilia, including World War II scrapbooks. Especially interesting is the society's video, *Yesterday on Film*, a 45-minute compilation of rare movies of the area from the 1920s and 1930s. It includes a 1928 travelogue; excerpts from the silent comedy *Mantoloking Moonshine*; and film of locals helping rescue passengers from the *Morro Castle*, the luxury liner that caught fire off Spring Lake Beach in 1934. The museum is open the second Thursday of each month, from 1:00 to 4:00 P.M.

Toms River Seaport Society Maritime Museum   Donation

Insiders' Tip
To beat the lines at Great Adventure, head for your first-choice rides just when the park opens—or wait until later in the day, say after 5:00 P.M.

Water Street and Hooper Avenue, Toms River
(732) 349–9209
If you love vintage boats and boating history—or if you'd like to learn more about these subjects—this museum will provide you with a pleasant hour or two. Its home is the 1868 carriage house that served the estate of Joseph Francis, the man who developed the "Lifecar," an unsinkable rowboat that proved invaluable in hazardous sea rescues. For his invention, Francis received a congressional medal in 1890, presented by President Harrison.

In the museum's two-story main building and sheds, you'll find artifacts of the area's marine history, a wartime library, a ship's store, boat models, and wonderful vintage boats. The collection includes the *Sheldrake*, a 12-foot Morton Johnson sneakbox sailed by F. Slade Dale from Bay Head to New York and then to Florida in 1925; a circa 1902 Perrine sneakbox; a Hankins rowing skiff; and a Beaton Sailing sneakbox. The museum is open Saturday and Tuesday from 10:00 A.M. to 2:00 P.M.

Other Attractions

Lakewood Blue Claws $$
2 Stadium Way, Lakewood
(732) 901–7000
www.lakewoodblueclaws.com
Ocean County baseball fans were tickled by the birth of this new minor league club, a Class A affiliate of the Philadelphia Phillies, and a member of the South Atlantic League.

Robert J. Novins Planetarium $$
Ocean County College, Dover Township
(732) 255–0342, (732) 255–0343 for recorded
information
www.ocean.cc.nj.us/planet/

If you suspect there's life we don't know about in the universe, the planetarium's program called "The Living Universe" will give you food for thought. It will also raise questions like: If there *is* intelligent life out there, where would we look for it—and how might we get in touch with an alien civilization?

If you'd simply like to get better acquainted with the sky above, the show called "A Sky for All Seasons" will help you explore the evening sky, the stars, and the constellations. Though these two shows aren't open to children under six, the planetarium does offer programs suitable for kids ages four to six, generally on Saturday afternoon. These cover what the sun and stars are and why they seem to move across the sky; lessons are liberally laced with tales like "King Soup and the Big Dipper" and "How the Little Bear Got His Long Tail." Call for a schedule of programs.

Show Place Ice Cream Parlor
202 Centre Street, Beach Haven
(609) 492–0018

If you're planning to take in a musical at the Surflight Theatre, what could be better than a pre- or post-show sundae or ice-cream soda? Just walk next door; you'll not only get your ice cream, you'll be serenaded by the singing serving staff. The ice-cream parlor, like many attractions in the area, is seasonal, open Memorial Day through Labor Day.

Atlantic and Cape May Counties

Amusement Parks

TW Sports Amusement Park
6115 Black Horse Pike, Egg Harbor
(609) 484–8080

This amusement complex is located in the Greater Atlantic City area and has activities to complement those you'll find on the Boardwalk in A.C. For example, in addition to a pool, miniature golf, and video games, it has bumper boats, laser tag, and batting cages. During the summer, it's open daily from noon to 11:00 P.M.; off-season, it's open Saturday from noon to 10:00 P.M. and Sunday from noon to 5:00 P.M.

Historic Sites

African-American Civil War Cemetery
Tabernacle Road, Lower Township

Gravestones found at Mount Moriah and Mount Zion Cemeteries in Lower Township indicate that African-American Civil War soldiers were buried here. There was once a church on this site.

Colonial House $
Greater Cape May Historical Society
653½ Washington Street (next to Cape May City Hall), Cape May
(609) 884–9100

This colonial house, circa 1775, is part of the Hughes Plantation and one of the only early houses on Cape Island that is open to the public. The historical society puts on changing exhibits; they have an annual Summer Exhibit, as well as one during Victorian Week. Call for hours.

Somers Mansion   Free
Shore Road, Somers Point
(609) 927–2212

Historians know this is the oldest house in Atlantic County, but since no records remain, no one is sure exactly how old it is. Historians estimate that it was built no later than 1725. It isn't really a mansion, just a big colonial house that was home to harbormaster Richard Somers, the man who operated the first ferry across Great Egg Harbor. The furnishings, plateware, and such are not original (it's something of a wonder that the house itself has survived, given all the calamities that befall old homes), but they are authentically 18th- and 19th-century and certainly depict a comfortable life of the period. The museum is open Wednesday through Sat-

The Historic Towne of Smithville

As you stroll Smithville's brick and cobblestone paths, consider the colorful and strange legends that surround this captivating little town, located on U.S. Highway 9 in Atlantic County. Smithville began life in 1787 as a stagecoach stop. Coaches would leave Cooper's Ferry in Camden at 3:00 A.M., bump along the rough trails created by the Lenni Lenape Indians, and, if all went well, arrive late the following day. Weary passengers got food, warmth, and hospitality at the Smithville Inn, which also served as the town's meeting place and town hall until 1876.

According to legend, Smithville was also a popular stop with such pirates as Blackbeard and Captain Kidd; apparently they liked to rest up here and perhaps bend an elbow when they weren't plundering unwary ships or burying their loot up and down the Jersey Coast.

Smithville is also thought to be the birthplace of the Jersey Devil (see the Close-up on page 128). It's not a hockey player, mind you, but a winged demon that has been spotted thousands of times over the past few centuries.

When the railroad put stagecoaches out of business, Smithville declined, and the inn fell into disrepair. In 1949, Fred and Ethel Noyes, both lovers of New Jersey history, restored the inn, which is now on the National Register of Historic Sites. Collecting historically significant structures from throughout the region, Fred and Ethel re-created the Historic Towne of Smithville.

Today, Smithville is a picture-postcard spot with an inviting village green. Ducks glide on tranquil Lake Meone, alongside the white swan boats that have delighted generations of children. On a quiet day, it's pleasant just to meander and explore the antiques shops, the authentic covered bridge, and the one-of-a-kind stores that are a refreshing change from cookie-cutter malls. Here, you'll find jewelry, collectibles, candles, and old-timey candies that used to sell for a penny but don't anymore. There's even a resale shop for bargain hunters. Stop for freshly baked goodies at the Smithville Bakers and relax on the boardwalk overlooking the lake. Feed the ducks or rent a paddleboat and join them. Ride the carousel and feel like a kid again. Visitors who actually are kids will have a swell time riding the miniature train. For some family fun, you can take in a performance of the Brownstone Puppet Players or view the enchanting puppet collection in their museum.

For a meal in a relaxed period setting, dine at the Smithville Inn, where you can choose old-fashioned dishes like chicken pot pie or meatloaf made from old family recipes. There are other, more casual, dining options, as well as ice-cream treats galore at Scoops. One of the newer attractions is The Showbarn, a dinner (or lunch or brunch) theater that serves up lighthearted productions like *Once Upon A Christmas*.

If you enjoy festivals and special events, Smithville has plenty, including antique car shows, historical reenactments, town crier contests, wool-spinning and decoy-making demonstrations, and fife-and-drum events. And at Christmas, the town does itself up in splendid holiday style.

The Smithville Inn is open for lunch and dinner daily, except for Sunday when brunch replaces lunch. The shops are open Monday through Friday from 10:00 A.M. to 6:00 P.M., Saturday from 10:00 A.M. to 7:00 P.M., and Sunday from 11:00 A.M. to 6:00 P.M. The attractions tend to keep the same hours as the shops. For more information on Smithville, call (609) 652–7777 or visit www.smithvillenj.com.

An Attraction on the High Seas

The 110-foot A. J. *Meerwald* is New Jersey's own tall ship, the flagship of the Delaware Bay Schooner Project. Authentically restored, the vessel is a living classroom of maritime history. Launched in 1928, the schooner was one of hundreds built along the Delaware Bay shore before the industry declined during the Great Depression. The *Meerwald*, rigging removed, served during World War II as a Coast Guard fireboat.

After the war, the *Meerwald* was used as an oyster dredge and as a surf clammer until it was retired in the 1970s. The once-lovely vessel languished in mothballs until it was taken over by the Schooner Project in 1989. Re-launched in 1996 after a complete restoration, the *Meerwald* now travels from its home port of Bivalve (2800 High Street, Port Norris/Bivalve, 856–785–2060) to various ports statewide, including Atlantic Highlands and Cape May. Check www.ajmeerwald.org for schedules and information about public sailings and special events aboard the ship.

urday from 10:00 A.M. to noon and 1:00 to 4:00 P.M., and Sunday from 1:00 to 4:00 P.M.

Museums and Libraries

Atlantic City Historical Museum   Free
Garden Pier, New Jersey Avenue and the
Boardwalk, Atlantic City
(609) 347–5839
www.acmuseum.org

This isn't just any old historical museum; it covers the history of Atlantic City, so know in advance that you're in for some fun. You'll be greeted by Mr. Peanut, once a familiar sight on many Shore boardwalks (young children in our family were known to scream at the sight of him).

Watch an entertaining video called *Boardwalk Ballyhoo*. You'll learn that Atlantic City's sea air was once prescribed as a cure for a variety of ailments, including insanity. And you'll glimpse Atlantic City entertainment at its biggest, boldest best—from the days of the diving horses to the Big Band era to the time when top show-business acts like Martin and Lewis played here. Enjoy the vintage photos in the Al Gold Photography Gallery, the Miss America memorabilia, and the quirky sou-

venir Heinz pickle pins. The museum is open daily from 10:00 A.M. to 10:00 P.M., and admission is free.

Atlantic County Historical Society   Free
907 Shore Road, Somers Point
(609) 927–5218

After you've reviewed the flashier side of life in these parts, you can visit the Atlantic County Historical Society's building for a look at how people lived in Victorian times. Though the building is 20th-century, you'll find authentically furnished Victorian rooms; the kitchen is equipped with period utensils, the dining room is suitably ornate, and so on. There are Native American artifacts, too, along with relics from the county's maritime past—and a desk that once belonged to Somers Point Mayor Chalky Leeds. Spend some time in this county—or in the society's library—and you'll notice how often the name "Leeds" comes up, in the past and the present. The museum and library are open Wednesday through Saturday from 10:00 A.M. to 3:30 P.M., and on the first Thursday of each month from 6:00 to 9:00 P.M.

Cape May County Museum $
504 U.S. Highway 9 North, Cape May Court House
(609) 465-3535
www.cmcmuseum.org

Like so many of the Shore's historical museums, this one offers visitors a peek at the small treasures of the past—the tools and implements that were part of everyday life from the 17th to the mid-20th centuries. Located in the historic John Holmes House, the museum has clothing, textiles, home furnishings, tools, and decorative objects. Survey the 18th-century kitchen and be glad for the tools we have today for preparing meals. In the Doctor's Room, you'll be equally glad that the antique surgical instruments have also been retired.

If you like war memorabilia, you'll find guns, swords, uniforms, and other items, from the Revolutionary through the Gulf Wars; the flag from the *Merrimack* inspires today, as it did a long time ago.

Going farther back in time, visit the Native American Room to view relics of the Lenni Lenape, the tribe that enjoyed the Shore long before any Europeans set foot on our sands.

In addition to the main house, you'll find a vintage barn from the 1800s; it houses tools and gadgets for home and farm, a maritime and whaling exhibit, and a natural history display. And to remind us of the transportation options available in days gone by, the museum has a handsomely restored doctor's sulky, a stagecoach, and a peddler's wagon. Lighthouse buffs will be interested in the original Fresnel lens from the 1859 Cape May Point Lighthouse.

If you're still not tired, there's more: The Genealogical Library includes collections of Cape May County family documents and bibles, historic maps, and books by local authors. Since many descendants of the *Mayflower* pilgrims still live in Cape May County, the genealogical material has been very useful to *Mayflower* researchers. The gift shop specializes in items that are associated with the history and lore of the county. From April through October, the museum is open Tuesday through Saturday from 9:00 A.M. to 4:00 P.M.; October through March, it is open only on Saturday from 9:00 A.M. to 4:00 P.M. Call for library hours.

Cape May Firemen's Museum   Free
Washington and Franklin Streets, Cape May
No phone

Nowadays, all Americans are most conscious of the special sort of bravery it takes to enter a burning building in order to save others. The history of many Shore communities has been altered by devastating fires, as well as by great storms. With its many wooden Victorian homes and hotels, Cape May has always been especially vulnerable; in the mid- to late 1800s, whole sections of the town were lost to fires.

This museum, housed in a Victorian-style building replica of the original firehouse, memorializes Cape May's big fires and the men who fought them. You'll see antique fire-fighting equipment; Cape May's first piece of mechanized equipment, the 1928 LeFrance; and pictures of some major fires, such as the one that took place on May 18, 1979, at the Windsor Hotel. During the summer, the museum is open every day; at other times, it's open on weekends when the weather is good. If you'd like to visit and find the museum closed, just talk to the friendly volunteer firefighters in the "real" firehouse behind the museum.

Discovery Seashell Museum   Free
2717 Asbury Avenue, Ocean City
(609) 398-2316

Even if you're not enchanted by seashells, this unusual museum and shop is worth a look. It's run by the Strange family, whose members are certified divers with a passion for collecting unusual shell varieties from around the world. You'll see such rarities as the Glory of India cone and the elusive golden cowry—as well as such anomalies as the only Siamese twin helmet shell known to exist.

In the Shell Yard, you'll find more than 10,000 varieties of seashells as well as 15 different types of coral, carved shells, and air plants that grow in shells without soil. If your hunt for pretty seashells has been in vain, you can buy them here. The museum is open daily

Saltwater Taffy

Though both salt and water are ingredients in saltwater taffy, it is not and never has been made with salt water; like many other things popularized in Atlantic City, the name was a gimmick that just really caught on. In 1883, taffy was a recent invention, and David Bradley had a candy stand that was drenched by sea water during a summer storm. The following day, the story goes, when a child asked to buy some taffy, Bradley replied: "You mean saltwater taffy, don't you?"

The name stuck, as does the candy. While Bradley's smart remark may have created a phenomenon, it was Joseph Fralinger who cashed in on it. When individual pieces of taffy were selling for a penny apiece, or six for a nickel, Fralinger got the bright idea of selling the candy in boxes, packaged as souvenirs that tourists could take home.

Fralinger's business took off, but he soon had competition. Enoch James, a candy maker from the Midwest, heard about the "taffy rush" in Atlantic City and came to set up shop on the Boardwalk. James' Candy has been Fralinger's biggest rival ever since.

To this day, hardly a visitor leaves the Boardwalk without a box of saltwater taffy, if only to show the folks back home that they didn't spend all their time in the casino. When it comes to taste-testing, we'd say that both Fralinger's and James' taffy are good, but then our favorite flavors are chocolate, licorice, and peppermint, while many prefer the fruit flavors. The main difference is in the presentation: Fralinger's taffy comes in slender logs that kids love to stretch out before completely consuming. If you prefer to decorously pop the whole candy into your mouth at once, then head for James' Candy. Their short, rectangular taffy is "cut to fit the mouth."

during the summer months; call for hours and for the off-season schedule.

Doo Wop Preservation League   **$$ for tours**
3201 Pacific Avenue, Wildwood
(609) 729–3700, ext. 150
www.doowopusa.org

Just in case you're not from Jersey or Philly, "doo-wop" refers to a musical style made popular by groups like The Ink Spots and The Turbans. Today the term is used to describe the unique architecture that evolved from the American pop culture of the 1950s and 1960s, known also as "googie" or "populux."

As we've explained in the Overview chapter, Wildwood has some 220 buildings in the doo-wop style—the largest concentration in the nation. The Doo Wop Preservation League was formed to promote and preserve this unique heritage. At the league's headquarters, you'll find such period relics as canvas butterfly chairs, an old jukebox, and appliances dating back to the 1950s. There are drawings by architecture students from Yale, Kent State, and the University of Pennsylvania; these students consulted with newer businesses like Subway and Pizza Hut to make their storefronts compatible with the existing doo-wop buildings.

If you have a poodle skirt tucked away in the attic, you may enjoy a trip down memory lane. The league can oblige with a trolley tour that will take you past motels and hotels that bring back the days of bright colors, gaudy neon, quirky geometric shapes, polished aluminum, and plastic palm trees. From mid-June through August, the tour runs on Tuesday, Wednesday, and Thursday, with a pickup at the above address at 7:45 P.M.; in September, there is a Sunday tour with an 11:45 A.M. pickup.

Emlen Physick Estate $$
1048 Washington Street, Cape May
(609) 884–5404
www.capemaymac.org

As New Jersey's only Victorian house museum, the Physick Estate is a snapshot of life among the affluent in Victorian Cape May. Emlen Physick Jr. was part of a wealthy Philadelphia family. His grandfather, Dr. Philip Syng Physick, developed surgical procedures and instruments (like the stomach pump) still in use today; U.S. Chief Justice John Marshall and Dolley Madison were among his famous patients.

Though the younger Physick also graduated from medical school, he never practiced and lived instead as a gentleman farmer. In 1879, he, his widowed mother, and his maiden aunt moved into the 18-room house that had been built by noted Philadelphia architect Frank Furness. An example of Victorian "Stick Style" architecture, the house is a veritable candy box of features like hooded dormer windows and massive upside-down chimneys.

Almost a century later, the house and outbuildings on the four-acre estate were rescued from the wrecker's ball by the Mid-Atlantic Center for the Arts (MAC), an organization that was formed to save the estate and preserve its architectural treasures.

What you'll see today is a dining room laid out with the finest in china and glass (a Victorian family's way of showing off its wealth), a parlor that is impressively furnished but was rarely used, and areas where the servants worked—at least a half-dozen were needed to keep this stately mansion running smoothly. There's more, of course, but be sure to save a little time for afternoon tea in the Twinings Tearoom, located in the estate's restored 1876 carriage house. You'll partake of tea sandwiches, salads, pastries, breads, scones, or other sweet and savory delights.

The Carriage House Gallery mounts changing exhibits, and in the adjoining Gallery Shop, you can buy some Twinings teas, teapots, and other tea-related items. If you enjoy the Victorian elegance of the tea room, inquire about the special events that are held there—for example, "Tea and Temperance," an afternoon repast seasoned by a lively debate among costumed actors about the evils of alcohol.

George F. Boyer Museum   Donation
Holly Beach Mall, 3907 Pacific Avenue,
Wildwood
(609) 523–0277
www.thewildwoods.com

The Boyer Museum has a remarkable collection of picture books—more than 150—filled with photographs that capture Wildwood's history, from its merger with Holly Beach City to the present. You'll find volumes devoted to the bars, the clubs—even the entertainers who played Wildwood in your father's (or your grandfather's) day. There's also a vast newspaper library on microfiche, dating back to the 1880s, an important resource for anyone who wishes to do serious research into Wildwood's past.

In a lighter vein, the museum is also the home of the Marbles Hall of Fame. You may know that generations of kids and adults have played marble games like Potsies, Poison, Passout, Chassies, Puggy, Black Snake, and Old Bowler (said to have been Abraham Lincoln's favorite). But perhaps you didn't know about the serious marble competitions that have been going on since 1922 (girls didn't get to play until 1947), when the Macy's store in Philadelphia sponsored a promotional event featuring the game. In 1923, the Scripps-Howard newspaper chain adopted the National Marbles Tournament and sponsored it for many years. In 1955, the city of Wildwood, along with a group of volunteers, took over the event, and here it remains. From May through October, the museum is open Monday through Saturday from 9:00 A.M. to 2:00 P.M.; from November through April, the hours are Thursday through Saturday from 10:00 A.M. to 2:00 P.M.

Boardwalks

To those of us who spent happy childhood summers at the Shore, the word "board-walk" is synonymous with excitement—gunning for friends or brothers in bumper cars, skeeball, hot-spun cotton candy. These days, in the words of the old Beatles song, some are gone and some remain. Long Branch and Asbury Park are just happy memories, while Point Pleasant and Seaside are still going strong. The boardwalks discussed here are not just for strolling or jogging, mind you, these are places with rides and amusements and food that's bad for you. We have mentioned some boardwalk attractions in the Overview chapter, so we'll try not to repeat.

In Ocean County, head for Point Pleasant Beach, where the Jenkinson's Board-walk area is kid-oriented, and where you could easily entertain your entire family without half trying. Jenkinson's motto is "Lots for Tots," and they do deliver such entertainment as baby parades, treasure hunts, pony rides, petting zoos, kiddie concerts, and a kiddie beach show with magic. They have weekly fireworks as well as weekly beach concerts (for adults). Call (732) 899–6686 or visit www.jenkinsons.com for current information.

Seaside Heights has a really big boardwalk, with even more arcades and rides, including New Jersey's only beach skyride. You can also ride a true museum piece: one of the only two surviving American-made classic carousels in New Jersey. Much of the Dr. Floyd L. Moreland Historic Dentzel/Looff Carousel dates back to 1910, though some of the horses go back as far as the 1890s. The 58 animals (36 move up and down) were hand-carved by master craftsmen William Dentzel of Philadelphia and Charles Looff of Coney Island. The carousel music is provided by the only continuously operating Wurlitzer Military Band Organ in the state; it has 105 wooden pipes and 51 keys, and plays from a style 150 band organ roll. Count 2,016 lightbulbs on the carousel, along with 18 paintings (15 original). Several weddings have taken place on the carousel, as have many birthday parties. Run by Dr. Moreland, professor of Classics and dean at the Graduate School and University Center of the City University of New York, the carousel and its shop, which is full of collectibles and carousel music, are a celebration of this vintage amusement. The carousel is open daily during the summer, from 10:00 a.m. to midnight, and on weekends and holidays year-round, from noon to early evening.

"On the Boardwalk, in Atlantic City. . ." (as the tinny old tune goes), you'll find all sorts of food stands and souvenir shops selling amazing items like bellybutton lights sandwiched in between 12 mammoth casinos. Skip the bad pizza and find Kohr's Custard, where pyramids of oranges are just waiting to be squeezed. Fralinger's and James' have taken their saltwater taffy battle into the 21st century. Walk the length of the Boardwalk and you'll find every sort of diversion: the Ripley's Believe It or Not! Museum, the Ocean One Shopping Mall, the "old" (renovated) Convention Hall, all manner of rides and games, the Atlantic City Art Center, and the Atlantic City Historical Museum. (See entries in this chapter and the Arts and Culture chapter for more on these.) At Virginia Avenue is the historic Steel Pier, where you'll find amusements like the heart-stopping bungee jump, and noisy, ringing arcade games.

Ocean City has two big boardwalks offering wholesome family fun. PHOTO: LILLIAN AFRICANO

Cape May County has two big boardwalks, in Ocean City and Wildwood. Ocean City's offers wholesome, family-oriented fun; this community, you'll recall, is "dry." You will find wall-to-wall games, souvenir and novelty shops, surreys for rent, arcades, water slides, a giant Ferris wheel, bumper cars, quirky, themed miniature golf courses, and outstanding candy shops. There's a branch of Fralinger's Salt Water Taffy here along with Shriver's, which has been in Ocean City since 1898 and is the oldest business in continuous operation on the Boardwalk. Johnson's, which has three locations, is our biggest temptation; we just can't stop eating their caramel popcorn until it's all gone. (You can also find Johnson's Caramel Corn in local supermarkets.)

The Music Pier is an Ocean City landmark, where you can see the annual Miss New Jersey pageant or hear concerts by the Ocean City Pops and other performers. Ocean City is known for wacky annual events, and some of them, like the Freckle Contest, take place on the Boardwalk.

When it comes to rides, the two-mile-long Wildwood Boardwalk wins, hands-down. It has five amusement piers and 100 rides (more than Disneyland), including such scream-inducers as the Tornado and the Great White, the tallest and fastest wooden roller coaster on the East Coast. Three water parks feature waterfalls, raft rides, tube floats, water guns for soaking, and even a 1,000-gallon dumping bucket that periodically douses those playing below. That should keep even easily bored kids happy. For more Wildwood Boardwalk information, call Morey's Piers at (609) 522–3900 or visit www.moreyspiers.com.

Ripley's Believe It or Not! Museum $$
Boardwalk at New York Avenue, Atlantic City
(609) 347–2001

If wacky, tacky, over-the-top stuff makes you smile, this is one museum you'll want to visit. Where else could you see what purports to be the Jersey Devil's skeleton? A roulette table made of jelly beans? Or the world's biggest model of a suspension bridge made of toothpicks (160,000)? You get the idea. Somehow this museum seems perfectly at home amid the honky-tonk Boardwalk attractions. It's open daily from 10:00 A.M. to 10:00 P.M.

Naval Air Station Wildwood Aviation Museum
Cape May County Airport,
500 Forrestal Road, Rio Grande
(609) 886–8787
www.usnasw.org

This museum is located at the former site of Naval Air Station Wildwood, a World War II dive-bomber training center. It's dedicated to the memory of the World War II airmen who died while training here. The facility was saved from demolition by a retired orthopedic surgeon, Dr. Joseph Salvatore, and his wife, a retired nurse. Dr. Salvatore bought the hangar he'd known as a boy for $1 and leased the surrounding land. Then came the hard work of repair and restoration.

Visit today and you'll walk into a cavernous 300-foot by 250-foot wooden hangar, which houses an orientation theater, exhibits, a gift shop, an extensive collection of aircraft photos, and vintage planes, including a MiG-15, an A-4 Skyhawk, and a Lockheed T-33. The museum offers educational programs and lectures; the big special event at this site is the Annual Fly-In, held the second Saturday in August. The museum is open Monday through Friday from 9:00 A.M. to 4:00 P.M. and on weekends by appointment.

Ocean Gate Museum   Free
Cape May and Asbury Avenues, Ocean Gate
(732) 269–0104

Back in 1881, when Ocean Gate was known as "Good Luck Point," the Pennsylvania Railroad cut a single track across a 600-acre farm and meadowlands owned by Captain Caleb Grant. Excursion trains passed through Good Luck Point on their way to beach resorts at Seaside Park and Bay Head. Early in the 20th century, some passengers got off the train, looked around, and decided to build their summer cottages here. A church and school soon followed, phone lines were installed, and by 1918, Ocean Gate was born.

The Ocean Gate Historical Society bought the railroad station in 1990 and moved it several blocks to its present location. Now restored, the two-room station has exhibits that recall the town's early days. You'll also see the station's old lamps, the original ticket counter, charts, maps, other railroad memorabilia, and the railroad's two-man fire-fighting hand pumper, used by local firemen. From May through September, the museum is open Saturday from 10:00 A.M. to noon, and Wednesday from 10:00 A.M. to noon and from 6:30 to 8:00 P.M.

South Jersey Railroad Museum   Free
Shoreline Railroad Historical Society
1721 Mount Pleasant Road, Tuckahoe
(609) 628–2850

Though perhaps not equal in number to the Shore's boat enthusiasts, there are dedicated railroad buffs in many area communities, and it's thanks to their efforts that we have train-related exhibits and events. What you'll find at this museum is a century of operating toy trains—fun for kids and adults alike. There are also rotating exhibits, displays of railroad memorabilia (you'll recall that railroad history goes back a long way in the Cape May area), and special events like the "Steam-Up," featuring real steam-operated model trains. The museum is open year-round, Wednesday and Saturday from 11:00 A.M. to 4:00 P.M. Between Thanksgiving and Christmas, it's also open on Sunday from 11:00 A.M. to 4:00 P.M.

Other Attractions

Atlantic City Surf Professional Baseball Club
$$
Sandcastle Stadium, 545 North Albany

The First Boardwalk

Did you know that our nation's first boardwalk was inspired by Alexander Boardman, a conductor on the Camden and Atlantic Railroad, and Jacob Keim, an Atlantic City hotelier? The two men came up with the idea because the well-heeled (and long-skirted) people who strolled on the beach in Atlantic City were constantly tracking sand into railroad parlor cars and hotel lobbies. In 1870, the city council voted to build a wooden footwalk along the beachfront. It was 10 feet wide and portable—laid down in time for Memorial Day, then taken up and stored after Labor Day. This first boardwalk was so popular, it was soon packed with people who delighted in the sand-free stroll.

Needless to say, the town fathers realized they would need to enlarge this popular attraction, and several more "footwalks" followed. About 1880, the famous rolling chairs came to the Atlantic City Boardwalk. At first they were the same simple wheeled seats that had been introduced at the Philadelphia Centennial of 1876 and were used primarily to carry invalids along the Boardwalk. Then, a local inventor brought out a romantic and graceful design, creating pretty wicker conveyances with sensuous curving fronts. In short order, these chairs became popular with courting couples, as well as with visiting "sports" who preferred riding to walking.

Even more well known than the chairs were the city's entertainment piers. Perhaps the most famous of these was Steel Pier 9 (still alive and well), which opened in 1898 and quickly became "The Showplace of the Nation." For a single admission, you could, if you had the stamina for it, enjoy 16 hours of continuous entertainment. The dress code called for full evening regalia, and the attractions included Big Bands, vaudeville acts—and the famous high-diving horses, which performed in the ocean stadium a half-mile out at sea.

Today Atlantic City is on its fifth boardwalk. The present Boardwalk is 4½ miles long and 60 feet wide. Constructed of thousands of two-by-fours of Bethabrara hardwood from Brazil and longleaf southern yellow pine, it is seated on concrete and steel pilings. Atlantic City's Boardwalk is not just an aimless stroll; it's really the main "street" of A.C., the heart of this rich and varied city.

Avenue (near Bader Field), Atlantic City
(609) 344-7010

Enhancing Atlantic City's image as a family travel destination, the new Sandcastle Stadium is the home of the minor league A.C. Surf from May through September. In this attractive setting, you can watch the game in pleasant surroundings—and see the beckoning glitter of Atlantic City from your seat. During the off-season, the stadium becomes the scene of such events as

"Surf's Halloween Parade and Fireworks," a fun-filled celebration that includes a parade, costume contest, trick-or-treating, pumpkin painting, and fireworks.

The Fishermen's Memorial
End of Missouri Avenue, Cape May

The Perfect Storm showed us the terrifying moments that fishermen at sea face. This monument shows us the pain of the fishermen's families: a woman and two chil-

The Jersey Devil

Although stories of the birth of the Jersey Devil vary, the most common account dates back to a stormy night in 1735, when a Mrs. Leeds was giving birth to her 13th child, some say at the Smithville Inn. During her labor, she cursed the baby: "Let this child be a devil!" A beautiful boy was born, the story goes, but to the horror of both mother and midwife, the boy began to mutate: his face elongated, his legs grew long, and his feet became hoofs. Dark wings sprouted from his shoulders. Suddenly the creature let out an ear-piercing scream and flew off into the night.

Since then, the Jersey Devil has been sighted regularly, in and around the Pine Barrens, in other New Jersey towns, and even as far away as New York. According to Devil lore, a courageous cleric performed an exorcism some years later, with "bell, book, and candle," and the ritual supposedly put the creature to sleep for a hundred years. And yet. . . . All in all, there have been more than 2,000 reported sightings of this mythic creature, some from eminently respectable and sober citizens.

In the early 19th century, one story goes, Commodore Stephen Decatur, a naval hero, was testing cannon balls on the firing range when he saw a strange creature flying across the sky. He fired and hit the creature, but it kept right on flying. Another distinguished sighter of this period was Joseph Bonaparte, former King of Spain and brother of Napoleon; he claims to have seen the Devil in Bordentown while he was hunting. Farmers of the time reported that many sheep and chickens were killed by a creature that emitted a piercing scream and left strange tracks.

The Devil appears to have been particularly busy during 1909; there were over a thousand sightings that year. Was it mass hysteria, the product of a thousand fevered imaginations? A Gloucester couple claimed to have watched the creature from their bedroom window for some 10 minutes. They described it as being three and a half feet tall, with a head like a collie and a face like a horse. It had a long neck and wings at least two feet in length. The creature walked on its back legs, which were long like a crane's, but with horses' hooves for feet, while its shorter front legs ended in dog-like paws. When the couple yelled "Shoo!" at this apparition, it reportedly barked—and then flew away.

According to superstition, the Jersey Devil appears before disasters, such as the outbreak of war. Supposedly he was sighted before the start of the Civil War, the Spanish American War, World War I, World War II, and the war in Vietnam. Some claim to have seen him on December 7, 1941, before Pearl Harbor was bombed. Believers say that it is the creature's demonic origins that make him a harbinger of disaster.

dren looking out to the harbor, waiting for the fishing boat that will never return. On the monument are the names of Cape May's lost fishermen, from as far back as the mid-19th century. Sad to say, new names are added from time to time. Yet this is one of the loveliest and most peaceful places to sit and contemplate the sea and the sailboats. And there even are a few parking places.

Historic Gardner's Basin
New Hampshire Avenue and the bay,
Atlantic City

Located on the inlet on the northern end of Atlantic City—well away from the smoke and noise of the casinos—is spruced-up Gardner's Basin. No bright lights here, just calm bay waters, a waterfront cafe, and the cedar-sided Ocean Life Center (see description on page 130). And instead of the ka-ching of myriad slot machines, what you'll hear are boat horns or the screech of gulls.

The rescue (in 1976) and ongoing restoration of what was a rundown area has created an inviting oasis that harkens back to the basin's early days. More than a century before the casinos arrived, the basin area was being billed as a healthy retreat, and during Atlantic City's earliest days, the first five hotels were built in this inlet area.

But those early days of glamour and elegance eventually gave way to somewhat seedier times. During Prohibition, the basin was a rumrunner's paradise; it's been estimated that some five million gallons of illegal booze came through here during that era. It was also once a haven for backroom gambling and other mob activity.

The smugglers' skiffs are no more; now you can hop aboard a party boat and try your luck with the bluefish and sea bass. From June through September, there are half-day deep-sea fishing excursions; daylong trips are available from April 1 to June 1 and October 2 to December 23. Call (609) 652-8184 for more information.

If you'd rather contemplate the sea and its inhabitants, take a morning skyline cruise on the *Cruisin 1*, enjoy a marine-mammal-watching adventure (whales in spring and fall, dolphins in summer), or savor the sunset with a cool drink in hand. For reservations and information, call Atlantic City Cruises, Inc. at (609) 347–7600.

For delightful waterfront dining, try the Flying Cloud. There's also a 10-acre maritime park here and an amphitheater for concerts and other shows. During the summer months, the basin is the site of several lively events: the New Jersey Fresh Seafood Festival (June), the Jazz Festival (July), the Atlantic City Ocean Marathon Swim (July), the Ocean Life Festival (August), and the Festival Latino Americano (September).

Lucy the Elephant $
9200 Atlantic Avenue at Decatur, Margate
(609) 823–6473
www.lucytheelephant.org

She's over 120 years old and stands six stories tall; she's survived hurricanes, a fire, and years of neglect. She's Lucy the Elephant, a National Historic Landmark beloved by generations of children and adults. Built in 1881 (when Margate was known as the City of South Atlantic City) as an advertising gimmick by James V. Lafferty, Lucy cost a whopping $38,000. Lafferty had hoped Lucy would attract buyers for the oceanfront lots he had for sale. Lucy was an instant success, but Lafferty's real-estate venture flopped. In 1887, he sold the elephant and his land.

Lucy's new owner was Anthony Gertzen. In the 83 years that Lucy was part of the Gertzen family, she remained a tourist attraction, but she did come down in the world. After a 1903 hurricane, she was moved a hundred feet inland and turned into a tavern. A couple of years later, a fellow who couldn't hold his liquor knocked down an oil lantern, causing the fire that nearly burned Lucy to the ground. In 1929, she lost her howdah, the riding cage on her back, in a storm (it was replaced with a simpler version), and then went on to weather even more storms in the next few decades.

Operated as a tourist attraction until 1970, Lucy was donated to the city and moved two blocks to city land. Thanks to the dedicated fund-raising efforts of the Save Lucy Committee, restoration began. Lucy now attracts an average of 15,000 visitors a year. She has her own Web site, and soon she'll have a camera mounted in her head, so you'll be able to get a Lucy's-eye view of Margate's beach and the Atlantic Ocean.

Inside the elephant, you'll find photos, memorabilia, and an eight-minute video about Lucy's "life." The fun, of course, is

Lucy the Elephant is over 120 years old and still delights children of every age. She attracts some 15,000 visitors a year and has her own Web site. PHOTO: COURTESY OF ATLANTIC CITY CONVENTION & VISITORS AUTHORITY

just being inside, and perhaps going up to her howdah to take in the panoramic view of Atlantic City's skyscrapers, the ocean, Ocean City, and the mainland. During the question-and-answer period, kids often ask if Lucy was ever alive. Adults sometimes ask if she was ever a hotel. (She wasn't, though that story persists.) From mid-June until Labor Day, Lucy is open Monday through Saturday from 10:00 A.M. to 8:00 P.M., and Sunday from 10:00 A.M. to 5:00 P.M. In April, May, early June, September, and October, she is open on weekends from 10:00 A.M. to 5:00 P.M. Lucy closes for the winter, with the following exceptions: Thanksgiving weekend and the Christmas season (when Santa is in attendance), and Presidents' Day weekend. If you visit Lucy in summer, you can adjourn to the I Love Lucy Beach Grille next door and enjoy a sandwich and cold drink on an outdoor deck.

Miss America RoseWalk
Michigan Avenue, Atlantic City

This pink-lit runway is a tribute to the Miss America pageant. (See Close-up on page 131.) Bronze plaques line the walkway, giving the name and year of every Miss America, along with a quote. Read them all and you'll get some idea of how much America's "ideal" woman has changed over the years. For skeptics, Debra Maffett, Miss America 1983, may be able to explain the enduring attraction of the contest: "I just felt there had to be something better out there for me. . . . So many people who grow up in small-town America never get to have a dream, a goal, or a star. The most wonderful feeling in the world is when one is striving for something."

Ocean Life Center $$
Historic Gardner's Basin, New Hampshire Avenue and the bay, Atlantic City
(609) 348-2880

If you love the ocean, here's an opportunity to get better acquainted with some of the creatures who live there. Peek into a horseshoe crab's eyes (all 13 of them), hold a green crab, or listen to the sounds of whales and dolphins. At this three-story, $4.5-million facility, the stars are the inhabitants of the 30,000 gallons of

Miss America's Hometown

The Miss America pageant, like the Convention Hall, was the brainchild of Atlantic City businessmen who wanted to extend the summer season (and fill the hotels) beyond Labor Day. The first pageant, in 1921, was an instant success, attracting not only the desired tourists, but also nationwide attention. The winner was 15-year-old Margaret Gorman of Washington, D.C. That first pageant had only eight contestants, clad in bathing regalia that covered most of their bodies. The following year, 58 beauties turned up, earning days of breathless coverage in *The New York Times*. The judges that year were artist Norman Rockwell and show business luminaries Flo Ziegfeld and Lee Shubert.

Over the years, the romantic notion of becoming Miss America captured the imagination of little girls everywhere, and Miss America toys and paper dolls became almost as popular as Barbie would be in her day.

The first Miss Americas were crowned at the Million Dollar Pier; later the pageant moved to Convention Hall. In 1955, Bert Parks became the master of ceremonies, and though he is no longer with us, we remember his voice crooning "There she is, Miss America. . ."

During the 1960s, feminists targeted the pageant as an event that exploited and distorted women. In fact, leading feminist Robin Morgan later said, "It was right here, in super tacky Atlantic City, that this wave of the feminist movement was born."

Nevertheless, Miss America endured, with some changes. Some Miss Americas achieved celebrity beyond the pageant: Joan Blondell, Vera (Ralston) Miles, Cloris Leachman, Bess Myerson, Lee Merriwether, Phyllis George, Vanessa Williams. (Anita Bryant, Miss Oklahoma in 1959, was only second runner-up, but she, too, has had a long public career.)

If you're interested in Miss Americas, past and present, stroll the RoseWalk on Michigan Avenue; there you'll find bronze plaques dedicated to all the Misses since 1921. Continue over to the Sheraton Hotel, which is now the headquarters of the Miss America organization. In the lobby, you'll find gowns from each decade as well as vintage photos. Upstairs, Carrie Bradshaw-wannabes can check out the Shoe Bar, a cocktail lounge where high-heeled shoes of various vintages provide the decor. Out front, there's a bronze statue of Bert holding a stainless-steel tiara. Duck under it and you can have a souvenir picture of your "crowning moment."

The last Miss New Jersey to wear the crown was Suzette Charles of Mays Landing. She was actually the first runner-up to Vanessa Williams in 1984 and took over after the publication of nude photos forced Williams to resign.

A Devil of a Drink

As befits its naissance in a tavern, the Jersey Devil is also a cocktail, invented by the bartender of the Smithville Inn. Down a few and you might well see a horrible vision, with the head of a dog, the face of a horse, and the wings of a bat.

Jersey Devil

1 ounce Laird's AppleJack
⅓ ounce Cointreau
⅓ ounce lime juice
⅓ ounce cranberry juice
½ teaspoon sugar
Shake ingredients with ice. Strain into a cocktail glass.

From: *Applejack: The Spirit of Americana,* published by Laird & Company, Scobeyville, New Jersey.

---

water in the aquarium tanks: fun-to-watch seahorses and pipefish, moray eels and sharks, and some fairly placid denizens, like Groman, the loggerhead turtle. All are a part of New Jersey's ecosystem; some are year-rounders, others only visit in summer.

You could easily spend a couple of hours in the 14,500-square-foot center, checking out the real-time weather and radar station on the observation deck, steering a real ship's wheel through the treacherous waters off Cape Horn, or taking a sailing lesson on the center's working model boat. If you can get your children away from the starfish and crabs in the touch tank, they can create their own ocean rubbings using crayons and paper. From the third-floor observatory, you can see where the ocean meets the bay. A glimpse of the Harrah's and Trump Marina Casinos will remind you that no matter how peaceful it is here, you're still in Atlantic City. The center is open daily from 10:00 A.M. to 5:00 P.M.

Renault Winery $
72 North Bremen Avenue, Egg Harbor City
(609) 965–2111
www.renaultwinery.com

Founded in 1864 by master winemaker Louis Nicholas Renault, this is the oldest continually operating winery in the United States. It's also the largest and most popular of the state's wineries. You'll understand why if you visit. With its new hotel and gourmet restaurants, plus a golf course in the works, Renault has evolved into a vacation destination rather than simply a place where wine is made.

Under Renault's expert guidance, the winery succeeded from the start. After it passed from his son to the D'Agostino family, it continued to prosper, even during Prohibition, when all other wineries closed. That was managed with a simple trick of labeling: The company began selling a new product, "Renault Wine Tonic," not to liquor dealers, but to drugstores all over the United States. This new patent "medicine" took off like a rocket; not only was it supposed to cure backaches and other problems, it had a 22-percent alcohol content!

When you tour Renault today, you'll learn more about the winery, past and present (it was bought by the Milza family in 1978). In the Glass Museum, you'll see hundreds of champagne glasses, some centuries old. Then you'll view this family-run operation, which grows the grapes, makes the wine, bottles it, and sells both wholesale and retail (on the premises). You'll be invited to taste, of course—isn't that half the fun? During October, the month of the annual Grape Harvest Festival, the winery is at its most active, with grape-stomping contests, hayrides, and other entertainment. There's a crafts festival in winter, and other events throughout the year. Guided tours and wine tastings are given Monday through Friday from 11:00 A.M. to 4:00 P.M., Saturday from 11:00 A.M. to 8:00 P.M., and Sunday from noon to 4:00 P.M.

U.S.S. *Atlantus* (concrete ship)
Off Sunset Beach, Cape May Point

Though we mentioned the *Atlantus* in our overview section, we'll remind you to look for it at low tide. This was one of 38 concrete ships planned by the United States because of a critical steel shortage during World War I. Only 12 were actually built. The *Atlantus* was a 3,000-ton, 250-foot-long freighter with a five-inch-thick hull of a special concrete aggregate. Launched on November 21, 1918, at Wilmington, North Carolina, and commissioned the following June, the *Atlantus* served for a year as a government-owned, privately operated commercial coal steamer in New England. After the war, when more effi-

Insiders' Tip

Only two roads access Point Pleasant Beach, N.J. Highways 35 and 88, so traffic can be horrendous at rush hour, especially on Friday evening. Check local traffic reports on 101.5 FM before heading for the Boardwalk.

cient steel ships were again available, it was decommissioned, stripped, and towed to Cape May by a firm that wished to start a ferry service between Cape May and Lewes. While awaiting positioning, the ship broke loose during a storm and ran aground. Attempts to free the hulking ship failed, and today the cracked, weatherbeaten hull is a tourist attraction that draws thousands of visitors to Sunset Beach each year.

Wyland's Whaling Wall
Boardwalk Mall at Garfield Avenue, Wildwood

When visiting Wildwood's Boardwalk, be sure to notice this 220-foot by 30-foot full-color mural painted by renowned environmental artist Wyland. The seascape features two life-size whales, a baby whale, dolphins, and other marine life.

Lighthouses

Jersey Shore Lighthouses
Delaware Bay Lighthouses

Like Lady Liberty holding aloft the golden flame of freedom, lighthouses are laden with symbolism: a glimmer of hope in the darkness. It's not hard to imagine storm-tossed mariners of years gone by, whose sole hope of making port is a tiny beacon that points the way toward a safe harbor. For many, this Guiding Light can have a religious connotation, while others remark on the typical conical shape of a lighthouse and put a more Freudian spin on its appeal.

All blather aside, there's no doubt that visiting lighthouses has become a popular pastime, even as many have fallen into disuse, made obsolete by more high-tech navigational aids such as LORAN. Local and national societies aimed at preserving these historic structures and opening them to the public have sprung up all over the country.

With 127 miles of coastline and a seafaring history that goes back to 1609, when Henry Hudson sailed the *Half Moon* down the coast of New Jersey, into Sandy Hook Bay and New York Harbor, the Jersey Shore is a must for dedicated lighthouse aficionados as well as casual fans who just like to climb up and enjoy gazing out to sea. From north to south, whether you're traveling by cabin cruiser or PT Cruiser, here's a rundown on what there is to see and how to see it. Admission to the lighthouses is generally free, though a donation may be requested.

Jersey Shore Lighthouses

Sandy Hook Lighthouse
Gateway National Recreation Area, Sandy Hook
(732) 872–5970

Sandy Hook Lighthouse is the oldest working lighthouse in the United States, having first lit its original beacon of 48 whale oil lamps on June 11, 1764. Held by the British during the Revolutionary War, the octagonal white tower survived American cannon fire to shine its light on the Bayshore for more than 200 years.

Volunteers from the New Jersey Lighthouse Society give tours to visitors on weekends on the half hour from noon to 4:30 P.M. from April until Thanksgiving. The tower can only accommodate eight at a time, so try to arrive between 11:30 A.M. and noon to put your name on the schedule for the day. You must also be at least 48 inches tall to climb the tower.

If you have to wait to tour the lighthouse, there's no shortage of things to do on Sandy Hook: walking or sunning on the beach, surf fishing, bird-watching on the salt marshes, or climbing the disused battlements of Fort Hancock are just a few suggestions.

Twin Lights of Navesink
Lighthouse Road, Highlands
(732) 872–1814

Overlooking Sandy Hook from an elevation of 200 feet above sea level, Twin Lights has the imposing mien of an old

Insiders' Tip

In 1880, a 35-foot-tall cast-iron tower was installed as Sandy Hook's North Beacon. By 1917 it was replaced, and the "Little Red Lighthouse" was moved to the northern end of Manhattan, where it still stands, now overshadowed by the George Washington Bridge.

fortress, with its solid brownstone construction and its castellated turrets. The towers are not really twins at all; one is octagonal and the other is square. They were built in 1862, but the first lighthouse on this site was erected in 1828.

In 1841, under orders from Commodore Perry, Twin Lights installed a first-order Fresnel lens the first in the United States, in the south tower. Designed by French physicist Augustin Fresnel (pronounced Fray-nel), the lens was a beehive-shaped construction of magnifying lenses and prisms that intensified the lighthouse's beacon so that it could be seen for many miles out at sea.

In 1898, the first Fresnel lens was replaced by a bivalve-shaped lens that was illuminated with an electric arc lamp, one of the first in the country. The huge bivalve lens, which is on view in Twin Lights' old generator room, produced a light that could be seen 22 miles away.

Twin Lights is also famous as the location of Guglielmo Marconi's first wireless telegraph antenna, erected atop this hill in 1899. Marconi demonstrated the new technology by reporting directly on the America's Cup yacht race, which was staged off Sandy Hook.

Twin Lights has an instructive visitor center with a well-chosen selection of books on lighthouses and New Jersey for sale. From Memorial Day to Labor Day, Twin Lights is open seven days a week, 10:00 A.M. to 5:00 P.M.; the rest of the year, it is closed on Monday and Tuesday.

Conover Beacon
Bayside between Leonard and Roop Streets, Leonardo

If you're a real devotee of lighthouses, you'll want to stop by here when visiting Sandy Hook or Twin Lights. Right on the beach, Conover Beacon looks like a big red and white periscope. It dates from the 1930s and was moved to this site from Keansburg. It was one of a pair of range lights that formed a line directing sea captains to the Chapel Hill Channel, the safest way into Sandy Hook Bay. The rear range light, Chapel Hill Lighthouse, situated 224 feet above sea level, is now a pri-

vate residence in Middletown. Neither light is open to the public.

Sea Girt Lighthouse
Beacon Boulevard at the ocean, Sea Girt
(732) 974-0514

For all appearances, Sea Girt Lighthouse is a comfortable red brick Victorian house with a welcoming porch that just happens to have a square light tower attached to it. Its interior is almost completely restored and furnished to reflect the lives of a lighthouse keeper and his family of the Victorian period.

Every lighthouse had a distinct signal beacon that allowed sailors to tell one from another, and Sea Girt's light turned red for two seconds out of every six. Sea Girt was also the first lighthouse in the country equipped with a radio fog signal.

Sea Girt Lighthouse is open to visitors Sundays from 1:00 to 4:00 P.M.

Barnegat Lighthouse
Barnegat Lighthouse State Park
Barnegat Light, Long Beach Island
(609) 494-2016

"Old Barney," the red and white tower that soars 170 feet over the sand dunes and the tricky inlet into Barnegat Bay, is a favorite subject of local artists and photographers and a familiar symbol of the Jersey Shore. Recent reports that the structure is listing due to ever-shifting tides and erosion have energized a $1.8-million project by the Army Corps of

Barnegat Lighthouse, affectionately called "Old Barney," is a familiar symbol of the Jersey Shore.
PHOTO: COURTESY OF OCEAN COUNTY PUBLIC AFFAIRS

Engineers to shore up its foundation with large rocks.

The lighthouse was, in fact, built by the Army Corps of Engineers back in 1856, designed by a Lieutenant George Meade who later rose to the rank of general and commanded the Union troops at Gettysburg in the Civil War. Meade felt that Barnegat needed a first-rate lighthouse not only to prevent the many shipwrecks that occurred in the hazardous shallows, but because it was an important landmark in transatlantic shipping. It was fitted with a first-order Fresnel lens, a 12-foot tall beehive structure made of 1,024 prisms, that produced a light so intense it could be seen up to 30 miles away. The lens is now on view in the nearby Barnegat Light Museum.

Barnegat was decommissioned in 1944 after its function was assumed by Barnegat Lightship, a vessel moored about eight miles east of Barnegat Inlet in 1927. Old Barney still served during World War II, though, as a lookout station. From its summit, military personnel watched for German submarines, which prowled the coastal waters—and sank two tankers in 1942.

Climb the 217 steps to the top and you'll see for yourself what a splendid lookout it is, with panoramic views of Long Beach Island, the ocean, Barnegat Bay, and Island Beach State Park. The lighthouse is open daily in the summer (June–August) from 9:30 A.M. to 4:30 P.M. and stays open on Saturday nights until 9:30 P.M. In the off-season, Barnegat is open daily from 9:00 A.M. to 3:30 P.M., except when very windy conditions prevail.

Tuckerton Seaport
120 Main Street (U.S. Highway 9), Tuckerton
(609) 296–8868
www.tuckertonseaport.org

At one time an eight-mile strip of land at the southern end of Long Beach Island, Tucker's Island became a distinct island when heavy winter storm tides created a channel through to Barnegat Bay. A small lighthouse was built on the island in 1848; in 1879, a bigger, better tower was built and equipped with a fourth-order Fresnel lens.

By that time, though, the shifting tides had already whittled the island down to just a mile. By 1927, the ocean had undermined the lighthouse and it collapsed into the briny. The rest of the island soon disappeared, too.

Tuckerton Seaport is a 40-acre living-history museum, located safely on the mainland, that is dedicated to the maritime heritage of New Jersey. In addition to a replica lighthouse, Tuckerton offers demonstrations of boatbuilding and decoy carving, and lessons in clamming and oyster harvesting. It's open daily from 10:00 A.M. to 5:00 P.M. except on Thanksgiving, Christmas, and New Year's Day. For additional details see the Living-History Farms and Historic Villages chapter.

Insiders' Tip

The New Jersey Lighthouse Society publishes a newsletter, holds meetings at various lighthouses, and organizes the Lighthouse Challenge every October, in which participants try to visit 11 lighthouses in a weekend. Some of the lighthouses open for the Challenge—East Point, Finn's Point, and Tinicum—are not usually open to the public. See the society's Web site, njlhs.burlco.org, or call Twin Lights to find out more.

Absecon Lighthouse
Vermont and Pacific Avenues, Atlantic City
(609) 441–9272
www.absecon.lighthouse.com

Nowadays, Absecon Light is dark—but passing boaters can surely see the hectic glare of the casinos' multicolored light towers. When it was built in 1857, also by Lieutenant Meade, designer of Barnegat Lighthouse, Absecon Lighthouse quickly became a huge attraction to the well-heeled tourists that frequented Atlantic City's posh hotels.

The 171-foot tower has seen a comprehensive restoration, including the rebuilding of the keeper's cottage. Visitors who scale its 228 steps will find its original first-order Fresnel lens still in place. The tower's hours are Thursday through Monday 11:00 A.M to 4:00 P.M., and it also can be opened by special arrangement. It is closed on major holidays.

Hereford Inlet Lighthouse
111 North Central Avenue, at First Avenue, North Wildwood
(609) 522–4520, (609) 522–2030

Except for its square, 50-foot light tower, Hereford Inlet Lighthouse would fit in perfectly among Cape May's lovely Victorian houses. Recently restored, Hereford is one of the state's prettiest lighthouses, surrounded by a lush garden filled with flowers and herbs. When it was built in 1874, it also afforded the keeper and his family one of the most comfortable residences they were likely to find, with ample living space and five fireplaces. It may well be that the keeper liked Hereford so much that he didn't want to leave—some folks have reported seeing his ghost.

Behind the lighthouse is a low boardwalk to the seawall overlooking the Hereford Inlet, where the view is quite beautiful. Hereford is a place to stop and smell the flowers and drink in the tranquil atmosphere before returning to the bustle of Wildwood's honky-tonk attractions. From May through September, Hereford is open seven days a week from 9:00 A.M to 5:00 P.M. From October through December and mid-March through April, hours are from 11:00 A.M. to 4:00 P.M. Monday through Thursday, and from 10:00 A.M. to 4:00 P.M. Friday through Sunday. From

The recently restored Hereford Inlet Lighthouse in North Wildwood, surrounded by flowers, is one of the state's prettiest. PHOTO: LILLIAN AFRICANO

Offshore Lights

Not all lighthouses are safely located on dry land. Sometimes a light is needed to warn sailors of a dangerous shoal or other obstacle to be avoided; they are often named after a ship or sailor who failed to do so. The following offshore lighthouses are all still in use and closed to the public, and are probably well known to your boating friends.

East of Sandy Hook is Ambrose Tower, which marks the Ambrose Channel into the New York–New Jersey Harbor along with Romer Shoal Lighthouse. Romer Shoal, a stolid red and white harbor light two miles north of the tip of Sandy Hook, can be glimpsed from the land at Mount Mitchill Scenic Overlook in Highlands.

Two miles northwest of Romer Shoal is the West Bank Lighthouse, which is technically in New York. Just southeast of Staten Island is the white cast-iron Old Orchard Shoal Lighthouse. Great Beds Lighthouse marks a dangerous shallow in the center of Raritan Bay.

Sailing up the Delaware Bay, you'll find five lighthouses marking hazards: the Brandywine Shoal Lighthouse, the Miah Maull Lighthouse, and the Cross Ledge, the Elbow of Cross Ledge, and the Ship John Shoal Lighthouses. The Miah Maull, named for Nehemiah Maull, who drowned here in a shipwreck in the 1700s, is a cool-looking, multistory, red cast-iron tower.

Another unique lighthouse is the Fourteen Foot Bank Lighthouse. It's a lovely, white three-story Cape May Victorian house that just happens to be set 13 miles out to sea.

January until March 15, the lighthouse is closed.

Cape May Point Lighthouse
Cape May Point State Park, Lighthouse Drive, Cape May Point
(609) 884–5404, (800) 275–4278 (Mid-Atlantic Center for the Arts)
www.capemaymac.org

Of the three lighthouses designed by George Meade for the Jersey Shore, Cape May is the only one that is still a working beacon, marking the important spot where the Delaware Bay meets the Atlantic Ocean. Nowadays, the 159-foot tower sports a reflector lens with a 1,000-watt bulb; its original Fresnel lens is on display at the Cape May County Historical Society in Cape May Court House.

Don't chicken out on climbing this one—the view of the ocean, the surrounding 140-acre state park, and the birds that pass through Cape May is not to be missed. At certain times, visitors are greeted at the summit by actors portraying the lighthouse's last keepers, Harry and Belle Palmer, who lived here in the 1920s. It's a sort of living-history play called *The Keeper's on Duty*.

At the base of the tower, in the old oil house, you'll find a visitor orientation center and a museum shop with books, videos, and souvenirs. Cape May Lighthouse is open from 9:00 A.M to 8:00 P.M. every day during the summer. Call to check hours for the off-season.

Delaware Bay Lighthouses

While these lighthouses are not technically on the Jersey Shore—they're on the Delaware Bayshore—they are well within driving distance for those dedicated to lighthouse-hopping. (Each is within two hours or so from some Shore town.)

East Point Lighthouse
Maurice River and the Delaware Bay, Millville
(856) 327–3714 (Maurice River Historical Society)

This remote location at the mouth of the Maurice (say Morris) River and the Delaware Bay, miles away from any sort of development, really gives visitors a sense of the isolation of the lighthouse keeper.

Insiders' Tip

New Jersey Travel & Tourism publishes an excellent brochure on state lighthouses. Call (800) VISIT NJ, ext. 0923 or go to www.visitnj.org to request this and other travel guides.

Built in 1849, the two-story red brick structure, with its weathered white paint, suffered fire and storm damage in the early 1970s. It is still undergoing restoration, but can be visited by special arrangement, when fund-raisers are held on the premises in midsummer (end of July or early August), and in October during the Lighthouse Challenge (when participants try to visit 11 lighthouses in a weekend).

Finn's Point Range Light
Supawna Meadows National Wildlife Refuge
197 Lighthouse Road, Pennsville
(856) 935–3218

Built in 1876, this odd, wrought-iron tower looks kind of like an oil well. From the top, there's a great view of the Delaware River. Finn's Point is quite close to Fort Mott State Park and is open to the public on the third Sunday of the month from April through October.

Tinicum Rear Range Lighthouse
Mantua and Second Streets, Paulsboro
(856) 423–1505, (856) 423–2545

First lit in 1880, Tinicum still shines a fixed red light to guide ships heading north to Philadelphia on the Delaware River. The 80-foot iron tower has a curious entry kiosk at its base that is also made of cast iron. The schedule varies, but summer weekends are your best bet. Call ahead before making the trip.

Revolutionary New Jersey

George Washington and the Continental Army spent almost half of the Revolutionary War in New Jersey, more time than they spent in any other state. The victories won here, in Trenton, Princeton, and Monmouth, were key events in the quest for independence, and today these and other localities have parks and historic sites where visitors can learn about and relive the early history of our democracy.

Some of these places—those relating to the Battle of Monmouth—are within the Shore area; others might be more of a daytrip. We've grouped key sites together, beginning with the ones that are most significant and closest to the Shore, in order to tell the story of these critical moments in American history. To help you keep track of the chronology, "A Timeline of the Revolutionary War in New Jersey" appears on page 148. Most of the places in this chapter are free or have a nominal admission charge.

Ten Crucial Days

Most schoolchildren have seen the famous painting of Washington crossing the Delaware River, but many adults probably don't remember why he was making the trip.

Picture the Christmas of 1776. Things were looking a lot bleaker than when the Declaration of Independence was trumpeted back in the middle of summer. The Continental Army—hungry, cold, ill-equipped, and much reduced in numbers due to disease and desertion—had little to celebrate. Washington's army had suffered a year and a half of defeats; the British had taken New York and were moving toward Philadelphia. After retreating through New Jersey, Washington stopped to regroup in Pennsylvania.

On December 25, he made his move. With 16 boats and 18 cannons, Washington crossed the ice-choked Delaware River at night, landing at Johnson's Ferry. At 4:00 A.M., the Continental Army marched to Trenton, where they surprised and defeated the garrison of Hessians (who had probably done a lot of holiday celebrating), taking more than 900 prisoners. On January 2, there was a second Battle of Trenton; once again, Washington outmaneuvered the British. The next day, Washington reached Princeton and defeated the British rear guard. The Revolution was saved.

Washington Crossing State Park
355 Washington Crossing–Pennington Road, Titusville
(609) 737–0623, (609) 737–9303 (visitors center)

Every Christmas Day, Washington's 1776 crossing of the Delaware River is reenacted here, and the recent wave of patriotism has resulted in record crowds. The event is a lively surprise for anyone expecting a dry recitation of historical facts. At the visitors center you can watch excellent films about war and view an extraordinary assemblage of Revolutionary items in the Swan Historical Foundation Collection. Curator Harry Kels Swan, a descendant of a colonial family that collected everything from letters to weapons, talks eloquently and vividly about the 10 crucial days that changed the course of the war. And if asked politely, he might show some of the precious items in his office: a piece of George Washington's coffin and an example of the first American money, coined from Martha Washington's silver tea service.

On the park grounds is the Johnson Ferry House, an 18th-century farmhouse and tavern that was probably used by Washington at the time of the crossing. Here, various aspects of life in colonial days are re-created. Depending on the time of year, colonial dames in costume might be cooking in the blazing fireplace, while the men outside make cider. If time and weather permit, you can walk part of the route the army took to Trenton, the 1½-mile Continental Lane. Summer hours are daily 8:00 A.M. to 8:00 P.M.; winter hours are 8:00 A.M. to 4:30 P.M.

Old Barracks Museum
Barrack Street, Trenton
(609) 396–1776

The beautifully restored barracks dates back to 1758; it was built for British soldiers during the French and Indian Wars, occupied by the Hessians before the Battle of Trenton, and eventually used as a hospital by the Continental Army. This is a place where history is fun—and gory enough to engage television-hardened teens. For example, a guide taking on the character of surgeon's assistant David McCaffrey gives the grisly details of how wounded limbs were amputated and how soldiers were inoculated against smallpox (with a feather quill). Chief historical interpreter Jeff Macechak might give a recruiting speech, appealing to the patriotism and youthful idealism of the crowd, then firing off a musket for emphasis.

The museum's "Point of View" section personalizes the war. Along with the historic image of Washington's crossing are

The restored Trenton barracks at the Old Barracks Museum date back to 1758; they were occupied by Hessian soldiers before the Battle of Trenton. PHOTO: LILLIAN AFRICANO

suggestions of what soldiers might have been thinking that cold and fateful night. One possibility: "Lord, let me survive this week so I may return to my home and a hot meal." Downstairs, along with an unrestored section of the original squad room, are the hands-on exhibits of the History Labs, where visitors can learn what it's like to be a researcher or an archaeologist. The museum is open daily from 10:00 A.M. to 5:00 P.M.

New Jersey State Museum
205 West State Street, Trenton
(609) 292–6464

Though this museum is filled with art treasures, cultural and natural history exhibits, and archaeology displays, many Revolutionary War buffs come here to see one thing: the replica by Robert Bruce Williams of Emmanuel Leutze's famous painting of General George Washington and his troops crossing the Delaware River. (The original is in the Metropolitan Museum of Art in Manhattan.) If you make a visit to the Barracks Museum (above), take the time to travel the short distance to this museum. The painting, which hangs in the museum auditorium, is stunning—but historically incorrect; it shows Washington in front of an American flag (which had not yet been created), crossing in fine weather during the daytime.

Elsewhere in the museum, you can further immerse yourself in the atmosphere of the period by viewing a fine collection of furniture and decorative arts of the Revolutionary War period. The museum is open Tuesday through Saturday from 9:00 A.M. to 5:00 P.M., and Sunday from noon to 5:00 P.M.

Trent House
15 Market Street, Trenton
(609) 989–3027

Trent House was a summer estate built in 1719 by William Trent, for whom Trenton is named. A wealthy Philadelphia merchant of Scottish origin, Trent was one of Philadelphia's 15 wealthiest men.

During the Revolutionary War, the house was occupied by a Dr. William Bryant, a suspected loyalist; it was known that some Hessian officers camped here, and that the cupola of the house was used as a lookout station. Like other house museums, Trent House can give you a sense of how the wealthy lived during colonial times. It's open daily from 12:30 to 4:00 P.M.

Trenton Battle Monument
North Broad and Warren Streets and Brunswick, Pennington, and Princeton Avenues, Trenton

This monument marks the spot where Washington positioned his artillery in the surprise attack on December 26, 1776.

Princeton Battlefield State Park/Clarke House
500 Mercer Road, Princeton
(609) 921–0074

On January 3, 1777, Washington's troops defeated a force of British regulars here. Today, a flag of white stars on a blue field—Washington's company flag—flies above this battleground.

Princeton wasn't the war's biggest battle, but it was one of the most fiercely fought, with heavy losses on both sides. American General Hugh Mercer, one of Washington's closest friends, was mortally wounded and died nine days later in Clarke House, located nearby. An Ionic colonnade on the battlefield marks the graves of the American and British dead.

As curator John Mills explains, "The Battles of Trenton and Princeton were the turning points of the war. The British fought extremely well. In fact, they won most of the battles. But they lost the war. For them, it was like America's Vietnam War."

Just as American veterans make pilgrimages to war sites such as Normandy, descendants of the soldiers of Britain's 17th Regiment occasionally turn up at Princeton, to visit the place where their forbears fought so valiantly.

The Clarke House, built in 1772 by Thomas Clarke, is another museum of colonial life; in addition to the living quarters, there's a display of Revolutionary War weapons, period artwork, and a collection of toy soldiers. In the room where General Mercer died, blood could be seen

Curator John Mills leads a tour of Clarke House at the Princeton Battlefield State Park. General Hugh Mercer died in the house following the battle. PHOTO: LILLIAN AFRICANO

on the floor well into the 20th century. The park is open daily, from dawn to dusk. Clarke House is open Wednesday through Saturday from 10:00 A.M. to noon, then 1:00 to 4:00 P.M.; Sunday hours are 1:00 to 4:00 P.M.

The Princeton Battle Monument
Stockton Street and Bayard Street, Princeton

Designed by sculptor Frederick MacMonnies and built in 1922, this frieze shows Washington in high relief, rising above the madness of the battle. It's dedicated to Princeton's dead from all wars.

Historic Morven
55 Stockton Street, Princeton
(609) 683–4495
www.historicmorven.org

This historic home (circa 1758) was built by Richard Stockton III, a signer of the Declaration of Independence, and his wife, Annis Boudinot Stockton, a published poet. Annis was the sister of Elias B. Boudinot, president of the Continental Congress. Though the stories can't be confirmed, it's been reported that Washington dined at the house, and that the Marquis de Lafayette visited here. The house is undergoing a renovation; when the workmen have finished, it's expected to be open Tuesday through Sunday from 10:00 A.M. to 4:00 P.M. Call ahead.

Bainbridge House
158 Nassau Street, Princeton
(609) 921–6748

Built by Job Stockton, this pretty Georgian home is one of the few remaining 18th-century houses in Princeton. Virtually all the woodwork—floors, stairs, and window frames—is original. On the first floor are three furnished exhibit rooms; upstairs is a small gift shop and the headquarters of the Princeton Historical Society. If you have questions about the house or the events that took place in Princeton, you can get them answered here; you can also pick up a pamphlet that will guide you through a walking tour of this historic area. Bainbridge House is open Tuesday through Sunday from noon to 4:00 P.M.

Nassau Hall
Nassau Street, Princeton University, Princeton

Across the street from Bainbridge House is Nassau Hall, which served as a barracks and hospital for both Continental and British troops. It was the scene of the last stand of the British in the Battle of Princeton. From June through November 1783, the Continental Congress convened in Nassau Hall.

Two Hard Winters

The American Revolution was won more by sheer endurance and spirit than by battles fought and won. Without proper clothing and nourishment, Washington and his army spent two hard winters in Morristown, New Jersey.

Morristown National Historical Park
Washington Place, Morristown
(973) 539–2085

George Washington and the Continental Army spent two frigid, disease-ridden winters in Morristown, which came to be known as the "Military Capital of the Revolution." After the brilliant victories at Trenton and Princeton, the British retrenched to New Brunswick, while Washington and the Continental Army arrived here on January 6 and hunkered down until the spring. Washington also spent the following winter here, in the Jockey Hollow Encampment Area. That second winter (1779–80) was the most severe of the 18th century, and the troops suffered greatly from cold, hunger, and diseases, namely dysentery, yellow fever, and smallpox. The enlisted men slept in huts or tents, and sometimes boiled shoes for soup when food was scarce.

Within the park is Fort Nonsense, the fortified hilltop from which sentries could watch for British raiding parties, and the Jacob Ford mansion, which became Washington's headquarters and a home to some of his officers. Near the mansion is the Washington Headquarters Museum, where you can revisit lessons you learned in school—like the fact that Benedict Arnold was tried for war profiteering in a

Molly Pitcher

Mary Ludwig Hays, called Molly, was married to Pennsylvania artilleryman William Hays and followed his unit into battle, fetching water to cool down the cannon barrels as they became overheated as well as the throats of the patriots. The Battle of Monmouth took place during a late-June heat wave, when temperatures reached 100 degrees, and men on both sides collapsed from heat exhaustion, including William Hays. Molly, the pitcher bearer, took her husband's place at the cannon and helped to forestall a Continental retreat.

local tavern, found not guilty, but reprimanded for misusing his office as military governor. It was after this trial that he turned traitor.

The park is open daily from 9:00 A.M. to 5:00 P.M. After you visit the park, you might want to visit the following four nearby sites, which all have Revolutionary War connections.

Old Dutch Parsonage
65 Washington Place, Somerville
(908) 725–1015

This was the birthplace and home of General Frelinghuysen, a member of George Washington's staff during the Revolutionary War. It is open Wednesday through Saturday from 10:00 A.M. to noon, then 1:00 to 4:00 P.M.; Sunday hours are 1:00 to 4:00 P.M.

Wallace House
38 Washington Place, Somerville
(908) 725–1015

A short distance from the Old Dutch Parsonage is Wallace House, which was leased by Washington as his headquarters during the winter encampment of 1778–79.

Rockingham
84 Laurel Avenue, Highway 603, Kingston
(609) 921–8835

George Washington occupied this 18th-century house from August 23 to November 10, 1783, while the Continental

Congress was meeting at Nassau Hall in nearby Princeton. It was here that he wrote his farewell orders.

The house was moved in July 2001 to this 27-acre site; it features artifacts and memorabilia (including war regalia and dragoon helmets) collected over a hundred years. An extensive restoration and refurnishing are under way. The intention is to expand all the interpretive programs and to make this site a living-history farm with a children's museum and a gift shop.

John Parker Tavern
2 Morristown Road, Bernardsville (Somerset County)
(908) 766–0118

This crossroads tavern was constructed in the mid-18th century. It was frequently used by Continental troops, including General "Mad" Anthony Wayne. The building now houses the Bernardsville Public Library.

Retreat and Defeat

In order to prevent the British from gaining river access to New England, the Americans built Fort Lee and Fort Washington on opposite sides of the Hudson River. But the colonists were unable to defend these forts from the better-trained and better-equipped British and German soldiers. On November 16, 1776, Fort Washington in

New York fell. Two days later, Washington evacuated his troops from Fort Lee in Northern New Jersey and headed west, across New Jersey, through Historic New Bridge Landing, crisscrossing the state from the Hudson River to the Delaware, eventually reaching Pennsylvania.

Fort Lee Historic Park
Hudson Terrace, Fort Lee
(201) 461–1776

This is a splendid park to visit in good weather, even if you don't have an abiding interest in Revolutionary War history. From several overlooks, you'll see spectacular views of the George Washington Bridge, the Hudson River, and the New York skyline. (People who live in the area pay a great deal of money to live in apartments with similar views.) After you've enjoyed the outdoors, adjourn to the two-story visitors center, where you can watch a video detailing the park's history and view exhibits that tell the story of Washington's retreat. The Fort Lee Revolutionary War Monument is located on a point where the original outworks of the old fort were located; it is believed to mark the original camp occupied by General Lee. The park is open dawn to dusk daily; the visitors center is open Wednesday through Sunday from 10:00 A.M. to 5:00 P.M.

Historic New Bridge Landing
1209 Main Street, River Edge
(201) 487–1739

The wooden bridge here helped the Continental Army flee to safety. Three historic houses grace the park, the 1774 Campbell-Christie House (201–343–9492), the 1678 Demarest House (201–261–0012), and the Steuben House (201–487–1739), a 1713 Bergen Dutch sandstone mansion presented to Prussian baron General Friedrich von Steuben in gratitude after the war.

Baylor Massacre Burial Site
Red Oak Drive, River Vale and Old Tappan Roads, River Vale
(201) 646–2780

On September 28, 1778, British troops under the command of Major General Sir Charles Grey attacked the Third Dragoons of Virginia. Five patriots were killed. Here, alongside the Hackensack River, is a small park memorializing their burial site.

Washington Rock State Park
Washington Rock Road, Green Brook Township
(201) 915–3401

From the vantage point of Washington Rock, there is a 30-mile panoramic view of the valley—which made this location a valuable lookout point for General Washington in June 1777.

Drake House Museum
602 West Front Street, Plainfield
(908) 755–5831

Here, Washington consulted with his officers during and after the Battle of Short Hills, which was fought over the entire Plainfield area June 25–27, 1777. The museum is open Sunday from 2:00 to 4:00 P.M., Thursday and Friday by appointment.

Dey Mansion
199 Totowa Road, Wayne
(973) 696–1776

Built between 1740 and 1750, this mansion served as Washington's headquarters in 1780. It is open Wednesday, Thursday, and Friday from 1:00 to 4:00 P.M., and Saturday and Sunday from 10:00 A.M. to noon and from 1:00 to 4:00 P.M.

Defense of the Delaware River

To protect the city of Philadelphia against a British attack by sea, the Continental Congress ordered the development of a river defense. Three land batteries were erected: Fort Mifflin on the Pennsylvania side of the Delaware River, Fort Mercer in Red Bank, New Jersey (not to be confused with Red Bank in Monmouth County), and a fortification at Billingsport, New Jersey. The remains of Fort Mercer are found at Red Bank Battlefield Park.

A Timeline of the Revolutionary War in New Jersey

For those of us who don't remember our American history as well as we should, this chronology will help place the events of the Revolution in context and clarify the significance of some of the historic sites discussed in this chapter.

1776

May 10, 1776—The Second Continental Congress convenes in Philadelphia.

June 21, 1776—The New Jersey Provincial Congress at Burlington votes 53–3 to sever ties with Great Britain.

July 4, 1776—The Continental Congress approves the Declaration of Independence in Philadelphia.

July, 1776—Washington's troops construct Fort Lee on the New Jersey side of the Hudson River and Fort Washington in New York.

November 16, 1776—Fort Washington falls to the British, and Washington evacuates Fort Lee.

November 20, 1776—Washington leads 2,000 troops from Fort Lee across the Hackensack River to New Bridge Landing and Steuben House.

November 23–December 3, 1776—Washington continues his retreat west across New Jersey, passing through Princeton, to the Delaware River.

December 7–8, 1776—Washington and his troops cross the Delaware River. The British and Hessians reach Princeton and Trenton.

December 13, 1776—General Lee is captured by the British in Basking Ridge.

December 25, 1776—On Christmas night, Washington and 2,400 troops cross the Delaware River and land at Johnson's Ferry, now Washington Crossing State Park.

December 26, 1776—In a predawn strike, the Continental Army marches to Trenton, surprising the Hessians in an attack at the Old Barracks in Trenton.

1777

January 1, 1777—Lord Cornwallis takes command of the British Army in Princeton.

January 2, 1777—The Battle of Trenton rages with heavy fighting along the Assunpink Creek.

January 3, 1777—At the Battle of Princeton, Washington strikes the British rear, and the Americans defeat a small British force.

January 6–May 28, 1777—Washington's troops spend a cold winter at Morristown.

September 26, 1777—The British take Philadelphia.

September–October, 1777—Washington builds up defenses at Red Bank on the lower Delaware River.

October 22, 1777—The Americans defeat attacking Hessian troops, then abandon Fort Mercer.

November 15, 1777—The British take Fort Mifflin in Pennsylvania.

December, 1777–March, 1778—Washington and 12,000 troops survive a bitter winter at Valley Forge, Pennsylvania.

1778

March 21, 1778—British and Loyalist troops raid Hancock's Bridge and American troops die at Hancock House massacre.

June 28, 1778—With the British retreating across New Jersey, Americans claim a critical victory at the Battle of Monmouth.

December 11, 1778—Washington sets up headquarters in Wallace House, while his troops spend the winter in Watchung Mountains in Middlebrook.

1779

August 19, 1979—Major Henry Lee attacks the British fort at Paulus Hood in Jersey City.

October 28, 1779—British Major John Simcoe leads raid through Elizabethtown to Bound Brook and Somerset Courthouse in Millstone.

December 1, 1779—Washington moves his army into winter quarters at Morristown for the most severe winter of the century.

1780

June 7–23, 1780—The Battle of Springfield sees the invasion of Elizabethtown and Springfield.

July 1–8, 1780—Washington establishes headquarters at Dey Mansion in Wayne.

1783

June 30, 1783—Congress leaves Independence Hall in Philadelphia and reconvenes at Nassau Hall in Princeton.

August 23, 1783—George and Martha Washington arrive at Rockingham.

September 3, 1783—The United States of America and England sign a Peace Treaty in Paris, France.

November 2, 1783—Washington writes his Farewell Address at Rockingham.

Fort Mercer/Red Bank Battlefield Park
100 Hessian Avenue, National Park
(856) 853-5120

Hold the fort at any cost, Washington ordered Colonel Christopher Greene in October 1777. The British had already won the Battle of Brandywine in September, but in order to move their warships and supply boats, they needed to destroy both Fort Mifflin and Fort Mercer.

To defend Mercer with only 400 men, Greene called on local farmers to supply him with logs. After more than 200 were gathered, he ordered his men to tie the logs together in sections of two, three, or four, then sheath them in iron. Next, Greene had his men float these stockades, or chevaux-de-frise, across the river, weight them, and anchor them so that the points of the logs rested about four feet below the surface—where they could pierce the bottoms of the King's wooden ships.

The second element in Greene's strategy was to build a second inner wall to the fort, which would reduce the perimeter to be defended and free up additional men to fight. The strategy worked; the American casualties in the Battle of Red Bank were 14 dead and 23 wounded; the attacking Hessians lost 514 men. Though the British eventually reached Philadelphia, they did so at great cost—which gave Washington's armies yet another sorely needed boost in morale.

The Battle of Red Bank gave the American cause yet another heroine, Ann Whitall. Ann and her husband, James, lived in a comfortable brick mansion overlooking the Delaware River. Parts of the Whitall property were commandeered by the colonial army in 1777. When the battle began and the house came under cannon fire, Ann refused to leave, saying, "I'll be needed after the battle is over." She was indeed needed, for the house became a hospital for the wounded. Ann tended the injured soldiers, both American and Hessian—and earned the nickname "Angel of the Battle of Red Bank."

The fort eventually had to be evacuated, and the Whitalls had to leave their home, but only temporarily. Though the house was looted and badly damaged, James and Ann returned. They, and later five generations of their descendants, occupied the property until 1868.

If you visit Red Bank Battlefield Park today, you'll find outdoor signs explaining the events during the battle, as well as sections of the chevaux-de-frise. The first floor of the Whitall house is open to the public; here you'll glimpse the lifestyle of an affluent merchant-farmer—and see a representation of the field hospital where Ann Whitall helped tend the wounded.

Though the park has a somewhat somber history, it is today a beautiful place. If you bring a lunch, you can picnic in one of the pavilions located in a grove of trees with a panoramic view of the Delaware River.

The park is open daily, dawn to dusk. The Whitall house is open Wednesday to Friday from 9:00 A.M. to noon and 1:00 to 4:00 P.M., and Saturday and Sunday from 1:00 to 4:00 P.M.; it is closed weekends November through March.

Hancock House
1 Front Street, Hancocks Bridge

Judge William Hancock and members of the American garrison were massacred here after being surprised by a force of British regulars and local loyalists. The house was built in 1734 by Judge Hancock's father. Call Fort Mott State Park at (609) 935-3218 to arrange a tour.

Laird's AppleJack, the Spirit of Early America

They say an army travels on its stomach, and Washington's army, plagued with drunkenness, barely rose without a pint. Since grapes and grain to make wine and whiskey were hard to come by in the colonies, the drinks of choice were hard cider and brandy distilled from apples, which were abundant.

The Laird family of Colts Neck, New Jersey, a town still known for its orchards, has been producing liquor made from apples ever since William Laird arrived from Scotland in 1698. Early stagecoach travelers could stop for a jug at the Colts Neck Inn, built in 1717 at the crossroads of present-day County Road (Highway 537) and New Jersey Highway 34 by a Laird relation.

During the American Revolution, Robert Laird was a soldier under General Washington, and when the army was in the vicinity (Battle of Monmouth), the Lairds did their bit by supplying the thirsty troops. Coincidently, Washington had written to the Laird family some years earlier, around 1760, to get their recipe for "cyder," which he began making.

Apple brandy spread west in the 1820s, with a preacher named John Chapman, a.k.a. Johnny Appleseed, and even appeared on a saloon license issued to Abraham Lincoln in 1833. Laird's distillery survived Prohibition by making sweet cider and apple brandy for "medicinal" purposes, and so today, Americans can enjoy the 100-proof applejack that got the patriots through those long, cold winters.

The Tea Burning Monument
Main Street and Market Square, Greenwich

Everyone knows about the Boston Tea Party, but few people realize that New Jersey had a tea-related protest, too. In December 1774, protestors burned a shipment of tea stored in the cellar of Dan Bowen, a British sympathizer. This monument was erected in 1908 by the State of New Jersey to mark the site.

Potter's Tavern Museum
49-51 West Broad Street, Bridgeton
(856) 455-5529

During the winter of 1775, it was at this tavern, a popular meeting place of the period, that the *Plain Dealer*, a handwritten newspaper supporting the struggle for independence, first appeared.

The Battle of Monmouth

In May of 1778, the British commander, General Sir Henry Clinton, was in Philadelphia. After France joined the war on the American side, strategy dictated that he reinforce New York City. On June 18, he began to evacuate Philadelphia, heading northeast across New Jersey with 20,000 troops and a 12-mile-long baggage train.

The British advance was slow and hard, their movement hampered by hot weather and American sabotage in the form of burned bridges, muddied wells, and roads blocked by felled trees. On June 26, the British reached Monmouth.

Pursuing the enemy from Valley Forge with a force of 15,000 men, Washington arrived in Englishtown on June 27, 1778. He ordered Major General Charles Lee to attack the British rear the following morning with his advance guard of 5,000 men.

General Lee thought that the British were better trained, and he did not want to engage them. Washington overruled him, believing that the British on the move were vulnerable. Reluctantly, Lee engaged the enemy on June 28. About mid-morning, he saw an opportunity to hem in 1,500 British soldiers, but was surprised by an additional 8,000 red coats, and his forces retreated in confusion.

Washington arrived to rally his demoralized troops. It has been reported that at one point, Lee protested that the Americans were not able to stand against the British. An enraged Washington replied: "Sir, they are able, and by God they shall do it!"

For the rest of the brutally hot day, the bloody conflict raged. Washington expected the fighting to continue the following day, but the British pulled up stakes and headed for New York during the night.

Monmouth was the largest land artillery battle of the war, and the last major battle of the north. Though losses were probably about even, it was a major political victory for Washington. Holding its ground against the feared British Army also gave the Continental Army a huge boost in morale.

A postscript: After the war, General Lee demanded a court-martial in an attempt to clear himself of any taint of misconduct. He was court-martialed and suspended from the army for a year. When he refused the suspension, he was removed from the army.

Monmouth Battlefield State Park
347 Freehold-Englishtown Road, Manalapan
(732) 462-9616

Every year on June 28, or the weekend closest to that date, there is a reenactment of the Battle of Monmouth here. One of the largest battle reenactments in the country, it features cannons and musket fire, authentically clothed soldiers in the field, as well as women, children, and merchants in period garb. Throughout the day, there are infantry, cavalry, and artillery demonstrations in the natural amphitheater next to the visitors center.

During the rest of the year, you'll find this 1,810-acre park preserves a splendid rural 18th-century landscape of hilly farmland and hedgerows, with miles of hiking and horseback riding trails, a picnic area, a playground, and a food concession. Deer hunting is allowed, with a permit, and in winter you can cross-country ski and sled.

On park grounds is Craig House, a restored farmhouse of the period, which was home to John and Ann Craig and their three children. During the battle, the Craig House was used as a field hospital by both armies. Legend has it that, before the battle, the Craigs hid their silverware at the bottom of their well before fleeing for safety. In the heat, British troops drained the well and found the silver.

A landscape restoration program here re-created the fences and lanes that existed at the time of the Revolutionary War. The exterior of the nearby 1745 Rhea-Applegate House has been restored, and the 1730s Sutfin-Herbert House, also close by, is next. The park is open from dawn to dusk daily; the Friends of Monmouth Battlefield give guided tours of the Craig House on Sundays during the summer and fall (call ahead for times).

Old Tennent Church
Adjacent to the Monmouth Battlefield, Tennent Road, north of Highway 522
(732) 446-6299

This Presbyterian Church, which was built in 1751-53, served as a temporary hospital for the American wounded. According to some stories, the church walls were pierced by musket balls during the battle. Near the church are monuments to the battle's war dead, including Colonel Henry Monckton, the highest-ranking British officer to die on Monmouth Battlefield.

The Old Tennent Church still holds Sunday services at 11:00 A.M., and visitors are welcome. If you'd like to explore the grounds, there's a new interpretive tape outside that you can use as a guide.

Covenhoven House
150 West Main Street, Freehold
(732) 462–1466

This comfortable colonial dwelling, built in 1752, was home to William and Elizabeth Covenhoven. The house, which is open to visitors, is included here because it was briefly occupied by British General Sir Henry Clinton before the Battle of Monmouth in June of 1778. You can read more about the house in the Attractions chapter. Covenhoven House is open May through September. The hours are Tuesday, Thursday, and Sunday from 1:00 to 4:00 P.M., and Saturday from 10:00 A.M. to 4:00 P.M.

Monmouth County Historical Association
70 Court Street, Freehold
(732) 462–1466
www.monmouth.com/~mcha

If you'd like to know more about the Battle of Monmouth and all the colorful characters who played a role in shaping American history, the headquarters of the Monmouth County Historical Association can be a valuable resource. Not only is there a permanent exhibition about the battle, but you will also find knowledgeable guides, changing exhibits, and fascinating archival material. The museum is open Tuesday through Saturday from 10:00 A.M. to 4:00 P.M., and Sunday from 1:00 to 4:00 P.M. The library and archives are open Wednesday through Saturday from 10:00 A.M. to 4:00 P.M. Across Court Street, you'll find the Monmouth Battle Monument, a depiction of Liberty atop a column, dedicated in 1884.

Other Revolutionary War Sites at the Shore

Sandy Hook Lighthouse
Gateway National Recreation Area,
Sandy Hook
(732) 872–5970

Though Sandy Hook is covered in the Lighthouses chapter, we mention it here because the lighthouse was occupied by the British during the war—and subsequently bombarded by Washington's troops.

Allen House
Sycamore Avenue and Broad Street (N.J. Highway 35 South), Shrewsbury
(732) 462–1466

Located at Shrewsbury's historic four corners, the Allen House was a tavern during the war years and before. Among the exhibits at this museum is one on the Battle of Monmouth. (For a fuller description of Allen House, see the Attractions chapter.)

Living-History Farms and Historic Villages

For kids who think that all food comes shrink-wrapped in plastic, or adults who can't remember when it didn't, a visit to one of New Jersey's living-history farms is a wake-up call to how good we've got it. Imagine having to chop wood and build a fire in the stove before you could get a cup of coffee! At these farms—Howell, Fosterfields, and Longstreet—workers in period clothes tend their animals and till the soil using 19th-century methods and equipment. Sometimes they even offer visitors the chance to pitch in with the chores.

A visit to a historic village is like a trip in a time machine. Seeing people in period costumes working and otherwise going about their daily routines really brings to life a bygone era in a way that just seeing some worn and rusty tools in a museum display case simply can't. Some of the villages and farms here date all the way back to the colonial era, while others offer a snapshot of life in the early Industrial Age, when bog iron was a high-tech industry.

Here at the Shore, folks have always looked to the ocean for their livelihoods. So it's fitting that one local living-history museum, Tuckerton Seaport, celebrates our maritime heritage and helps to pass on some of the seafaring know-how of previous generations.

With the exception of Cold Spring Village and Tuckerton, which each have an $8.00 entrance fee, admission to the places in this chapter is free or less than $5.00.

Batsto Historic Village
Wharton State Forest, Hammonton
(609) 561-3262

Imagine scattered 19th-century iron-workers' cottages, a sawmill, a tiny post office, a modest general store, and other historic structures, all set in a majestic forest, and you have a pretty good picture of Batsto Village. Located in Wharton State Forest, which is part of the Pinelands National Reserve, Batsto is free of honking autos, billboards, strip malls, and fast-food restaurants. The historic site is a moment frozen in time, reflecting both the early Industrial Age and this region's agricultural period.

Founded in 1766 by Charles Read, the most noted ironmaster in West Jersey prior to the Revolution, Batsto became the site of the Batsto Iron Works, which supplied Washington's Continental Army during the American Revolution. In the late 18th century, William Richards bought the ironworks and switched to the production of window glass when the iron industry

began to fail. When the glass industry also declined some 90 years later, Philadelphia financier/industrialist Joseph Wharton bought the property and converted it into a "gentleman's farm." He built the sawmill and the underground silo, and enlarged the mansion. In 1954, the State of New Jersey bought the entire village, which is listed on the National Register of Historic Places.

Today Batsto's 33 historic buildings are like time capsules. Visit the workers' simple cottages, which typically had three rooms downstairs and two rooms upstairs. During the Wharton era, the rent was just two dollars a month. Stroll to the post office, which opened in 1852. It still flies the 32-star American flag—and is only one of three post offices in the country where you can have your stamps hand-canceled. Because of the site's historic significance, no zip code is required here.

Move on to the general store. The labels on the goods are strange and unfamiliar—but if you have great-grandparents, they might remember Harlon's Baking Powder,

Batsto Village is a restored 19th-century ironworkers' village set in majestic Wharton Forest. PHOTO: LILLIAN AFRICANO

Flaccus Brothers' Catsup, or Brick's Nonpareil Mincemeat.

Peek into the sawmill. The giant antique saw can still cut through heavy logs as if they were made of cardboard. On weekends, the resident potter and weaver might demonstrate their crafts, harkening back to a time when people made the clothes they wore and the utensils they used. Whenever his schedule allows, the blacksmith fires up his forge. There are barns and stables, of course, as well as a piggery, a wood house, and an ice and milk house.

At the heart of Batsto is the mansion that was home to generations of ironmasters until it was bought by Joseph Wharton. The original house dates back to the mid-17th century, but when Wharton expanded it, he transformed it into a much grander Italianate-style home. Today 14 of the 32 rooms are open to the public, including parlors, bedrooms, the kitchen, the library, and servants' quarters. Reflecting the grand entertaining that was done here, the dining area has 14-foot ceilings, a gorgeous crystal chandelier, and a table that seats 22. The fireplace is a reminder that these old houses were often cold and drafty.

At the visitor center, there's a gift shop and an exhibit area featuring such artifacts as the Stewart quilt, which escaped the village fire of 1874. Batsto is open year-round except for New Year's Day, Thanksgiving, and Christmas. The grounds are open from dawn to dusk, and most of the buildings are open from 9:00 A.M. to 4:30 P.M. However, the mansion has reduced hours during the winter months, so call ahead.

Historic Allaire Village
Highway 524, Wall Township
(732) 919-3500
www.allairevillage.org

The bog-iron industry is long dead, but Allaire Village brings to life the days in the 1830s when the furnaces roared and James P. Allaire's Howell Iron Works was a major industrial center. Allaire, you may know, was the New York brass-founder who created the air chamber for Robert

Fulton's steamship *Clermont*—and later for the transatlantic steamship *Savannah*.

Allaire purchased this land, which had large quantities of bog iron, and set up the ironworks to supply his engine works in New York. At one time more than 500 workers lived here.

When the bog-iron industry died, the workers left, and the village declined. The land was bought by Arthur Brisbane, one of William Randolph Hearst's editors, and later was donated by his widow to the state.

Today you can spend a pleasant few hours touring the village and enjoying its wooded setting. Start at the visitor center, which occupies two of the original row houses. Learn about the bog-iron industry and see a slide show about the village. In another of the row houses, you'll find period furnishings, linens, and toys. The Episcopal Church that Allaire built for his workers was free (other churches charged pew rents), and today it's a popular wedding site for couples who want to be married in a romantic period setting.

As you explore, you'll see the stream-fed millpond that supplied power for the mill, the 18th-century farmhouse that housed the works' manager, the working blacksmith shop, the general store, the bakery, and other elements of village life. The grounds are inviting, and you can stroll among the laurel, sweet gum, and holly, or enjoy a picnic lunch.

We like Allaire because there are educational programs and special events all year long: antique shows, flea markets, car shows, re-enactments, and more. A park favorite is the vintage Pine Creek Railroad, the first operating steam train exhibit in New Jersey. If you'd like a ride, call (732) 938-5524 for a current schedule. The park also has a wonderful nature center and campgrounds. From May through Labor Day, the village is open daily from 10:00 A.M. to 5:00 P.M. Hours are abbreviated the remainder of the year; call ahead.

Historic Cold Spring Village
720 U.S. Highway 9, Cape May
(609) 898–2300
www.hcsv.org

The sparkling water bubbling out of the ground in a salt marsh near Cape May was called Cold Spring; it was a precious commodity in days long past, especially since there was no freshwater spring south of it in Cape May. The village of Cold Spring grew up near the water, and when Cape May became a popular resort, the village supplied the cottages and hotels with fresh produce during the summer months; it even delivered water from the spring before the resort's own waterworks was built. The waters of Cold Spring were said to have healing powers, especially for kidney diseases and rheumatism.

What you'll find today on this 22-acre wooded site is a 19th-century open-air living-history museum with 25 restored buildings. Costumed interpreters ply their trades—spinning and weaving, farming and gardening, making paper and so on—demonstrating life during the mid-1800s in a rural South Jersey town. Women prepare meals over an open hearth, men work tin or wood, and the innkeeper entertains one and all with oft-told tales. Children will get a kick out of the strict discipline imposed in the one-room schoolhouse, and grown-ups may feel a twinge of nostalgia for the days when the jail was used not as a prison, but as a place where men too drunk to get home could sleep it off.

During the summer, the village has a busy schedule of weekend family-friendly events: a Revolutionary War weekend, a Civil War weekend, a Native American weekend, an antique auto show, children's festivals, and musical events. The village has a restaurant, bakery, and ice-cream parlor. It is open June through most of September from 10:00 A.M. to 4:30 P.M. daily.

Adjoining the village is a nature trail at Bradner's Run, a freshwater stream dividing the village from adjoining land. You can pick up a free brochure for a self-guided walk at the U.S. Highway 9 or Seashore Road gatehouse. As you explore this swamp forest, you'll find sweet gum and swamp maples, white cedars, and other trees; keep an eye out for white-tailed deer, raccoons, possums, skunks, foxes, and ever-present birds.

Historic Walnford and Crosswick Creek Park
Walnford Road, off Highway 539, Allentown
(609) 259–6275

At the heart of Crosswick Creek Park is the 36-acre historic district of Walnford. This former mill village consists of Walnford House, the 1774 Georgian-style mansion that was home to the Waln family; an 1879 carriage house; an 1873 gristmill; and various outbuildings. Surrounding the village are more than 1,000 undeveloped acres of parkland, purchased by the county to protect the water table. There are no trails, so this wilderness is suitable for admiring, rather than trekking.

As the village represents some 270 years of history, there's a big range of interpretive programs for all ages, from archaeology to papermaking. You can visit any day from 8:00 A.M. to 4:30 P.M.; the house is open from 11:00 A.M. to 4:00 P.M., and the gristmill operates on weekends from April to November. There's a brochure and map to guide you, as well as staff to answer your questions.

Longstreet Farm
Holmdel Park, Roberts and Longstreet Roads
Holmdel
(732) 946–3758

Longstreet Farm, with its 495 acres assembled by Hendrick Longstreet in 1806 from several smaller properties, was among the most prosperous farms in Monmouth County. The farm remained in the Longstreet family until it was purchased by the county in 1967. Among Longstreet's outbuildings are a well house, which covers a 30-foot well; a chicken house; a corn crib; a cow house; and a potato house. A display in the carriage house includes farm scenes and illustrations of community life in the 1890s.

The farmhouse, which was built in three sections between 1775 and 1840, has 14 rooms. The nine rooms open to the public include the back parlor, where the gentlemen of the house retired for cigars and brandy; the sitting room, where ladies might write letters or play cards; and the kitchen, which boasted such "modern" conveniences as apple peelers, egg poachers, fruit presses, and waffle irons.

Longstreet has a full program of activities such as blacksmithing demonstrations, quilting bees, and an annual Halloween party. From Memorial Day to Labor Day, the farm is open daily from 10:00 A.M. to 4:00 P.M. The farmhouse is open weekends and holidays, March through December, from noon to 3:30 P.M.

Tuckerton Seaport
120 West Main Street, Tuckerton
(609) 296–8868
www.tuckertonseaport.org

Among New Jersey's living-history sites, Tuckerton Seaport is one of the gems. The seaport was the first American port of entry chartered by President George Washington in 1790. (Boston and Philadelphia had been previously chartered by England's King George III.)

The seaport you'll see today is the dream come true of a group of southern Ocean County sportsmen who feared that progress and development in the area would drive the traditions of bay life into extinction. Their first thought was to buy some land and create a gunning club, a place to teach the baymen's tradition of waterfowling. That modest goal lead to a bigger one. So today we have a working seaport village and museum that showcase the environment, folklore, and rich maritime history of the southern Jersey Shore.

You could easily spend a half-day here, strolling along the boardwalk and exploring the buildings that bring to life the men and women who lived and worked on the water.

Visit the Tucker's Island Lighthouse to see how New Jersey's lighthouse keepers lived. Peek into buildings with colorful names like Napoleon Kelly's Oyster House, Jay C. Parker's Decoy Carving Shop, and Parsons' Clam & Oyster House, and learn about the whalers and shrimpers, the oystermen and the clammers. Find out why Tuckerton was once known as "Clamtown"—and learn how to catch clams by "treading" or "tonging." Watch decoy carvers work in styles that are generations old. See how the famous Barnegat Bay Sneakbox was constructed and find out why its unique features were suited for the shallows of the bay and tidal creeks. There is much more, of course, including the Skinner/Donnelly Houseboat, where you can get a glimpse of the houseboating lifestyle, one that's all but forgotten.

Tucker's Island Lighthouse at Tuckerton Seaport re-creates Ocean County's maritime history.
PHOTO: COURTESY OF OCEAN COUNTY PUBLIC AFFAIRS

If you get hungry, you can dine on seafood or burgers. And if you like crowds and festivities, visit the seaport during one of the special events: the Annual Seafood Festival in June, the Annual Classic Boat Show in July, or the Bayman's Annual Boat Parade in August.

In spring and summer, the seaport is open daily from 10:00 A.M. to 5:00 P.M.; in the off-season, it is open Wednesday through Friday from 10:00 A.M. to 4:00 P.M., and Saturday and Sunday from 10:00 A.M. to 5:00 P.M.

Wheaton Village
1501 Glasstown Road, Millville
(800) 998–4552
www.wheatonvillage.org

"Down in southern New Jersey, they make glass. By day and by night, the fires burn on in Millville, and bid the sand let in the light." So wrote Carl Sandburg in "In Reckless Ecstacy." The fires still burn in Millville and they are still making glass. If you have an interest in glass, you'll find

that Wheaton Village is a leading resource. In addition to glass, you'll find a variety of arts and crafts items here—including ceramic, carved-wood, and tin pieces, paintings, and folk art.

The Museum of American Glass, which is housed in a 20,000-square-foot Victorian-style building, is the largest museum in the country dedicated to the history of American-made glass. The exhibits, chronologically displayed, begin with a 1739 piece from the Wistarburgh Glass Works, America's first glass factory. Some pieces are decorative, some functional. You'll find humble bottles and beautiful work by Tiffany and Steuben. There's a collection of some 300 paperweights—and such curiosities as the world's largest bottle, created on September 26, 1992, in the village's glass factory. The bottle, featured in the *Guinness Book of World Records,* is seven feet, eight inches tall; it can hold 188 gallons.

The museum offers daily guided tours at 2:30 P.M. You can also wander through on your own and visit the research library, which holds more than 2,000 books, documents, and photographs on glassmaking history.

The T. C. Wheaton Glass factory is a working facility modeled after the original 1888 factory. You can watch one of the three narrated daily shows, and then try your hand at glassblowing; under the guidance of an expert artisan, visitors can make original paperweights. There are special programs for schoolchildren. The factory is also an important resource for emerging glass artists, who teach and serve in various programs here.

After you've toured the museum and the glass factory, visit Crafts and Trades Row to observe regional New Jersey crafts being created. Watch potters turn lumps of clay into vases and bowls, see a glassworker manipulate glass rods in intense flame to make colorful miniatures, and look on as an expert carver shapes a block of wood into a striking decoy. On weekends, the tinsmith demonstrates his craft; his wares are sold at the General Store.

Kids of school age will get a kick out of the Centre Grove Schoolhouse. Built in 1876, this single-room school had students in the first through the ninth grades; on Sundays, it served as the local church. The original school bell still hangs in the tower.

Love to shop? There is a lot to buy here, at the Gallery of American Craft (which has five or six exhibitions each year), the Arthur Gorham Paperweight Shop, and the Brownstone Emporium. The Christmas Shop is open year-round, selling exquisite glass ornaments and everything you need for the holiday season. The General Store offers dry goods, children's games, penny candy—and lots of nostalgia.

The Down Jersey Folklife Center, which opened in June 1995, is concerned with preserving the cultural heritage of southern New Jersey, including such living traditions as African-American oyster-shucking songs and Pinelands fox-chasing. The areas that are the focus of the center's research includes two Shore counties (Atlantic and Cape May), as well as six others that make up the southernmost part of the state, from the Pine Barrens to the Delaware Bay. Programs at the Folklife Center and Wheaton Village include ongoing exhibits that highlight traditional artists and area folklife. They also sponsor performances and demonstrations by area musicians, dancers, and craftspeople. From April through December, the village is open daily from 10:00 A.M. to 5:00 P.M.; in January and February, it's open Friday through Sunday from 10:00 A.M. to 5:00 P.M.; in March, the hours are Wednesday through Sunday from 10:00 A.M. to 5:00 P.M. The village is closed on Easter, Thanksgiving, Christmas, and New Year's Day.

Road Trip

The following two destinations are about an hour's drive from Shore towns in Monmouth County.

Fosterfields Farm and The Willows
73 Kahdena Road, Morristown
(973) 326-7645

Fosterfields Farm in Morristown has a somewhat grander pedigree than Titusville's Howell Farm (see page 160). The manor house, called The Willows, was built in 1854 by General Joseph Warren Revere (grandson of Paul Revere) for the princely sum of $7,100. Its Gothic Revival style and lavish landscaping made The Willows a standout, even among neighboring Vanderbilt and Rockefeller properties.

During the docent-guided tours of the house (which was later occupied by the affluent Foster family), you may hear about the customs of the local gentry, including the use of calling cards, folded a certain way to invite a visit or black-bordered to indicate a caller in mourning. The carriage house also reflects the Fosters' affluence: this was a three-carriage family, with a vehicle for everyday travel, a fancier one for Sunday, and a sporty tandem gig for showing off. On the farm you'll see butter being churned, corn being ground for chicken feed, and perhaps a ram relaxing in the sun. A 10-minute film and photo display give a vivid picture of life on this gentleman's farm.

Demonstrations of old-time activities ranging from cooking to blacksmithing to

At Fosterfields, the land is farmed the old-fashioned way. PHOTO: LILLIAN AFRICANO

flower pressing run from April through October. Since General Revere was a retired Civil War officer, there's a Civil War weekend in October, featuring infantry drilling, skirmishes, and the demonstrations of combat medicine of the time. The Willows is also open during the first weekend in December, when Morristown's finest historic house museums are decorated for the holidays. The farm is open Wednesday through Saturday from 10:00 A.M. to 5:00 P.M., and Sunday from noon to 5:00 P.M. It is closed November through March.

Howell Living History Farm
101 Hunter Road, Titusville
(609) 737-3299.

Visit the Howell Living History Farm in Titusville and you'll glimpse what life might have been like in 1900, when horses and buggies traveled the lanes of Pleasant Valley. In those days, farm families worked sunup till sundown, and the horse was the most powerful farm machine. Sheep graze peacefully, but everyone else will be hard at work. Near the stable, you might see a field hand shoveling manure into a spreader. Another might be plowing for winter wheat, sitting on an old-fashioned plow pulled by two draft horses, making slow, steady progress through a large field.

Stroll this pastoral setting and you'll see a "snake" fence, built by visitors and volunteers. If you ask, a staff member will inform you that the "snake" was more popular with local farmers than the post and rail fence because it was stronger and easier to build.

If there's a school outing going on, you might spot groups of kids visiting the hen house to see where eggs really come from. If it's fall, they might be lining up for a hayride. Howell's horses are really big; most of them come from Amish country in Pennsylvania, as does the farm's buggy.

The pond looks like a setting for a Winslow Homer painting, replete with ducks and geese. During the cold winter months, when the water freezes, slabs of ice are cut and stored in the icehouse, then covered with sawdust for insulation. Back in the days before refrigerators, Howell was called the "ice farm" because it provided neighbors with chunks of ice for their iceboxes.

You also can watch volunteers demonstrate the old-fashioned method of threshing wheat with a wooden tool called a flail. Seeing how long it takes to get a handful of grain will make adults and children appreciate the fragrant wheat bread that gets baked in the farmhouse's wood-burning stove. Taste a chunk of this bread, which will certainly be better than any store-bought version you've eaten. Pick up a pamphlet called "A Celebration of Wheat." It will remind you that a year of hard work goes into these simple loaves. Not a bad thought for folks who think it's a pain to make a supermarket run more than once a week.

With 30 or so points of interest, including beehives and apple orchards, a self-guided farm tour takes from 60 to 90 minutes. On weekends there are organized hands-on activities, everything from planting seeds to shearing sheep to tapping trees for syrup. While adults participate, kids can do related crafts. During "Popcorn Harvest" (in November), for example, adults can pick their own ears of corn—and then see a demonstration of husking, shelling, and popping over an open fire, while children make popcorn balls.

What's especially interesting about Howell is that it isn't simply a tourist attraction. Since the equipment and technology used on the farm correspond with the state of agriculture in many Third World countries, Howell operates a training program for interns who plan to work in agricultural extension programs overseas.

A free brochure gives a brief history of the 126-acre property, which has been farmed for more than two and some half centuries, ever since blacksmith John Phillips bought the land from his brother. One of the free pamphlets, "The Potato: The Food of Love," includes not only a history of the vegetable, but also such Victorian recipes as Potato and Cider Soup, and Chocolate Potato Truffles. Among the interesting souvenirs for sale in the farmhouse are whole-wheat flour, pumpkins and gourds, cornstalks, Indian corn, and popcorn.

The farm is open most of the year except for a break between December and January. Tuesday through Saturday, the hours are 10:00 A.M. to 4:00 P.M. (Saturday programs run from 11:00 A.M. to 3:00 P.M.); Sunday hours are noon to 4:00 P.M.

Farms and Wineries

"Pick Your Own" and Other Farms
Apple Orchards
Wineries

Driving by the oil refineries on the New Jersey Turnpike has prompted many a New Jersey visitor to think, "Garden State, my foot!" But you'll have a different outlook if your car takes you by a roadside farm stand and you take home some tender, sweet Jersey corn, or juicy Jersey tomatoes with a depth of flavor that'll make you swear off those starchy cellophane things forever.

The fact is, New Jersey is an agricultural state, with a long farming tradition. New Jersey has always had quite a few apple orchards, for instance, going way back to colonial days, when hard cider was the only alcoholic beverage that was cheap and readily available. (See Close-up on Laird's AppleJack in the Revolutionary New Jersey chapter.) These days, most people just make pies.

Down south, the uniquely mild climate has proved hospitable to a number of crops, including peaches, berries, and beans. Thanks to its sandy soil, the Pinelands has become a major producer of cranberries and blueberries.

The biggest surprise, though, may be that New Jersey has vineyards, and while they may not quite have the cachet of Napa Valley, they produce some respectable wines and gladly welcome visitors for tastings.

"Pick Your Own" and Other Farms

If we've whet your appetite for the very freshest fruits and vegetables, peruse this list of the Shore area's "pick your own" farms, as well as a list of the dates when you might expect to do the picking. (Some farms also sell already-picked produce, if your pickin' days are behind you.) Not all the fun is in the food, though. There are often pony rides and hayrides, and some enterprising farmers have created a fall post-harvest business boom by cutting elaborate mazes in their corn fields. Just think how long you can lose your kids in one of these!

Hours of operations are provided, when available, but since weather and other conditions affect the harvest, and since many of these farms don't necessarily have regular hours for picking, call ahead to avoid disappointment. Farms will charge by the bushel or pint; prices will vary each harvest season.

Monmouth County

Antonio Casola Farms
178 N.J. Highway 34 and Schanck Road, Holmdel
(732) 332–1533
www.casolafarms.com

At the big green and white barn, you'll find all kinds of things to buy, including nursery stock, bedding plants, gourds, hay, straw, cornstalks, and flowers. In the appropriate seasons you can pick various vegetables, pumpkins, fall squashes, and Christmas trees. You can picnic here whenever the weather is good—or you can take a hayride during pumpkin season. The farm is open from March 1 to December 25.

Atlantic Farms
506 Atlantic Avenue (Highway 524), Wall
(732) 528–8680

Here you can pick peppers, eggplants, tomatoes, plum tomatoes, squash, pumpkins, chrysanthemums and other flowers, cornstalks, and Christmas trees. There's a picnic area, a petting farm, a corn maze in the fall, pony rides for kids, and hayrides for everyone during pumpkin season. The farm is open daily year-round from 9:00 A.M. to 7:00 P.M.

Battleview Orchards
91 Wemrock Road, Freehold
(732) 462–0756

Pick sour cherries, peaches, nectarines, apples, and pumpkins—though not all at the same time. You'll also find yummy pies and doughnuts in the bakery and a variety of fruits and vegetables in the farm market. Hayrides are given, too.

The Berry Farm
N.J. Highway 34 (behind Delicious Orchards), Colts Neck
(732) 294–0707

Pick luscious strawberries, raspberries (red and black), and blackberries. Then adjourn to Delicious Orchards next door (see below) and buy some fresh cream, and maybe the fixings for shortcake.

Boyce Berry Farm
Highway 537, Clarksburg
(609) 259–9198

Blueberries are what you'll find here; if you don't want to do the picking yourself, you can buy five-pound freezer-ready bags, picked to your order. It's recommended that you call ahead.

C. Casola Farms
489 Highway 520 East, between Highway 79 and N.J. Highway 34, Marlboro
(732) 946–8885

In fall, you can pick your own pumpkins, wend your way through the corn maze, and enjoy a hayride; youngsters can ride the little pony, too. The farm market sells flowers, bedding plants, hanging baskets, sweet corn (July till November), vegetables and other produce, hay, straw, and Christmas trees.

Delicious Orchards
36 N.J. Highway 34, Colts Neck
(732) 462–1989

Delicious Orchards isn't really a "pick your own" farm at all, but it is a favorite

place for great produce in Monmouth County. In fact, it has become the Balducci's of the Jersey Shore, adding boutique delicacies such as imported cheeses and chocolates to mainstays like fresh apple cider and orange juice. The baked goods alone are worth the trip; we recommend the biscuits, apple-cider doughnuts, pecan cookies, and butter-crust pies.

Earth Friendly Organic Farm
17 Olde Noah Hunt Road, Cream Ridge
(609) 259–9744

Pick blueberries and thornless blackberries from late June through mid-August, daily from 9:00 A.M. to 5:00 P.M. Buy eggs here as well. Bring a lunch to enjoy in the shaded picnic area.

Eastmont Orchards
Highway 537 (one mile east of N.J. Highway 34), Colts Neck
(732) 542–5404

Here you can pick apples, peaches, and pumpkins. The farm is open from late July through October, but always call ahead.

Laurino Farms
773 Sycamore Avenue, Tinton Falls
(732) 842–3470, (732) 842–3125

Depending on the season, you can pick strawberries, beans, tomatoes, okra, and

Cranberries

Unlike many agricultural crops, the cranberry likes the Pinelands' sandy soil, which protects its roots from rotting. Introduced to New England's pilgrims by the Native Americans in 1620, the cranberry is one of New Jersey's most important crops. In fact, the state is our nation's third-largest producer of cranberries, after Massachusetts and Wisconsin.

Up until the 1960s, the berries were handpicked by a method known as dry harvesting, which is slow and painful. Nowadays, when the crop is ready to harvest, the bogs are flooded, then churned by tractor-like machines; this allows the fruit to float to the surface. Cranberry farming here is a family affair, involving some 40-odd South Jersey families; some have farmed cranberries for as many as five generations. It was once a seasonal business, but cooperatives have made it stable—and Ocean Spray has made it big business by introducing blended juices, cranberry "cocktails," and cranberry snacks. Today the cranberry's reputation, like the apple's, is high, and not just as a snack or beverage, but as a health aid, one that's particularly beneficial in maintaining good kidney function.

If you'd like to immerse yourself in cranberry culture—and taste dozens of cranberry permutations, attend the annual Cranberry Festival, which takes place in Chatsworth every October. It's a two-day event that draws as many as 25,000 people. The festival sometimes includes fun tours of the cranberry bogs; you'll see men in waders and the big machines that scoop the fruit from the flooded bogs. It has been described as a symphony in red. Once you've seen the fruit in its natural (and bitter)

New Jersey is our nation's third-largest producer of cranberries. PHOTO: LILLIAN AFRICANO

form, you can taste all sorts of sweetened versions at the festival: cranberry muffins, cranberry cake, cranberry preserves, cranberry salsa, and...well, you get the idea. You'll also find arts and crafts vendors, antiques dealers, country-style music all day long, and plenty of hats and aprons and souvenir shirts for sale. On one of the days there's an Antique and Classic Automobile Show. Some years, there's even a special visit by the Jersey Devil (the fabled demon is like Santa Claus or the Easter Bunny in this area, making frequent guest appearances). For general information and directions, call (609) 726–1907 or (609) 726–1890.

If you have a yen to handpick cranberries yourself, the old-fashioned way, you can do so at Lipman Farm, off Highway 530 in Toms River; it offers public picking on Saturdays and Sundays in October from 8:00 A.M. to 5:00 P.M.

pumpkins. The farm is open June through October, daily from 9:00 A.M. to 6:00 P.M.

Menzel Brothers
N.J. Highway 34, Holmdel
(732) 946–3060
Pick strawberries, peas, pumpkins, and other vegetables.

Slope Brook Farms
213 Heyers Mill Road, Colts Neck
(732) 462–5775, (732) 772–1772
During the fall, you can pick pumpkins and hop on a hayride.

Stattels' Brookrest Farm
Highway 520, Marlboro
(732) 946–9666
Pick pumpkins in season and enjoy hayrides in October. Call for hours.

Sunny Acres Pumpkin Patch
Burlington Path Road, Cream Ridge
(609) 758–7817
Here you'll find pumpkins, gourds, winter squash, and mums; visitors get a hayride to the pumpkin patch.

Wemrock Orchards
300 N.J. Highway 33 West (across from Battleground Park), Freehold
(732) 431–2668
www.wemrockorchards.com
Depending on the season, you can pick strawberries, gourds, cornstalks, mums,

and pumpkins. The farm is open year-round, so you can also buy (already picked) produce and fresh fruit, pies, and apple-cider doughnuts. Activities offered at the farm include hayrides through the apple trees, hot-air balloon launches, and a corn maze in fall.

Westhaven Farm
725 Highway 524, Allentown
(609) 259–2186
This farm has strawberries, pumpkins, cornstalks, and Christmas trees, though not all at the same time. The kids will have fun admiring the farm animals and trying to find their way through the corn maze. There are hayrides, too.

Ocean County

DeWolf's Farm
10 West Colliers Mill Road (off Highway 539), New Egypt
(609) 758–2424
Pick strawberries, raspberries, blackberries, tomatoes, beans (fava, snap, and long), peas, field peas, melons, hot peppers (all types), bitter cilantro, potatoes (white and sweet), and pumpkins.

Emery's Berry Farm
346 Long Swamp Road (off Highway 539), New Egypt
(609) 758–8514
www.netpie.com
The pickin' menu at this NOFA-certified

organic farm includes strawberries, heritage blueberries, raspberries, and pumpkins. You can also buy produce and such goodies as homemade ice cream from the farm market—or navigate the corn maze, if you're in the mood. The farm is open from early April until just before Christmas.

Hallock's U-Pick Farm
38 Fischer Road (off Highway 528), New Egypt
(609) 758–8847
www.hallocksupick.com

Here you'll find strawberries, tomatoes, peas (black-eyed and field), beans (green, flat, wax, butter, and lima), potatoes (white and sweet), okra, onions, cabbage, broccoli, collards, peppers, greens (mustard and turnip), bitter balls, jute leaves, sweet potato leaves, and more.

Holly Hill Nursery
2211 Lacey Road, Forked River
(609) 693–5215

During the month of December, you can pick out your own Christmas tree and they'll cut it down for you.

Silverton Farm
1520 Silverton Road, Toms River
(732) 244–2621

If you prefer organic produce, you'll find it here: strawberries, raspberries, cherry tomatoes, green beans, and pumpkins. Flowers are available, too, as well as hayrides in fall (call for reservations). The farm is open from mid-May to early November, Tuesday through Sunday from 10:00 A.M. to 5:00 P.M.

Atlantic County

Daystar Nursery and Greenhouses, Inc.
250 South Mannheim Avenue, Egg Harbor
(609) 965–4351
www.daystarnursery.com

Here you can pick blueberries, and you'll also find flowering plants and shrubs. Call between 8:30 A.M. and 5:00 P.M.

Gold Seal Farm
901 Darmstadt Avenue, Egg Harbor
(609) 965–2413

The specialty crop at this "pick your own" farm is blackberries.

Mays Landing Florist and Greenhouse
315 Clarkstown Road, Mays Landing
(609) 625–2600

On offer here are blackberries, strawberries, and various vegetables and herbs; you can also buy cut flowers and bedding plants.

Shady Brook Farm
5800 White Horse Pike, Egg Harbor
(609) 965–4696, (609) 965–1285

Pick pumpkins, wend your way through the corn maze, or take a hayride.

Surf and Turf Farm
251 South Odessa Avenue, Pomona
(609) 965–4607

Pick strawberries, peas, spinach, or lettuce. The farm is open daily from 8:00 A.M. to 6:00 P.M.

Cape May County

Allen Family Farm
265 Tarkiln Road (gravel road at fire tower), Belleplain
(609) 465–7221, (609) 861–3778
www.blueberrykidz.com

The pickin' crops here are blueberries, apples, white peaches, tomatoes, and corn.

George's Farm Market
Highway 631 (one mile west of U.S. Highway 9), Marmora
(609) 390–9119

Pick strawberries and pumpkins; take a hayride in the fall.

Macellaro's Orchard
145 Macellaro Road (between Handmill and Hoffman Roads), Woodbine
(609) 861–2068

The crops here are strawberries, tomatoes, cucumbers, hot peppers, squash, and other vegetables. The farm is open July through early November, daily from 8:00 A.M. to 6:00 P.M.

Blueberries

Blueberries are the Pinelands' other fruit. You may have heard that blueberries are cholesterol-free, low in calories (a half-cup has 42), a good source of fiber, and most important, have the highest overall antioxidant score of some 40 fresh fruits and vegetables. New Jersey is second to Michigan in blueberry production; the fruit is grown primarily in Atlantic and Burlington Counties.

It was a young farm woman, Elizabeth White, who was responsible for turning the blueberry into a serious cash crop. Perhaps she was carrying on a family tradition, for it was her grandfather, James Fenwick, who was one of the first to cultivate the cranberry in the mid-1800s. Elizabeth, along with researcher Frederick Coville, enlisted locals to help her locate the best wild blueberry bushes in the Pinelands; she named each bush after the person who found it. Known as "Miss Lizzie" to the "pineys" who taught her about berry size, flavor, and ripening, she paid locals from one to three dollars to mark the largest berry on each bush. She took thousands of cuttings to create new varieties, and in 1916, she and Coville produced the first commercial blueberry crop.

Elizabeth White was the first farmer to put a clear wrapper over the small baskets of blueberries when they were shipped for sale. In 1927 Elizabeth helped organize the New Jersey Blueberry Cooperative Association. She died at the age of 83 on November 11, 1954, at her home, called Whitesbog.

The blueberry is celebrated in June, which officially kicks off blueberry season. The Red, White and Blueberry Festival takes place in downtown Hammonton, just off N.J. Highway 54. (Wharton Forest and Batsto Village are also located in Hammonton, so the festival could be a pleasant addition to a balmy day outdoors.) The event includes a stage show, an antique car show, food vendors, arts and crafts, lots of fresh-picked blueberries, all kinds of blueberry baked goods—and, of course, a blueberry pie-eating contest. For information, call the Hammonton Chamber of Commerce at (609) 561–9080. Hammonton considers itself the (unofficial) blueberry capital of the world.

These muffins are great with New Jersey blueberries:

Blueberry Muffins

1¼ cups all-purpose flour	1 egg white
¾ cup whole-wheat flour	3 tbsp. honey
2¾ tsp. baking powder	3 tbsp. oil
¼ tsp. baking soda	1¼ tsp. vanilla extract
⅓ cup sugar	⅛ tsp. finely grated orange or lemon zest
¾ cup skim milk	1 cup fresh blueberries

Preheat oven to 425 degrees F. Coat 12 standard muffin-tin cups with nonstick spray. Sift the flours, baking powder, and baking soda into a large bowl. Stir in sugar. In a small bowl, beat together the milk, egg white, honey, oil, vanilla, and zest until well mixed. Gently stir the blueberries into the flour mixture. Add the milk mixture and stir just until the dry ingredients are moistened; do not overmix. Divide batter evenly among the muffin cups. Bake on the center oven rack for 13 to 16 minutes, or until the muffins spring back when touched lightly. Let stand for five minutes before removing from the pan. Makes 12 muffins.

Recipe from the New Jersey Department of Agriculture

Apple Orchards

After the strawberries and tomatoes have gone, autumn brings an abundance of New Jersey apples. We've listed those orchards that fall within the general Shore area. The apple-picking season generally ends in late October or early November. Because conditions and hours may vary, always call ahead to avoid disappointment. Orchards generally charge by the bushel, with prices varying each harvest season.

Battleview Orchards
91 Wemrock Road, Freehold
(732) 462–0756, (800) 662–3075

Pick all varieties of apples here, and other fruits as well (see "Pick Your Own" section). The farm market is open daily from 9:00 A.M. to 6:00 P.M. Fall picking hours are from 10:00 A.M. to 5:00 P.M.

Butterhof's Shady Brook Farm
5800 White Horse Pike, Egg Harbor
(609) 967–1285

Pick Golden Delicious, McIntosh, Red Delicious, and Stayman/winesap daily from 10:00 A.M. to 5:00 P.M.

Donato Brothers
337 Weymouth Road, Landisville
(856) 697–0404

Here you'll find gala, Golden Delicious, Jonathan, McIntosh, Red Delicious, and Stayman/winesap apples.

Eastmont Orchards
169 County Road East (Highway 537), Colts Neck
(732) 542–5404

At Eastmont you'll find the following varieties: empire, Fuji, Golden Delicious, Jonathan, Macoun, McIntosh, Red Deli-

Jersey apples are good sources of dietary fiber. If you'd rather have someone else do the work for you, you can buy them at one of the Shore's farm markets. PHOTO: LILLIAN AFRICANO

When to Pick

Want to gather gallons of blueberries? Looking for the perfect pumpkin? The following lists let you know when your favorite fruits and veggies are ripe for the pickin'. Since conditions change from year to year, always call ahead.

Fruits and Berries
Apples: September 1 to October 25
Blackberries: July 15 to July 30
Blueberries: July 5 to August 10
Cherries: June 10 to June 25
Grapes: September 10 to September 20
Peaches and Nectarines: July 20 to September 1
Pears: August 10 to August 31
Plums: July 15 to August 15
Red Raspberries:
  Traditional: July 5 to July 21
  Fall-bearing: September 1 to September 20
Strawberries: June 1 to June 10

Vegetables
Asparagus: May 1 to May 30
Beets: July 1 to October 31
Broccoli: July 1 to October 31
Cabbage: June 10 to October 31
Cauliflower: October 5 to November 20
Collards: August 20 to October 31
Cucumbers: July 5 to August 15
Eggplant: July 20 to September 30
Lettuce:
  Late-spring: May 20 to July 15
  Early-fall: September 15 to November 15
Lima Beans: July 15 to August 31
Okra: August 15 to September 15
Onions: June 25 to July 31
Peas: June 15 to June 25
Peppers: July 15 to October 31
Potatoes: July 20 to September 30
Pumpkins: October 1 to October 15
Snap Beans: June 20 to July 20
Spinach: May 5 to June 25
Squash: June 25 to September 1
Sweet Corn: July 5 to August 31
Tomatoes: July 10 to September 15

cious, and Stayman/winesap. Also available for sale: Paula red, Rome, Ida red, Arkansas black, braeburn, and pippin. Fall picking hours are Monday through Friday from 9:00 A.M. to 5:00 P.M., Saturday and Sunday from 9:00 A.M. to 6:00 P.M.

Geiser's Farms
1859 New Bedford Road, Wall
(732) 449–1862

Pick Cortland, empire, Golden Delicious, and Red Delicious apples here, from 9:00 A.M. to 6:00 P.M.

Pleasant Valley Farm
4520 Harding Highway (U.S. Highway 40),
Mays Landing
(609) 625–8463

Pleasant Valley grows the following apple varieties: Cortland, Fuji, Granny Smith, Golden Delicious, Jonathan, McIntosh, Red Delicious, and Stayman/winesap. And you can buy cider, too.

Wineries

All right, maybe you've never heard anyone walk into a liquor store and say, "Give me a bottle of your best Jersey red." But that doesn't mean our state's vintners don't produce good wines, only that Jersey grapes haven't yet been "discovered" by one and all.

Though New Jersey doesn't spring to the lips in discussions of wine the way Napa or the Loire Valley might, Jersey winemaking is not a Johnny-come-lately.

Did you know that the first New Jerseyans began cultivating vineyards back in the mid-1700s? In fact, in 1767 London's Royal Society of Arts recognized two New Jersey vintners for their success in producing the first bottles of high-quality wine derived from colonial agriculture. And the state's vintners still win awards in both national and international competitions.

New Jersey's 16 wineries produce between 130,000 and 180,000 gallons a year, putting New Jersey among the top 15 or 20 wine-producing states. Soon there will be more. Says Donna Csolak of the Garden State Wine Growers Association, "We expect the number of wineries to double within the next few years; every couple of months, we have a new one. Lots of farmers are realizing that they can grow grapes—so they're pulling out the squash and planting grapes instead."

To give you the full picture of Jersey viticulture, we've listed wineries from all over the state, in addition to those in the four Shore counties.

Most of the tastings and tours are free, although some wineries charge a small fee.

Shore Area

Balic Winery
U.S. Highway 40, Mays Landing
(609) 625–2166

Sample the wines in the tasting room, then treat someone (or yourself) to a gift basket of whatever you most enjoyed. Open Monday through Saturday from 9:30 A.M. to 5:30 P.M. and Sunday 10:30 A.M. to 5:00 P.M. Closed Sundays in November and December.

Cape May Winery & Vineyard
709 Townbank Road, Cape May
(609) 884–1169

In addition to a tasting room and indoor and outdoor event areas, you'll find a gourmet food and gift shop; custom labeling for wines is available, too. Open Sunday for wine tasting, sales, and for tours of the vineyard and wine cellar. Call for an appointment. Closed November through April.

Cream Ridge Winery
Highway 539, Cream Ridge
(609) 259–9797
www.creamridgewinery.com

Here you can taste wine, order custom labeling, shop at the gourmet shop, take a private tour, or set up a private event or grape-stomping party. Several outdoor festivals are held at Cream Ridge every year; call for information or to receive their newsletter. The wine-tasting room and gift shop are open daily from 11:00 A.M. TO 6:00 P.M.

Renault Winery
72 North Breman Avenue, Egg Harbor
(609) 965–2111
www.renaultwinery.com

The Renault Winery is New Jersey's oldest continuously operating winery, dating back to 1864. Visit the Glass Museum and ooh and aah over the enormous collection of wine goblets and champagne glasses, some centuries old. Tour this impressive winemaking operation, taste this and that, then shop for gifts or order custom labeling. In addition to a winery, the Renault complex includes a gourmet restaurant and a hotel, with a golf course on the way (see Attractions chapter). We recommend the blueberry Champagne. The winery is open Monday through Friday from 11:00 A.M. to 4:00 P.M., Saturday from 11:00 A.M. to 8:00 P.M., and Sunday from noon to 4:00 P.M.

Sylvin Farms
24 North Vienna Avenue, Germania
(609) 965–1548

This is a small but pleasant operation, so your time here will be spent tasting—and perhaps buying a bottle or two of the wines you like. Visitors are welcome by appointment.

Tomasello Winery
225 White Horse Pike, Hammonton
(800) MMM–WINE
www.tomasellowinery.com

This Mediterranean-style villa has a tasting room and banquet facility. The Vintners Room, decorated in French country style, is an appealing site for a party. You

can buy wine-related gifts, gift baskets, or custom labels for weddings, holidays, or corporate gifts. The winery is open Monday through Saturday from 9:00 A.M. to 8:00 P.M., Sunday from 11:00 A.M. to 6:00 P.M.; tours by appointment.

Other New Jersey Wineries

Alba Vineyard
269 Highway 627, Milford
(908) 995–7800
www.albavineyard.com

The vineyard has a tasting room and a gift shop. Private parties can be arranged, and there are banquet facilities for special events. The surroundings are especially lovely, so bring lunch and enjoy it in the outdoor picnic area. The vineyard is open weekdays by appointment, Saturday from 10:00 A.M. to 6:00 P.M., and Sunday from noon to 5:00 P.M.

Amalthea Cellars
209 Vineyard Road, Atco
(856) 768–8585

The vineyard has a tasting room and a gift area. Hours vary by season, so call ahead.

Amwell Valley Vineyard
80 Old York Road, Ringoes
(908) 788–5852
www.amwellvalleyvineyard.com

In addition to a tasting room, a gift shop, event areas, and picnic facilities, the vineyard offers custom labeling for its wine. It's open Saturday and Sunday from 1:00 to 5:00 P.M.; other days by appointment.

Bellview Winery
150 Atlantic Street, Landisville
(856) 697–7172
www.bellviewwinery.com

This relatively young winery (opened the summer of 2001) has already won three bronze medals in state competition. It has a tasting room that can accommodate about 15 people. Gift baskets and gift certificates are available. Check for special events like festivals and grape stomping. It's open Friday from noon to 7:00 P.M., Saturday from noon to 5:00 P.M., Sunday from noon to 3:00 P.M., and by appointment.

Four Sisters Winery at Matarazzo Farms
10 Doe Hollow Lane (Highway 519),
Belvidere
(908) 475–3671
www.foursisterswinery.com

After you've tasted the wines, visit the gift shop, relax in the outdoor picnic area, order custom labeling, or arrange a special event: a grape-crushing party, a moonlight hayride, or a private tasting for your very best friends. The winery is open daily from 9:00 A.M. to 6:00 P.M. for tasting and retail sales, Saturday and Sunday for tours from 10:00 A.M. to 5:00 P.M. Call for extended holiday hours.

King's Road Vineyard
360 Highway 579, Asbury
(800) 479–6479
www.kingsroad.com

At King's Road, you can do your tasting indoors or on an attractive deck overlooking the vineyard. If you like the setting, you can have a private party or a wedding here. The vineyard is open Wednesday through Sunday from noon to 5:00 P.M.; tours are offered on weekends in April through October.

La Follette Vineyard and Winery
64 Harlington Road, Belle Mead
(908) 359–9234
www.lafollettewinery.com

This winery is open for tastings only on weekends in May through September. Call for hours.

During a King's Road Vineyard winery tour, you'll learn how the vineyard's grapes become New Jersey wine. PHOTO: LILLIAN AFRICANO

Poor Richard's Winery
220 Ridge Road, Frenchtown
(908) 996–6480
www.intac.com/~poorrich/

Tours are offered on weekends from noon to 6:00 P.M. At other times, call ahead for an appointment.

Unionville Vineyards
9 Rocktown Road, Ringoes
(908) 788–0400
www.unionvillevineyards.com

The decorating theme at Unionville is fox-hunting, and the tasting room and gift shop are housed in a converted barn dating back to 1858. Several outdoor festivals are held here every year; call for details or to receive the winery's newsletter, which provides information on private wine tasting, barrel lectures, and other events. It's open Thursday through Sunday from 11:00 A.M. to 4:00 P.M. for tasting and sales; winery tours are held on the weekends or by appointment.

Valenzano Winery
340 Forked Neck Road, Shamong
(609) 268–6731
www.valenzanowine.com

Sample the wines in the tasting room, buy whatever you enjoyed—and perhaps order personalized labels for your own wine cellar. The winery is open by appointment.

Insiders' Tip

For a lively and inexpensive day out, attend one of the state wine industry festivals, which are generally held in the spring and the fall. Most will have a scenic setting (especially in fall), and in addition to local wines, you can expect good food, crafts, and children's activities such as pony rides and petting zoos. For a schedule of these events, call (609) 588-0085 or check www.newjerseywines.com.

The Arts and Culture

Visual artists have been attracted to the beauty of the Jersey Shore for a long time, but in Winslow Homer, the Shore found a true interpreter. His *Long Branch, New Jersey* is considered the first painting of the so-called "New Jersey Impressionists." It's a tradition that was carried on by Ida Wells Stroud and her daughter, Clara Stroud. Mother and daughter founded the Manasquan River Artists, an organization that still exists; both worked hard throughout their lives to promote struggling New Jersey artists. You can learn more about the New Jersey Impressionists in classes and lectures given at the Noyes Museum in Oceanville, which has exhibited their works.

Today many fine painters, as well as artists in other media, work here and exhibit their work at Shore galleries and art shows. The crafts, too, have a long tradition at the Shore, dating back to the quilting of colonial days and the varied handiwork of the Lenni Lenape Indians, now exhibited in area museums. The Jersey Shore also has a strong history of glassmaking, partly thanks to the ready supply of sand. (See "Wheaton Village" in the Living-History Farms and Historic Villages chapter.) Many area artists choose to sculpt in this fragile medium.

The performing arts—music, theater, and film—have been well represented at the Shore and have seen dramatic growth over the past few decades. We have theater and musical groups, both amateur and professional, in every county, presenting productions of new and classic works.

Live theater has prospered at the Shore, judging by the number of local companies made up of gifted community players and Equity actors. Prices for their productions are considerably lower than what you would pay in the city; tickets are easier to obtain; the atmosphere is relaxed; and there's the added bonus of getting to know more about your community when you attend a performance.

A word about the music scene: There are wonderful performances by opera companies, chorale groups, and first-rate orchestras on the Shore. But when we talk about the Jersey Shore sound, we mean rock 'n' roll—Bruce Springsteen, Jon Bon Jovi, and Southside Johnny and the Asbury Jukes. In this section, you'll find the larger venues like the Count Basie Theatre in Red Bank and the PNC Bank (formerly the Garden State) Arts Center in Holmdel. Music clubs like the Tradewinds and the Fast Lane are listed under "Nightlife" in the individual county chapters.

Monmouth County

Performing Arts

Algonquin Arts Theatre
173 Main Street, Manasquan
(732) 528–9211
www.algonquinarts.com

The Algonquin is not only a theater, it's an educational resource for the area. Several companies perform here on a regular basis: the Premier Theatre, the Two River Theatre Company, and the Dunbar Repertory (see the entries on each, below). The theater also hosts a variety of other performances, including dance, classical and modern music, and children's shows.

Convention Hall
1300 Ocean Avenue, Asbury Park
(732) 502–4581

Back in its palmy days, Convention Hall used to hear the Big Band sounds of Glenn Miller and Harry James. In the '60s, the Rolling Stones, Jefferson Airplane, The Who, and the Doors played here, putting Asbury Park on the rock map and inspiring the local talent. Recently, some repairs were made to the hall's magnificent Art Deco exterior; inside, it's like a huge club, with an open floor and seating around the perimeter. The space can be adapted to hold circuses, trade shows, boxing matches, basketball games, and other sporting events as well as concerts. In summer, big-name bands like Everclear and the Goo-Goo Dolls pass through here; check the *Asbury Park Press* and free local papers to find out who and when. Before embarking on their recent world tour, Bruce Springsteen and the E Street Band did several warm-up shows here. During one rehearsal, fans began gathering out-side, and the Boss let them come inside where they could hear a little better.

Count Basie Theatre
99 Monmouth Street, Red Bank
(732) 842–9000

Built in 1926 as a vaudeville theater and movie house, and formerly known as The Carlton Theatre, this 1,435-seat house went dark in 1970. It was acquired by the Monmouth County Arts Council in 1973 and renamed in 1984 after the death of Red Bank native William James "Count" Basie. Since then, the theater has been one of Monmouth County's busiest halls. During any given season, about 150 events might be booked here, including performances of Shakespeare's plays, concerts by the award-winning New Jersey Symphony Orchestra, opera, children's shows, and of course, gigs by New Jersey's rockers. Phoenix Productions (732-747-0014) has performed such musicals as *Joseph and the Amazing Technicolor Dream-coat* and *Brigadoon* at the Count Basie.

During the summer, big bands like Everclear and the Goo-Goo Dolls play Asbury Park's Convention Hall. Bruce Springsteen recently did a concert series here. PHOTO: NINA AFRICANO

The Count Basie Theatre, a former vaudeville house, is a major venue in Monmouth County.

PHOTO: NINA AFRICANO

Dunbar Repertory
Algonquin Arts Theatre
173 Main Street, Manasquan
(732) 780–6694

The credo of this repertory company is: "Theater from the heart of African-American culture." It performs the works of new playwrights as well as plays by such well-known writers as Langston Hughes and August Wilson. During the holiday season it stages *Black Nativity*, a Christmas story. The company also performs smaller works at various venues in the county and surrounding areas.

Fellowship Theatre
22 Pilgrim Pathway, Ocean Grove
(800) 773–0097

This 550-seat theater is part of the new $1.6-million Young People's Temple and Conference Center. Recent seasons included such productions as Oscar Wilde's *The Importance of Being Earnest* and Shakespeare's *A Midsummer Night's Dream*, performed by the resident company.

First Avenue Playhouse
123 First Avenue, Atlantic Highlands
(732) 291–7552

At this small community theater, you'll see grown-up offerings such as *The Seven Year Itch* (served with dessert), and kids' shows like *The Snow Queen*, performed by the Paper Moon Marionette Theatre.

Jersey Shore Arts Center
"Old" Neptune High School, N.J. Highway 71
and Main Avenue, Ocean Grove
(732) 502–0050

Once a boarded-up high school, the center now rings to the sound of Broadway show tunes, bluegrass music, theatrical drama, and other performing arts events. The Pine Tree Players perform here, as does the Night on Broadway Company.

Lauren K. Woods Theatre
Monmouth University, Cedar Avenue, West
Long Branch
(732) 263–5730

This 145-seat theater (one of two at Monmouth University) has a busy year-round schedule. Its program includes a drama in the fall; a musical in spring; and a comedy, drama, and mystery during the summer season.

Metro Lyric Opera
40 Ocean Avenue, Allenhurst
(732) 531–2378

The Jersey Shore's venerable opera company performs throughout Monmouth and Ocean Counties, at venues like the Count Basie Theatre in Red Bank (see page 175) and the Paramount Theatre in Asbury Park (see below). Among its recent productions were *Carmen* and *Don Pasquale*. The company also presents educational programs for kids and seniors, in public schools and libraries.

Monmouth Civic Chorus
Red Bank
(732) 933–9333
www.monmouthcivicchorus.org

For more than 50 years—the last dozen or so under the artistic direction of Mark Shapiro—the chorus has delighted audiences throughout Monmouth and Ocean County, as well as in Carnegie Hall. It performs choral music, both classical and modern; opera; operetta; and musical theater selections. A three-concert subscription series at the Count Basie Theatre (see page 175) is offered each year.

Monmouth County Park System Summer Musical Theatre
Thompson Park, Newman Springs Road, Middletown
(732) 842–4000

If you'd like to see theater in a barn (the way they did it in old Judy Garland movies), try a show in Thompson Park. The season runs from June through August. Some recent productions were *She Loves Me* and *Funny Girl.*

New Jersey Repertory Company
Lumia Theatre, 179 Broadway, Long Branch
(732) 229–3166
www.njrep.org

Located in the heart of Long Branch, this professional theater is dedicated to developing and producing new plays with diverse themes. In addition to their stage productions, the company presents 20 to 30 staged readings a year; these readings give playwrights the opportunity to hear their work, discuss it with an audience, and develop it as needed. Recent original works have been *Harry and Thelma in the Woods*, a comedy by Stan Lachow, and *Naked by the River*, by Michael Folie. The theater offers a package that includes a show and dinner at Joe & Maggie's, one of the area's top restaurants.

Ocean Grove (Great) Auditorium
Pilgrim Pathway, Ocean Grove
(732) 775–0035, (800) 773–5689
www.oceangrove.org

In 1894, the Great Auditorium (as it's commonly known) was constructed at a cost of almost $70,000. This stunning Victorian wooden structure could seat 10,000 on bleachers (it now accommodates fewer than 7,000 in regular theater seats). Religious leaders like Billy Sunday, Norman Vincent Peale, and Billy Graham preached in the auditorium; Caruso gave his first American concert here. In the ensuing years, the Great Auditorium would become a seasonal venue featuring such performers as Peter, Paul and Mary, and the Preservation Hall Jazz Band every Saturday night. During the summer season, there are also classical music concerts, light opera performances, and recitals by Dr. Gordon Turk on the world-famous Hope-Jones pipe organ.

Paramount Theatre
Sunset and Ocean Avenues, Asbury Park
(732) 502–4581

This splendid Art Deco treasure is the venue for dance programs, jazz, opera, classical music, comedy, and even classic rhythm and blues. Performances here are not always well-advertised, and we often find out about them after they're over, when we pass by the sign in the park on Main Street and Sunset Avenue in Asbury that posts announcements of events here and at Convention Hall.

The First Avenue Playhouse in Atlantic Highlands is a small community theater offering both adult's and children's productions. PHOTO: NINA AFRICANO

PNC Bank Arts Center
Garden State Parkway (exit 116), Holmdel
(732) 335–0400
www.artscenter.com

Summer brings a full schedule of rock headliners, from classic bands like Aerosmith or Steely Dan to performers with a younger appeal like Jewel and Lenny Kravitz, to this outdoor amphitheater. If the weather's nice, lawn seats are just fine; if it rains, you'll wish you'd sprung for the more expensive, covered section. The atmosphere is relaxed; concertgoers arrive hours early to picnic on the grounds and in the parking area. You'll also find dance productions, opera, and classical music concerts here. In the "shoulder season," before the weather turns cold, special events such as ethnic festivals are also held at the center. There are picnic facilities and a nature trail at Telegraph Hill Park. During the holiday season, the regional power company puts on a dazzling display of lights that can be seen as you whiz by on the Parkway.

Pollak Theatre
Monmouth University, Cedar Avenue,
West Long Branch
(732) 571–3483

The Pollak presents high-quality live entertainment; among the recent performers here were Dr. John, pianist George Winston, and Natalie MacMaster.

Premier Theatre
Algonquin Arts Theatre, 173 Main Street,
Manasquan
(732) 223–7122

During April, October, November, and December, the Premier company performs at the Algonquin Arts Theatre. In summer, the company performs at the Henderson Theatre on the Christian Brothers Academy campus in Lincroft. Among its recent productions: *West Side Story, Camelot,* and *Scrooge.*

Red Bank Arts Theatre (Clearview Cinema)
36 White Street, Red Bank
(732) 747–0333
www.clearviewcinemas.com

This boutique two-plex in the heart of Hip City (Red Bank) is the place to go for French movies and other art-house fare that doesn't make it to the mall.

Spring Lake Theatre Company
Third and Madison Avenues, Spring Lake
(732) 449–4530

Even if you're not staying in Spring Lake, you might want to catch a performance at this popular theater during the summer, when the town is in full bloom—or during the winter holidays, when it twinkles and sparkles like a Victorian Christmas card. Among the recent productions: *Carousel, Private Lives,* and *Scrooge.*

Two River Theatre Company
223 Maple Avenue, Red Bank
(732) 345–1400
www.tworivertheatre.org

This professional theater company performs classics and new works at the Algonquin Arts Theatre (see page 174). Recent plays were John Guare's *The House of Blue Leaves* and Edward Albee's *A Delicate Balance.* The season generally runs from September through May.

Visual Arts

Art Alliance of Monmouth County
33 Monmouth Street, Red Bank
(732) 842–9403

This co-op gallery of painters, sculptors, and photographers has a new theme exhibit each month, with lively openings attended by artists and friends on the first Saturday of every month. Annual juried shows attract entries from across New Jersey. Classes in drawing and painting are open to the public. Hours are irregular, so call ahead.

Art Forms
16 Monmouth Street, Red Bank
(732) 530–4330

In addition to painting and sculpture, this gallery showcases ceramics, glass, and jewelry that is more art than craft. Call for hours.

Be
704 Cookman Avenue, Asbury Park
(732) 774–2411
www.beinasburypark.com

Have coffee, check out the classes for kids, view works by young Shore artists—or just hang out and talk about the positive changes going on in Asbury Park. This gallery is at the heart of it all, sponsoring events that draw residents and visitors alike. It is open Wednesday from 11:00 A.M. to 5:00 P.M., Thursday through Saturday from 11:00 A.M. to 11:00 P.M., and Sunday from noon to 5:00 P.M.

Evergreen Gallery
308 Morris Avenue, Spring Lake
(732) 449–4488

Here you'll find works on canvas and paper by New Jersey artists. Commissioned artwork and decorative painting can be done on request. The gallery is open Monday through Saturday from 10:00 A.M. to 5:00 P.M., and Sunday from noon to 4:00 P.M.

Main Street Gallery
113 Main Street, Manasquan
(732) 223–1268
www.mainstreetgallery.com

One of the largest galleries in the Shore area, MSG represents many local and regional artists, including Paula Kolojeski. The gallery is open Monday through Saturday from 10:00 A.M. to 5:00 P.M. (Friday until 6:00 P.M.).

Manasquan Art Gallery
1407 Atlantic Avenue, Wall
(732) 292–0656

Located in the Circle Factory Outlet Center, this gallery carries prints and lithographs by such renowned artists as Howard Behrens and Delacroix. It is open Sunday through Wednesday from 10:00 A.M. to 6:00 P.M., and Thursday through Saturday from 10:00 A.M. to 8:00 P.M.

Performing Arts

Albert Music Hall
125 Wells Mills Road (Highway 532), Waretown
(609) 971–1593

If you love bluegrass and country music, you'll have a swell time here on Saturday night, when The Pinelands Cultural Society presents its weekly program: "Sounds of the Jersey Pines." The show starts at 7:30 P.M. In addition to the weekly musicales, the Albert hosts a number of festivals, including the Ocean County Bluegrass Festival (February) and the Ladies of Country and Bluegrass Music (June).

The Fine Arts Center
Ocean County College, College Drive, Toms River
(732) 255–0500

The programming here is varied: dramatic plays such as *The Side Man,* by Warren Leight, holiday favorites like *The Nutcracker,* band concerts, and children's events.

Strand Theater
400 Clifton Avenue, Lakewood
(732) 367–7789

At this vintage 1922 theater, expect to find just about every form of entertainment, from concerts by popular singers like Natalie Merchant to children's shows. The Garden State Philharmonic (732–349-6277, www.islandhts.com/garden) performs here and at other venues such as Toms River High School. The Strand Theater Project, a new community theater group, presents such musicals as *Carousel* and *Bye, Bye Birdie.*

Surflight Theatre
Engleside and Beach Avenues, Beach Haven
(609) 492–9477
www.lbinet.com/surflight

The 450-seat Surflight has been presenting high-quality summer stock for more than half a century. Recent seasons have featured *Jekyll & Hyde, West Side Story,* and *Annie.* Groups of 15 or more may purchase dinner packages or lunch-and-matinee packages. The season here runs from May through mid-October; the theater reopens for the Christmas season, when it presents such seasonal shows as *A Christmas Carol.*

Visual Arts

Anchor & Palette Gallery
45 Mount Street, Bay Head
(732) 892–7776
www.anchorandpalette.com

At this gallery you'll find many of the state's fine artists, including Dick LaBonte, whose paintings and prints represent life on the Shore at the turn of the century. During the fall and winter, the gallery offers art classes and workshops in oil painting, watercolor, basic drawing, and other media taught by local artists. The gallery is open Monday through Friday from 10:00 A.M. to 4:30 P.M., Saturday from 10:00 A.M. to 5:00 P.M., and Sunday from 11:00 A.M. to 2:00 P.M.

The Fine Arts Center
Ocean County College, College Drive, Toms River
(732) 255–0500

The art gallery hosts shows for local and national artists. Past exhibits have featured photography, quilts, and work by young adults. Call for information on current shows and hours.

Gull Studio
70-72 Bridge Avenue, Bay Head
(732) 892–3503

Enjoy browsing in this quaint and picturesque gallery; it's chock-full of seascapes and other appealing scenes by New Jersey artists. Gull represents local talent Robert A. Loder Jr., who does paintings and sketches of the Jersey Shore, Maine, Cape Cod, and the Chesapeake Bay. Gull Studio is open daily from 10:30 A.M. to 5:00 P.M.

Jane Law's LBI Art Studio and Gallery
2001 Long Beach Boulevard, Surf City
(609) 494–4232

The gallery carries original watercolors and oils by local and nationally known artists, as well as wildlife sculptures. Art classes for adults and children are given year-round, but in the summer, they are outdoors—with the ocean in the background. The gallery is open daily from 10:00 A.M. to 5:00 P.M. in summer; off-season, it is closed on Tuesday and Wednesday.

Lavallette Heritage Committee
13 Camden Avenue, Lavallette
(732) 793–3652

The committee sponsors festivals, concerts, and special events throughout the summer. Its Arts & Crafts Show takes place in July, and the Heritage Day Festival is in September.

Long Beach Island Foundation of the Arts and Sciences
120 Long Beach Boulevard, Loveladies
(609) 494–1241
www.lbifoundation.org

Founded in 1948 by Boris Blai, the foundation is a cultural hub and recreation center for the island. Throughout the year there are classes and workshops in various creative arts such as drawing, painting, and ceramics; after-school classes are offered for children. During the busy summer season, there's also a children's camp, as well as lectures, films, swing dancing, art exhibitions, and other programs. The foundation has two popular fund-raisers, which take place in August: a house tour, which allows visitors a peek at some of the area's truly splendid homes, and the Loveladies Arts and Crafts Festival, a juried event that attracts more than 100 artists, crafters, and vendors, featuring everything from jewelry to paperwork to ceramics.

M. Christina Geis Gallery
Georgian Court College, Lakewood
(732) 364–2200 ext. 348 or 330

Visit the gallery on this college campus and you'll have the added pleasure of seeing the former Jay Gould estate. The architecture is Georgian and Renaissance, enhanced by elaborate gardens and fountains. In 1924, the Sisters of Mercy converted it into a four-year institution of higher learning.

The art gallery has featured the work of such Shore artists as Laurence Waxberg, Karen Pomeroy, and Alison Amelchenko. With a new exhibit each month, you might see paintings, photographs, or sculptures by students, professors, or artists from New York or Philadelphia. The gallery is open to the public Monday through Friday from 9:00 A.M. to 8:00 P.M.

M. Thompson Kravetz Gallery
517 Main Avenue, Bay Head
(732) 295–4040

Nineteenth-century American and European art is displayed here; call for an appointment to tour the gallery.

Ocean County Artists' Guild
Ocean and Chestnut Avenues, Island Heights
(732) 270–3111
www.islandhts.com/guild.htm

Works by members and guest artists (from the Shore and southern New Jersey) are exhibited in this charming Victorian house. Workshops are given here, as are classes for adults and children. The guild's exhibits may be viewed Tuesday through Sunday from 1:00 to 4:00 P.M.

Out of the Blue
1225 Bay Avenue, Point Pleasant
(732) 899–2200

If you love art depicting surf, sand, and ships, visit this gallery to view the works of painter Stanley Meltzoff and sculptor Ken Ullberg. It's open Monday through Friday from 10:00 A.M. to 2:00 P.M., and Saturday and Sunday from 10:00 A.M. to 5:00 P.M.

Picture Perfect Gallery
1307 N.J. Highway 37 East, Toms River
(732) 929–3636
www.pictureperfectgallery.com

A longtime area favorite, Picture Perfect features prints by Island Heights artist Virginia Perle. Among Perle's many shore seascapes are her *Along the Shore* series and *Island Beach*. It is open Monday, Tuesday, and Saturday from 10:00 A.M. to 5:00 P.M.; Wednesday, Thursday, and Friday from 10:00 A.M. to 6:00 P.M.

Atlantic and Cape May Counties

Performing Arts

Atlantic Cape Community College
5100 Black Horse Pike, Mays Landing
(609) 343–4907
www.atlantic.edu

The programs at this community college include art exhibitions, student theater productions, and music and speaker series. A popular program is Careme's Cafe Series, which starts with a yummy four-course gourmet dinner in the 65-seat restaurant operated by the college's Academy of Culinary Arts. After dinner comes a second "dessert"—a show spotlighting contemporary acoustic musicians like Philadelphia's Ben Arnold.

Atlantic Contemporary Ballet Theatre
612 East Pine View Drive, Absecon
(609) 748–6625
www.acbt.org

This chamber ballet company has a repertoire of classical and contemporary ballets. A seasonal favorite, *The Nutcracker* is offered every year during the last week of November and the first week of December; a Nativity ballet is performed in December.

Avalon Performing Arts Council (APAC)
Avalon
(609) 967–3066

The council sponsors a number of activities at various venues, including a juried art show, cabaret nights, music and movies at the beach, concerts featuring the Langley Air Force Clarinet Quartet, children's holiday programs, and weekly summer performances for children.

Boardwalk Living Theatre
55 South Dover Avenue, Atlantic City
(609) 348–4048
www.boardwalklt.com

The Boardwalk players create a living history of Atlantic City, from the 18th to the 21st century. They have performed in Historic Gardner's Basin and are available for themed group tours or parties, indoors or out. Among the plays in their repertoire is a fun production called *RumRunners!* This comic romp about Atlantic City during the Prohibition era is alive with gangsters, flappers, rumrunners—even singing Irish cops.

Cape Harmonaires
North Cape May Center, Townbank and Shunpike Roads, North Cape May
(609) 884–4234

If you like four-part harmony and barbershop stylings, catch the rehearsals of this group every Tuesday from 7:30 to 9:30 P.M. at the above address. All men are welcome to join. They perform in the area, too.

Cape May Jazz Festivals
416 Portsmouth Road, Cape May
(609) 884–7200

In April and November, the Cape May Jazz Festivals are held in Convention Hall. These are major events featuring the finest mid-Atlantic musicians performing jazz in all its permutations, from straight-ahead jazz in small-club settings to high-energy jam sessions to gospel and blues.

Cape May Stage Professional Equity Theatre
31 Perry Street, Cape May
(609) 884–1341
www.capemaystage.com

Cape May's only professional Equity theater company appears from June through December in the Cape May Welcome Center, an intimate 75-seat converted church at Bank and Lafayette Streets. It generally performs new scripts or such contemporary plays as *Shirley Valentine* and *Talley's Folly*. Cape May Stage also participates in educational programs in college and high school settings.

Cape Shore Chorus Sweet Adelines, Inc.
(609) 463–1618

The men have the Harmonaires, the women have the Sweet Adelines, singing four-part harmony in the barbershop style. If you'd like to join, rehearsals are in South Seaville every Thursday night at 7:15 P.M. Call for directions. The group

The Jersey Shore and the Silver Screen

Asbury Park may not exactly rival L.A.'s Griffith Park for its screen appearances, but the Boardwalk's bleak expanse has attracted a number of locations scouts. Recently, while *The Sopranos* was filming at Convention Hall, Robert DeNiro was across town shooting *City by the Sea*. *The Sopranos* has also shot scenes at the Channel Club marina in Monmouth Beach and Monmouth Park Race Track in Oceanport.

Going back a few years (1980), Woody Allen filmed parts of *Stardust Memories* at the Great Auditorium in Ocean Grove, as well as at the Boardwalk and the old carousel in Asbury. A year later, *Ragtime* featured the century-old Victorian houses of Ocean Grove, too. Daddy Warbucks's Fifth Avenue mansion in *Annie* was actually Woodrow Wilson Hall, the administrative building for Monmouth University in West Long Branch.

Louis Malle captured A.C.'s poignant contrasts of money and poverty in *Atlantic City,* which starred Edison native Susan Sarandon and Burt Lancaster. *The Color of Money, The Pick-up Artist,* and *Wiseguys* all shot scenes at Merv Griffin's Resorts Casino. *The Lemon Sisters* featured the Boardwalks of Asbury and A.C., too. *The Amityville Horror, Baby, It's You,* and episodes of *The X Files* also had scenes shot at the Shore. *Stealing Home,* with Jodie Foster and Mark Harmon, was shot in Island Beach State Park.

The Shore has its local success story, too: Red Bank's Kevin Smith, director of *Mall Rats, Chasing Amy, Dogma,* and *Jay and Silent Bob Strike Back.* Smith financed his first film, *Clerks,* with credit cards and shot it at the Keansburg convenience store where he worked. Scenes from *Chasing Amy* were shot in Rumson's Victory Park. Many locations in Red Bank appear in *Dogma,* which starred Matt Damon and Ben Affleck, including St. James Church at Red Bank Catholic High School.

Smith, whose work is now celebrated at Shore film festivals, is an inspiration to other area independent filmmakers. If you're a fan, drop by his store, Jay and Silent Bob's Secret Stash, in Red Bank and check out the movie memorabilia.

You may soon be seeing a lot more of the Garden State on the silver screen; negotiations to bring a film studio to Trenton are progressing. In a way, moving pictures would finally be coming home, since it was Thomas Alva Edison, the genius of Menlo Park (New Jersey), who invented the medium.

performs in Cape May County and surrounding areas.

Center for Community Arts
712 Lafayette Street, Cape May
(609) 884–7515

This organization sponsors a year-round Youth Arts Program and a Community History Project, which mounts exhibits and programs about Cape Island's African-American history. Annual events include a Dr. Martin Luther King Jr. Memorial Celebration in January and a Youth Arts Fair in May.

East Lynne Company, Inc.
Cape May
(609) 884–5898

No nudity, nothing vulgar—wholesome family entertainment is this professional Equity company's specialty. Specifically, it performs American works written before

1935, or new works written about that period. One popular show was *The Dictator,* a comedy first produced on Broadway in 1904, featuring John Barrymore in his debut performance. Another crowd-pleaser was the *Spoon River Anthology,* reprised by popular demand. The season generally runs from July to October; the company also runs educational programs and benefits in the community.

Elaine's Dinner Theater
513 Lafayette Street, Cape May
(609) 884–4358
www.elainesdinnertheater.com

If you watch the Food Network's *Best of . . .* series, you may already know that they named Elaine's one of the country's top five dinner theaters—as much for the fun as for the food. For example, during a recent show, *The Secret of the Sphinx,* diners were treated to talking camels, mummies, and all manner of magic and mayhem.

At the same location is the Haunted Mansion theme restaurant, which operates from Easter to Halloween. It features the same menu as Elaine's, but the entertainment here, mixed media and live, appeals to kids and to folks who liked *Beetlejuice.*

Ocean City Pops Orchestra
Ocean City
(609) 398–9585
www.oceancitypops.org

This professional summer orchestra has brought music and fun to the historic Boardwalk Music Pier for the better part of a century. It performs from June through September, offering a variety of treats, from Beethoven to Broadway, as well as children's programs. The orchestra can also be seen at other Cape May County venues.

Performing Arts Center of Middle Township
1 Penkethman Way, Cape May Court House
(609) 463–1924

The only performing arts center in Cape May County, this 1,000-seat venue is part of Middle Township High School. Among the headliners here: the Ocean City Pops and the New Jersey Pops, as well as opera and choral and theatrical groups.

Sea Isle City Players
Townsend's Inlet Civic Center, Sea Isle City
(609) 263–2400

In the fall, this community theater group produces a comedy, in the spring, a musical—and in summer, just in time for school vacation, there's children's theater.

The Showbarn
The Village Greene, Historic Smithville
(609) 748–7799
www.theshowbarn.com

One of the newer attractions in the Towne of Historic Smithville is this appealing dinner theater, which serves up such whimsical fare as *Once Upon A Christmas,* along with dinner, lunch, or a buffet brunch.

Stockton Performing Arts Center
Richard Stockton College of New Jersey
Jimmy Leeds Road, Pomona
(609) 652–9000, (609) 652–4607
www.stockton.edu

At this 550-seat theater, South Jersey's premier center for the performing arts, professional artists display their talents in theatrical and dance productions, and in a variety of concerts, including jazz, classical, and blues. ACT (Atlantic Contemporary Theatre) performs Shakespearean plays and other classical theater here. Children's shows are staged as well.

Visual Arts

Accent Gallery
956 Asbury Avenue, Ocean City
(609) 398–3577
www.accentgallery.com

See the seascapes of Shore artists like Kim Weiland, as well as works in paper, glass, ceramics, and sculpture by nationally known artists. The gallery is open Monday through Saturday from 10:00 A.M. to 5:00 P.M., Sunday from 11:00 A.M. to 3:00 P.M.

Atlantic City Art Center
Garden Pier, New Jersey Avenue and the Boardwalk, Atlantic City
(609) 347–5837
www.aclink.org/acartcenter

A few steps away from the Atlantic City

Shore landmarks have inspired generations of artists. This watercolor of Chalfonte Hotel in Cape May is by artist Carol Clarke. PHOTO: COURTESY OF THE CHALFONTE HOTEL

Historical Museum is this small but inviting art gallery. The center hosts monthly exhibits by noted national and regional artists and artisans. In the three galleries, you'll find paintings, paper sculptures, drawings, and etchings. The gallery is open daily from 10:00 A.M. to 4:00 P.M.

Mid-Atlantic Center for the Arts (MAC)
The Emlen Physick Estate, 1048 Washington Street, Cape May
(609) 884-5404
www.capemaymac.com

If Cape May is today one of the Shore's most vibrant year-round destinations, then MAC can take much of the credit. Established in 1970 as an all-volunteer organization, it now employs 130 people and has a million-dollar budget. MAC has vigorously promoted the arts in Cape May, presenting theater, concerts, lectures, and special events in various venues—and introducing thousands of visitors to the community's Victorian heritage.

The center makes its headquarters in a historic 18-room Victorian house and offers walking tours and trolley tours of Cape May's historic district. Among its most popular annual events are the Victorian Week Celebration (October) and the Christmas Tour. A recent addition to the estate is the Twinings Tearoom (for more about the house and the tearoom, see the Attractions chapter).

The Noyes Museum of Art
Lily Lake Road, Oceanville
(609) 652-8848
www.noyesmuseum.org

Though the Noyes is the smallest of New Jersey's art museums, it is one of the most appealing. Located between Smithville and Absecon on Lily Lake Road, it's adjacent to the Edwin B. Forsythe National Wildlife Refuge—and about 15 minutes away from Atlantic City. The Noyes, the only fine arts museum in the southern part of the state, was founded by American folk artist Fred Noyes and his wife, Ethel. (The couple was also responsible for re-creating the historic village of Smithville.)

The museum is built on the Noyes' personal collection of some 450 works of art: paintings, sculpture, photography, folk art in various media, and crafts such as baskets, glass, and fiber art. The Noyes also has an outstanding collection of vintage American bird decoys—more than 360 pieces dating from the mid-1800s to the 1970s. Assembled by the museum's founder, it's considered one of the finest in the country. To complement the decoys, there are about 130 related prints by contemporary artists and 540 duck-stamp prints.

The emphasis at the Noyes is on New Jersey artists. One past exhibit focused on Jersey Shore photographs; another, called "Mother and Daughter Impressions," featured the work of New Jersey Impressionists Ida Wells Stroud and her daughter, Clara.

In addition to its permanent collections and changing exhibits, the museum offers some appealing programs, including classes in sand painting and Mexican yarn painting for youngsters, and lectures on American Impressionism for middle and high school students. If you're in the Atlantic City area, or if you plan to visit Smithville or the Forsythe Refuge next door, you might want to include the Noyes in your itinerary, not just for the art, but also for the peaceful and beautiful surroundings. The museum is open Tuesday through Saturday from 10:00 A.M. to 4:30 P.M., and Sunday from noon to 5:00 P.M. Admission is $3.00.

Ocean City Arts Center
1735 Simpson Avenue, Ocean City
(609) 399–7628
www.oceancityartscenter.org

The center sponsors monthly gallery exhibits, weekly classes (more than 35), workshops, lectures, bus trips, and concerts. In addition to annual arts and crafts-shows on the Ocean City Boardwalk in August and September, there are children's programs and artists' receptions. The center is open Monday through Thursday from 9:00 A.M. to 9:00 P.M., Friday from 9:00 A.M. to 4:00 P.M., and Saturday from 9:00 A.M. to noon.

Ocean Galleries
9618 Third Avenue, Stone Harbor
(609) 368–7777
22nd Street and Ocean Drive, Avalon

(609) 967–4462
www.oceangalleries.com

Original contemporary art in all media, by local and international artists, is featured at these two galleries. For those who enjoy Shore seascapes, the galleries have limited-edition prints of Avalon and Stone Harbor scenes by artist Doris Zogas. The Stone Harbor gallery is open from 10:00 A.M. to 10:00 P.M. daily during the summer season and from 10:00 A.M. to 5:00 P.M. the rest of the year. The Avalon gallery is open from 9:00 A.M. to 5:00 P.M. daily year-round.

William Ris Galleries
9400 Second Avenue, Stone Harbor
(609) 368–6361

Here you'll find original art—watercolors, oils, and pastels—as well as limited-edition prints by local and national artists. There is also a selection of pottery, glassware, jewelry, and various gift items. During the summer season, the gallery is open from 10:00 A.M. to 10:00 P.M. daily; the rest of the year, the hours are 10:00 A.M. to 4:00 P.M. Friday through Sunday.

Insiders' Tip

Founded in 1991, the South Jersey Cultural Alliance (8 North Mississippi Avenue, Atlantic City, 609-441-1700) is an umbrella group of arts and cultural organizations whose members include more than 100 museums, performing arts resources, and historical associations. You can find out about all sorts of arts events on the Southern Shore at their Web site: www.sjca.net.

Annual Events and Festivals

You might think that swimming, surfing, building sand castles, and just hanging around the beach would leave folks at the Shore with little time to do anything else. But you would be only partly right. Shore residents and visitors are busy, busy, busy during the summer, doing everything from birding to flying kites to taking part in the myriad competitions that are part of the season's fun here. And let's not forget the flea markets and sidewalk sales, beloved by all local bargain hunters (we've had friends visit us just for these events).

Some events are nearly universal in these parts—like the vintage car celebrations held up and down the Shore. They're often called "Cruisin' with the Oldies," and they're usually full-blown parties with live music (often doo-wop). Red Bank has two such events, one in spring and another in fall. Ocean City has an antique auto event in June; Cold Spring Village has one in August.

Seafood festivals also abound—this is the Shore, after all. In this chapter, we've listed but a chosen few.

Calaveras County had its jumping frogs; the Jersey Shore has crab races—don't ask us why. In Harvey Cedars, there's an August race to determine the fastest crab on Long Beach Island. If you don't own a crab, you can rent. Barnegat has a similar competition in September, part of its big seafood festival.

During July and August, a number of towns offer free outdoor evening concerts. Belmar has them on Tuesdays at 8:00 P.M. (Taylor Pavilion) and on Fridays at 7:00 P.M. (Main and Ninth). On Point Pleasant Beach (Jenkinson's North Pavilion), concerts conducted by Father Alphonse take place on Wednesday evenings at 7:30. In Red Bank, you can listen to jazz in Marine Park every Thursday at 7:30 P.M., and on Sandy Hook, there are beach concerts on Wednesdays at 6:00 P.M. Asbury Park's summer concerts take place on Thursday nights at the Arthur Pryor Pavilion (Ocean and Fifth Avenues). Long Branch has "Jazz and Blues at the Beach" on Sunday evenings, at Laird and Ocean Avenues. On Barnegat's Municipal Dock on East Bay Avenue, you and your sweetie can enjoy music under the stars on Saturday nights.

Also common are lifeguard and beach-patrol competitions, which take place from Sandy Hook down to Cape May County. One of the biggest is at Sandy Hook, and we've listed that one in this chapter.

Around the Fourth of July, there are fireworks in just about every town. The biggest and most impressive display takes place on the Red Bank riverfront on July 3 (weather permitting); it's the work of the Grucci family, which also does the Macy's fireworks show in New York on the Fourth. Some towns have weekly fireworks displays during the summer: Point Pleasant Beach has them (at Jenkinson's South Beach) on Thursday evenings; Seaside Heights has fireworks on the Boardwalk at Webster Avenue on Wednesday evenings.

After the swimsuits have been put away, fall brings forth another round of activities: fishing competitions, Halloween parades, and other autumnal festivities. Things get a bit quieter during the winter. But as the December holiday season approaches, homes and businesses come to life with lights and decorations. Almost every little town has a tree-lighting and/or menorah-lighting ceremony and special events like visits from Santa. Later in the month, towns with sizeable African-American populations—like Asbury Park and Atlantic City—have Kwanzaa celebrations. On New Year's Eve, some towns hold First

Cruisin' with the Oldies is one of Red Bank's most popular events. PHOTO: ANDREW HASSARD

Night celebrations, which are generally alcohol-free, family-oriented festivities. Check with your local town hall or Chamber of Commerce to see if there's a First Night event near you.

In February, you'll find various events relating to Black History Month as well as celebrations of the birthdays of Presidents Washington and Lincoln. Local newspapers generally provide listings of the month's events.

During the Easter holiday season, many towns have Easter egg hunts, visits from the Easter Bunny, and similar celebrations. We've mentioned a few, listed under April, but sometimes they're in March, depending on when Easter falls.

We've given the months when various annual events and festivals occur; to get the specific dates, call the appropriate town hall or check your local newspapers.

January

Atlantic SAIL EXPO
Atlantic City Convention Center
One Ocean Way, Atlantic City
(609) 449–2012
www.sailamerica.com

The Atlantic City Convention Center is the site of many major shows throughout the year. This chapter includes a few that are of special interest to Shore residents. SAIL EXPO is the premier East Coast show for sailboats and sailing-related hardware, clothing, and gear. You'll find not only the hottest new items, but also concept displays on what the future of sailing might hold.

February

Annual Polar Bear Plunge
41st Street Beach, Sea Isle City
(609) 263–8687
www.seaislecity.org

You've heard the expression, "Go jump in the lake." Well, these folks take things a bit further, gathering in the middle of winter to jump into the ocean en masse. After their teeth stop chattering, the "polar bears" adjourn to the LaCosta Lounge on JFK Boulevard and Landis Avenue for a post-plunge party that includes food, music, and prizes.

Atlantic City Classic Car Event
Atlantic City Convention Center
One Ocean Way, Atlantic City
(856) 768–6900
www.acclassiccars.com

Since this annual celebration of horsepower takes place in the enormous new convention center, it bills itself as the world's largest indoor classic car show. If you're a car buff, you'll have a swell time at this event, which brings in hundreds of vendors and includes a car auction and a swap meet, where you might just find that elusive bit of chrome you need to restore your 1955 Thunderbird. The 2002 event included a display of the legendary Tucker automobile of 1947.

Atlantic City International Power Boat Show
Atlantic City Convention Center
One Ocean Way, Atlantic City
(856) 768–6900
www.acboatshow.com

This boat show is big—bigger than New York's or Miami's, covering just about every square foot of the convention center's 596,000 square feet of exhibit space. In 2002, there were some 800 boats, worth a total of about $100 million, on display. The boats seem to get bigger and more luxurious all the time, regardless of the so-called recession that affects the rest of the economy. A case in point: the Sunseeker Predator 61, made in the United Kingdom and priced at $1.8 million. Now you know: If you love boats, catch this show.

Black History Month Event
Atlantic City Art Center
Boardwalk and New Jersey Avenue,
Atlantic City
(609) 347–5837

Every year during Black History Month, the Art Center hosts a relevant art show; a past example was "Threads That Bind," an exhibition of Ghanian kente cloth.

Black History Month Events
Cape May Court House Museum
504 U.S. Highway 9 North, Cape May Court House
(609) 465–3535
www.cmcmuseum.org

During Black History Month, the museum joins with the Whitesboro Historical Foundation to present various programs on four Saturdays. These might include musical performances, lectures, or panel discussions. The museum also exhibits photographs, documents, and historical objects related to black history.

Black History Month/Presidents' Weekend
Monmouth Battlefield State Park
347 Freehold-Englishtown Road, Manalapan
(732) 462–9616

Both Black History Month and Presidents' Weekend are commemorated at the park over a three-day period. Events include walking tours of the battlefield, and a presentation on black heroes of the American Revolution, including soldiers like Salem Poor and Oliver Cromwell, and the men of the nearly all-black First Rhode Island Regiment. About 900 African-American soldiers fought at Monmouth; you can read about them in *Men of Color,* available at the park's gift shop. Within the park is Bethel AME Cemetery, where six black Civil War veterans are buried.

Crafts and Antiques in Winter
Cape May Convention Hall
Beach Drive at Stockton Place, Cape May
(800) 275–4278
www.capemaymac.org

To liven up this quiet time of year, about 40-odd crafters and a similar number of antiques dealers from the mid-Atlantic region assemble in the convention hall. Among the offerings are antique jewelry, furniture, crystal, glass, porcelain. Many items are from the Victorian period, as befits any event in Cape May.

The Deep Cut Orchid Show
Monmouth Mall
N.J. Highways 35 and 36, Eatontown
(732) 531–5058
www.deepcutorchids.com

The Deep Cut Orchid Society, which is based at Deep Cut Gardens in Middletown, sponsors this show. Exhibits feature scenes of tropical rain forests, woodland paths, and Japanese gardens. And, there are vendors selling orchids of every type and hue. It's a terrific opportunity to admire or acquire these exotic blooms.

Discover Cape May Houses Tour
Throughout Cape May
(800) 275–4278
www.capemaymac.org

The Mid-Atlantic Center for the Arts co-sponsors two self-guided walking tours of Cape May's Victorian architectural gems: one in February, the other in November. You decide which time of year appeals most. This is a good way to peek into more than a dozen bed-and-breakfast inns and private homes.

Filmmakers Symposium
Monmouth Mall
N.J. Highways 35 and 36, Eatontown
(732) 870–6010, (800) 531–9416

Do you like to be the first kid on the block to see the hot movies? If so, check out this 12-week event, which is divided into two six-week sessions, one in winter and the other in autumn. It's moderated by Chuck Rose and features celebrity guests like Danny Aiello, Dustin Hoffman, Wendy Wasserstein, and local-lad-made-good Kevin Smith. The symposium has hosted more than 700 film premieres. The 2000 symposium premiered 51 movies that later earned a gaggle of awards. It invites participants to become students of film; first to view the movies, then to discuss them with filmmakers and actors.

Ocean County Bluegrass Festival
Albert Music Hall
125 Wells Mills Road (Highway 532),
Waretown
(609) 971–1593

Take in this lively annual bluegrass concert, and you'll be tapping your toes and clapping your hands in no time at all. Organizers say this event features "the greatest bluegrass, country, and pineland music this side of Nashville."

Polar Bear Plunge
Jenkinson's Pavilion
Parkway and Ocean Avenue, Point Pleasant Beach
(732) 899–6686

Is jumping into the frigid Atlantic in the middle of winter your idea of fun? Then freeze for a good cause. Almost 2,000 hardy souls show up each year to raise thousands of dollars for the Special Olympics of New Jersey.

Washington's Birthday at Allaire Village
Allaire Village
Highway 524, Wall Township
(732) 919–3500
www.allairevillage.org

If your kids think that commemorating Washington's birthday means rushing to the mall, take them to this reenactment of Washington's birthday as it might have been celebrated circa 1830. Amid the games and merriment, George himself makes an appearance.

March

Annual Ocean Drive Marathon
Cape May to Sea Isle City
(609) 523–0880
www.odmarathon.com

This annual run begins in Victorian Cape May, continues, via the Ocean Drive, over four drawbridges, then through the Wildwoods (where contestants run the length of the Boardwalk), through the island communities of Stone Harbor and Avalon, and finishes on the promenade at JFK Boulevard in Sea Isle City.

"Atlantique City" Spring Festival
Atlantic City Convention Center
One Ocean Way, Atlantic City
(800) 526–2724
www.atlantiquecity.com

This indoor art, antiques, and collectibles show claims it's the largest in the world. It is certainly big, with upwards of 1,500 booths on 10½ indoor acres.

Jazz at the Point Festival
Various locales, Somers Point
(609) 927–7161
www.oceancityvacation.com/jazzfest.htm

At this four-day event, more than a dozen musicians, some local and some fairly well known (like guitarists Tony Do Rosario and Jimmy Bruno), appear at five area restaurants, clubs, churches, and schools. A weekend ticket will get you into all venues and shows. If you don't want to buy a ticket, there's a free concert on Saturday afternoon.

Leprechaun Contest
Casino Arcade
Grant Avenue and Boardwalk, Seaside Heights
(732) 793–6488
www.casinopier-waterworks.com

Here's an opportunity for your kids to dress up as leprechauns and compete for prizes. Winners get to ride the Casino Pier float in the St. Patrick's Day Parade.

St. Patrick's Day at Allaire Village
Allaire Village
Highway 524, Wall Township
(732) 919–3500
www.allairevillage.org

While many Shore towns hold parades in honor of St. Pat, here you'll find a re-enactment of an 1830 celebration. The costumes are authentic, and the fun includes good things to eat, games, and other diversions.

St. Patrick's Day Parade
Boardwalk, Atlantic City

As you may have guessed, St. Patrick's Day generates parades all over the Shore. This one starts at New Jersey Avenue and the Boardwalk.

St. Patrick's Day Parade
Boulevard, Seaside Heights
(800) SEA–SHOR
www.seasideheightstourism.com

Celebrating Irish heritage in a big way, this parade features some 20 marching bands, about a dozen floats, and 75 marching groups from around Ocean County.

St. Patrick's Day Parade
Lake Como to Sixth Avenue and Main Street, Belmar
(732) 280–2648
www.belmar.com/stpat

They start celebrating early in Belmar—usually a week or so before St. Patrick's Day (March 17)—and they have one of the biggest parades in the state. One year, even with cold and rain and the threat of a major snowstorm, some 60,000 Irish or near-Irish showed up (in decent weather, the parade draws about 160,000 spectators). With more than 20 bagpipe bands, a similar number of high school bands, and festivities throughout the town—and in many local bars and restaurants—a good time is had by all.

Sherlock Holmes Weekend
Cape May
(609) 884–5404, (800) 275–4278, ext. 185
www.capemaymac.org

The game's afoot during Sherlock Holmes Weekends, which take place in March and in November, when the weather in this most Victorian of towns is most London-like. But if you don't mind a little chill, this is truly a fun way to experience a brand-new Holmes mystery. You'll don Victorian attire and prowl the gaslit streets in search of clues. When the case is closed, you'll dine with the cast on Saturday evening and learn how these mysteries are created. The event, sponsored by the Mid-Atlantic Center for the Arts, also features a theatrical production and a tour of historic homes.

April

Annual Doodah Parade
Sixth to 12th Avenues, Boardwalk, to Music Pier, Ocean City
(609) 525–9300

We're not exactly sure what a "doodah" is, but what the hey, it's as good a reason as any to put on silly clothes and march around town. The cortege begins at Sixth Street, proceeds along the Boardwalk, and ends at the Music Pier. In years past, the theme of the parade involved animals, and folks would dress as different woodland creatures. Recent parades, though, have honored famous comedians, drawing forth an array of Groucho and Harpo Marxes, Laurels and Hardys, Mae Wests, and W. C. Fieldses. If you're willing to be silly and you don't care who sees you, you'll get a free T-shirt and a hot dog lunch.

Easter Celebrations
The beach at Franklin Avenue Stage and Boardwalk, Seaside Heights
(800) SEA–SHOR
www.seasideheightstourism.com

Kids love an Easter egg hunt, and this is a big one. Every year on Palm Sunday, the Easter bunny buries more than 15,000 prize-filled eggs in various locations on the beach. Kids age 10 or under are welcome to hunt for the goodies donated by Boardwalk merchants.

On Easter Sunday, put on that Easter bonnet and your best duds and join the mayor and town council for the annual Easter Promenade. Women receive a corsage and everyone can enjoy the live entertainment.

Easter Parade
Boardwalk and Fifth Avenue, Asbury Park
www.asburypark.net

No matter what else was going on in this troubled city, the Easter Parade has gone on. For more than 65 years, folks have put on their Easter Sunday best and set out to parade among neighbors and onlookers, to be photographed by local papers, and perhaps to win a prize.

New Jersey Seafood Festival
Silver Lake Park, Belmar
(800) 523–2587

Another excuse to eat clams and shrimp, this festival features two days' worth of some of the Shore's best seafood, accompanied by live jazz and blues music. More than 30 of the Shore's top seafood restaurants are represented. The state's wine growers show off their vintages at the wine-tasting tent. After you've eaten, check out the artists' and crafters' booths, the model boat demonstrations, and the environmental displays. Your kids will no doubt want to head for the petting zoo and the pony rides.

May

Music Festival
Various locations, Cape May
(609) 884–5404
www.capemaymac.org

Classical music, chamber music, jazz, and even the occasional doo-wop are on offer during the five-week festival. An Atlantic City mini concert series is part of the festival, with performances taking place in that city's Convention Hall and other locations.

National Long Distance Casting Championship
Wildwood
(609) 624–9375

Contestants from the United States and as far away as Japan travel to Wildwood to participate in this event. But during the sport's venerable history, it was never, until recently, promoted as a spectator event. Casting demonstrations are staged at night, lit by strobes and floodlights, so all can see the ultra-high-tech rods and the outfits of the fly fishermen. Men, women, juniors, and seniors vie for top honors in certified distance casting. In case you didn't know, the sport started in Cape May County under the banner of the "Ocean City Cup Tournament" and the authority of the Association of Surf Angling Clubs in 1916. The first event took place when the Ocean City Fishing Club challenged the Asbury Park Fishing Club to a team distance-casting competition. The Ocean City Cup is solid silver, valued at $45,000; it predates the Americas Cup.

Town-wide Garage Sale, Sidewalk Sale, and Donation Day
Belmar
(732) 681–2900
www.belmar.com

Are you in the market for some lawn furniture? How about a lamp or a beach umbrella? On this weekend in early May, anyone who wants to get rid of stuff, does. People have been known to furnish summer rentals with things they buy cheap. Name your price.

Wildwoods International Kite Festival
Beach and Convention Center, Wildwood
(215) 736–3715.

Though it started as a two-block competition, this event is now America's biggest kite festival; it's also the world's only official kiting event held on a beach. Competitors from the United States, Canada, and Europe converge here to compete in a variety of categories. Sport kite teams with names like "Captain Eddy's Flying Circus" (Ohio) and "Chicago Fire" (Illinois) perform flight routines synchronized to music. These hardy competitors strap themselves to their kites, using waist belts to control kites that dance in the air at speeds in excess of 200 miles an hour. In the Extreme Kite Board/Wild Wheels Bug Blast competition, specially designed three-wheel land cruisers, affixed with kites designed to harness wind power, blast across the sand at speeds of up to 40 miles an hour. Additional events include surfing demonstrations, tractor kiting, and land-sailing demonstrations. The finale, inside the convention center, is a competition featuring kite ballet and synchronized flying.

During Wildwood's Kite Festival, you'll see kite races and some impressive kite ballet. PHOTO: COURTESY OF CAPE MAY COUNTY TOURISM

World Series of Birding
Cape May
(609) 884-2736
www.njaudubon.org

Long recognized as one of the premier birding spots in the world, Cape May attracts enthusiasts from around the country in May for the World Series of Birding. Timed for the spring migration, the event brings birders together to witness thousands of birds passing through Cape May en route to their northern nesting spots. This official event is organized by the New Jersey Audubon Society; categories include teams, individuals, youth/school groups, and novice backyard birders. Participants search for as many bird species as they can within a defined geographic area. Teams usually average about 165 species, but the totals vary according to weather, experience, skill, and just plain luck. Since 1984, a total of 314 species have been observed and officially recorded during the event. A nice sidebar to this event: teams raise money for favorite environmental causes by gathering pledges, based on the number of birds they see.

June

Annual Mariner's Blessing
Historic Gardner's Basin, Atlantic City
(609) 348-4040

This isn't just a tourist event. Wherever you find fishermen, the boat parade and ceremonial blessing for a safe and prosperous season have real meaning. Though anyone who makes a living at sea knows that boats and their crews are lost every year, this is a happy occasion, with music and vendors and all the other trappings of Shore festivals.

Annual New Jersey Fresh Seafood Festival
Historic Gardner's Basin
New Hampshire Avenue and the bay, Atlantic City
www.gardnersbasin.com

In mid-June, this festival turns the basin into a family playground for two entire days. Dozens of vendors offer a succulent selection of ocean fare, including Cajun fried shrimp, clams and oysters on the half shell, and chowders and soups. There's music and entertainment, too. And when the last finger-licking morsel has been consumed, you can relax and watch a gorgeous sunset.

Battle of Monmouth Reenactment
Monmouth Battlefield State Park
347 Freehold-Englishtown Road, Manalapan
(732) 462-9616

We've talked about the 1778 battle in our Revolutionary New Jersey chapter; it was one of the war's critical engagements and it made a heroine of Mary Hays, better known as Molly Pitcher. Once a year, on a weekend in late June, the park once again becomes a battlefield. Men, women, and children in period dress live in tents and cook over campfires. The patriots march and drill—and then go off to meet General Henry Clinton's redcoats. If history in books seems dull to your kids, the reenactment will bring it stirringly to life.

Baymen's Clam Bake
"Tip" Seaman Park (Ocean County Park)
U.S. Highway 9, Tuckerton
(732) 296-8868
www.tuckertonseaport.org

You may have guessed that Shore folk like events where lots of food is served. We don't need an excuse to eat seafood, but it's nice to have one—along with an excuse to enjoy the company of friends and neighbors, and some lively entertainment. You'll find all that at the Baymen's Clam Bake, as well as hot dogs and pork barbecue for those who don't like the fruits of the sea. There are children's activities like sand art and face painting. Proceeds benefit the Barnegat Bay Decoy & Baymen's Museum.

BeachFest
Atlantic City
(609) 484-9020
www.acbeachfest.com

Late in June, Atlantic City kicks off the summer with the biggest beach party on the East Coast: hundreds of thousands of visitors come to A.C. for this three-day

The magnificent sand castles that compete during Atlantic City's Beachfest are works of art.

bash. You can splash in the still-cool surf; you can build sand sculptures (you'll see some spectacular creations); and you can sample the many Boardwalk festivities. There are free concerts, shows, a parade, wrestling, dance parties, sky-diving shows, fireworks, and more.

Miss New Jersey Pageant
Boardwalk, Ocean City
(609) 399–2629
www.oceancityvacation.com

There she is, Miss New Jersey. Young ladies from all over the Garden State vie for some $90,000 in scholarship money in this swimsuit and talent competition. But the big prize is the chance to move on to the big show next door, the Miss America Pageant in Atlantic City.

National Marbles Tournament
Ringer Stadium (on the beach), Wildwood
(609) 729–9000

Boys and girls (ages 8 to 14) from all over the country meet at Ringer Stadium on the beach to compete for some $4,000 in

scholarship money and prizes—and the title of King and Queen. Tournament marbles originated in 1922 with this event, originally sponsored by Macy's department store in Philadelphia. If you'd like to know more, visit the George F. Boyer Museum on the Holly Beach Station Mall, which is home to the National Marbles Hall of Fame.

Red, White and Blueberry Festival
Downtown Hammonton (just off N.J. Highway 54)
(609) 561–9080

Hammonton considers itself the (unofficial) blueberry world capital, and so officially kicks off blueberry season with this celebration in June. The event includes a stage show, an antique car show, food vendors, arts and crafts, lots of fresh-picked blueberries, all kinds of blueberry baked goods—and, of course, a blueberry pie-eating contest. Wharton Forest and Batsto Village are nearby, so the festival could be a pleasant addition to a visit to those attractions.

Riverfest
Marine Park, Red Bank
(800) 438–FEST

Jazz and blues and food from area eateries are on the menu for this annual festival held on the banks of the Navesink River. It's the state's largest free music event, and it goes on for three (with luck) balmy, tune-filled days. You'll also find crafts vendors and a play area for children.

ShopRite LPGA Classic
Seaview Marriott Resort
U.S. Highway 9, Absecon
(609) 383–8330
www.shopritelpga.org

Every year, the top women professional golfers compete in this prestigious event, held on Seaview's Bay Course. Past winners include Annika Sorenstam, Betsy King, Se Ri Pak, and Juli Inkster. It's a great opportunity to see the golfers up close and even grab an autograph or a photo.

July

All-Women Lifeguard Tournament
Gateway National Recreation Area, Sandy Hook
(732) 872–5940

This competition is the largest all-women lifeguarding contest in the world. About 200 young women on 20-odd teams, most from the East Coast and Canada, swim, run, paddle, and row; the competition for golden bowl trophies, team plaques, and silver, glass-bottomed tankards is intense. Even if you don't have a sister or cousin entered in the competition, it's fun to watch—and a good excuse to spend time in this beautiful park.

Annual Barnegat Crab Race and Seafood Festival
Veterans' Field
Bay Boulevard, Seaside Heights
(732) 349–0220

If you have no desire to race a crab, you might come to eat one: steamed crabs and other delicacies are on offer during this late-September festival. And just to keep things lively, there is entertainment, a flea

market, a craft fair, and a pageant for youngsters ages two to eight.

Cape May County 4-H Fair
Cape May County 4-H Fairgrounds
355 Court House/South Dennis Road (Highway 657), Clementon
(609) 465–5115

In addition to animal shows and sales, there's always live entertainment and plenty of good stuff to eat, including a fish fry and chicken barbecue.

Classic Boat Show Weekend
Tuckerton Seaport
120 West Main Street, Tuckerton
(609) 296–8868

Shore folk love their classic boats almost as much as their classic cars, and this day celebrates the beauty of the wooden crafts of the past, which were powered by sails or antique engines. There is also a boat-building class, a sailing competition for model boats in the Tuckerton Creek, and face-painting for kids who want to look like pirates or pussycats for the day.

Elvis Day
Jenkinson's, Point Pleasant Beach
(732) 892–0600

Elvis Day may not have the earth-shaking importance of, say, D-Day, but there's sure to be plenty of hip-shaking going on. Celebrate the King with an army of guys in pompadour wigs and white jumpsuits who come for the look-alike contest. In a slight departure from reality, there's also a skydiving Elvis and, later on, a laser light show with an Elvis theme.

Festival of the Sea
St. Francis Center
4700 Long Beach Boulevard, Brant Beach (LBI)
(609) 494-8861

This weeklong festival has all the ingredients of a typical Shore affair: rides, amusements, games, and lots of feasting.

Monmouth County Fair
East Freehold Park Showgrounds
Kozloski Road, East Freehold
(732) 842-4000

Pet a pregnant cow and admire the ducks, goats, and sheep raised by youthful 4-H-ers at this old-fashioned agricultural fair. Folks compete for ribbons and trophies in over 1,000 categories, including baked goods, quilting, canning, and needlework. Prizes are given for goats and sheep and other livestock, too. Even if your farming expertise begins and ends with begonias, you'll find lots to see and do: visit the petting zoo, browse the home and garden tent for exotic orchids and bonsai plants, admire antique cars, and view demonstrations of interesting farm machinery—like incubators that hatch chicks. There is entertainment, a scattering of midway rides, and of course, lots of stuff to eat.

Ocean County Fair
Robert J. Miller Air Park
Highway 530, Berkeley Township
(732) 914-9466
www.oceancountyfair.com

If you want more than the usual midway attractions from your county fair, you'll find some odd ones here—skunk racing and pig racing, for instance. (What is it with us Shore folk? Will we race any critter that we can coax or cajole toward a finish line?) Like the Monmouth County Fair, this one shows off the skills of 4-H-ers and the quality of their animals. In addition to a dog show and a horse show, there's entertainment galore, including guitar and calliope playing and an oldies music event. Are you good with a chain saw? Compete in the carving contest. If you have a beautiful baby, enter him or her in the baby contest. And if you have a two-year-old who likes to run—you guessed it, there's a toddler race. It's all in good fun, as the crowds who turn out for the annual event can attest.

Oceanfest
Promenade, Long Branch

Long Branch goes all out for this Fourth of July event, the city's biggest of the summer. There are bands, dancing, entertainment, pony rides, arts and crafts, a basketball tournament, and lots of food of every ethnic persuasion. It's finished off with a spectacular fireworks display. If you like the bustle of crowds, this one's for you: attendance can run about 300,000.

St. Paul's Annual Antiques Show
St. Paul's United Methodist Church
Bridge and West Lake Avenues, Bay Head
(732) 892-5926
www.bayhead.org

There are lots of terrific church-sponsored sales throughout the Shore, but we single out this one because it's been going on for a half century and is one of the most popular antiques shows in the area. It draws dealers from all over the state—and some interesting out-of-town customers, too (we heard that Katharine Hepburn made a purchase here some years ago). In addition to the usual antiques—furniture, glassware, jewelry, silver, and the like—you'll find boutique tables laden with arts and crafts, and an art show presented by the Manasquan River Artists' Group.

Sand Castle Contest
18th Avenue Beach, Belmar
(732) 681-3700

One thing we've got plenty of at the Shore is sand, and so you'll find sand-castle contests up and down the coast throughout the warm months. The Belmar competition is serious business, though, with $25,000 in prizes and some 3,000 participants, including professionals from all over the country. There are children's age-group divisions and a 16-and-over category. While some competitors use the

Sidewalk Sales by the Sea

Sidewalk sales are a big part of Shore culture; almost every town (and mall) has them. Some are notable: Red Bank's, in July, is a biggie, with virtually the entire downtown area participating. The bargains are real and the atmosphere is festive. Deal's sale, also in July, is much smaller, because there aren't many shops, but the shops there are selling high-end designer merchandise, and the bargains are irresistible if you have a taste for names like Moschino and Armani. In sedate Spring Lake, there's an August sale that serves as a good excuse to visit the town. Stone Harbor does one in August; Cape May has two—one in May, another in September. Point Pleasant has a good one, too. Wherever you live or spend your summer vacation, watch the local paper or call the local Chamber of Commerce to find out when these bargain fests take place. Bring cash (some places don't take credit cards during these cut-to-the-bone events) as well as cards, wear comfortable shoes, and start your engines.

old-fashioned pail-and-shovel approach, master builders like Pennsylvania resident Chuck Feld employ such implements as a masonry trowel and cake-decorating tools. Chuck, incidentally, has created such wonders as a sand Godzilla and a castle that was featured in tourism commercials with former governor Christine Todd Whitman. Feld works full-time at this craft and shovels from six to 20 tons of sand a day.

Sara the Turtle Festival
Sea Isle City
(609) 262–TOUR

As we mentioned in our Overview chapter, Sea Isle City makes a point of caring for its turtles. From June until the end of July, female terrapins leave the marshes and cross a busy street to reach the higher ground, where they lay their eggs. To create public awareness and to save the turtles from being killed in traffic, Sea Isle has adopted Sara the Turtle as its official mascot. This annual festival, which is named for her, raises funds for the Sea Isle City Environmental Commission and the Wetlands Institute. It celebrates Sara with a puppet show, a shell exhibit, a Diaper Derby, races for children, and face-painting.

August

Atlantic City Film Festival
2921 Atlantic Avenue, Atlantic City
(609) 646–1640
www.atlanticcityfilmfestival.com

The Atlantic City Film Festival accepts entries from independent producers, major studios, and students, offering prizes in a number of different categories—feature films, documentaries, shorts, and animation. In past years, screenings and award ceremonies have been held at the Showboat Casino.

Atlantic County 4-H Fair
David C. Wood Youth Center
N.J. Highway 50 (between Mays Landing and Egg Harbor City), Egg Harbor City
(609) 625–7000, ext. 6158

At this fair, the emphasis is more on traditional 4-H activities than on midway-type attractions. But in addition to the horse show, the dog show, and the other animal competitions, there are such fun events as frog jumping and turtle races, an antique tractor parade, model railroad demonstrations, and magic shows.

Clearwater Festival
Asbury Park
(732) 872–9644
www.clearwatermc.org/clearwater-festival.htm

If you're a baby boomer, you may remember folk singer Pete Seeger sailing his sloop *Clearwater,* a replica of a 19th-century vessel, down the Hudson River, stopping along the way to speak out about environmental concerns. The Clearwater Festival was inspired by Seeger's work; today the organization is involved in environmental issues, fighting, for example, the proposed dumping of contaminated dredge material from New York Harbor into the ocean off Sandy Hook. In 2001, the 26th festival moved from Sandy Hook to Asbury Park—a move that brought out Bruce Springsteen, who made a surprise appearance and boosted not only the festival, but also Asbury Park. The three-day affair features environmental displays, food and crafts booths, children's activities, and several music stages.

Italian Festival
Joe Palaia Park
Deal and Whalepond Roads, Ocean Township
(732) 695–2971

When it's August in and around Ocean Township, folks know it's time to let out the belt a notch and get ready to feast on sausage and peppers, portobello mushrooms, clams on the half shell, meatball subs, and fried calamari. This ethnic festival, which runs for two days, has been around for more than a quarter of a century. After you've eaten till you can't manage another morsel, there are rides, amusements, games of chance, fireworks and a "big 50-50," a game of chance with prizes that run as high as thousands of dollars.

Jersey Cape Shell Show and Sale
The Wetlands Institute
1075 Stone Harbor Boulevard, Stone Harbor
(609) 368–1211

Conchologists have shows wherever shells are found. This weekend event includes lectures, craft demonstrations, and shells from around the world. Rare and decorative shells and shell arts and crafts are also on display. Shells from New Jersey, as well as from more exotic places, are featured in competitive and educational exhibits. You'll also see demonstrations of shell craft. You, too, can compete by bringing in a wondrous clam, oyster, whelk, or moon shell.

Miss Crustacean Hermit Crab Beauty Pageant
12th Street Beach, Ocean City
(609) 525–9300

Other towns simply have crab races, but Ocean City has the world's only hermit crab beauty pageant. It is followed, of course, by hermit crab races for the Cucumber Rind Cup.

Red Bank International Film Festival
Clearview Cinema
White Street, Red Bank
(732) 843–7972
www.freedomfilmsociety.org

Sponsored by a number of local businesses, this summer event features the work of independent filmmakers, including some from the Shore area. More than 50 films, including documentaries and experimental works, are shown during the three-day festival.

World's Oldest Baby Parade
Sixth Street and the Boardwalk, Ocean City
(609) 525–9300

This baby parade is almost a century old. But the format remains the same. Some 300 kids—infants to 10-year-olds—compete for prizes and the chance to get their pictures taken by the local paper.

September

Antique Wooden Boat Show
Bay Head Yacht Club Basin
Centennial Park, Bay Head
www.bayhead.org

There are bigger antique wooden boat shows than this one, but on a beautiful fall day, you might enjoy a visit to this picturesque town with a long history of boat-building. The New England atmosphere and the gray-shingled cottages make for a romantic setting that matches perfectly with the romance of wooden boats.

Chowderfest Weekend
Ninth Street and Taylor Avenue, Beach Haven
(609) 494–7211

Manhattan or New England? You can settle this burning question once and for all at this showcase for clam chowder. Taste to your heart's content as restaurants compete for prizes in a chowder cook-off. (Prizes are also given for the best booth.) You'll get music while you slurp; there's entertainment for kids, too.

Crazy Hat Parade
Euclid Avenue Beach, Loch Arbour
(732) 531–4740

For some 30 years, this tiny town has been getting silly and giddy on Labor Day weekend. This annual parade isn't a big event, but if you're in the area, it's fun to watch 70 or 80 people march along the sand wearing hats that resemble the one worn by Dr. Seuss's Cat in the Hat, or baskets of eggs, or cornucopias of fruit. Most paraders are veterans, notably the descendants of Arthur Kaplow, who originated the parade as an end-of-summer ritual.

Festival of the Sea
Beach and Boardwalk, Point Pleasant Beach
(732) 899–2424

Named one of the "Top 100 Events in North America" by the American Bus Association, this funfest takes advantage of the beautiful days and warm water temperatures that September at the Shore is known for. There are arts and crafts, food galore, and entertainment, too. But what makes this festival stand out from all the other food-and-entertainment events is the "Hey Rube Get a Tube" inner-tube race on the ocean. Thrills (well, not too many of those actually) and spills (much more likely) make for a rollicking good time. With prizes, of course.

Everyone has fun at Point Pleasant's "Hey Rube Get a Tube" race. PHOTO: COURTESY OF OCEAN COUNTY PUBLIC AFFAIRS

Giant Fall Flea Market
Ocean Pathway, Ocean Grove
(732) 774–1391

There are flea markets all over the Shore, almost year-round. This one, sponsored by the local Chamber of Commerce, is a big one, a real trash-and-treasures affair, with more than 300 vendors. Some sell new merchandise—sweatshirts, socks, sunglasses, and the like. But regular folks bring their no-longer-wanted stuff here, too, so you might spot (as we have in the past) such finds as an unusual Art Nouveau lamp and an antique alligator vanity case—at considerably less than antiques shop prices.

Latino Festival
Historic Gardner's Basin
Atlantic City
(609) 209–6862
www.gardnersbasin.com

This two-day affair is one of the biggest festivals at Gardner's Basin. Hosted by the Hispanic Alliance of Atlantic County, it celebrates Hispanic cultural heritage with colorful costumes, live music, and Latino foods. If you like to dance, musicians like merengue artist Tono Rosario and salsa specialist Obie Bermudez will supply the beat.

Ocean County Decoy and Gunning Show
"Tip" Seaman County Park, Pinelands Regional High School, 565 Nugentown Road, and Middle School, 590 Nugentown Road, Tuckerton
(609) 971–3085

This event reflects South Jersey's strong waterfowling heritage. You'll find displays from past and present, with an emphasis on working and antique decoys, model boats, sneakbox building, and waterfowling on the Barnegat Bay. Hundreds of exhibitors display their works of art and merchandise in all three locations. Competitions and contests are always part of this event on Lake Pohatcong and along the shoreline at "Tip" Seaman County Park. The musical entertainment features the sounds of the Pine Barrens,

and the food reflects the tastes of the bay (along with burgers and chicken for land-lubbers). There are dog and puppy retriever contests and duck- and goose-calling competitions.

Thunder on the Beach Monster Truck Competition
The beach, Schellenger to Young Avenues, Wildwood
(609) 523–8051
www.njhra.com

Monster Trucks race for the "King of the Beach" title. This is a whole weekend of Monster Truck rides, exhibits, autograph sessions with the drivers—and lots of food, for what is a beach weekend without it? If trucks on the beach are not for you, there are power-boat races on Sunset Lake in Wildwood Crest this month, often on the same weekend.

Wings 'n' Water Festival
The Wetlands Institute
1075 Stone Harbor Boulevard, Stone Harbor
(609) 368–1211

In September, the institute sponsors this, its biggest fund-raising event. The work of nationally acclaimed decoy carvers, and paintings of wildlife and the sea are displayed; guided beach and marsh tours are given, too.

October

Annual 18-Mile Commemorative Run
St. Francis Community Center
4700 Long Beach Boulevard, Brant Beach (LBI)
(609) 494–8861
www.stfranciscenterlbi.com

Runners who have their eyes on the Boston and New York Marathons train at this USA Track and Field–certified event. It begins at the southern end of Long Beach Island, in beautiful Holgate Nature Preserve, and runs the length of LBI to historic Barnegat Lighthouse State Park in the north. Applications are available at the Web site.

Annual Firefighters Memorial Run
Promenade and Kennedy Boulevard,
Sea Isle City
(609) 861–0674
www.seaislecity.org

This has been a popular event for almost 30 years. The run is five miles long; there's a one-mile jog for children and joggers.

Annual Long Beach Island Surf Fishing
Tournament
265 West Ninth Street, Ship Bottom
(609) 494–7211
www.discoversouthernocean.org

It's impossible to keep your lucky spots secret for long when area fishermen fan out all across the beaches of Long Beach Island, trying to land the biggest bluefish or striper (bass). There are thousands of dollars to be won in daily, weekly, and grand prizes. If you love to fish, here's a chance to show off your prowess and win money, too.

Annual Pine Barrens Jamboree
Wells Mills County Park
905 Wells Mills Road (Highway 532),
Waretown
(609) 971–3085
www.oceancountygov.com

Celebrate the culture of the Pine Barrens with music, environmental activities, and crafts.

Annual Pumpkin Festival
Historic Cold Spring Village
720 U.S. Highway 9, Cape May
(609) 898–2300

If you need an excuse to visit Cold Spring Village in autumn, this might be it. There's a Halloween parade, music, games, food, a craft show, and yes, pumpkin-painting.

"Atlantique City" Holiday Megafair
Atlantic City Convention Center
One Ocean Way, Atlantic City
(800) 526–2724
www.atlantiquecity.com

Here's another of the huge shows that take place in the convention center. This one, featuring art, antiques, and collectibles, draws some 1,600 exhibitors

from the United States, Canada, Europe, and Asia.

Barbershop Quartet Weekend
Wildwoods Convention Center
Burk Avenue and Boardwalk, Wildwood
(609) 729–9000
www.harmonize.com/mad

If you like the old-fashioned sound of barbershop quartets, you might want to take in one of the evening competitions that are part of the Barbershoppers' Mid-Atlantic District Convention. There are quartet and chorus performances; take your pick.

Clean Ocean Action Fall Beach Sweep
Gateway National Recreation Area, Sandy Hook
(732) 872–0111
www.cleanoceanaction.org

This is the largest statewide beach clean-up. Volunteers fill giant trash bags with waste left on the beach and catalogue what they've found. These records help to pinpoint the sources of pollution, for example, the medical waste that washed up on our shores some years ago. The organization also holds a fund-raiser in the fall; it's just about having fun and supporting a worthy cause. There's music and food donated by local restaurants, as well as a silent auction featuring gifts and art donated by area businesses and artists.

Coast Day NJ
Fisherman's Cooperative Dock
Channel Drive, Point Pleasant Beach
(732) 872–1300, ext. 22
www.njmsc.org

The New Jersey Marine Science Consortium sponsors Coast Days along the Shore. Each provides an opportunity to learn about the marine environment here through exhibits, demonstrations, and tours.

Coast Day N.J.
Various locations, Cape May
(732) 872–1300, ext. 22
www.njmsc.org

Since you are at the Shore, wouldn't it make sense to learn a little more about the ecosystem here? This is one of a series of events sponsored by the New Jersey Marine Sciences Consortium and held along the Shore. It includes marine exhibits, guided tours, and hands-on activities.

Corvette Show
Towne of Historic Smithville
U.S. Highway 9 and Moss Mill Road, Smithville
(609) 652–7777
www.smithvillenj.com

If you own a Corvette (or yearn to own one), you'll find a hundred or more of these gorgeous autos, both classic and new, to drool over at this annual event. If you happen to be on the Atlantic City Expressway as a caravan of 'vettes heads toward Smithville (as we were one year), it's a glorious sight.

Cranberry Harvest Tours
Whitesbog Village (Lebanon State Forest)
120-13 Whitesbog Road, New Lisbon
(609) 893–4646
www.whitesbog.org

Cranberries, as we explain in the Farms and Wineries chapter, are the treasures of the Pine Barrens, and it is a wonder to see them. At this festival you'll get a slide presentation on the history of cranberry cultivation in New Jersey and trips to the bogs. The harvest of these ruby red berries by the millions is a great photo opportunity.

Fall Flea Market
Historic Allaire Village
Highway 524, Wall Township
(732) 919–3500
www.allairevillage.org

One good reason to attend this event is that it supports the operation of Allaire Village. Another good reason is that dozens of vendors turn up, which makes for some interesting shopping.

Halloween Festival
Bayview Park
68th Street and Long Beach Boulevard, Brant Beach (LBI)
(609) 361–1000, ext. 246

Long Beach Islanders come out for this daytime Halloween celebration, which features a haunted house, clowns, a trackless train, and lots of balloons.

Halloween Parade
Lyle Lane to the Emlen Physick Estate, Cape May
(609) 884–9565

Cape May puts on one of the Shore's splashier Halloween parades, featuring bands, floats, and performing groups. There are costume contests, with prizes and trophies. It takes place during the day, so you don't have to worry about keeping the kids up late.

Haunted Seaport
Tuckerton Seaport
120 West Main Street, Tuckerton
(609) 296–8868
www.tuckertonseaport.org

If you happen to be near this area of Ocean County in late October, celebrate Halloween with the kids in a safe (yet scary) environment. There's a costume parade, a sing-along, hot cider, and creature cookies. The scary part comes with tales of terror, convincingly told.

Ocean County Columbus Day Parade and Italian Festival
Boulevard (parade) and Grant Avenue (festival), Seaside Heights
(732) 477–6507
www.ameri-com.com/columbus

The highlight of this three-day festival is the parade along the Boulevard. Like many other Shore happenings, it's a great excuse to enjoy good things to eat.

Octoberfest
Bay Avenue, Highlands
(732) 946–2711

The char-grilled bratwurst smells like heaven to German-food lovers. There are potato pancakes, sauerkraut, baked goodies, and a beer truck dispensing Spaten on tap. Oompah music inspires some neighbors to step into a polka. There may also be a fireworks display on the final night of this lively event.

The Chatsworth Cranberry Festival

Chatsworth, in Burlington County (about a 20-minute drive from Long Beach Island), is the capital of the Pine Barrens. With an area of over 73,000 acres and a population of nearly 2,000, it's the largest township with the smallest population of any in the county. Though early settlements date back to the late 1700s, it wasn't until a century later that cranberries became important here.

Once known as Shamong, the town was renamed Chatsworth in 1901. Back in the late 19th century, it was a high-society hot spot, boasting a country club with such distinguished members as the Vanderbilts, Drexels, and Astors. The glamour is long gone, and the only remaining landmarks are Bizby's General Store and the partially restored White Horse Inn, still in need of interior repair. The Cranberry Festival is a way to raise funds to restore it.

The cranberry harvest here is the third largest in the United States. And it's here, at this two-day event that draws as many as 25,000 visitors, that you can immerse yourself in cranberry culture—and taste dozens of cranberry concoctions. The event, which takes place in October, includes tours of the cranberry bogs, which are really fun. You'll see men in waders sloshing through flooded bogs working along with big machines; the scene has been described as "a symphony in red."

Once you've seen the fruit in its natural (and bitter) form, you can taste all sorts of sweetened versions at the festival: cranberry muffins, cranberry cake, cranberry preserves, cranberry salsa, cranberry...well, you get the idea. You'll also find arts and crafts vendors, antiques dealers, country-style music all day long, and plenty of hats and aprons and souvenir shirts for sale. On one of the days there's an Antique and Classic Automobile Show. Some years, there's even a special appearance by the Jersey Devil (the mythical demon, not a hockey player).

For more about the Chatsworth Cranberry Festival, call (609) 726–1907 or (609) 726–1890 or visit www.cranfest.org.

Octoberfest
Towne of Historic Smithville
U.S. Highway 9 and Moss Mill Road, Smithville
(609) 652–7777
www.smithvillenj.com

Smithville hosts one of the biggest Octoberfests we've ever seen, with hundreds of exhibits, crafters, food vendors, rides, and entertainment. It does get crowded, but if the weather cooperates and you find a parking place, you'll have a good time.

Red Bank Art Walk
(888) HIPTOWN
www.redbankrivercenter.org

If you need an excuse to explore Red Bank, this is a good one. Stroll the brick sidewalks, sip a latte, and enjoy the mix of stores, ranging from upscale home shops like Duxiana and Renovation Hardware to Domenick's Barber Shop, where a haircut will set you back eight bucks. You'll find most of the galleries, like Art Forms, the Art Alliance, and Afridesia, on Broad Street, Monmouth Street, or White Street, so you can make a little circuit. There are also a number of places on the route to stop for a drink or a snack, including the Dublin House and the Broadway Diner.

Victorian Week
Emlen Physick Estate
1048 Washington Street, Cape May
(800) 275–4278
www.capemaymac.org

A 10-day celebration of Cape May's Victorian heritage, Victorian Week is one of the reasons this picturesque town is often busier in the fall than it is in summer. This event includes a Victorian dance weekend, historic house tours, living-history reenactments, and much more.

Women's Surf Fishing Tournament
Municipal Marina
42nd Place and the bay, Sea Isle City
(215) 855–3411

If you're a female fisher, try your luck. Compete for the Mayor's Trophy, given for the most fish, or for one of the prizes awarded in other categories.

November

Annual Bicycle Hub Mountain Bike Race
Allaire State Park
Wall Township
(732) 946–9080
www.bicyclehub.com

If you're a mountain biker who enjoys a challenge, enter the state's oldest and largest event; the competitors range from beginners to pros.

Cape May Jazz Festival
Historic District
Beach Drive, Cape May
(609) 884–7277
www.capemayjazz.com

If you're a jazz buff, you won't want to miss this three-day festival that features such greats as Chuck Mangione, McCoy Tyner, and Ray Barretto. There are usually about 20 jazz, blues, and gospel performances as well as jam sessions.

Holiday Light Spectacular
PNC Bank Arts Center
Garden State Parkway, exit 116
(732) 335–8698
www.artscenter.com

From mid-November though January 1, you'll find a spectacular display of holiday lights—the largest in the state—at the PNC Bank Arts Center. This is a drive-through event; the entrance fee is per car. At the end of the drive, there's a Holiday Village, where you can step out and get some refreshments or have your picture taken with Santa. The hours are from dusk until 10:00 P.M. Sunday through Thursday, and from dusk to 11:00 P.M. on Friday and Saturday.

Holiday Season
Emlen Physick Estate
1048 Washington Street, Cape May
(800) 275–4278
www.capemaymac.org

Beginning in mid-November (or thereabouts), the county launches seven weeks of special events and activities—including candlelight house tours and a Christmas feast—to celebrate the season. To make sure you don't miss out, call for a schedule or check the Web site.

December

Annual Long Beach Island Christmas Parade
Long Beach Boulevard, Ship Bottom
(609) 494–1614, ext. 116
www.shipbottom.org

Long Beach Island gets pretty quiet in late fall and winter, but there are moments during the holiday season when everyone who's still around comes out to have a good time. The Christmas Parade is one of those times, with floats, bands, antique cars, and the requisite visit by Santa Claus.

Christmas at Allaire Village
Allaire Village
Highway 524, Wall Township
(732) 919–3500
www.allairevillage.org

By now you will have guessed that there are many special events at Allaire all year long. We've listed a few, but you can call or check their Web site for a complete schedule. During the holiday season, the village offers a costumed reenactment of Christmas as it might have been celebrated back in the 1830s, when the village was "real." Since Santa will be there, this event might make a nice alternative to those visits with the department store versions.

Christmas Celebrations
Bay Head
(800) 4–BAYHED
www.bayhead.org
As we mentioned earlier, almost every Shore town wakes up for the Christmas season. Just choose one you'd like to visit and call the local town hall to find out what special events are planned. Bay Head launches the season with a weekend of events. It kicks off with an open house at the town shops, a tree lighting, caroling, a visit from Santa, musical entertainment, and refreshments and raffle drawings all night long. Festivities continue the next day with the Bay Head Christmas Walk, an all-day parade, and a Christmas symphony concert by the Orchestra of St. Peter's by the Sea, conducted by Father Alphonse Stephenson. The weekend concludes with a tour of the local inns, which serve refreshments.

Christmas Parade
Convention Hall
714 Beach Avenue, Cape May
(609) 884–9565
Cape May loves to have a parade and Christmas is a good excuse for one. There are floats, performing groups, and strolling vendors, and of course Santa Claus always shows up to join the fun.

Sindia Day Celebration
1735 Simpson Avenue, Ocean City
(609) 399–4131
In the early-morning hours of December 15, 1901, the _Sindia_, a four-masted 329-foot barque en route from Kobe, Japan, to New York City, ran aground off the coast of Ocean City. A century later, the anniversary is observed with storytelling, music, displays, and a visit from the ghost of Captain MacKenzie, the ship's master.

Kidstuff

Fun from Aquariums to Zoos

Miniature Golf

Skating

Bowling

Fun Food

Parks

The Jersey Shore's 127 miles of beach are a natural playground for kids and their parents. During the summer months, many Shore towns offer beach-oriented activities like sand-castle contests, nature walks, and fireworks displays; you'll find some of the bigger happenings listed in the Annual Events and Festivals chapter.

Boardwalks and amusement parks are almost synonymous with summers at the Shore, and you'll find them described in the Attractions chapter. There you'll also find many museums that will appeal to the younger set, including Ripley's Believe It or Not! Museum and the Ocean Life Center at Gardner's Basin in Atlantic City. And don't forget Lucy the Elephant in Margate or the Towne of Historic Smithville, another winner with kids that's just minutes from Atlantic City.

When trying to amuse the enfant terrible, don't overlook our Living-History Farms and Historic Villages chapter, which includes Tuckerton Seaport, a swell place to spend a half day or so. In the Outdoor Activities chapter, we tell you about seagoing safaris: whale watches, excursions on paddlewheel boats, and other fun stuff that kids will enjoy as much as you do. Also check the various theater groups we've listed in the Arts and Culture chapter, as many regularly offer children's productions.

With all of these options, how can kids sit there and say, "Mom, I'm bored" or, worse yet, sit around watching the tube and playing video games on a beautiful, sunny day? This we cannot answer, but in this chapter, we've tried to arm you with some unsnubbable suggestions. You'll find children's museums, zoos, and aquariums, and special places like Storybook Land, which you will remember as fondly as your toddler. One sure-fire Shore favorite is miniature golf, and we've listed a bunch of places, probably one near you.

This chapter also offers some things to do on days that are cold, rainy, or just too darn hot for the beach, like bowling or skating. We've also included a selection of entertainment-oriented restaurants, for—as the old TV ad goes—when you're hungry for fun. Keep in mind, too, that the county and state parks are not just a place to play outside, but places to hook up with all sorts of organized sports and other activities for children. We've compiled the contact information to get you started.

Price Codes

$ . . . . under $5
$$ . . . . $5 to $10
$$$ . . . . $10 to $20
$$$$ . . . . over $20

Fun from Aquariums to Zoos

Monmouth County

Imagine That! Discovery Museums for Children
$$
N.J. Highway 35 North and Harmony Road, Middletown
(732) 706–9000

For those rainy days when you're in no mood for clanging amusements and boardwalk arcades, here's an alternative with dozens of hands-on educational activities. Your kids can examine rocks and fossils, play with magnets, sit in the cockpit of an airplane, or pretend to care for patients in an ambulance. When you want an alternative to babysitting, Imagine That! also offers Adventure Programs that keep the kids happily engaged and supervised for a couple of hours. It's open Sunday through Thursday from 10:00 A.M. to 6:00 P.M., and Friday and Saturday from 10:00 A.M. to 8:00 P.M.

Ocean County

Jenkinson's Aquarium $$
300 Ocean Avenue, Point Pleasant Beach
(732) 899–1212
www.jenkinsons.com
We've mentioned Jenkinson's before, in connection with its Boardwalk attractions. Their motto is "Lots for Tots," and they do deliver on it, with baby parades, treasure hunts, pony rides, petting zoos, kiddie concerts, and a kiddie beach show with magic and fireworks on Thursday night.

One of Jenkinson's most popular attractions is the aquarium, which is home to sharks, seals, alligators, stingrays, penguins, and other denizens of the deep. We rarely have the urge to touch aquatic creatures, but if your kids do, there is a touch tank, which allows them to get their hands on a sea star or a baby shark. In addition to exhibits that teach kids about sea creatures and their habitats, the aquarium has workshops for children of all ages. Since it's especially fun to be around at feeding times, call or check the Web site for a schedule. Another fun possibility: You can book a Perky the Penguin Birthday Party for children four or older. The aquarium is open daily year-round, closing only on Christmas and New Year's Day. Hours are 10:00 A.M. to 5:00 P.M., with extended hours in summer.

Popcorn Park Zoo $
Humane Way and Lacey Road, Forked River
(609) 693–1900
This very special zoo was founded in 1977 to rescue and shelter animals that are sick,

elderly, abandoned, abused, or injured. Since Popcorn Park isn't a planned zoo, the inhabitants are an eclectic lot. Each one has a story, and the zoo publishes tales that are sad and often heart-wrenching. Lacey the Lion, for example, lost his job as part of a magic act; Sam the Jaguar was abandoned by his owner and left to starve; and Dudley Morris, the pot-belly pig, simply outgrew his home.

All of the 200-odd animals have names: monkeys, rabbits, horses, sheep, goats, and even an elephant. At this zoo, your kids can meet and mingle with the deer and goats that wander freely. And they can learn lessons about human kindness—and human carelessness and cruelty. Be warned: If your child has always wanted a pet, you may face extra pressure here. The Humane Society has a shelter on the property, with lots of lovable creatures looking for homes.

Robert J. Novins Planetarium $$
Ocean County College, Dover Township
(732) 255–0342, (732) 255–0343
www.ocean.cc.nj.us/planet/
In addition to its offering for adults and older kids, the planetarium runs programs for children between the ages of four and six. Your kids will learn what the sun and stars are and why they seem to move across the sky. To make the lessons fun, they'll hear stories about the stars and constellations. You're asked not to bring infants or children younger than four, because they won't understand the material and may be frightened by the darkness and the unfamiliar environment. For more details on the planetarium, see the Attractions chapter.

Atlantic and Cape May Counties

Birch Grove Park and Wildlife Zoo $
Burton Avenue, Northfield
(609) 641–3778
This inviting 275-acre park has 21 lakes for fishing, a playground, walking paths, picnic areas, and a small zoo. It's open daily from 9:00 A.M. to 7:00 P.M. in sum-

mer and from 9:00 A.M. to 4:00 P.M. in winter. Admission to the zoo is free during the week, $1.00 on weekends.

Brownstone Puppet Theatre and Museum
$$
Towne of Historic Smithville
U.S. Highway 9 and Moss Mill Road, Smithville
(609) 652–5750
Round out your trip to Smithville with a visit to the Brownstone, a charming theater housed in a 19th-century music hall. If there's a show going on, you'll meet adorable characters like Annabel the Bear and Sara the Turtle, and you'll see some imaginative puppetry, too. The museum displays a collection of puppets from around the world. Here's another good spot to consider for a birthday party. For more on Smithville, see the Attractions chapter.

Cape May County Park and Zoo $
U.S. Highway 9 and Crest Haven Road, Cape May Court House
(609) 465–5271
You and your kids can wander through the zoo along a series of boardwalks; the animals are below and there are no bars to mar the experience. In the African Savannah section, you'll find ostriches, giraffes, and zebras roaming freely on an open plain. The new climate-controlled Aviary boasts 75 bird species, including exotic flamingoes. The Reptile House is home to snakes, turtles, alligators, lizards, and arachnids. There's an exhibit of New Jersey Animals, which includes such natives as river otters and red foxes. At the Petting Zoo, your kids can pet and feed goats, llamas, and sheep.

The zoo is accredited by the American Association of Zoological Parks and Aquariums—which puts it in the same category as some of the world's finest zoos. It has more than 150 animal species, including red pandas, reindeer, bears—and the capybara, the world's largest rodent. It draws more than 300,000 visitors each year.

In addition to the zoo, the park complex offers fishing, hiking, biking, and outdoor concerts. There are covered pavilions for picnics and open-pit barbecues. The zoo is open every day except Christmas. In spring and summer, the hours are from 10:00 A.M. to 4:45 P.M.; in late fall and winter, the zoo closes at 3:45 P.M. Admission is free during the week, $1.00 on weekends.

Children's Museum $
3112 Fire Road, Egg Harbor Township
(609) 645–7741
The Children's Museum is an amazing place for children ages 10 and under to play pretend—with all the props they could imagine. There's a post office where kids can put Velcro stamps on envelopes and move them from the mailbox to the post office box. Would-be firefighters can try on the gear: hat, coat, boots, and all. Among the other activity areas are a bubble station that lets visitors make giant bubbles, a sand table with dinosaurs, a music center, a car factory, a hospital emergency room, even a television studio. It's open Monday through Saturday from 10:00 A.M. to 5:00 P.M., and Sunday from noon to 5:00 P.M.

Storybook Land $$$
Highway 322 (Black Horse Pike), Egg Harbor Township
(609) 641–7847
www.storybookland.com
About 10 miles west of Atlantic City, a world away from clanging slots and neon lights, is a sweet, old-fashioned (circa 1955) amusement park set on 20 wooded acres. The park is clean and bright, there are no long lines, and there are no electronic games. What you'll find are the simple pleasures you (and your parents) enjoyed—and often yearn to share with the younger generation. You'll find The Three Bears' house, giant likenesses of fairy-tale characters—and just a few concessions to modern technology, like the talking wolf in Little Red Riding Hood's house.

At Halloween, there's a trick-or-treat weekend and hayrides. At Christmas time, Santa visits the beautifully lit park, and there are a number of holiday events. In

The Marionette Cottage is a collection of vintage marionettes at the Brownstone Puppet Theatre.
PHOTO: COURTESY OF THE BROWNSTONE PUPPET THEATRE

May and June, Storybook Land is open weekdays from 10:00 A.M. to 3:00 P.M., weekends from 11:00 A.M. to 5:00 P.M.; July through Labor Day it's open Thursday and Friday from 10:00 A.M. to 3:00 P.M., and weekends from 11:00 A.M. to 5:00 P.M. Call or check the Web site for hours the rest of the year, including special holiday hours during the Easter and Christmas seasons.

Miniature Golf

Miniature golf and the beach go together. The kids in our family used to enjoy nothing more than a round or two after a satisfying day in the surf.

Mini-golf courses, like many seasonal businesses at the Shore, tend to open when the weather warms up. Some may start with weekend hours around Easter, while some don't open until Memorial Day. During the summer, they open up in the morning and stay open late every day. Our advice: If you have a yen to play a round in the off-season, call ahead. Course fees are generally well under $10.00—usually more like $5.00 or $6.00.

Monmouth County

Putt-Around Miniature Golf
800 Ocean Avenue, Bradley Beach
(732) 774–6222

Having learned the game at the Shore, we always see miniature golf as a game that belongs right by the sea—like the original links of Scotland, if you will. Soaring real-estate prices have doomed other mini golfs in Monmouth County; Putt-Around is one of the few remaining.

Twin Brook Golf Center
1251 Jumping Brook Road, Neptune
(732) 922–1600

While the kids putter around on the miniature golf course, grown-ups can work on their golf swings. Twin Brook also has a two-level driving range, an excellent nine-hole par 3 course, a pro shop, and a grill.

Ocean County

Beacon Miniature Golf Course
Long Beach Boulevard between 17th and 18th Streets, North Beach Haven (LBI)
(609) 492–7719

This vintage (more than a half-century old) course offers the old-time style of miniature golf that you don't see around so much anymore. Your kids might not care, but you might enjoy the familiar windmill, the mini Ferris wheel and the mini biplane, whose spinning propellor is the obstacle.

Hartland Miniature Golf & Arcade
2903 Long Beach Boulevard, Ship Bottom (LBI)
(609) 494–7776

The course is small but pretty, one of the better ones in the area. Regulars describe it as mildly challenging and fun.

Mr. Tee's Golf and Games
Engleside and Bay Avenues, Beach Haven (LBI)
(609) 492–8689

Mr. Tee's has an 18-hole course that adjoins an arcade with kiddie rides and lots of games, including pinball and skeeball.

Settler's Mill Adventure Golf
806 North Bay Avenue, Beach Haven (LBI)
(609) 492–0869

Settler's Mill has been described as the Augusta National of Shore miniature golf courses, and rightly so. This not-just-for-kids course has long fairways and historical markers; while you're playing, they let you know, for example, that the Lenni Lenape Indians were the Shore's first summer visitors.

Smuggler's Quay
Grant and Central Avenue, Seaside Heights
(732) 830–4724

Known for its amusements, Seaside Heights does not lack for miniature golf.

This pirate-theme layout is two blocks from the Boardwalk.

Atlantic and Cape May Counties

Atlantic City Miniature Golf
Boardwalk and Mississippi Avenue, Atlantic City
(609) 347–1661

Atlantic City's best, this premier 18-hole course on the Boardwalk is located opposite the old Convention Hall. It's not tough, and the sea breezes are a bonus.

Congo Falls Adventure Golf
1132 Boardwalk, Ocean City
(609) 398–1211

Theme miniature golf courses are part of the fun at the beach. This one has King Kong towering over the two 18-hole courses: Congo Queen and Solomon's Mine. Special effects include waterfalls, caves, and a snake pit. Since Solomon's Mine takes you indoors (through caves), it would be fine on a rainy day.

Enchanted Lagoon
321 East 17th Avenue, North Wildwood
(609) 729–3633

Just off the Boardwalk, this attractive 36-hole course has some entertaining and challenging holes.

Gillian's Island Adventure Golf
Boardwalk at Plymouth Place, Ocean City
(609) 399–0483

This course, which is part of a bigger entertainment complex, sets out to give you a jungle adventure, with 18 holes of waterfalls, rock formations, and scenic landscaping.

Goblin Golf
1244 Boardwalk, Ocean City
(609) 399–5927

Horror is the theme here: giant rats in a big hunk of Swiss cheese, a skeleton chained to a wooden well, a mummy under glass. Look for Dracula, and a torture wheel, too.

Drop a Line

We cover fishing more extensively in the Outdoor Activities chapter, but here's a great outing for parents and children (over 10 years of age) who'd like to take up fishing together. It's a family tour and hike of the Pequest Fish Hatchery, offered by the Monmouth County Park System (732–842–4000). The Hatchery and Natural Resource Education Center is located in Warren County, and the program includes transportation from the designated park pickup site. You don't need to bring any equipment, just wear hiking boots or shoes with good traction; all fishing gear is provided. You can buy your bait for the day near the hatchery. Learn more about fish habitats, and maybe you'll get lucky and experience the thrill of reeling in a tasty rainbow trout.

Island Fun Park Miniature Golf
N.J. Highway 147, Middle Township
(609) 523–1386

The course is tucked into an amusement complex guarded by a gorilla. It's a tough course that goes uphill and downhill, and includes such challenges as a gravel pit.

Junk Yard Golf
1336 Boardwalk, Ocean City
(609) 398–0046

The kids can play this one even on rainy days; the course is under cover.

La Mer Mini Golf
Pittsburgh and New Jersey Avenues, Cape May
(609) 898–2244

La Mer is a pretty and compact garden-style 16-hole course, featuring a waterfall and rock formations.

Pirate Island Golf
33rd Street and Landis Avenue, Sea Isle City
(609) 263–8344

This 36-hole multilevel course lives up to its name—the greens run through a replica of a ship's hull.

Putter's Beach
63rd Street and Landis Avenue, Sea Isle City

Putter's Beach has a beach-style layout with a fine putting surface called omni-grass. It won the "Best Course" award for the 1999 Miniature Golf Tour (based in Ocean County).

Tee Time Mini Golf
239 96th Street, Stone Harbor
(609) 967–5574

This fun and challenging facility in Stone Harbor is one of only five American Tournament Standard (ATS) courses in the United States. Since the Master National Pro Minigolf Association announced that the 2004 Summer Olympics to be held in Athens have accepted mini golf as a provisional sport, this is the place for serious putt-putters to hone their game. Tee Time, the first tournament course of this design open for public play, offers rooftop miniature golf.

Skating

For the young with no fear of fractures, in-line skating is cool, and four-wheel roller skates are practically antique. Roller blades permit skating at higher speeds, with enough maneuverability to play real hockey games and attempt tricks akin to those done by skateboarders. Plus, it's tremendous exercise. Insist that your skaters wear proper protective gear—knee pads, elbow pads, helmets, wrist guards, even gloves when appropriate.

Ice-skating, too, has taken off in recent years, and really there's no better way to cool off on a hot summer day. With the growth of organized hockey, however, ice time is at a premium, and rinks now have more limited "open skates," so call before you drive over. Costs are rising, but skating is still a pretty affordable outing, running about $10 per person, including skate rental.

Monmouth County

American Hockey & Ice Skating Center
1215 Wyckoff Road (Highway 547 at N.J. Highway 33), Farmingdale
(732) 919–7070
www.american-hockey.com

If your little girl yearns to be the next Sarah Hughes or Michelle Kwan, sign her up for figure skating clinics here. Olympic hopefuls can be inspired—the Russian gold medalist Alexei Yagudin actually trained at this facility. For your future Wayne Gretzkys, there are clinics, and for more serious immersion, Hockey Camp. Or the whole family can simply skate around for fun. Call ahead for public skating hours.

Eatontown Roller Skating Center
105 N.J. Highway 35 North, Eatontown
(732) 542–5858

Roller disco came and went, but this skating center has endured this and other trends. In keeping up with the times, it now offers hip-hop nights and skateboard sessions.

Ocean County

Acme Surf and Skate
1 South Main Street, South Toms River
(732) 286–4055

This indoor skate park with ramps caters to aggressive-style in-line skaters, skateboarders, and BMX bikers. It's $13.00 a day if you've got your own pads and gear, $21.00 if you need loaner pads. You can also rent your choice of wheels for $8.00.

Ocean Ice Palace
197 Chambers Bridge Road, Brick Township
(732) 477–4411

The facilities here include one ice-skating rink, bleachers, a pro shop, and a snack bar.

Recreation Station
1 South Main Street, South Toms River
(732) 244–9191

Right next door to Acme Surf and Skate, this is a headquarters for in-line (roller) hockey leagues.

Winding River Skating Center
1211 Whitesville Road, Toms River
(732) 244–0720

This outdoor ice-skating rink is open from November through March. Skate rentals are available.

Atlantic and Cape May Counties

Flyers Skate Zone
501 North Albany Boulevard, Atlantic City
(609) 441–1780

In addition to one ice-skating rink, Skate Zone has a snack bar and pro shop.

Parkway Skating Center
3133 Fire Road, Egg Harbor
(609) 383–1800

This roller-skating center has family nights, sessions for young children, and group lessons.

Ventnor City Recreation Center
Atlantic and New Haven Avenues, Ventnor
(609) 823–7947

The Ventnor municipal ice rink shares a building with the town's Cultural Arts Center, the library, and the community center. There is no snack bar.

Young's Skating Center
Park Road and 13th Avenue, Mays Landing
(609) 625–1191

This roller rink offers blade and old-fashioned four-wheel skate rentals. Bring the kids on Thursday, Family Night, when admission is $4.00, but adults get in for free.

Bowling

You may associate bowling with beer bellies and cigarettes, but we've never met a kid who didn't enjoy a day at the lanes. In fact, there are some areas where bowling is in danger of becoming downright trendy. Should your child really take a shine to the sport, look into the bowling leagues and programs that some of the county parks run in cooperation with participating bowling centers.

The going rate is about $3.00 to $4.00 per person per game, and another $3.00 for shoe rentals, but rates may vary, so it's a good idea to call ahead. You'll also want to avoid busy league nights, often Monday and Thursday. Many Shore alleys offer family packages, which may include rental shoes and refreshments. Some have "family bowling clubs," which are multiweek packages entitling you and your child to instruction, practice games, a set number of games a week, and bowling shoes, for a flat fee. You can also find "twofer" coupons in your local newspaper, which let you buy one game and get one free. You'll also find such deals in the *Entertainment* book, a collection of discount coupons for dining and other activities, including bowling, available through local fund-raising groups or directly from the company (800–681-1915, www.entertainment.com).

Monmouth County

Brunswick Bradley Beach Bowl
1217 Main Street, Bradley Beach
(732) 774–4540

Brunswick Monmouth Lanes
700 Joline Avenue, Long Branch
(732) 229–1414

Lanes at Sea Girt
N.J. Highway 35, Wall
(732) 449–4942

Ocean County

Ocean Lanes
2085 Lanes Mill Road (at N.J. Highway 88), Lakewood
(732) 363–3421

Playdrome Lakewood
101 Locust Street, Lakewood
(732) 364–8080

Playdrome Point Pleasant
2307 N.J. Highway 88, Point Pleasant
(732) 892–0888

Playdrome Toms River
821 Conifer Street, Toms River
(732) 349–5345

Thunder Bowl
U.S. Highway 9, Bayville
(732) 349–8844

Atlantic and Cape May Counties

DiDonato Lanes
1151 White Horse Pike, Hammonton
(609) 561–3040

Gardiner's Wildwood Bowl
3400 New Jersey Avenue, Wildwood
(609) 729–0111

Harbor Lanes
1400 White Horse Pike, Egg Harbor Township
(609) 965–2299

Mouse Trap Lanes
51 Dennisville-Petersburg Road, Woodbine
(609) 861–2695

Showboat Bowling Center
Boardwalk and Delaware Avenue, Atlantic City
(609) 343–4040, (800) 621–0200

Fun Food

While adults peruse the wine list and try to choose between the Dover sole and the rack of lamb, fidgety kids have their own ideas about what makes for a good place to eat out. If you'd like to take the off-spring to a restaurant where sitting quietly and using the proper fork are not exactly de rigueur, here are a few suggestions.

C. B. Huntington Railroad Restaurant
140 U.S. Highway 9, Bayville
(732) 505–1294
In addition to a full menu of chicken, steaks, pizza, and pasta, C. B. Hunting-ton's has more than 160 square feet of running model trains to entertain railroad buffs young and old.

Chuck E Cheese's
1107 N.J. Highway 35 North, Middletown
(732) 615–9091
Brick Plaza, Brick Township
(732) 262–9200
With all the great pizzerias in this area (see the Close-up in the "Restaurants" section of the Monmouth County chapter), it would only be under duress that one would choose Chuck E Cheese's—but hey, it happens. Anyway, the attraction is hardly the food, but the whole arcade-while-eating experience—the skeeball, video games, and other kid fun.

Hard Rock Cafe
Trump Taj Mahal
1000 Boardwalk at Virginia Avenue,
Atlantic City
(609) 441–0007
With a state-of-the-art sound system and walls covered with funky rock memora-bilia, the Hard Rock appeals to kids and adults alike. The menu ranges from steaks and pasta to sandwiches and finger food, and the burgers are picked by some as the "Best of the Shore." There's also a large selection of souvenir merchandise. It's open daily from 11:00 A.M. to 2:00 A.M. Say hello to Elvis out front.

Planet Hollywood
Caesars Atlantic City
2100 Pacific Avenue, Atlantic City
(609) 347–7827
This theme restaurant on the Boardwalk boasts a nifty collection of movie memora-bilia that includes a beaten-up "Termina-tor" outfit worn by Arnold Schwarzenegger, part-owner of the chain. The food is pretty good, too, especially if you stick to the basics—burgers and fries and salads. Open daily from 11:00 A.M. to 2:00 A.M.

Parks

Is your baby a budding couch potato? Get that little butt in gear—sign him or her up for one of the many sports programs offered (at quite reasonable prices) by the Shore's county parks. You'll find dozens of choices: Basketball, baseball, tennis, soccer, karate, cheerleading, and sailing are just some of the possibilities. For the competitive lot, there are various kinds of races—biking, running, and canoeing. But sports are only the beginning of what's on offer; our parks organize field trips, cooking classes, various crafts workshops, and even theme birthday parties.

To find out about programs in your area, pick up an activity directory at a county park or call one of the phone numbers listed below. For information on programs at state and national parks, call the numbers given in the Natural World chapter.

Atlantic County Park Headquarters
Estell Manor
109 N.J. Highway 50, Mays Landing
(609) 645–5960

Cape May County Parks
U.S. Highway 9 and Crest Haven Road, Cape May Court House
(609) 465–5271

Monmouth County Park System
805 Newman Springs Road, Lincroft
(732) 842–4000
www.monmouthcountyparks.com

Ocean County Department of Parks and Recreation
1198 Bandon Road, Toms River
(732) 270–6960, (877) OC–PARKS

Daytrips

For the first 20 years or so that we summered at the Jersey Shore, you could count the number of times we strayed more than 10 miles from the coast. How silly! We were missing out on lots of fun things to see and do that are out there in the great Garden State—all close enough to enjoy on a day's excursion from the Shore.

In this section, we'll tell you about some of the many historical and cultural attractions that are within daytrip distance (less than a two-hour drive) from some part of the Jersey Shore. Now, you know that Shore people go to New York City and Philadelphia for a day, but we're going to focus mostly on lesser-known places in New Jersey.

The New Jersey Office of Travel and Tourism divides the state into six regions: Shore, Southern Shore, Greater Atlantic City, Delaware River, Gateway, and Skylands. The first three encompass the counties we've focused on in this book: Monmouth, Ocean, Atlantic, and Cape May. The Delaware River region covers a vast swath of southwestern New Jersey, rural areas from Salem to Burlington County as well as busy and historic towns like Princeton and Trenton in Mercer County. The Gateway is basically the northeast part of the state, bordering on the Hudson River, plus Essex and Passaic Counties. The poetical Skylands is the mountainous area of the northwest, as well as Morris and Somerset Counties.

The places you can visit are as diverse as the state itself: up north, you'll find lions and tigers and bears (and wolves); out west, there's a genuine rodeo and a re-created Wild West town. Historic ships and sites offer glimpses of the state's past. We have homes and museums dedicated to famous New Jerseyans like Thomas Edison and Yogi Berra, and exquisite gardens grown to please an eccentric heiress, Doris Duke. Really, whatever you enjoy, you'll find it in the Garden State.

Price Code

$	under $5
$$	$5 to $10
$$$	$10 to $20
$$$$	over $20

Delaware River Region

Battleship *New Jersey* $$
Beckett Street, Camden
(856) 966–1652
www.battleshipnewjersey.org

Lovingly referred to as "Big J," the battleship *New Jersey* settled into her berth in Camden in October 2001—just a mile upriver from the Philadelphia Naval Shipyard where she was built in 1940. Big J was opened to the public soon after the attack on the World Trade Center, so you can well imagine the patriotic fervor that greeted the world's most decorated ship. Public officials made stirring speeches and former crewmen wept.

Big J saw more years of service and traveled more than any other U.S. Navy vessel, having served in World War II as the flagship for Admiral William F. Halsey Jr.'s Pacific operations, in Korea, in Vietnam, and in the Middle East in the 1980s. During its years of service, the *New Jersey* was awarded 19 stars for battles and campaigns. Today you can tour Big J, either on your own or with a docent; guided tours around the upper and lower sections take about two hours. If you're not able to climb the decks, you can take a virtual tour in the ship's multimedia room. In the future, there will be a museum at the ship's dockside. From April through September, the ship is open from 9:00 A.M. to

5:00 P.M.; October through March from 9:00 A.M. to 3:00 P.M.

Cowtown Rodeo
N.J. Highway 40, between Woodstown and the Delaware Memorial Bridge
(856) 769–3200

Neither a theme park nor an "attraction," this is the only honest-to-goodness real-life weekly rodeo on the East Coast. It's also the longest-running regular Saturday night rodeo in the United States, dating back to 1929. You'll see real cowboys and good old bareback bronco riding, steer wrestling, calf roping, and Brahma bull-riding—all the stuff of cowboy movies. The Saturday night show begins at 7:30 P.M. and runs about three hours, more or less. There's a Western store on-site, in case you're inspired to make a slight identity adjustment. The Cowtown Rodeo begins in May and runs through late September. Arrive early for the best seats. If you have time to drive around on the back roads, you'll see miles and miles of open fields and fertile farmland, populated mostly by cattle and horses. New Jersey, you say? Yup. There's also a flea market every Tuesday and Saturday.

Crosswicks Village
Main Street, Chesterfield
(609) 324–1337

In September, the Crosswicks Village Festival lets you experience what life was like in colonial and Civil War–era America. Tour historic homes and buildings such as the old Chesterfield Firehouse and the Ellisdale United Methodist Church. There are encampments by both Revolutionary and Civil War reenactors, colonial American music, and 18th-century dancing. There's also a juried craft and art show featuring local artists and artisans, and a bit of *Antiques Roadshow*–style fun with $5.00 appraisals. You can ride in a horse-drawn carriage or play games like marbles or quoits, a precursor of horseshoes. There are demonstrations of traditional women's crafts like embroidery and sampler making, and talks about such historic movements as the ones for women's rights and against slavery. Call for dates and details.

Drumthwacket   Free
354 Stockton Street, Princeton
(609) 683–0057

The Drumthwacket estate is the New Jersey governor's magnificent official residence; it is the only governor's mansion in the United States not located in the state's capital city. Built in 1835 by Charles Smith Olden, a Quaker who served as New Jersey governor in 1860, this splendid home has a grand portico and six massive pillars topped by Ionic capitals. The Celtic name "Drumthwacket" was given to the mansion by Moses Taylor Pyne, a later owner who also added two wings, one of which includes the wood-paneled library. In 1966, the State of New Jersey acquired the house, and in 1981, it was designated the official Governor's Residence. It is managed as a historic site by the Drumthwacket Foundation, which provided the mansion with superb examples of 18th- and early-19th-century furnishings. Public tours are given every Wednesday between noon and 2:00 P.M., except for the Wednesday before Thanksgiving and the Wednesday between Christmas and New Year's Day; the house also is closed to the public during the month of August.

Fort Mott   Free
Pennsville
(856) 935–3218

The 104-acre Fort Mott complex is part of New Jersey's Coastal Heritage Trail, which begins here and runs south along the Delaware River, then north along the Atlantic Coast, highlighting places that are part of the state's maritime history (also see the Close-up on page 36). Fort Mott, Fort Delaware (on Pea Patch Island in the middle of the river), and Fort DuPont in Delaware were all constructed in the 1800s to protect Philadelphia and other cities on the Delaware River from possible attack from a naval power like Spain.

Today, when you take a walking tour of the gun emplacements, you'll see that the fort's secret weapon was this: the guns "disappeared" when they were not being fired because they were hidden below the walls. Just outside the park is Finns Point Lighthouse, which is open for visits April

Princeton

Princeton isn't just a university town, it's a cultural center, as well as a treasure trove of historic sites. We've mentioned Drumthwacket and the Princeton University Art Museum, but there's so much more, including the splendid library and Nassau Hall, an important Revolutionary War site (see our chapter on Revolutionary New Jersey). If time permits, visit Bainbridge House, birthplace of William Bainbridge, commander of the U.S.S. *Constitution* during the War of 1812, and now headquarters of the Historical Society of Princeton. Other nearby places of interest are Clarke House on the Princeton Battlefield, and Morven, home of the New Jersey Historical Society. To round out your day, take in a show at the renowned McCarter Theatre.

through October, on the third Sunday of the month, from noon to 4:00 P.M. If you're a Civil War buff, take note of the Finn's Point National Cemetery, which is accessible by Fort Mott's main road. Here you'll find the graves of almost 2,500 Confederate solders who were held at Fort Delaware as prisoners of war; buried in the same cemetery are the Union soldiers who guarded them. If you'd like to visit Fort Delaware, it's an easy trip by ferry. Fort Mott is open daily; summer hours are from 8:00 A.M. to 7:00 P.M.; winter hours are from 8:00 A.M. to 4:00 P.M.

New Jersey State Aquarium   **$$$**
1 Riverside Drive, Camden
(800) 616–JAWS
www.njaquarium.org

There is much to see and do at this awesome multimedia complex, so plan to make your visit a leisurely one. After your orientation at the Ocean Base Command Center, you can move on to the Shark Zone to see the stars of this and any aquarium. Marvel at the monsters of the past, like the 50-foot carcharodon megalodon from the Pliocene era, then visit with (and even stroke) the more benign sharks and rays in the Shark Touch Tank. Learn more about sharks on touch-screen computers or watch an interactive video showing humans and sharks together. You might be tempted to linger, but so much more awaits. See periwinkles and hermit crabs

in the Mangrove Lagoon. Climb through the coral-encrusted hull of a replica of the R.M.S. *Rhone*, an iron-clad ship that sank in 1867. Learn more about the Pine Barrens and the Delaware River. View the aquarium's 760,000-gallon Open Ocean Tank, the second largest in the United States. Its 24-foot by 18-foot window will give you a splendid view of more than a thousand fish, including quite a few sharks. Spend some time in the amphitheater at the Deep Atlantic window and listen to the divers talk to you on their SCUBAphones. If you still want more, visit the Sea Lab research station some 50 feet below the surface via a remote control camera. In addition to the exhibits, the aquarium offers a daily schedule of activities, including performances by divers, seals, sharks, and other denizens of the deep. The aquarium is open from mid-September through mid-April from 9:30 A.M. to 4:30 P.M. on weekdays, and from 10:00 A.M. to 5:00 P.M. on weekends.

New Jersey State Museum   **Free**
205 West State Street, Trenton
(609) 292–6464
www.state.nj.us/state/museum/musidx.html

Everything you wanted to know about New Jersey (well, almost), you're likely to find here, starting with the history and daily lives of the Lenni Lenape, or Delaware Indians. The state's cultural history can be traced through the decorative arts, as the museum displays works from colonial times to the present.

Moving beyond state borders, the fine arts galleries feature 20-century American art, with works by such artists as Georgia O'Keeffe, Alexander Calder, John Marin, and Louise Nevelson. (New Jersey artists are represented, too.) Kids will enjoy exploring the world inhabited by New Jersey's dinosaurs in the Natural History galleries. View the skies above during regularly scheduled shows at the state-of-the-art Planetarium. The museum is open Tuesday through Saturday from 9:00 A.M. to 4:45 P.M, and Sunday from noon to 5:00 P.M.

A trip to the museum can be combined with visits to the State House, the William Trent House, and the Old Barracks Museum.

New Jersey State Police Museum   Free
River Road, West Trenton
(609) 882–2000

Are *CSI* and *NYPD Blue* among your favorite television shows? If so, you might enjoy a behind-the-scenes look at how real crimes are investigated at this law-enforcement museum. First you'll learn that the first class of 120 state troopers was selected in 1921 and trained by 25-year-old H. Norman Schwarzkopf (yes, that's "Stormin' Norman") at a camp in Sea Girt. The 81 trainees who completed the course were deployed on horseback and motorcycle to enforce the laws in the state's 7,500 square miles.

Among the most fascinating exhibits here is material relating to one of New Jersey's most notorious crimes, the Lindbergh kidnapping; you can see the actual ransom notes, the ladder used by the kidnapper, and trial footage on the Fox Movietone News. There is also an extensive research library on the case, which can be examined by appointment.

The exhibit on Criminal Investigation shows the equipment used by the real-life Crime Scene Identification Unit. You'll see surveillance equipment, forensic lab implements, and fingerprint-lifting tools. You can even use the microscopes to look at your own fingerprints. And if you never got over that childhood wish to be a police officer, you can sit behind the wheel of a cruiser, turn on the "cherry tops," and listen to the police radio. The museum is open Monday through Saturday from 10:00 A.M. to 4:00 P.M.

Princeton University Art Museum   Free
McCormick Hall, Princeton
(609) 258–1860

Princeton packs a world-class collection into a boutique-size museum, with galleries of ancient, Renaissance, and contemporary art. Especially noteworthy are the collections of Chinese art: bronzes, tomb figures, paintings, and calligraphy. Pre-Columbian art—the art of the Olmec and Maya—is also well represented, as is the art of African and Native American cultures. You'll find Greek and Roman antiquities, medieval stained glass, and paintings from the early Renaissance through the 19th century, including some exquisite Dutch still lifes. The collection of works on paper ranges from photographs to Old Master prints and drawings. The museum is open Tuesday through Saturday from 10:00 A.M. to 5:00 P.M., and Sunday from 1:00 to 5:00 P.M.

Smithville Mansion & Industrial Village
$
Burlington County Park
Easthampton
(609) 265–5068

During the 18th century this area in rural Burlington County was an active milling site. It became known as Shreveville in the early 19th century, when the Shreve brothers turned it into a cotton-milling complex. In 1865 it was purchased by Hezikiah B. Smith, a Massachusetts industrialist from Lowell who later served in the U.S. Congress. Smith renamed the complex Smithville and converted it to the production of woodworking machinery. He expanded this model community to include a school, an opera house, boarding houses, parks, a railroad station, and a 300-acre farm. He established an employees' credit union and closed his factory at noon on Saturday—both remarkable innovations.

In 1975, the county acquired the property and developed it as the first Burlington County Park. Smithville's 25 surviving buildings are now part of that park and

Rolling on the River

At the Jersey Shore, we've got the whole Atlantic Ocean to play in, and you'd think that would be enough—but no. A road trip to go tubing on the Delaware River is a favorite way to cool off when days heat up. Bucks County River Country in Point Pleasant, Pennsylvania (PA Highway 32, eight miles north of New Hope) calls itself the "World's River Tubing Capital." A trip with this company certainly can seem crowded at the starting point, but once you're out on the beautiful Delaware, the people tend to spread out nicely. The float downriver takes a few hours, depending on the flow of the river, which averages from one to four feet in depth here, with a comfortable water temperature of about 80 degrees. Rafting, canoeing, kayaking, and hayrides are also available. Call (215) 297–5000 or visit www.rivercountry.net for more information.

greenway system. The 19th-century mansion, which is at the center of the complex, has been restored; plans are under way to restore other structures.

State House   Free
125 West State Street, Trenton
(609) 292–4840, (800) 792–8630 (from New Jersey)

Built in 1792, New Jersey's State House is the second-oldest (after Maryland) capitol in continuous use. Enlarged and modified over the years, it is a magnificent building with re-created period rooms in 19th- and early-20th-century styles.

Do note such highlights as the 145-foot domed ceiling of the Rotunda; the splendid chandelier (made by Thomas Edison's General Edison Electric Company) that lights the Assembly Chamber; the wall of intricately designed inlaid wood by noted New Jersey artist Hiroshi Murata; and the stained-glass skylights of the Senate Majority Conference Room. You'll find an exhibit area on the third floor, with historical artifacts and memorabilia related to the State House and the Legislature.

You can tour the State House on your own with the aid of an interpretive map (free), but when official business is being conducted, some areas may be closed to you. Days when the legislature is not in session (Tuesday, Wednesday, and Friday)

are the best times to visit. You may also take a guided tour, but you will need to make a reservation.

Gateway Region

American Labor Museum $
Botto House National Landmark
83 Norwood Street, Haledon
(973) 595–7953

If you're part of a working-class family, this museum will talk to you. (As our family history includes an immigrant silk worker, it's especially relevant to us.) During the great labor unrest of 1913, immigrant silk worker Pietro Botto offered his home as a meeting place for the strikers. From its balcony, champions of the labor movement—including Elizabeth Gurley Flynn and Upton Sinclair—addressed thousands of workers.

The house, which is now a National Landmark, has been restored, and you can explore the period rooms and the gardens for a glimpse of how turn-of-the-century immigrant workers lived. The museum has had exhibits on various figures important to the labor movement, like Cesar Chavez. It is open Wednesday through Saturday from 1:00 to 4:00 P.M. Though closed on major holidays, it is open, appropriately, on Labor Day, when it celebrates America's workers with a special program.

Aviation Hall of Fame $
Teterboro Airport, Teterboro
(201) 288–6344

Maybe Wilbur and Orville didn't launch the *Kitty Hawk* here, but New Jersey can still lay claim to two centuries of aviation history, and you can learn all about it here. You'll see displays relating to such famous aviators as Charles Lindbergh, Amelia Earhart, Buzz Aldrin, and Wally Schirra. You can view films about major aviation events, examine jet and rocket engines, walk around a Martin 202 airliner, and listen to air-traffic controllers at work. In short, you can experience a real airport. The hours are from 10:00 A.M. to 4:00 P.M. Tuesday through Sunday.

Fairy Tale Forest $$
140 Oak Ridge Road, Oak Ridge
(973) 697–5656
www.fairytaleforest.com

Long before Disney created his theme parks, New Jersey had some quaint "once-upon-a-time" parks that delighted kids and their parents. Fairy Tale Forest, which dates back to 1957, was one of them. It was created by German immigrant Paul Woehle Sr., who handcrafted each of the exhibits.

Woehle's granddaughter and her partners have recently revived the park, and today you'll find more than 20 life-size cottages and scenes from classic fairy tales. You'll recognize such characters as Goldilocks (sleeping in Baby Bear's bed), the Three Little Pigs, Cinderella, Rapunzel, Snow White, and other childhood favorites. There are no electronic games or exciting rides, but there is an old-fashioned merry-go-round and a fire truck ride. This is a place to stroll and use your imagination, and perhaps adjourn to the Hot Diggity Grill for a snack. At Christmastime, the forest is decked with lights, giving it a real fairy-tale quality.

Hackensack Meadowlands Environment Center   Free
Two DeKorte Plaza, Lyndhurst
(201) 460–8300

Historically, the meadowlands of New Jersey is an ecosystem that has been little appreciated, even mocked. But at the Environment Center, you may learn that one man's swamp is a heron's wetlands. You'll be greeted by a sprawling diorama that depicts an urban salt marsh, complete with brackish creek water and the creatures that live there, including snapping turtles, diamondback terrapins, and fiddler crabs. You'll also see exhibits on the birds and animals who inhabit the wetlands. More than 200 species of birds have been sighted here, as the area is a rest stop for ducks, geese, and shorebirds. There's a gallery featuring the history of Meadowlands development, and a glassed-in visitor center that extends into the salt marsh, affording you a great view of the wildlife. A series of boardwalks lead through the cattails and reeds. How, you may ask, is this different from what you have at the Shore? Well, it's a different environment, and it's a place you could visit if you go to one of the other attractions "up North." And there's a lot to do with kids here. The museum store has birding supplies, books, and educational games. The museum is open from 9:00 A.M. to 5:00 P.M. on weekdays, and from 10:00 A.M. to 3:00 P.M. on Saturday.

Jane Voorhees Zimmerli Art Museum   Free
Rutgers, The State University of New Jersey
George and Hamilton Streets, New Brunswick
(908) 932–7237
www.zimmerlimuseum.rutgers.edu/

Like the Princeton Art Museum, the Zimmerli is a terrific resource. If you're going to take in a Rutgers football game, plan on spending another hour or two viewing art collections from the late 18th century to the present. You'll also find a collection of stained glass that includes examples of New Jersey windows from 1880 to 1940, drawings of stained-glass designs, and a window designed by Frank Lloyd Wright. The Rutgers Collection of Original Illustrations for Children's Literature features original art from the 1920s to the present; many of the works are by New Jersey artists. The museum also has a full calendar of lectures, events, and changing exhibits. Among the past exhibits: "The

Victor Weeps: Photographs by Fazal Sheikh of Afghan Refugees, 1996–1998" and "Art of the Baltics," featuring modernist art during the post-war Soviet period. The museum is open Tuesday through Friday from 10:00 A.M. to 4:30 P.M., and weekends from noon to 5:00 P.M.; it is closed on Saturdays in July and for the entire month of August.

Liberty Science Center (LSC) $$
Liberty State Park
201 Phillip Street, Jersey City
(201) 200–1000
www.lsc.org

If your kids don't believe science can be fun, bring them to the Liberty Science Center. Three themed exhibition floors are loaded with hands-on displays. For example, in The Green House on the Environment Floor, you can study rare insects and take part in experiments conducted by the staff. Kids will ooh and aah while checking out such creepy-crawlys as giant Madagascar roaches in the Micro-Zoo. (And you thought the bugs in your house were bad!) Since kids like to touch things most of us would run from, they'll be delighted by the Touch-A-Bug exhibit.

On the Health Floor, you can make the point that your kids need more exercise without saying a single word: Just lead them to the testing stations at Bodies in Motion, where they can check their own flexibility, strength, and balance. On the Invention Floor, you and your kids can take apart the very machines—like computers—that daunt you in real life. And you can make stuff, using the available tools.

There are always traveling exhibits, and in choosing these, the museum folk seem to have an unerring instinct for what kids will like. For example, one past exhibit was called "'Grossology,' the (Impolite) Science of the Human Body." It featured barf, burps, boogers, and other gross stuff that kids love to giggle about. The center also houses an IMAX Dome theater, the largest in the country, showing films such as Cirque du Soleil's *Journey of Man*. LSC hours are from 9:30 A.M. to 5:30 P.M. Tuesday through Sunday. Call for extended summer hours.

From Liberty State Park, you can also take the ferry to the Statue of Liberty, which is in New Jersey, and Ellis Island, which we graciously share with the Empire State.

New Jersey Naval Museum (U.S.S. *Ling* 297)
$
Court and River Streets, Hackensack
(201) 342–3268
www.njnm.com

For devotees of wartime weaponry, this museum displays sea craft from various wars, like the patrol boat *Riverine,* an example of the boats used in Vietnam. (You may have seen some like it in *Apocalypse Now*.) As other boats of this class have been stripped for parts, destroyed, or sold to foreign navies, the *Riverine* is the only one left in the northeastern United States. Another interesting exhibit is the Japanese Kaiten, a suicide torpedo boat; and a German Seehund (meaning sea-dog or seal), a World War II two-man coastal sub. But the star of this museum is the U.S.S. *Ling* 297, a 312-foot-long Balao Class World War II submarine. Like all other subs of that war, the *Ling* was named after a fish. Commissioned on June 8, 1945, it never saw active duty in the Pacific, but served as a training vessel. Now the *Ling* is open for public tours. If you do go inside, you'll quickly understand just how frightening it could be when 95 men shared such limited space so many fathoms under the sea. The museum is open Wednesday through Sunday from 10:00 A.M. to 5:00 P.M. (last tour begins at 4:00 P.M.).

Thomas Alva Edison Memorial Tower and Menlo Park Museum   Free
37 Christie Street (Menlo Park section), Edison
(732) 549–3299
www.menloparkmuseum.org

In 1938, the state dedicated a monument to honor Thomas Edison at his former laboratory site: a 130-foot concrete column that towered over Menlo Park. Edison, known as "The Wizard of Menlo Park" moved to the town in 1876. It was here that he was granted more than 400 patents for his inventions, which included the incandescent light bulb, the phonograph, and the electric rail car.

The museum, which is adjacent to the tower, houses products from the Thomas A. Edison Co., photographs of Edison's laboratory, and the inventor's death mask, made in 1931 by noted American sculptor James Earl Fraser. There are plans to construct a new $4-million museum building, a replica of the old laboratory. An archaeological dig, focused on the boardinghouses where Edison's employees lived, is also planned; any artifacts that are found will go to the museum. The present museum is open Wednesday through Sunday from 10:00 A.M. to 4:00 P.M.

Yogi Berra Museum & Learning Center   **$**
Montclair State University
8 Quarry Road, Little Falls
(973) 655-2377
www.yogiberramuseum.org

Lawrence Peter Berra is one of America's national treasures. The diminutive Yankee is a Hall-of-Famer, a three-time Most Valuable player, holder of more world championship rings (10) than any player in baseball history, and part of baseball's Golden Age. America loves Yogi for all of that, and for making us laugh with his Yogi-isms, his screwy statements that have become part of everyday speech. Now we all know: "It ain't over till it's over," and "You can observe a lot just by watching," and: "It's deja vu all over again." But how many will agree: "The future ain't what it used to be?"

This museum, on the campus of Montclair State University, is dedicated to Yogi, who was born in 1925 and retired from baseball in 1992. See him as a Navy recruit who went on to fight in the D-Day invasion, as a star catcher, as a humanitarian who has given time and money to many causes. Among the museum's priceless collection of artifacts are Yogi's 10 world championship rings and the mitt he used to catch Don Larsen's perfect game in the 1956 World Series. You can watch a film of Yogi's life, as well as other baseball documentaries in the museum's Canon Theater; under the big screen is a replica of the Yankee Stadium scoreboard on September 19, 1959, the first Yogi Berra Day.

You'll also find exhibits relating to the history of baseball, covering its pre-Civil War origins, how it became the national pastime in the late 19th century, and later how integration changed the game. You'll see displays about such early greats as Babe Ruth and Lou Gehrig. If you want a baseball souvenir, head for the museum gift shop, where you'll find pictures and other memorabilia signed by Yogi himself. We'd love to tell you that the museum is open unless it's closed, but the hours are from noon to 5:00 P.M. Wednesday through Sunday. It is closed during the university's winter holiday break.

Next door to the museum is Yogi Berra Stadium, home of the minor league New Jersey Jackals, so you can take in a ball game after visiting Yogi's memorabilia.

Skylands Region

Black River and Western Railroad
Stangl Road (off N.J. Highway 12), Flemington
(908) 782-6622
www.BRWRR.com

On a balmy spring or summer day, explore the rural Hunterdon County countryside on this short-line railroad, which runs some 16 miles from Flemington to Ringoes. The railroad dates back to 1854, when the Flemington Transportation Company built the line from Flemington south to Lambertville, where it met the Pennsylvania Railroad. At the time there was substantial passenger and freight traffic, generated largely by the dairy and fruit production in the area. But rail traffic eventually dwindled and the line ceased operation in 1953.

In May 1965, the town of Flemington decided to operate a tourist line, complete with vintage coaches and diesels, on the old freight rails. You can ride this museum on wheels on weekends from April through December; Thursday and Friday rides are added during July and August. There are also many special train events throughout the year, including The Easter Bunny Express, The Great Train Robbery, Halloween Special, October's Fall Foliage runs, and The Santa Express.

Flemington Is for Shoppers

Flemington in one word: shopping! When visiting the attractions in this area, it would take an iron will not to at least check out some of the bargain opportunities that this area is known for. For instance there's Liberty Village Premium Outlets on Church Street (908–782–8550), where you'll find Brooks Brothers, Cole Haan, Tommy Hilfiger, Ralph Lauren, Donna Karan—and much, much more. Shoppers also flock to nearby Lambertville—just across the Delaware River from better-known New Hope, Pennsylvania—not for designer clothes, but for antiques.

Duke Gardens $
Highway 206, Somerville
(908) 243–3600

The tragic story of Doris Duke's lonely final years and her death, virtually alone, seems to prove the old saw that "money can't buy happiness." But in her heyday, the heiress to tobacco millions lived the kind of fairy tale that is the stuff of romance novels. One of her several homes was this Somerville estate, inherited from her father, James Buchanan Duke, who bought the land in 1893 and spent, according to some estimates, about $10 million to create roadways, hills, lakes, and fountains here. He imported millions of shrubs and trees from all over the world for his personal Shangri-la. After Mr. Duke's death, his daughter Doris took over the estate, employing as many as 400 people to maintain it. She added an 18-hole golf course and an indoor skeet shoot, and she also developed exotic display gardens in her father's honor, using Longwood Gardens in Pennsylvania as her inspiration. She began the project in 1959, and in 1964, the gardens were opened to the public. For the next 20 years, Duke oversaw the work of 15 full-time gardeners.

When you visit this magical place, you'll see magnificent garden displays inspired by all corners of the globe; there are English, Chinese, Japanese, French, Italian, Indo-Persian, Colonial, Edwardian, American Desert, and Tropical Jungle styles. It's easy to picture the heiress

enjoying the sanctuary of her gardens; you can see her personal touch in the Edwardian garden, which is filled with gorgeous orchids. Miss Duke was an expert on these blooms, most of them in the mauve color that was popular with wealthy Americans in the late 19th century.

The gardens are open daily, from October through May, but you must call and reserve a day and time for your tour. Call (908) 243–3600 on weekdays between 9:00 A.M. and 4:00 P.M. to reserve.

If you're not exhausted from your garden tour, you might want to visit nearby Wallace House (38 Washington Place, 908–725–1015), which served as Washington's headquarters during the Middlebrook encampment of 1778–79. See the chapter on Revolutionary New Jersey for more background.

Franklin Mineral Museum $
32 Evans Street, Franklin
(973) 827–3481

Of particular interest to geology buffs, this museum offers a comprehensive display of the 300 species of minerals from the Franklin-Ogdensburg area, site of the zinc mines of the New Jersey Zinc Company. The Franklin ore body, the world's richest in zinc content (it contained 30 minerals not found anywhere else in the world), was depleted in 1954, after being mined for more than 100 years.

There's a lot to see here, including the world's largest fluorescent display, where ores and minerals are shown under regular light and then long- and shortwave ultraviolet light. The result is a dazzling display of brilliant colors. There are also polished and set gemstones, both common and rare.

The museum's Jensen Wing houses a collection of fossils, Native American relics, and rocks and minerals. For a more intimate geology experience, you may explore the Mine Replica, which has been constructed with timber, rails, ore carts, drilling equipment, and other items actually used in the zinc mines of Franklin Sterling Hill. If you like, you can even scout the mine tailings in the Buckwheat Dump next door and search for mineral specimens. The museum is open to the public April through November, Monday through Saturday from 10:00 A.M. to 4:00 P.M., and Sunday from 12:30 to 4:00 P.M.

Lakota Wolf Preserve $$$
89 Mount Pleasant Road, Columbia
(877) SEE–WOLF
www.lakotawolf.com

You won't be able to dance with wolves at this preserve, but you will have an opportunity to observe and photograph tundra, timber, and arctic wolves in natural surroundings. (Bobcats and foxes also live here.)

During a Wolf Watch, you'll take your place in the observation area, among four packs of wolves, and see them play and interact with each other. From the people who raise and care for these beautiful animals, you'll learn about the social structure of wolf packs, their eating habits, and their interaction with people.

The Wolf Watch program takes place twice daily: during the summer at 10:30 A.M. and 4:00 P.M.; during the fall and winter at 10:30 A.M. and 3:00 P.M. Call for reservations Monday through Friday. No pets are allowed at the preserve. It is open year-round, but call ahead to confirm your reservation if the weather is inclement.

Land of Make Believe $$$
Great Meadows Road (Highway 611), Hope
(908) 459–9000
www.lomb.com

It's another old-time park dating back to the 1950s, but the Land of Make Believe goes for the "something for everyone" approach. Located on some 30 acres of a converted dairy farm, this is New Jersey's biggest children's amusement park, with a multitude of rides, shows, and attractions; a water park; and an appealing picnic grove. You'll find traditional arcade games and rides like the roller coaster, the Tilt-A-Whirl, and the carousel, as well as some unusual ones such as the Red Baron Airplane Ride and the Civil War Locomotive and Train Ride. The Pirate's Cove water park, which has a wading pool and an infant water-play area, features a life-size pirate ship.

If your kids like interactive fun, they can be part of the show at the Middle Earth Theatre, assuming the roles of knights and princesses in medieval times. Take an old-time hayride and look for deer along the foothills of Jenny Jump Mountain. If you don't bring a picnic, you can buy kid favorites like hot dogs, cheese fries, and pizza. The park is open Memorial Day weekend and the first two weekends in June; after that, it's open daily from 10:00 A.M. to 6:00 P.M. through the summer season; it's also open the weekend after Labor Day.

Mountain Creek $$$$
200 N.J. Highway 94 North, Vernon
(973) 827–2000
www.mountaincreek.com

There aren't lots of places where you can ski (day and night) and snowboard without leaving the state; Mountain Creek, in the northwest corner of the state, is your best bet. It has more than 165 skiable acres and 45 trails. In 2001 some $2.5 million in improvements were made, including new snowmaking guns. Eleven high-speed lifts can move more than 16,000 passengers each hour.

We like the Drop Zone Tubing Center, which has a dedicated lift so you can have the fun of snow tubing without having to walk up the hill. There's a Snow Sports School if you're a beginner, with dedicated beginner terrain and Magic Carpet lifts (these are like moving sidewalks). They have a Ladies Club program, which meets on Tuesday mornings for a two-hour

If you don't ski, take a downhill run in a tube at Mountain Creek. PHOTO: LILLIAN AFRICANO

clinic; during this club time, the Kids Kamp is free, and you also get parking privileges and rentals if needed. The Kids Kamp is for youngsters ages 4 to 12; the program includes instruction (skiing and snowboarding), lunch, lift tickets, and rentals. There's also an online reservation system.

In the summer, Mountain Creek sheds its ski togs and offers amusements of another kind. Foremost is Water World, a park that offers rides, slides, and pools. A fairly mild brand of splashy fun, suitable for youngsters, can be found in Kidz World, which offers a wading pool, kids' bumper boats, and the like. For adults and older kids, there's more heart-pounding stuff at Adventure Ridge, for example, the white-water thrill of the Colorado River and the high-speed plunge down Cannonball Falls.

On dry land, the warm weather brings all kinds of outdoor activity. Mountain bikers will find 30 miles of trails offering various levels of challenge; access them in style with the cabriolet gondola. The park has some 150 front- and full-suspension rental bikes.

If skating or skateboarding is your pleasure, the Square One Skate Park's 12,000-square-foot playground includes mini-ramps, launch ramps, and fun boxes. There is also an in-line skating path that winds around the mountain, and an 18-hole mini-golf course.

Northlandz $$$
495 U.S. Highway 202 South, Flemington
(908) 782–4022
www.northlandz.com

Young at heart or young in age, you'll be captivated by this miniature world that took almost 30 years to create. A labor of love by Bruce Williams and his wife, this 16-acre attraction began with the Great American Railway: 135 trains and eight miles of track, 35-foot mountains and 40-foot bridges, thousands of handcrafted buildings, and more than 10,000 freight cars. Later additions include: the La Peep Dollhouse, a 94-room miniature mansion complete with indoor swimming pool and two-story library; the Raritan River Railway, a ⅔-scale steam replica that travels through tunnels and over bridges; the Doll Museum, with more than 200 collectible dolls from around the world; the Music Hall, where a 2,000-pipe organ is the centerpiece of a 500-seat theater and is played several times daily. The Club Car Cafe, however, is full-size, and offers stuff to eat that kids like—pizza, Nathan's Famous hot dogs, ice cream, popcorn, and Otis Spunkmeyer's muffins and cookies. Northlandz is open weekdays from 10:30 A.M. to 4:00 P.M., and weekends and holidays (except Easter, Thanksgiving, and Christmas) from 10:00 A.M. to 6:00 P.M.

Pine Creek Miniature Golf $$
394 N.J. Highway 31 (east of Lambertville and south of Flemington), West Amwell
(609) 466–3803
www.pinecreekgolf.com

Pine Creek Miniature Golf is no ordinary miniature golf course; it's miniature golf raised to the ultimate level. Sprawling over 28 acres, Pine Creek is one of the largest and most beautiful courses in the United States, with nary a windmill in sight. Its two 18-hole courses (a par 55 and a par 65) ramble over acres of beautiful countryside in a picturesque country-club setting complete with flowers, trees, streams, ponds, waterfalls, and even a Danish-style clubhouse (with a dining area, fireplace, and dance floor). This place not only appeals to kids, it draws "real" golfers as well. There are no easy holes-in-one here, but holes so challenging that each course takes over an hour to play. With targeted lighting, Pine Creek also offers night play. After your round, you can adjourn to the clubhouse for pizza and other treats. Pine Creek is open daily, weather permitting, from April through October; hours vary, so call ahead. The course also has limited hours between November and March; again, call to inquire.

The Great American Railway at Northlandz features 135 trains, eight miles of track, and thousands of handcrafted buildings. PHOTO: COURTESY OF NORTHLANDZ

Space Farms Zoo & Museum $$
218 Highway 519, Beemerville
(973) 875–5800
www.spacefarms.com

Imagine ancestors who saved everything: antique cars and wagons, tools, toys, and weapons. Add to the picture some 500 live animals, a gargantuan stuffed bear, and an Indian Museum, and you have some idea of what this curious and quirky place is like.

It all started back in 1927, when Ralph and Elizabeth Space ran a small general store, gas station, and repair shop. Ralph supplemented his family's income by trapping predators that threatened farm animals for the state Game Department. As Ralph caught bobcats, foxes, and raccoons, his children wanted to keep the animals. In time, his menagerie grew and grew; now it's the largest private collection of North American wildlife in the world. It

Lizzie River Otter gets a big hug from Lindsey Space at the Space Farms Zoo Nursery.

PHOTO: COURTESY OF SPACE FARMS ZOO AND MUSEUM

now also includes such exotics as lions, Bengal tigers, llamas, jaguars, monkeys, and more. The star attraction is Goliath, who died in 1991, but who lives on in the Guinness record book as the largest bear in the world (2,000 pounds and 12 feet tall); thanks to the wonders of taxidermy, he is on display here.

After visiting with the animals, you can have a buffalo burger in the restaurant, picnic outside, play some miniature golf, or wend your way through the museum displays of antique autos, carriages, farm tools, toys, Civil War weapons, and all sorts of odds and ends. In case you're wondering, the Spaces started these collections during the Great Depression, when folks traded their belongings for food from the general store. Space Farms is open daily May through October from 9:00 A.M. to 5:00 P.M.

Sterling Hill Mining Museum $$
30 Plant Street, Ogdensburg
(973) 209–7212
www.sterlinghill.org

Have you ever had a yen to visit an actual mine—but without the danger and dirt? Indulge your fantasy here. Less than a half century ago, this mine encompassed one of the world's largest concentrations of zinc ore. Today you can learn all about metal mining by touring underground tunnels and studying the exhibits, the educational material, and the mining artifacts and machinery. If you or your youngsters have an interest in geology, this museum will afford you an interesting couple of hours (it's not recommended for children under six). It is a seasonal attraction, open daily March through November from 10:00 A.M. to 5:00 P.M.; tours are given at 1:00 and 3:00 P.M.

United States Equestrian Team (USET)
Headquarters   Free
Hamilton Farm
Pottersville Road (just west of U.S. Highway 206), Gladstone
(908) 234–1251
www.uset.org

If you've ever thrilled to the performances of the U.S. Olympic team, you'll probably

Insiders' Tip
You'll find more information on many of the attractions listed in this chapter and on other places to go in New Jersey at www.visit nj.com. Or call (800) VISIT NJ for a free travel guide.

enjoy a visit to the USET headquarters. This nonprofit organization selects, equips, trains, and finances equestrian teams to represent us in international competitions like the Pan American and Olympic games. A tour of the stable, built in 1916, is an amazing experience; we would gladly live in these sumptuous quarters, which have been rightly described as one of the largest and most lavish facilities in the United States. Built with brick and concrete, reinforced with steel, the ornate interior includes carriage rooms (which are now USET executive offices), corridors, and harness rooms with tile walls, terrazzo floors, and brass fittings. There are 54 box stalls with cork brick floors; during the annual Gladstone Antiques Show (mid-September), they become booths for top antiques dealers.

In the trophy room, which has glass-enclosed walnut cases, stained-glass ceiling lights, and oak flooring, you'll see ribbons and awards won by equestrian teams over the years. To schedule a visit, call the office, which is open Monday through Friday from 8:30 A.M. to 4:30 P.M.

USGA Golf House and Museum   Free
77 Liberty Corner Road (Highway 521),
Far Hills
(908) 234–2300
www.usga.org

If you're a golfer, you owe yourself at least one visit to Golf House. It's more than a museum, it's a veritable shrine to the game, home to the world's largest public collection of vintage golf memorabilia, books, and fine art. Where else could you see such remarkable items as the original club used by Alan Shepard on his Apollo 14 mission? Or the 1-iron used by Ben Hogan in the 1950 U.S. Open at Merion? There's an entire room devoted to golf legend Bobby Jones, but memorable golfers from Mary, Queen of Scots, to Tiger Woods are covered—and that includes exhibits on U.S. presidents, along with their clubs.

In addition to being golf's historical repository, the facility also includes a research center dedicated to the testing of new golf clubs and balls, with equipment so hi-tech that it's beyond us to explain. You can take a self-guided tour and watch some of the testing while you learn how the equipment is manufactured. Although visitors aren't permitted on the testing range or in the lab, there is an observation deck. Golf House is open during the week from 9:00 A.M. to 5:00 P.M., and from 10:00 A.M. to 4:00 P.M. on weekends.

Wild West City $$
Highway 206, Netcong
(973) 347–8900
www.wildwestcity.com

Shoot-outs and stagecoach rides in New Jersey? Yes, indeed, and if you don't believe us, mosey on over to Wild West City, an authentic reproduction of Dodge City in the 1880s. All day long (between 11:00 A.M. and 6:00 P.M.), there's some kind of action going on: gunfights at the O.K. Corral, Pony Express riders thundering into town—and even a holdup, starring the infamous outlaw Jesse James.

Bring a picnic or have a meal in the Golden Nugget Saloon. Then sample the other attractions: train rides, pony rides, an Old West stagecoach ride, a petting zoo. In the Indian Museum and Frontier Museum, you'll find collections of artifacts from the real Old West. From late April to mid-June, Wild West City is open to the public on weekends only, from 10:30 A.M. to 6:00 P.M. (weekdays are reserved for school groups). From mid-June to Labor Day, it's open daily for everyone, from 10:30 A.M. to 6:00 P.M.

Monmouth County

Accommodations
Restaurants
Nightlife
Shopping

Years ago, Monmouth County was very seasonal, with a large summer population that disappeared after Labor Day. Over the past couple of decades, as commuters discovered they could live at the Shore and work in Manhattan or "up North," Monmouth's beach communities have become year-round towns. What this means to you is that you'll find fewer cheap beach motels and more high-quality hotels and charming bed-and-breakfast inns, particularly in Highlands, Avon, and Spring Lake. There are plenty of high-end restaurants and shops, too.

Accommodations

During the busy summer season, prices for Monmouth County hotels, bed-and-breakfast establishments, and good-quality vacation rentals are on the high side, unless, of course, you compare them to the Hamptons. Among hotels and inns, you won't find much that's pleasant for under $100 a night, which is why our price ratings begin at "Under $125." Though New Jersey doesn't have an occupancy tax (the kind that sends your hotel bill way up in New York City), you will pay the standard six percent sales tax on your stay in a hotel or inn.

Unless otherwise noted, all the establishments listed here provide parking for guests and a telephone in each guest room. The hotels and most of the bed-and-breakfast inns can supply you with Internet access even if the guest rooms aren't equipped with modem ports.

Area hotels generally have both "smoking" and "no smoking" rooms, but ask in advance if this is a concern. At the bed-and-breakfast inns, the general rule is no smoking on the premises. Some places allow smoking on the porch, others will ask you to go into the garden or at least away from the house. If you're a smoker, ask in advance where you will have to go to smoke.

Most, but not all, the establishments we've listed have air-conditioning. Be aware that in recent years, summers at the Shore have produced some hot days, so if you need more than open windows and ceiling fans to cool off when the temperature climbs, choose your accommodations accordingly.

Many, if not most, inns do not accommodate children. The reason isn't meanness on their part. As one innkeeper explained, his place is furnished with real antiques, including many fragile pieces, which makes it suitable for adults only. Another said that guests (often parents themselves) tend to come to an inn for a quiet, relaxing, sometimes romantic getaway. And the quiet—not to mention the romance—can be disturbed by the normal exuberance of young children. Whether you agree or not, that's the way it is. In case you want to bring your kids to an inn, we have listed a few places that will welcome them.

Our price ratings reflect the cost of a standard double room in season (Memorial Day through Labor Day); in most cases, there's a big price spread between the standard room and rooms or suites offering such options as a whirlpool bath or a fireplace. If you're coming to the Shore in the off-season, you'll get considerable savings—anywhere from 20 percent to 40 percent—

depending on where you stay and when you travel. Usually children under a certain age (six to eight, so ask) will stay free in their parents' room; there's generally a modest surcharge for older kids.

Virtually all the inns require minimum stays (usually two or three nights) on weekends and during holiday periods. Some offer discounts for extended stays, usually a week or longer. Be sure to ask about cancellation policies: Some are quite liberal, allowing a full refund of your deposit if you cancel within a specified time period before your arrival date; some establishments will charge a cancellation fee regardless of when you notify them.

Hotel Price Code

For one night in a standard double room in high season.

$	Under $125
$$	$125 to $200
$$$	$200 to $300
$$$$	Over $300

Hotels

Berkeley Carteret Hotel $–$$
1401 Ocean Avenue, Asbury Park
(732) 776–6700, (888) 776–6701
www.berkeleycarterethotel.com

This oceanfront dowager has entertained visitors to the Shore since 1924. Some of our older relatives remember it fondly as Asbury's "in" place, an elegant hotel that was always bustling and nearly always booked solid during the summer season. Today the hotel is like Sleeping Beauty; when Asbury Park revives, there's no doubt that the Berkeley Carteret will once again be the queen of hotels in this area, with prices to match. The property, which includes 250 rooms and suites, a restaurant, a lounge, a swimming pool, a fitness center, and banquet rooms with 12-foot ceilings and crystal chandeliers, has undergone extensive renovation and refurbishing over the years. Compared to places with similar amenities it's a bargain, and when you book over the Web, you may even get a lower price. These days, many of its guests are business folk, but soon the

balance may once again shift to tourists from "up North" or New York. Even now, it's a convenient place to stay if you're taking in a concert or special event at Convention Hall or the Paramount.

The Breakers $$$
1507 Ocean Avenue, Spring Lake
(732) 449–7700
www.breakershotel.com

You can't beat the Breakers for location: right on Ocean Avenue in Spring Lake, where the beach and the Boardwalk promenade are just across the the street. The hotel also has a smallish pool, a nice alternative when the weather is hot and the ocean is choppy. The Breakers also welcomes children, while many of Spring Lake's other lovely bed-and-breakfast establishments do not. It's even possible to get adjoining rooms if you're traveling with friends or extended family.

The century-old hotel has lovely graceful porches, and many a warm-weather bride has chosen to be married outdoors before adjourning to her reception inside. The excellent Breakers on the Ocean restaurant specializes in Italian cuisine and seafood, serving a variety of pastas as well as several shrimp, veal, and chicken dishes. We're fond of the sunny poolside Veranda restaurant, which serves breakfast and lunch. It's a nice place to survey the beach scene while savoring eggs Benedict and sipping orange juice.

Though the guest rooms aren't as interesting as those you'll find in some of the town's bed-and-breakfast establishments, they do have all the typical hotel amenities: private baths, air-conditioning, mini-refrigerators, and television. The pricier luxury rooms, however, are pretty posh, with ocean views, whirlpool baths, fireplaces, and VCRs.

Molly Pitcher Inn $$
88 Riverside Avenue, Red Bank
(732) 747–2500, (800) 221–1372
www.mollypitcher.com

Named after the heroine of the Battle of Monmouth, the Molly Pitcher is sited smartly on the Navesink River. Built in 1928, it was designed to resemble Philadel-

The Breakers is a family-friendly oceanfront hotel in beautiful Spring Lake. PHOTO: ARTHUR AFRICANO

phia's Independence Hall. Within walking distance of Red Bank's train station and antiques district, "the Molly" is convenient for New Yorkers who arrive without cars. If you have your own boat, you can arrive in style and dock it in the Molly's own marina.

After the Garden State Arts Center (now the PNC Bank Arts Center) was built in 1968, the hotel hosted many of the entertainers who performed there: Jack Benny, Bob Hope, Lena Horne, and the Beach Boys, to name just a few. In recent years, Bruce and Bon Jovi have often housed band members at the Molly. Over the years, the hotel has had extensive renovations, and today it's a well-run, modern establishment. The rooms are cheerful and appealing, furnished with reproduction period pieces. You'll find a fitness room indoors and an appealing outdoor pool promenade that overlooks the marina. The elegant Navesink Dining Room also overlooks the river, as does the International Bar, which serves light fare and espresso and cappuccino.

The hotel frequently offers packages that include accommodations, food and beverages, and special offers from the area's antiques dealers and boutiques. On July 3 (weather permitting), the hotel has a terrific outdoor barbecue. The food is quite good, and the promenade offers a dead-on perspective of Red Bank's impressive fireworks display over the Navesink River. If you're interested, call to find out when tickets go on sale, as they generally disappear within hours.

Ocean Place Conference Resort $$$
One Ocean Boulevard, Long Branch
(800) 411–7321
www.oceanplace.com

This 12-story oceanfront hotel is very, very popular during the summer months, and understandably so. The ocean is on your doorstep, so is an inviting pool, and there's an attractive oceanfront dining patio when you need a burger or a salad.

The 254 climate-controlled rooms and suites are well furnished and decorated in sunny pastels that reflect the colors of the beach outside. The hotel has an upscale restaurant, the Palm Court Dining Room, that specializes in fine seafood. More casual is the Ocean View Dining Room, which serves a luncheon buffet in an airy oceanside setting. The Captain's Quarters & Mariner's Lounge, furnished with over-stuffed chairs and billiard tables, is a place to meet-and-greet. Guests can have a workout in the fitness center, a swim in the indoor pool, a soak in the Jacuzzi, or play a round of tennis on one of the two lighted courts. A bonus here is the Ocean Place Spa, a full-service establishment where you can indulge in every imaginable form of pampering: massage therapy, wraps, facials, hydrotherapy, and more. If it's a spa getaway you want, Ocean Place offers day and overnight packages.

Oyster Point Hotel $$
140 Bodman Place, Red Bank
(732) 530–8200, (800) 345–3484
www.oysterpointhotel.com

The Oyster Point Hotel is right on the Navesink River, practically next door to the Molly Pitcher Inn (see page 230), and its name and history are equally interesting. It stands on land that was once inhabited by the Navesink Indians, a tribe of the Lenni Lenape. The Navesink cultivated oysters, and over the years, the discarded shells formed a 30-foot mound at the river's sharpest point. By 1704 the site became known as "Oyster Shell Point."

From a distance, the hotel almost looks like an old-fashioned ocean liner, jutting into the river. The public areas are light and airy, and the soaring ceiling and a wall of windows make the sun-filled atrium an inviting place to congregate or to read the morning paper. The 58 guest rooms and three suites are furnished in dark wood, with pale walls and fabrics. Many rooms have water views, as do the restaurant and bar and the ballroom/banquet room. Predictably, the hotel is popular for weddings, business meetings, and conferences. We hear that Rumson resident Bruce Springsteen once held a birthday party for his mother-in-law here.

Sheraton Eatontown Hotel & Conference Center $$$
N.J. Highway 35 North and Industrial Way, Eatontown
(732) 542–6500
www.sheratoneatontown.com

Though N.J. Highway 35 isn't exactly scenic, this modern, well-maintained hotel does a brisk year-round trade with meetings, weddings, and business travel. In summer many Shore residents send their overflow guests here. The hotel is conveniently located, a short drive from Long Branch beaches, Monmouth Park Raceway, and the entrance to the Garden State Parkway. The Sheraton also has many appealing amenities and services. The 208 rooms and suites are spacious and nicely furnished in dark woods and attractive prints; coffeemakers and complimentary coffee are provided. There's an indoor/outdoor pool with a whirlpool and a fitness room. Guests who stay on the Executive VIP level enjoy such extra perks as a private lounge, complimentary continental breakfast, and complimentary evening hors d'oeuvres.

The hotel's Concorde Cafe has an appealing and airy atrium setting; it serves breakfast, lunch, and dinner. JR's Pub has a sports bar atmosphere, complete with four big television screens that let you keep up with your favorite team. Complimentary hors d'oeuvres and reduced-rate drinks are served during happy hours, from 5:00 to 7:00 P.M. Monday through Friday.

Bed-and-Breakfast Inns

Carriage House $–$$
18 Heck Avenue, Ocean Grove
(732) 988–3232
www.carriagehousenj.com

As the Carriage House has undergone a complete renovation, its eight rooms are among the freshest in Ocean Grove. Some have balconies and ocean views, the larger ones have working fireplaces, and all have private baths, air-conditioning, and television. The decor is a blend of French and English, and the atmosphere here is light and airy, less "done" than some, and very comfortable.

The ample breakfast is served buffet style; it includes orange juice, fresh fruit, French toast or quiche or homemade cheese cake. Hot and cold cereals are also available. Since the Carriage House is just a block from the beach and a block from town, you won't have to take your car everywhere. The inn will provide discounted beach badges and towels, as well as beach chairs if you request them.

Cashelmara Inn $$–$$$
Ocean and Lakeside Avenue, Avon-by-the-Sea
(800) 821–2976

We have friends who invariably pick this bed-and-breakfast inn for their romantic weekends, and we can see why. Everything here is so deliciously cozy and intimate: You wake up to the sound of the waves, watch the sunrise from your bed, soak in a Jacuzzi for two, then adjourn for breakfast, served seaside at a table for two. As is the case at the good bed-and-breakfast inns, breakfast is a delight, featuring farm-fresh eggs, fruit-filled pancakes, scrumptious French toast, and home-baked muffins.

Cashelmara was once a grand summer estate, built almost a hundred years ago by William G. Wilcox. It's been beautifully restored to a state of Victorian elegance, with ornately carved mirrors, Oriental carpets, marble-topped mahogany furnishings, and lots of period bibelots. They've also installed such mod cons as air-conditioning and Jacuzzis; all the guest rooms have private baths.

Most of the rooms have ocean views; the larger suites have fireplaces, sitting areas, and whirlpools-for-two. When you stay here, you'll get a badge for the Avon beach and towels to take there. After your day at the beach, you can settle into one of the pretty white porch rockers and enjoy the view. Or settle in for a good read in the Victorian parlor. There's much to do in town in the evening, but if you don't feel like going out, you can watch a movie in the inn's own Mulligan Grand Victorian Theater. No reclining seats, but you can sink into a velvet chair or loveseat—and the soda and popcorn are on the house.

If romance is not on your agenda, Cashelmara, unlike many of the Shore's elegant bed-and-breakfast inns, does welcome "well-behaved children," if your kids are up to that challenge. (There is a small surcharge.)

Laingdon Hotel $
8 Ocean Avenue, Ocean Grove
(732) 774–7974
www.laingdonhotel.com

Ocean Grove has so many quaint inns that it may be hard to choose. The Laingdon, built in the late 1800s, is one of the town's original Victorian hotels, with some of the best ocean views. The lobby is like a postcard, all red velvet and mahogany. The rooms are simple and clean, and many (but not all) have private bathrooms. Most rooms have ocean views, and all have access to the hotel's big terrace. Rooms do not have air-conditioning; they're cooled instead by ocean breezes and ceiling fans, which are usually enough. Rates here are considerably lower than at fancier establishments; a room with a double bed and bath starts at well under $100.

The Lillagaard Bed & Breakfast Inn $–$$
5 Abbott Avenue, Ocean Grove
(732) 988–1216
www.lillagaard.com

This historic inn was recently renovated and decorated with hand-painted murals. Rooms here are air-conditioned and have ceiling fans; many also have private baths and ocean views. Each room offers its own touch of whimsy, like the Watermelon Room, which is decorated with painted hunks of watermelon, some whole, some half eaten, others down to the rind. That cooling image should make you smile on a warm summer day. The house has a library, a television and game room, and those most appealing Shore hangouts—two porches. There's a Victorian garden, too. If you want to go to the beach, the inn supplies discounted badges.

You'll be served a continental breakfast in the "English Kitchen" dining room, which is furnished in dark wood and antiques. The meal might include homemade muffins or other baked goods, cereal, fresh fruit, and perhaps a soufflé or a baked omelette; on the weekends there are bagels and lox.

A recent addition to the inn is Mrs. BLT's Tea Room, where you can linger over a pot of tea or indulge in the full catastrophe: a stanchion piled with little sandwiches, scones, and other desserts, accompanied by lemon curd and clotted cream. The cost, depending on what you order, is between $2.00 and $15.00.

Nathaniel Morris Inn $$
117 Marcellus Avenue, Manasquan
(732) 223–7826
www.nathanielmorris.com

If you like historic inns, note that this one was built in 1882 by William Longstreet and later occupied by Gilbert Marcellus; both men are considered to be Manasquan town fathers. The inn is featured on the town's historical register and has been named one of Manasquan's "Centennial Homes." During its long life, the house was the summer cottage of a wealthy Philadelphia family, a hat shop, and housing for the military during the two World Wars. Now it's Manasquan's nicest bed-and-breakfast inn.

The public areas of the house include a Victorian parlor furnished with antiques, a comfortable living room with a big-screen television, a formal dining room, and two sunny, enclosed porches. The wicker furniture on the porches invites you to relax and linger, reading your favorite beach book or one of the many magazines collected here. Breakfast is part of the fun of staying at an inn, and this one is indeed filling: It includes juices, fruit, cereal, baked goodies, and a hearty entree.

All the inn's guest rooms have private baths, television, and air-conditioning. Antique furniture mixes comfortably with reproductions, and pretty floral-printed spreads and window treatments complement the soft colors of the walls. If you choose one of the second-floor rooms, you'll have a private verandah. And if you're traveling with another couple or older children (guests must be over 13), you can have a two-room suite. For your trips to the beach, the innkeepers will supply you with badges, towels, chairs, and bikes.

Sea Crest by the Sea $$$
19 Tuttle Avenue, Spring Lake
(732) 449–9032, (800) 803–9031
www.seacrestbythesea.com

Time spent at this restored 1885 Queen Anne bed-and-breakfast inn just a half-block from the beach is like visiting a

Sea Crest by the Sea is one of Spring Lake's most romantic bed-and-breakfast inns. PHOTO: COURTESY OF SEA CREST BY THE SEA

well-off relative. Make that a relative who has furnished your room with antiques and interesting collectibles, and who is thoughtful enough to lay in a big supply of bikes, beach chairs, towels, and umbrellas for your personal use.

All the rooms are named and themed, as is the case in many inns. The first-floor bedroom/sitting room, called the Queen Victoria, has a canopied featherbed and billowy cotton linens. It's decorated with furniture of appropriate vintage and pictures of Britain's late monarch. Modern touches include private baths, air-conditioning, a television/VCR tucked into an antique cabinet, a CD player, and a mini-fridge filled with complimentary Pellegrino water (replenished daily), soft drinks, and juices. Most rooms have fireplaces; many have Jacuzzis and ocean views.

At breakfast time, you'll find the antique French sideboards laden with goodies: fresh orange juice, fresh fruit, yogurt and granola, warm buttermilk scones, a hearty entree (perhaps a quiche), exceptional coffee, and a yummy dessert. That should set you up for a day of frolicking in the surf. The innkeeper will give you a free badge for the Spring Lake beach, one of the nicest in Monmouth County.

If you happen to be around at tea time (4:00 P.M.), you can partake of some Earl Grey (or another tea of your choice) and more baked treats. Take them out onto the porch, settle yourself into a rocker, and let the cool ocean breezes refresh you while you contemplate dinner in one of the area's fine restaurants.

Water Witch House $–$$
254 Navesink Avenue, Highlands
(732) 708-1900
www.water-witch-house.com
Located in the hills of Highlands, the Water Witch is a convenient place to stay if you'd like to spend time at Sandy Hook, visit such nearby attractions as the Twin Lights Lighthouse, and sample the area's fine seafood restaurants. It's also minutes from the fast ferries to New York.

When it was built of local "Lenox" bricks in 1910, this small family-run bed-and-breakfast inn was a summer cottage. Twenty years later, it became an obstetri-cal hospital run by Dr. Mary Reed. Now thoroughly restored, it has the warmth of a private home. As is usually the case with bed-and-breakfast inns, all of the three rooms are different. But each has a queen-size bed and a twin-size daybed with a trundle in the sitting area, a private bath (which may be outside the room), and a stocked mini-refrigerator. The furnishings are antique, mostly dark woods. The large front room offers a partial water view and a glimpse of New York City, while the large two-room suite (which can accommodate three adults or two adults with up to two children) affords you sweeping water views (the private bath here is within the suite). The suite also has a wonderful antique solid-brass bed.

Breakfast here is hearty, and includes juice, fresh fruit, homemade baked goods, eggs, and breakfast meat. After a day in the sun at Sandy Hook, you can relax on the rear patio or in the front parlor before you head out for lobster at Bahr's or Doris and Ed's (see the "Restaurants" section of this chapter). If you're wondering about the name, it comes from a novel written in 1830 by James Fenimore Cooper called *The Water Witch, or the Skimmer of the Seas*. It is a story of piracy and derring-do, and since there was plenty of that here, the area became known as Water Witch.

Seasonal Rentals

If you plan to spend the whole summer at the Shore, your best choice would probably not be a hotel or inn; the cost would be prohibitive and you would soon feel very cramped. As they have for years, well-off city folk "take a house" for the season.

In Monmouth County, you can find seasonal rentals of motel-type efficiency apartments as well as substantial seashore homes. Prices vary from town to town, and of course, according to the size of the house. You can rent an 11-room Victorian in Belmar for the summer for $20,000, a three-bedroom home in Sea Girt for $16,000, or a Manasquan cottage for $11,500. In Spring Lake, a two-bedroom guest house on the grounds of a Victorian inn right on the lake will set you back $20,000. We've seen a larger Spring Lake lakefront home renting for $32,000 for the season. In Avon-by-the-Sea, a fully equipped, three-bedroom apartment in a pretty house on Sylvan Lake with ocean views goes for $23,000 for the summer, but can be rented by the week or by the month.

But you don't have to pay five figures to spend the summer in Monmouth. For example, a cozy one-bedroom garage apartment in Avon-by-the-Sea on a quiet shaded lane three blocks to the beach and Boardwalk was $7,500 for a long summer season (mid-May to mid-October).

The "season" at the Shore has traditionally been defined as from June 15 through Labor Day, but obviously, you can work out dates with the homeowner. Many choice rentals are booked early, before March, and often to returning vacationers. But if you're not overly picky and would rather have a bargain than a big selection, wait. Landlords who don't have a tenant by May or June are likely to be more flexible on price and, if you want to rent for a period of weeks, on term of occupancy.

When shopping for a rental, you can check ads in the *Asbury Park Press* or contact a broker in your town of choice. Check the Relocation chapter for an extensive list of area real-estate agencies.

Restaurants

There are hundreds of restaurants in Monmouth County, so this list is necessarily selective; we've tried to give a sampling of what's available in different price ranges, from diners to fine dining.

Of course you expect to get fresh fish at the Shore—there are dozens of seafood restaurants here, from Highlands to Belmar to Brielle. Many are good; a few, superb. What may come as a surprise is the variety of ethnic cuisines represented at the Shore—Caribbean, Japanese, German, Mexican, French, and plenty of Italian. Some area Italian restaurants have been around forever, and still sport their 1950s roadhouse decor, complete with jukeboxes and pine paneling. Some of the Italian restaurants here have combined the traditional large portions with cuisine that reaches well beyond the old red-sauce-on-everything days.

One thing about the Shore—good restaurants don't go out of style; places like Jimmy's, Doris & Ed's, and the Old Mill Inn stay busy year after year. We suggest you find out why for yourself.

We've mentioned some of the restaurants in the hotels and bed-and-breakfast inns earlier, so we won't repeat them here. You'll find more of these charming places to stay and eat in Spring Lake and Avon, two very scenic towns.

Restaurants Price Code

Ratings reflect the average price for two entrees, excluding drinks, appetizers, dessert, tax, and tip.

$ . . . . under $25
$$ . . . . $25 to $40
$$$ . . . . $40 to $55
$$$$ . . . . over $55

Bahr's Restaurant & Marina $$–$$$
2 Bay Avenue, Highlands
(732) 872–1245
www.Bahrs.com

Jack Bahr started making his spicy clam chowder way back in 1917, and now you can buy cans of Bahr's Manhattan and New England–style chowders in your supermarket. Of course you'll miss the restaurant's wonderful view of Sandy Hook and the N.J. Highway 36 drawbridge, not to mention the lobster, softshell crabs, and the biscuits and coleslaw. Bahr's is open daily for lunch and dinner.

Barnacle Bill's Marina $$
1 First Street, Rumson
(732) 747–8396

Barnacle Bill's is a happy combination—a happening bar with really good food. Better yet, the kitchen is open until midnight and the grill until closing at 2:00 A.M. Our favorites are the sweet steamers, sauteed brook trout, and spicy blackened anything. The burgers with grilled mushrooms ain't bad either. Expect to wait in the bar eating peanuts on weekends or any night during the summer. You can bring your drink out on the porch or pass the time by feeding the ducks from the dock. (They like peanuts, too.) It's open daily for lunch and dinner.

Blue Marlin $$
714 Main Street, Bradley Beach
(732) 988–7997
www.bluemarlin-restaurant.com
Jamaican favorites like jerk pork and conch fritters bring a slice of the Caribbean to the Jersey Shore. Bring your own rum to add to the nonalcoholic tropical drinks, sit outside on a warm night, and enjoy live music on Fridays and Sundays.

Boathouse Bar & Grill
1309 Main Street (N.J. Highway 71), Belmar
(732) 681–5221
www.boathousebarandgrill.com
This nautical-themed restaurant, done in a sort of early-lifeguard style, has an outdoor patio, a full bar, and happy hours that are happy and loud. There is a big menu, plus nightly dinner specials, but many come just to nosh on bar food like chicken wings, stuffed potato skins, sloppy joes, and pizza. The Boathouse is

open from 11:00 A.M. to 2:00 A.M. daily, and has live entertainment, which means you have to be over 21 to be in the bar after 8:30 P.M.

Broadway Diner $
45 Monmouth Street, Red Bank
(732) 224–1234
One of the few Shore restaurants that's open 24/7, the Broadway Diner is at the heart of "Hip City" (Red Bank). The young and pierced crowd heads for the smoking section in the rear, while cops hang out up front. We resent the disappearance of chicken a la king on Monday nights, but still, you can't beat hearty dinner specials like meat loaf or beef stroganoff that come with soup (we love the chicken orzo and yankee bean), salad, and dessert for about $10.

Captain Jack's $$–$$$
68 Main Avenue, Ocean Grove
(732) 869–0770
Captain Jack's is a comfortable storefront eatery set amid Ocean Grove's pretty shops and boutiques. It has attractive artwork on the walls, and tables, booths, and

The Broadway Diner will serve you breakfast whether it's 9:00 A.M. or 9:00 P.M. It's open 24 hours.
PHOTO: ANDREW HASSARD

banquette seating. Menu selections include Chesapeake crab cakes, crispy chicken in plum sauce, and bistro salad with bacon and egg. Finish your meal with coffee-toffee ice-cream pie or well-made carrot cake. As Ocean Grove is dry, you'll have to bring your own bottle.

Carlos O'Connor Mexican Restaurant $
31 Monmouth Street, Red Bank
(732) 530–6663

Whether you love it or hate it, the "decor" at Carlos O'Connor is an assault on the senses. With strings of red-chili-pepper lights draped across the room, Mexican tchotchkes covering every inch of wall space, and oddball tables and chairs, it's Mamma Leone meets Pancho Villa. But the food is good. Favorites are the crispy chips and salsa, black bean soup, quesadillas, and steak and chicken fajitas. Be sure to bring your own tequila or cold beer, and say hello to Carlos. You can't miss him—just look for the black hat.

Crown Palace $$
1285 N.J. Highway 35 North, Middletown
(732) 615–9888

There are not many good Chinese restaurants at the Shore, so the Crown Palace is worth schlepping to. We love the pan-browned wontons with sesame, beef with pan-fried noodles, and the sesame chicken. The whole Dragon Sole is an extraordinary treat. In addition to the regular menu, be sure to ask for the Chinatown menu—that's where you'll find all the seafood dishes that the Chinese people next to you are tucking into. It's open daily for lunch and dinner.

Doolan's Restaurant $$
700 N.J. Highway 71, Spring Lake Heights
(732) 449–3666

Doolan's is a big hall that's popular for weddings and other parties. Though not exactly cutting-edge in its cuisine, the restaurant does a good job with classic American dishes like prime rib, and the salad bar is a wonder. It's open for lunch during the week and for dinner daily, and offers early-bird dinners every day except Saturday.

Doris & Ed's $$$$
348 Shore Drive, Highlands
(732) 872–1565

There are many good seafood restaurants at the Shore, but Doris & Ed's is in a class by itself. Each fish dish is incredibly fresh, perfectly prepared, and beautifully presented. The servers are informed enough to help you select from an extensive wine list. Try to get a window table with a water view. The restaurant is open Wednesday through Sunday for dinner.

Eggimann's Tavern $–$$
2031 N.J. Highway 71 South, Spring Lake Heights
(732) 449–2626

Eggimann's has been in business for more than 115 years, and some of the clientele have been coming about that long, too. The magic formula here is home cooking and cocktails, with basic steak and seafood getting the nod. Eggimann's is open seven days a week for lunch and dinner, with piano entertainment on Fridays and Saturdays, and unlike many early-to-bed joints, the kitchen stays open until 11:00 P.M.

Fromagerie $$$$
26 Ridge Road, Rumson
(732) 842–8088

One of the few area restaurants to require a jacket and tie for men, Fromagerie offers French cuisine of the old school, presenting classic dishes like tournedos with béarnaise sauce, and beef Bourguignonne. Consider the crispy quail for your appetizer. We love Fromagerie for a special lunch, when the offerings are a little lighter; the kitchen creates wonderful salads with grilled steak or chicken, unbelievably rich cream soups, and superb desserts. The restaurant also is known for its large (and expensive) selection of vintage wines.

Hofbrauhaus $$–$$$
301 Ocean Boulevard (Scenic Drive), Atlantic Highlands
(732) 291–0224
www.hofbrauhausnj.com

Oompah bands and Wiener schnitzel are not exactly trendy, but the Hofbrauhaus has remained popular for decades. Its

Eggimann's Tavern has been serving meals to Spring Lakers for more than 115 years. PHOTO: ARTHUR AFRICANO

splendid location near Mount Mitchill Scenic Overlook, with its vistas of Sandy Hook and New York City, is one reason. Enjoy one (or more) of the genuine German beers on tap,. and you, too, may find yourself swinging into a polka. In the off-season, you'll find discount dinner coupons in the *Asbury Park Press.*

Indigo Moon $$$–$$$$
171 First Avenue, Atlantic Highlands
(732) 291–2433
www.indigochef.com

A departure from the prevalent seafood on the Bayshore, this new Country French bistro serves provocative dishes such as rosemary-roasted rack of lamb with ratatouille, citrus-grilled free-range chicken breasts with roasted vegetables and potato puree, and seared tuna in pastry crust. Save room for crème brûlée or tiramisu. BYOB.

Jimmy's Italian Restaurant $$–$$$
1405 Asbury Avenue, Asbury Park
(732) 774–5051

Jimmy's is the standard by which locals measure all new restaurants, as in, "Well, it's not as good as Jimmy's...." You can order anything on the menu and it'll be great, from the chicken with prosciutto, mushrooms, and artichoke hearts to steaks worthy of a New York steak house. Again and again we order the veal francese, light-as-a-feather sole juliet, and the stuffed sole oreganata. The good wine list with reasonable prices is also a plus. Jimmy's serves lunch and dinner every day but Tuesday.

Joe & Maggie's Bistro on Broadway $$$
591 Broadway, Long Branch
(732) 571–8848
www.joeandmaggiesbistro.com

At this cozy continental/American restaurant, owner and chef Joe Romanowski changes the menu often, coming up with innovative dishes that taste as good as they sound. There are always a few interesting seafood options, from cioppino to lobster thermidor. We recommend the duck-leg confit, if it's on the menu. Delicious desserts are worth every calorie. If you like to eat on the early side, take advantage of the twilight dinner specials, which offer a complete three-course meal for the price of an entree.

A Tale of Two Weiners: Max's and the Windmill

Coney Island made Nathan's famous, and the Jersey Shore has its own tale of the tube steak—a couple of tales, in fact.

Years ago, Max's was a fixture on the Long Branch Pier, serving great hot dogs, corn on the cob, fried clams, and peach melba, all served up with an attitude worthy of Ratner's in Manhattan. The pier disappeared (burned down) but Max's rose from the ashes and found a new home (see below), where it was business as usual.

My grandmother's favorite meal, especially after a not-too-successful day at Monmouth Park, was nicely charred hot dog at the cheerful, red Windmill. Oblivious to the thousands of yellow jackets that swarmed the trash cans full of discarded sodas, she would insist on dining alfresco, on the topside deck of the familiar "Moulin Rouge" of the Jersey Shore.

Long story short, many other Shore folk must have agreed with my grandmother, as the Windmill is now a successful local franchise, with 10 locations at the Shore and throughout the state. In addition to the near-foot-long dogs, we love the Windmill's char-grilled burgers and the fried mushrooms with tangy horseradish sauce; others indulge in hip-expanding cheese fries.

Max's Hot Dogs
25 Matilda Terrace, Long Branch
(732) 571–0248

Windmill
Original location:
586 Ocean Avenue at Brighton,
West End (Long Branch)
(732) 229–9863

Other locations:
200 Ocean Avenue, North Long
Branch
(732) 870–6098

Junction N.J. Highways 35 and 71,
Belmar
(732) 681–3628

22 North Bridge Avenue, Red Bank
(732) 530–7223

Junction N.J. Highways 88 and 70,
Brick
(732) 458–7774

N.J. Highway 9 South and Adelphia
Road, Freehold
(732) 303–9855

N.J. Highway 35 North, Hazlet
(732) 264–0101

1650 Stelton Road (Fairway Golf
Center), Piscataway
(732) 777–7933

48 Maple Street, Summit
(908) 598–9814

256 East Broad Street, Westfield
(908) 233–9242

Jose's Mexican Restaurant $$
101 N.J. Highway 71, Spring Lake Heights
(732) 974–8080
Located in a strip mall, Jose's is colorful and friendly on the inside, with walls decorated with sombreros. The emphasis is on "healthy Mexican food," with menu items such as chicken and broccoli quesadillas, vegetarian tacos, and chimichangas made with cholesterol-free soybean oil. Mexican

The original Windmill, located in the West End section of Long Branch, sells swell fast food: char-grilled burgers, giant hot dogs, French fries, and more. PHOTO: NINA AFRICANO

pizza is a big fried tortilla topped with lots of stuff—chicken, beans, lettuce, cheese, tomatoes, sour cream. Mere steps away is the Ice Hut, with fruit-flavored ices and fat-free ice cream. Jose's is open seven days a week for lunch and dinner and also accepts take-out orders.

Kelly's Tavern $$
N.J. Highway 35 South, Neptune City
(732) 775–9517

Kelly's is a big, loud Irish tavern that keeps the barflies well fed with its famous artery-choking Reuben. We choose the lesser evil, corned beef and cabbage. Homemade soups are always good, especially (surprise!) the creamy potato. In summer and on weekends, there's a raw bar, and the jumbo shrimp and sweet oysters are not to be missed. It's open daily for lunch and dinner.

Klein's Waterside Cafe $$$
708 River Road, Belmar
(732) 681–1177

Back in 1924, Ollie Klein Sr. peddled fish from his truck; a few years later he opened a fish market on Belmar's River Road, where his wife, Elizabeth, prepared fresh-off-the-boat seafood dinners. Now Ollie II runs the place, with such additions as a take-out menu, expanded dockside dining, a white-tablecloth grill room, and sushi, oyster, and raw bar. Our favorite: the luscious lobster.

La Nonna Piancone's Cafe $$$
800 Main Street, Bradley Beach
(732) 775–0906

For years, Piancone's Bakery was like the Balducci's of Bradley Beach, selling fresh rolls, stuffed breads, and great Italian cold cuts. So when the owners opened a restaurant next door, it was an overnight success, with lines snaking around the corner. And it's still busy, especially in the summer. The food is traditional Italian, but with a little zip. We especially like the housemade pastas.

Mahogany Grille $$–$$$
142 Main Street, Manasquan
(732) 292–1300

When fast food and casual seafood joints won't do, the Mahogany Grille offers grown-up fare and a sophisticated white-tablecloth ambience. You might start with artichoke and Granny Smith apple soup, then move on to porcini-dusted venison chops with fingerling potato–sausage stew or the pork loin stuffed with goat cheese and spinach. Finish with one of the highly styled desserts like the Tony Tux, a chocolate brownie garnished with peanut butter mousse and glazed with chocolate, served with vanilla ice cream and peanut butter crème anglaise.

McLoone's Rum Runner $$$–$$$$
816 Ocean Avenue, Sea Bright
(732) 842–2894

When we have visitors, we take them to McLoone's to show off the fabulous view: the sunset on Shrewsbury River, highlighting the mansions on the Rumson side. The high-end American menu does not quite deliver on expectations, though. One way to enjoy the view without the hefty tab is to sit outside, where both attire and the menu are more casual. Be prepared for big waits in season. It's open daily for lunch and dinner.

Memphis Pig Out $$
67 First Street, Atlantic Highlands
(732) 291–5533

Stroll down First Street and the smell of those ribs will stop you in your tracks—and they're every bit as good as they smell. Though you can pig out at the ample salad bar, the name applies more to the restaurant's decor; hundreds of piggy pictures and stuffed animals cover the walls and populate a souvenir stand at the register. On Mondays and Wednesdays, the place offers an unbeatable movie deal—free tickets to Atlantic Triplex across the street with your meal when you pay cash.

Mom's Kitchen $–$$
1129 Fifth Avenue, Neptune
(732) 775–4823

While other restaurant jack up their prices for special occasions like Valentine's Day or Mother's Day, Mom's actually comes out with specials that are even more of a bargain than the regular menu. If you like dishes with red sauce and waitresses that call you "Hon," try Mom's. P.S. The pizza's good, too.

Moonstruck $$$–$$$$
517 Lake Avenue, Asbury Park
(732) 988–0123

Moonstruck is the hottest new restaurant in Asbury. The gifted chef has a way with dishes such as chicken with garlic and rosemary, and shrimp with garlic ginger and soy sauce that has 'em lining up in the street. (No reservations.) As of this writing, Moonstruck was moving from its original location in Ocean Grove to Lake Avenue, so call to confirm. BYOB.

Old Mill Inn $$$–$$$$
Old Mill Road, Spring Lake Heights
(732) 449–1800
www.oldmillinn.com

For decades, the Old Mill has been *the* place to treat Mom, with its Sunday-best service and lovely lake views. Yet chef Tim Murphy, who trained with Wolfgang Puck, keeps things fresh with a California-style emphasis on fish and veggies, in addition to offering the classics like prime rib. It can get expensive here, especially if you enjoy cocktails or one of the very nice wines; a good buy is the twilight dinner, if you don't mind eating early. There are often shows at dinnertime, perhaps doo-wop music or a comedian like Pat Cooper, as well as special events such as Big Band Night.

Parkhill's $$
601 Main Street, Loch Arbour (on Deal Lake)
(732) 660–0040

This casual bar and restaurant overlooking Deal Lake stays open late and attracts a fairly young crowd, especially on weekends when there's live entertainment, or when there's some sort of TV event like Monday night football. When the weather is nice, though, head right for the patio. The menu doesn't quite live up to some of its ambitions, so stick with the basics. The burger with blue cheese is our favorite.

Ranoosh $$$
612 Second Avenue, Long Branch
(732) 483–9300

If you've never tried Lebanese food, stop depriving yourself. Order the grape leaves stuffed with lamb and rice, or kibbe, super-lean lamb blended with cracked wheat. The belly dancing and different flavors of hookahs (water pipes) at Ranoosh will transport you to a different place and time.

Salt Creek Grille $$–$$$$
4 Bingham Avenue, Rumson
(732) 933–9272
www.saltcreekgrille.com

Rumsonites love this chic California-casual retreat not only for its excellent food, but for its unique ambience. The valet parking, the gas fireplace in the outdoor waiting area, the wall of riverfront picture windows, the subdued lighting and tasteful decor, and even the daily newspaper tacked up over the urinals in the men's room reflect an attention to "atmosphere" unrivalled in this area. The food lives up to expectations; we recommend the seared ahi salad, lobster, flame-grilled steaks, and blue cheese burgers. Save room for dessert, and note that you must order the double-chocolate soufflé 25 minutes in advance.

Sand Bar $$$
Union Lane, Brielle
(732) 528–7750

Downstairs at the Sand Bar is a casual pub where folks snack on nachos, calamari, clams, buffalo shrimp, and other bar food. Upstairs is an upscale dining area that overlooks the Brielle Marina. Here the menu leans toward seafood like scallops, shrimp, and mahimahi, but you can also get pasta or a burger, and there is an extensive kids' menu.

The Sandpiper $$$
7 Atlantic Avenue, Spring Lake
(732) 449–4700

Set in a quaint Victorian hotel just steps from the ocean, the Sandpiper is so appealing, especially on summer evenings when a piano player adds a little mood music. The continental/American fare can be only fair at times, but if you use one of the "twofer" coupons that you'll often find in the *Asbury Park Press*, your meal will be reasonably priced. The Sandpiper is open for lunch and dinner seven days a week and will serve the bottle of wine that you bring along.

Seagull's Nest Deck Bar & Grill $
Sandy Hook area
(732) 872–0025

You don't really come to the Seagull's Nest for the food—you come to enjoy the breeze and the views of the ocean and Sandy Hook Bay from the second-floor open-air restaurant. The burgers and snacks are okay, and they really go down well with a cold beer and the guitar player singing about Margaritaville. Stay for the sunset over the bay, and sing "God Bless America" along with the old Kate Smith recording.

Shiki Japanese Steak House $$$
1735 N.J. Highway 35 North, Middletown
(732) 671–9500
www.shikisteakhouse.com

Years ago, the Shiki's shoji screens, sushi bar, and hibachi cooking must have been the height of exotic. It's all more familiar these days, but the food is still great, and the skilled chefs still give you a great show—and a little hot sake or a wacky tropical drink doesn't hurt, either. Be sure to order the fried rice or you'll end up enviously eyeing your more foresighted neighbor's plate. Expect to wait in the bar if you don't arrive early on weekends.

Something Fishy Restaurant $$–$$$
140 Ocean Avenue, Sea Bright
(732) 747–8340

Right at the entrance to Sandy Hook is this quaint and casual seafood joint with the motto "From the docks to your table." Along with your fresh lobster, crab cakes, soft-shell crabs, or steamers, you'll enjoy wonderful water views, especially when it's nice enough to sit outside. For landlubbers, the menu offers pasta as well as some steak and chicken dishes. If you prefer to eat on your own deck, order your food to go.

Sonny's Southern Cuisine $$
Press Plaza, Cookman Avenue, Asbury Park
(732) 774–6262

Come for the Southern fried chicken and stay for the crab cakes with mango sauce. Crawfish poppers are another Southern touch, as are side dishes like fried okra. Or just order some really good macaroni and cheese.

Sunset Landing $$
1215 Sunset Avenue, Asbury Park
(732) 776–9732

This appealing spot on Deal Lake is our favorite place for Sunday brunch, serving homemade muffins, interesting omelettes, and even fresh coconut juice to go along with its Hawaiian surfer theme. Kids love to feed the ducks when they get bored with eating. Sunset Landing is open for breakfast and lunch.

Thompson's Fish-N-Chips of Kearny $
1142 Ocean Avenue, Sea Bright
(732) 219–0888

As you may have guessed, the specialty at this come-as-you-are storefront right across the street from Sea Bright beach is fish and chips. You also can get broiled fish and British-style fast food like pasties (small meat or fish pies).

Uptown Restaurant & Bar $$$$
611 Broadway, Long Branch
(732) 229–2480

Uptown, with its giant martinis and cutting-edge cuisine, brings New York attitude to downtown Long Branch. It's expensive, but there's a prix-fixe menu offered Tuesday through Friday that gives you great value for your money. Wednesday nights there's live jazz.

What's Your Beef $$–$$$
21 West River Road, Rumson
(732) 842–6205

At this casual eatery, you order your steak or fish by the ounce, directly from the

Tomato Pies (a.k.a. Pizza)

For us, great pizza and the Jersey Shore are practically synonymous, and after you visit some of our favorite places, we hope you'll agree. For us, the perfect pizza is thin and crispy, with the edges ever so slightly burned. Even with extra toppings, a slice of pizza should not sag into a cheesy mess, but keep its shape when you fold the crust. The sauce should be tangy and flavorful, not just a bland red puddle. When it emerges from the hot pizza oven, the cheese should be bubbling on top, molten hot enough to exfoliate your over-eager palate. If we had to pick the "Best Pizza," it would have to be Federici's, but these places are all good, and each has its own particular charm.

Freddie's $
563 Broadway, Long Branch
(732) 222–0931

This was our regular haunt for many years. Freddie's pizza has changed a bit over time; we think the sauce is a little less tangy now. The pizza is still pretty good, though, especially the Extra Special, with sausage, peppers, and mushrooms. Freddie's salad, practically an antipasto with lettuce, is enough to feed the whole table. Freddie's has no liquor license, but diners can pop next door to Val's Tavern to pick up a cold six pack.

Federici's $–$$, no credit cards
14 East Main Street, Freehold
(732) 462–1312

The pizza here is well worth the ride to Freehold, and we're not the only ones who think so. The sauce is tangy, and the real Italian pepperoni crisp up just right, forming greasy little cups. Try our own innovation—pizza with fresh garlic and roasted red peppers. We like to sit outside in nice weather or in the bar area, where the painting of the original restaurant hangs. Mom and Pop Federici started this place in 1921, and most of their original recipes are still being used. The priceless pizza recipe has been the same for more than half a century, thank goodness.

Pete & Elda's Bar/Carmen's Pizzeria $–$$
N.J. Highway 35 South, Neptune City
(732) 774–6010

All of the pizzerias here make a thin-crust pie, but Pete & Elda's must hold a world record; the crust is so thin it's like a matzoh. So thin is this pizza, in fact, that you can eat a whole pie on your own, and if you do tackle a whole extra-extra large pie single-handedly, they'll give you a free Pete & Elda's T-shirt. Light on the sauce, this flavorful pizza is like an Italian quesadilla. When we get a topping here, it's usually sausage and peppers. Pete & Elda's is open daily for lunch and dinner.

Vic's Bar & Restaurant $–$$
60 Main Street, Bradley Beach
(732) 774–8225

The little neon sign that reads "Tomato Pies" tipped us off that this place might be a find. Inside, it's retro without even trying, with its aged pine paneling, fish tank, and the only real telephone booth we've seen in years. On summer evenings there's a big family crowd that arrives early, some coming to Vic's before hitting a flick at the equally vintage Beach Cinema next door. Aside from the thin-crust pizza, we love the hearty pasta fagioli and the escarole and bean soups. The housemade manicotti are pretty good, too. If you order wine, be sure to get it by the bottle or half bottle—trust us. Vic's is closed Monday, open the rest of the week for lunch and dinner.

Mad Hatter Pub & Eatery $$
10-E Ocean Avenue, Sea Bright
(732) 530–7861
Right in the midst of the Sea Bright bar scene, the Mad Hatter's very creditable thin-crust pizza was a pleasant surprise to us. After all, the place isn't even Italian—and they have karaoke.

Maria's Colonial Inn $–$$
165 Main Street, Manasquan
(732) 530–7861
Maria's pizza and other dishes are recommended by locals-in-the-know. It's one of those restaurants that's been around forever and is still always busy.

Squan Tavern Restaurant & Pizza $$
21 Broad Street, Manasquan
(732) 223–3324
Manasquan natives often tout the Squan Tavern as *the* best pizza, and even Federici's fans will admit that it's good—very good, in fact. And everyone loves the restaurant's old roadhouse atmosphere.

Tony's Baltimore Grill $, no credit cards
Iowa and Atlantic Avenues, Atlantic City
(609) 345–5766, (609) 345–9461
If you're sensitive about secondhand smoke, don't come to Tony's, a no-frills bar that serves old-fashioned Italian food and the best thin-crust pie in A.C. As far as Tony is concerned, you can leave home without American Express—it's cash only here.

chef, so there's no confusion about how you want it done. While it's cooking, help yourself at the ample salad bar.

Coffeehouses and Ice-Cream Parlors

Cravings Gourmet Desserts
310 Main Street, Allenhurst
(732) 531–7122
Bring someone a Decadence chocolate mousse cake from Cravings and you will surely be invited back. Locals love to stop in for a great cup of joe and maybe a banana nut muffin. For a quick sugar rush, try the shortbread cookies or a lemon square.

Days
48 Pitman Avenue, Ocean Grove
(732) 988–3297
We remember when Days served their homemade ice cream in old glass dishes on white table linens. Things may have changed, but Days is still one of the nicest places to go for ice cream, its covered porch opening onto the quaint streets of Ocean Grove.

Hoffman's
569 Church Street, Spring Lake Heights
(732) 974–2253
We've made plenty of pleasant pit stops at Hoffman's. The only trouble is that their housemade ice cream is so popular, there are often long lines.

The Inkwell
665 Second Avenue, West End (Long Branch)
(732) 222–6886

Back in the 1960s, The Inkwell was the ultimate hippie hangout, a dark and smoky coffeehouse. In its new location it also has a new salad-oriented menu and a new clientele: lots of hyper-dressed teenagers with designer attitude.

Jersey Freeze
120 Manalapan Avenue, Freehold
(732) 462–3008

It's not like you're going to drive all the way to Freehold for an ice cream, but if you're in town anyway—at Freehold Raceway, the Mall, or Federici's—the Jersey Freeze is the place to stop for a cold one—an ice cream, that is. They also have hot dogs and hamburgers and the like.

Schneider's Restaurant
801 Main Street, Avon
(732) 775–1265

Schneider's is really a restaurant, with German dishes like sauerbraten on the menu. But we love it for its old-fashioned soda fountain, where they turn out real ice-cream sodas, gooey sundaes, and the like.

Nightlife

On a summer night at the Shore there's plenty to do: Boardwalks, fireworks, movies, shows—and those diversions have been detailed in other chapters. This little section aims to give you an idea of what's going on in the area clubs—music, comedy, drinking, etc. We know there's no pleasing everyone, as one guy's idea of an ear-splitting good time is another person's nightmare. All we can do is try to point you in the right direction.

The cover charge at most local clubs is about $10—more for a well-known band. There's often no cover before 9:00 P.M., but you'll have a while to wait until the band takes the stage. Bars in New Jersey close at 2:00 A.M.

Bar Anticipation
703 16th Avenue, South Belmar
(732) 681–7422

What's in a name? Plenty. Check out some of the bands that appear here: Dicky Love, Size Matters, The Monster, Foxy Iguana. Are we reading too much into this? Maybe. Sometimes a foxy iguana is just a foxy iguana. But in fact, Bar A, as it's called, is a well-known meat market.

Dublin House Pub & Restaurant
30 Monmouth Street, Red Bank
(732) 747–6699

The Dublin House, in a very cool-looking historic building, is a great place to stop for an Irish coffee and listen to some music. There's live entertainment Wednesday through Sunday, often acoustic. Enjoy the passing crowd on the outdoor patio in summer; when it's chilly, explore the Irish Lounge upstairs. If you're hungry, there's a fair selection of food.

Jason's Jazz & Blues Niteclub
1604 Main Street, Belmar
(732) 681–1416

Jason's is a departure from the rowdy tourist bars that Belmar is known for. Here, customers from 20 to 70 years old enjoy performances by touring acts and local artists like Randy Preston, Billy Hector and the Fairlanes, and the High Voltage Brothers. Everybody knows owner Mel Hood, a jazz singer and one of the founders of the Jersey Shore Jazz and Blues Foundation. Pals like B. B. King have even been known to stop by and jam.

The Gay Scene in Asbury Park

Back in the 1970s, most tourists avoided Asbury Park, having fled the town in the wake of the race riot of July 4, 1970. But then a queer thing began to happen in Asbury—literally. An underground gay nightlife began to emerge in the '70s, starting with a few small clubs like the Blue Note, Key West, and Club Odyssey, drawing customers from both New York and Philadelphia.

In 1981 the owner of Club Odyssey, Ray Palazzo, started an event that outlived his once-successful bar, the Miss Gay New Jersey Pageant. The pageant carries on to this day, having moved on to other Asbury clubs like the old Down the Street bar (now Anybody's) and Club Paradise before going big-time in 2001 and taking over the ballroom at the Sheraton Eatontown. (For more on this, check out www.miss gaynj.com.)

Now the gay scene in Asbury Park is much more than just a few clubs that are busy in the summer. There's a real gay community consisting of year-round residents and New Yorkers and Philadelphians who have bought second homes here. Folks have really put down roots, buying and renovating some of the wonderful old Victorian houses and bed-and-breakfast inns here and in Ocean Grove. Along with the growing number of artists who have found space to live and work in Asbury, the gay community is one of the forces driving the long-overdue renaissance of this seashore resort.

Here is a small selection of spots that are worth checking out.

Asbury Park Lanes
209 Fourth Avenue, Asbury Park
(732) 776–6160
Asbury has a gay city councilman and it hosts the New Jersey Gay Pride Day (in June), but an even more significant breakthrough is Gay Bowling Night, held the last Saturday of every month at the Asbury Lanes. Call to double-check dates, though, before you order a bowling shirt with your name on it just for the occasion.

Cameo Bar
1213 Main Street, Asbury Park
(732) 774–9516
There are those who say, "Nothing surprises me anymore." Well, check out the Cameo Bar, and then we'll talk.

Georgie's
810 Fifth Avenue, Asbury Park
(732) 988–1220
This bar by the railroad tracks, a place where guys and gals unwind, is known for its happy hour. There are two pool tables and a jukebox. Fridays are the happening nights here, starting about 8 o'clock.

Paradise
101 Asbury Avenue, Asbury Park
(732) 988–6663
Paradise in the old Empress motel is easily the queen of Asbury nightspots. The crowd (primarily gay men) gets bigger every year, and the club keeps things fresh with special events, changes of scenery around its 7,000 square feet, and good-looking bartenders. It's the place to go on Saturday night.

The Talking Bird
222 Cookman Avenue, Asbury Park
(732) 775–9708
When late night turns into early morning, the boys head to The Talking Bird, right next door to Anybody's, for the after-hours breakfast, served until 3:00 A.M. on weekends. The food is good and cheap, and the place knows its audience, with plenty of Streisand on the jukebox.

The club is open from 8:00 P.M. to 2:00 A.M. Wednesday through Sunday; the usual cover is $8.00, but it can be a bit higher, depending on the musicians featured.

Osprey Nite Club
201 First Avenue, Manasquan
(732) 528–1800
There's always a young crowd in Manasquan, and it doesn't haul up to Belmar just to have a brew. At the Osprey there's always live music on the weekends, with bands like the Wallbangers and Papa Squat.

Pat's Tavern
715 Main Street, Belmar
(732) 280–2266
You'll see a few shamrocks in this place, and there are sure to be plenty for Joe Finn Irish Night. Pat's is also the center of the action on St. Patrick's Day.

Paul's Tavern
Main Street, South Belmar
(732) 280–9411
The outdoor bar can be a lovely relief on a summer night, and the bar food—steamers, ribs, wraps, quesadillas, even steaks—can be a treat. There is sometimes live music, but Paul's is more of a disco (welcome back to the 1970s).

Rascals Comedy Club
1500 N.J. Highway 35 South, Ocean Township
(732) 517–0002
www.rascals.net
Part of a national chain, Rascals features comics that you might have seen on *The Tonight Show* or on *Showtime*. Check the newspapers or the club's Web site for show schedules and ticket prices, which vary depending on whether the headliner is local New Jersey boy Rick Corso or a national name like Jackie Mason or Brett Butler.

The Saint
601 Main Street, Asbury Park
(732) 775–9144
www.thesaintnj.com
This old-line Asbury club, located on gritty Main Street, has seen many Jersey bands come and go. But then you might hear a fresh accent like Dem Brooklyn Bums here, too.

The Stone Pony
913 Ocean Avenue, Asbury Park
(732) 502–0600
www.stoneponyonline.com
What can we say about a joint that's practically synonymous with Asbury Park, Bruce Springsteen, and the Jersey Sound? Back in the 1970s, Southside Johnny and the Asbury Jukes were the house band here—that's when they weren't opening for Jon Bon Jovi across town at the Fast Lane. Elvis Costello, Gregg Allman, Cyndi Lauper, and the Ramones are just a few of the acts that have played here. The place is so renowned that when *Gladiator* star Russell Crowe got his Australian band, Thirty Odd Foot of Grunts, together, he told his agent that the place he wanted to play was this stage, where Springsteen played. These days, the Pony is much more pleasant than it used to be, thanks to an interior renovation and an outdoor stage. Check the paper and you might see names like Jimmie Vaughan (brother of Stevie Ray), Nils Lofgren, or saxophonist Clarence Clemons on the list of those appearing here. When E Streeters like Clarence or Lofgren appear, Bruce-watchers fly to the box

office, hoping that the Boss will drop in, as he often does.

Tradewinds
1331 Ocean Avenue, Sea Bright
(732) 842–7300
www.thetradewinds.com

The Tradewinds is busy just about every night in the summer. It features local groups, well-known bands like Everclear, and some big-name acts that can't quite fill Madison Square Garden anymore, like Hootie and the Blowfish, Blue Oyster Cult, and Billy Idol. Bruce has even dropped in on occasion.

Shopping

When Monmouth County was more of a summer vacation destination, stores would stock plenty of sunglasses and beach toys. Nowadays, with a substantial year-round population, the Shore has everything you'd find in suburban areas: great big malls, smaller strip malls, a few lively Main Streets, and so on.

We won't go into great detail about the malls, because we assume, if you live in America, you probably have an idea of what you can expect. Like malls elsewhere, the Shore malls are typically anchored by a major department store such as Macy's; they also house the usual suspects: Banana Republic, Gap, chain drugstores, restaurants, and multiplex movie houses.

In compiling this chapter, for the most part, we've listed places that make for more interesting shopping, either because they offer exceptional value or because their products or services are worth a look.

In compiling our listings, we haven't limited ourselves to stores in the coastal communities. We believe that shoppers, like golfers, are willing to travel a bit, and so we've included stores that might be a 15- or 20-minute ride or so from one of our Shore towns.

Antiques

If your pleasure is antiques and collectibles, you'll find a shop to suit you in almost every Shore town. Here we've listed a few places where you'll find a substantial concentration of dealers.

The Antique Center of Red Bank
West Front Street and Bridge Avenue, Red Bank
(732) 842–4336

The oldest antique center in the United States, encompassing three buildings and more than 100 dealers, this is a wonderful place to search out treasures in china, silver, linens, furniture, and vintage everything. It was voted "best all-around, not-to-be-missed antique center in New Jersey" by the *Star Ledger* and "Best of the Best" by the *Asbury Park Press*. The center is open daily from 11:00 A.M. to 5:00 P.M., and Sunday from noon to 5:00 P.M. P.S. After you've shopped here, you'll find a number of freestanding antiques shops in the same neighborhood.

Freehold Antiques Gallery
21 West Main Street, Freehold
(732) 462–7900

In this one spot, you'll find 60 dealers offering everything from vintage clothing and linens to fine silver and period furniture. The gallery is open Monday through Saturday from 10:00 A.M. to 5:00 P.M., and Sunday from noon to 5:00 P.M.

Surrey Lane Antiques
280 Norwood Avenue, Deal
(732) 531–6991

Though this is a single shop, we mention it for two reasons: One, it has an interesting selection of hand-painted beds, armoires, and vanities, along with linens and soaps and gift items. Two, it's alongside one of our favorite shoe stores, so we get to double our pleasure on a single shopping trip. The store is open Monday through Friday from 10:00 A.M. to 6:00 P.M., and Sunday from noon to 5:00 P.M.

Books

If you like to buy your books at chains like B. Dalton and Barnes and Noble, you will find them well represented, with stores in various malls. Listed below are a few of the independent shops that we like.

Antic Hay Books
605 Mattison Avenue, Third floor, Asbury Park
(732) 774-4590
www.antichay.com

Do you have a taste for Shore memorabilia? You'll find a treasure trove here: hundreds of authentic Jersey Shore prints, maps, and postcards. But most of the stock is books: some 17,000 titles. If you want something special that's out of print, just ask (or shop online). The shop, which is located in the former *Asbury Park Press* building, is open Tuesday through Saturday from 10:00 A.M. to 5:00 P.M., and Sunday from noon to 4:00 P.M.

The Book Pit
17 Wallace Street, Red Bank
(732) 747-4635

The name says it all: This funky, quirky bookstore is tucked behind Dorn's photography shop, so it's easy to miss. But if you like books, treat yourself to a browsing session; you may find that hard-to-find vintage cookbook, a good copy of a novel you loved 20 years ago, or an unusual photography or archaeology book. Prices are on the low side, so expect a bargain or two. The shop's posted hours are Friday from noon to 6:00 P.M., Saturday from 10:00 A.M. to 6:00 P.M., Sunday from noon to 5:00 P.M., and Monday from noon to 6:00 P.M. In fact, Russ, the owner, is something of a night owl, and you'll often find the shop open well into the evening, especially in the summer.

Fair Haven Books
759 River Road, Fair Haven
(732) 747-9455

This small shop appeals to area residents who dislike the chains and want to buy their books in a more personalized setting. The store has a kids' corner and often hosts book signings with local authors. It's open Monday through Saturday from 9:30 A.M. to 5:30 P.M.

Pyramid Books
23 Monmouth Street, Red Bank
(732) 758-0010

We like the bargain tables at this popular Red Bank shop. You may find last year's bestseller drastically marked down—along with last year's self-help book, and so on. The place is well organized, so it's fun to browse. It's open from 10:00 A.M. to 6:00 P.M. on weekdays, from 10:00 A.M. to 7:00 P.M. on Saturday, and from 11:00 A.M. to 5:00 P.M. on Sunday.

Clothing and Accessories

Camel's Eye
1223 Third Avenue, Spring Lake
(732) 449-3636

You'd expect to find a shop like this in an upscale Shore town. It carries fine resort wear (Lilly Pulitzer, et al.) and functional attractive accessories: handcrafted leather sandals, capacious tote bags, and handmade jewelry that looks swell with a tan. The shop is open weekdays from 11:00 A.M. to 5:00 P.M. and Saturday from 10:30 A.M. to 5:00 P.M.; it occasionally opens on Sunday.

CoCo Parì
270 Norwood Avenue, Deal
(732) 517-1227
17 Broad Street, Red Bank
(732) 212-8111

Fendi, Chloe, and Michael Kors are but a few of the top designers represented here. It helps if you're as slim as a fashion model and can carry clothes with attitude. But even if you're not and you can't, you might be tempted by the bargains in the basement of the Red Bank store, where you'll find drastic reductions on highly stylish clothes and shoes. The Deal store takes part in the town's big sidewalk sales in July.

The Red Bank store is open Monday and Tuesday from 11:00 A.M. to 6:00 P.M., Wednesday and Thursday from 11:00 A.M. to 9:00 P.M., Friday from 11:00 A.M. to 10:00 P.M., Saturday from 10:00 A.M. to 11:00 P.M., and Sunday from noon to 6:00 P.M. The Deal store is open Monday through Friday from 10:00 A.M. to 6:00 P.M., Saturday from 11:00 A.M. to 5:00 P.M., and Sunday from noon to 5:00 P.M.

The Country Fair
266 Norwood Avenue, Deal
(732) 531-8009

Understated good taste and classic clothes you can wear season after season are what you'll find at this fine shop. Women from Deal and surrounding towns have been coming here for years; have a look and you, too, may become a regular. The store is open Monday through Saturday from 10:00 A.M. to 5:30 P.M.; on Wednesday it stays open until 8:00 P.M.

Footnotes
280 Norwood Avenue, Deal
(732) 531–9734

We love shoes (family members refer to our respective closets as the "Imelda collections"), but we will never pay retail. That's why we like this store, which always discounts designer shoes—and sells them downright cheap during the legendary Deal sidewalk sales. Footnotes is open Monday through Saturday from 10:00 A.M. to 6:00 P.M., and Sunday from noon to 5:00 P.M.

Funk & Standard
40 Broad Street, Red Bank
(732) 219–5885

If you thought you had to go to SoHo or Tribeca for hip, retro clothes and accessories, browse this Broad Street favorite. The young at heart (or age) will like the offbeat clothes and gifts. The store is open Monday through Thursday from 10:00 A.M. to 9:00 P.M., Friday from 10:00 A.M. to 11:00 P.M., and Sunday from 11:00 A.M. to 6:00 P.M.

Garmany
105 Broad Street, Red Bank
(732) 576–8500
www.garmany.com

Upscale menswear bearing such labels as Ermenegildo Ziegna, Dolce and Gabbana, and Brioni is sold here. Offering old-fashioned service, Garmany has an on-site tailor shop so that everything purchased here will be a perfect fit. There's a shoe-shine service as well. The store is open Monday through Friday from 10:00 A.M. to 8:00 P.M., Saturday from 9:30 A.M. to 7:00 P.M., and Sunday from 11:00 A.M. to 6:00 P.M.

Nové
9 Broad Street, Red Bank
(732) 842–7784

This upscale women's boutique is part of the "up-scaling" of Red Bank's main street. It carries the kind of designer clothes you'd find in a very chic SoHo boutique, trendy but eminently wearable. If you get sticker shock, wait for the seasonal sales, when wonderful things become more affordable.

Pitti Bimi
264 Norwood Avenue, Deal
(732) 531–3676

For the child who wears only designer clothes, Pitti Bimi is the place to shop. Fond grandmothers packing full wallets may think nothing of spending upwards of $200 for a cute little dress, but for the more fiscally conservative, there are always the sales. The store is open Monday through Friday from 10:00 A.M. to 6:00 P.M., and Saturday from 10:00 A.M. to 5:00 P.M.

Skuby & Co.
1106 Third Avenue, Spring Lake
(732) 449–3700

Both corporate and casual menswear are on offer here, with labels like Tommy Bahama, Cutter and Buck, and Barry Bricken. You'll find accessories, too. The store is open Monday and Wednesday through Friday from 10:00 A.M. to 6:00 P.M. (closed Tuesday), Saturday from 10:00 A.M. to 5:00 P.M., and Sunday from noon to 4:00 P.M.

Steev 19
280 Norwood Avenue, Deal
(732) 531–9299

The men's and women's clothing here is sleek and sophisticated, with European flair. Designer clothing by Moschino and Armani and the like grace the racks; the styles tend to look best on the fit and trim. If you're not so trim, check out the accessories, which are also top-of-the-line. If Steve himself is around, he might be willing to tell you a story or two about Bruce Springsteen; the two were pals back in Bruce's West End days. The store is open weekdays from 10:00 A.M. to 6:00 P.M.; and Saturday and Sunday from noon to 5:00 P.M.

Consignment Shops

Alan & Suzi, Inc.
711 Cookman Avenue, Asbury Park
(732) 988–7372

If Asbury Park does come back soon, it will be thanks to pioneers like Alan and Suzi (who also have a shop on Manhattan's West Side). They've helped the town along not just by opening here, but by running over-the-top fashion shows and other events. Their shop carries vintage men's and women's designer clothing, as well as new things from interesting contemporary designers. It's open Thursday through Saturday from 11:00 A.M. to 5:00 P.M., and Sunday from noon to 5:00 P.M.

Farm House
952 Broadway, West Long Branch
(732) 263–1124

You'll find furniture and interesting home items along with the high-quality clothing, jewelry, and accessories. The shop has excellent sales twice a year. It's open Monday through Friday from 10:30 A.M. to 5:30 P.M., and Saturday from 10:00 A.M. to 4:00 P.M.

Living Posh
1607 Main Street, Belmar
(732) 681–9211

You'll find a little bit of everything here: clothing for the entire family, baby furnishings, furs, and bridal wear. The shop is open from 9:00 A.M. to 6:00 P.M. on Monday, Wednesday, Friday, and Saturday, and from 1:00 to 5:00 P.M. on Sunday.

Nearly New Shop
70 Monmouth Street, Red Bank
(732) 747–2772

If you enjoy the hunt as much as the treasure, you'll like the action here. We've found everything from Armani pants (for men) to vintage sunglasses to designer handbags, all at bargain prices. The store is open Tuesday through Friday from 10:00 A.M. to 4:30 P.M., and Saturday from 11:00 A.M. to 4:00 P.M.

Once Is Not Enough
304 Morris Avenue, Spring Lake
(732) 974–0076

We like consignment shops in posh towns because they're likely to have clothing and accessories from the closets of the affluent. Sometimes we hit gold here, and sometimes we don't. But that's how it is with consignment shops. The store is open Monday, Tuesday, and Thursday through Saturday from 11:00 A.M. to 5:00 P.M.

Delectable Edibles

Caramel Shop
1215 N.J. Highway 35 and Allaire Avenue, Ocean Township
(732) 531–3477

Though boardwalks are the best places to buy candy apples and saltwater taffy, there are times when a boardwalk just isn't handy. That's when you can visit this sweet, old-fashioned candy shop for the taffy and apples, as well as gourmet chocolate, licorice, and what used to be penny candy (it now costs 10 cents or more). You'll find a good selection of sugarless candy, too, as well as many gift box selections. Valentine's Day brings lots of heart-shaped confections, and Easter brings bunnies and baskets galore.

Delicious Orchards
N.J. Highway 34, Colts Neck
(732) 462–1989
www.deliciousorchardsnj.com

Back in the 1950s, Delicious was a 1,200-square-foot roadside stand. Now it's a splendid food emporium that sells some of New Jersey's best produce, as well as good stuff from other places. The baked goods here are the stuff of legend: breads, brownies, cakes, mouth-watering fruit pies, and biscuits that are better than most homemade ones. There's a butcher shop, a deli, a mouthwatering selection of produce, and many of the items (like olive oils and mustards) found in gourmet shops. The hours are from 10:00 A.M. to 6:00 P.M. Tuesday through Sunday.

we buy Rudy's dough, his fresh mozzarella, his marinara sauce, and freshly grated parmesan cheese. We let the dough rise, shape a pie, add all the other ingredients, and bake. Then we take a bow—and dig in. The store is open Monday, Tuesday, and Thursday through Saturday (closed on Wednesday) from 8:30 A.M. to 6:00 P.M., and Sunday from 8:30 A.M. to 1:00 P.M.

Sickles Farm
Harrison Avenue, Little Silver
(732) 741–9563
sicklesmarket.com

Sickles started life as a wholesale truck farm delivering to local shops. Now this family-run complex includes a large farm market and deli that sells tasty baked goods and lots of heat-and-eat goodies, and a garden center. During the summer, Sickles runs a summer "blues" festival, featuring a blueberry pie-eating contest. The market is open Monday through Saturday from 9:00 a.m. to 6:00 p.m. and some Sundays (call ahead).

Flea Markets

Collingwood Auction and Flea Market
N.J. Highways 33 and 34, Wall Township
(732) 938–7941

Collingwood is smaller than Englishtown (see next listing), and the opportunities for authentic treasures are fewer, but you'll still find several hundred indoor and outdoor stands here. You never can tell what you'll find: It could be a part to an old appliance, a set of tires, or some interesting vintage clothes. The market is open Friday from noon to 8:00 P.M., Saturday from 10:00 A.M. to 8:00 P.M., and Sunday from 10:00 A.M. to 5:00 P.M. However, the outdoor vendors are generally in place and selling by 9:00 A.M.

Englishtown Auction
90 Wilson Avenue, Englishtown
(732) 446–9644
www.englishtownauction.com

Dating back to 1929, Englishtown is the granddaddy of flea markets around these parts. Devotees of the market (and dealers)

Piancone's
804 Main Street, Bradley Beach
(732) 775–4870
www.piancone.com

Whether it's a half-pound of prosciutto, a container of Sicilian olives, or a serving of heat-and-eat lasagna, you'll find what you crave at Piancone's. When you don't want to cook, drop into the restaurant next door, La Nonna Piancone's Cafe (see the "Restaurants" section of this chapter). The store is open Monday through Saturday from 8:00 A.M. to 7:00 P.M., and Sunday from 8:00 A.M. to 4:00 P.M.

Primavera Italian Specialties
140 Brighton Avenue, Long Branch
(732) 229–1518

We've been buying Rudy Primavera's delicious homemade bread, excellent cold cuts, and superior sandwiches for years; we recommend them to you. When we want to show off our pizza-making skills,

show up at the crack of dawn hunting for buried treasure. There are hundreds and hundreds of vendors sprawled over this 50-acre market. A lot of stuff is ho-hum—socks and T-shirts, et cetera—but if you make a trip, chances are you'll buy something, whether it be an antique camera or an irresistible piece of costume jewelry. Englishtown is open on weekends year-round: Saturday from 7:00 A.M. to 4:00 P.M., and Sunday from 9:00 A.M. to 4:00 P.M.

Home

Kate & Company
1100 Third Avenue, Spring Lake
(732) 449-1633
If you're lucky enough to own a country house, this shop can help you dress it with English and Irish pine furniture. There are also hand-painted pieces, needlepoint items, and lots of unusual accessories from Italy and Mexico. The store is open Monday and Wednesday through Friday (closed Tuesday) from 10:00 A.M. to 5:00 P.M., and Sunday from noon to 4:00 P.M.

Ovale
8 Broad Street, Red Bank
(732) 933-0437
www.ovalemodern.com
A decade or so ago, you wouldn't have found a shop like this in Red Bank; it carries highly styled and innovative designer furniture, lighting, and accessories—the kind of stuff that a decorator would help you locate in the showrooms of Manhattan. You'll find names like Herman Miller, Knoll, and Noguchi. The store is open Tuesday through Thursday from noon to 5:00 P.M., Friday from noon to 6:00 P.M., and Saturday from noon to 5:00 P.M. It's also open some Sundays from noon to 4:00 P.M.; call ahead.

Prown's
32 Broad Street, Red Bank
(732) 741-7500
This rambling family-run hardware store has been around since 1925; it offers the kind of old-fashioned atmosphere and

service you won't find at the big mall stores. So if you need a screw, a knob, or a made-to-measure window shade, the knowledgeable clerks here will help you find exactly what you want. They also carry small appliances, lawn furniture, air conditioners, and all kinds of odds and ends. Prown's is open Monday through Saturday from 8:30 A.M. to 5:30 P.M., and Sunday from 11:00 A.M. to 4:00 P.M.

Rumson China & Glass Shop
125 East River Road, Rumson
(732) 842-2322, (888) 800-0020
www.rumsonchina.com
Perfect wedding gifts, future heirlooms, and all manner of lovely things made by Waterford, Baccarat, and Wedgewood—that's what you'll find at this appealing shop. The hours are from 10:00 A.M. to 5:30 P.M. Monday through Friday, and from 10:00 A.M. to 5:00 P.M. on Saturday.

Insiders' Tip
If you're the kind of shopper who never, ever pays retail, you'll find outlets not only in the Shore region, but also all over the state. The biggest outlet mall in New Jersey is the Jersey Gardens Outlet Mall, open Monday through Saturday from 10:00 A.M. to 9:00 P.M., and Sunday from 11:00 A.M. to 7:00 P.M. It's in Elizabeth, about a 40-minute drive from northern Monmouth. For more information, call (877) 729-8258.

Salton Block China Outlet Store
75 B-C Brighton Avenue, Long Branch
(732) 222–1144

If the word "discount" pleases you more than fancy trappings, you'll like this jumble of a storefront outlet, which sells Block China at reductions of up to 50 percent. Also sold here are small appliances, crystal, and other housewares. What we like about this store (other than the discounts) is that it's steps from the West End beach and several good restaurants. The store is open Monday through Saturday from 10:00 A.M. to 5:00 P.M., and Sunday from 11:00 A.M. to 4:00 P.M.

T. Berry Square
20 Broad Street, Red Bank
(732) 576–1819

Fans of the Rachel Ashwell "shabby chic" phenomenon can create their own version of the look at home with the merchandise here. The store carries fabric, linens, baby bedding, and window treatments—almost everything except the upholstered furniture. It's open Monday through Saturday from 11:00 A.M. to 6:00 P.M., and Sunday from noon to 5:00 P.M.

Malls and Shopping Centers

Brook 35 Plaza
2150 N.J. Highway 35, just north of Atlantic Avenue
(732) 974–2284
www.brook35plaza.com

Combine a trip to the beach at Sea Girt or Spring Lake with a stop at this upscale shopping center, which features about 20 stores. You'll find, among others, a Chico's, a Victoria's Secret, a Williams-Sonoma—and a Zebu for post-shopping refreshments. The hours are from 10:00 A.M. to 9:00 P.M. Monday through Friday, from 10:00 A.M. to 6:00 P.M. Saturday, and from noon to 5:00 P.M. Sunday.

Circle Factory Outlet Center
1407 West Atlantic Avenue, Manasquan
(732) 223–2300

Harry and David, Mikasa, Izod, and Geoffrey Beene are but a few of the names you'll find at this popular discount outlet. When it has one of its big sidewalk sales—usually Memorial Day and Labor Day weekends—the prices become even more alluring. The outlet is open Sunday through Wednesday from 10:00 A.M. to 6:00 P.M., and Thursday through Saturday from 10:00 A.M. to 8:00 P.M. During the summer season, Sunday hours remain the same, but from Monday through Saturday the outlet is open from 10:00 A.M. to 9:00 P.M.

Freehold Raceway Mall
3710 U.S. Highway 9 South, Freehold
(732) 577–1144
www.freeholdracewaymall.com

Located across from the Freehold Raceway, this mall has more than 215 stores and eateries, including Nordstrom, Lord & Taylor, Sears, and Macy's. If you're on the hunt for bargains, across from the mall is a strip mall housing a Marshall's and a Linens 'n' Things store. The Raceway Mall is open Monday through Saturday from 10:00 A.M. to 9:30 P.M., and Sunday from 11:00 A.M. to 7:00 P.M.

The Grove at Shrewsbury
N.J. Highway 35 North, Shrewsbury
(732) 530–1200
www.thegroveatshrewsbury

With shops like Williams-Sonoma, Coach, and Eddie Bauer, this is a mall for upscale tastes and pocketbooks. When shopping palls, you can relax and dine at the Pasta Fresca Cafe & Market, which offers Italian and New American cuisine (dinner Tuesday through Saturday). The mall is open Monday through Saturday from 10:00 A.M. to 9:00 P.M., and Sunday from 11:00 A.M. to 6:00 P.M.

Jackson Outlet Village (formerly Six Flags Factory Outlets)
537 Monmouth Road, Jackson
(732) 833–0680
www.jacksonoutletvillage.com

Located just a mile from Six Flags Great Adventure, this outlet features some 70 stores selling women's designer clothing,

Kevin Smith's Red Bank

If you're a fan of film director/writer and local lad Kevin Smith (*Clerks, Mall Rats, Chasing Amy, Dogma,* and *Jay and Silent Bob Strike Back*), you might want to visit these Red Bank spots while you're checking out the many interesting shopping opportunities in town.

Jack's Music
30 Broad Street, Red Bank
(732) 842–0731
Even if you have no musical talent, drop in and look around. Jack's is a Red Bank institution, and many of the Shore's musicians have passed through its doors at one time or another. In fact, when Bruce Springsteen fans showed up here to buy copies of the Boss's "Live in New York City" album in April of 2001, the man himself made a surprise appearance. Not only did he meet and greet hundreds of surprised fans, he signed their albums and posed for photos.

However, for purposes of your Kevin Smith tour, you'll want to know that scenes from *Chasing Amy* were shot here; in fact, Holden and Banky lived in the apartment above the store. The store is open Monday and Tuesday from 9:00 A.M. to 6:00 P.M., Wednesday through Friday from 9:00 A.M. to 9:00 P.M., Saturday from 9:00 A.M. to 6:00 P.M., and Sunday from 11:00 A.M. to 5:00 P.M.

Jay & Silent Bob's Secret Stash
35 Broad Street, Red Bank
(732) 758–0020
www.viewaskew.com
This shop is a treasure trove for Kevin Smith fans. You'll find *Clerks* T-shirts, *Mall Rats* posters, and all kinds of things that Kevin bought from the inventory of a defunct comic book shop. A lot of the stuff is signed by Kevin himself. The store is open Monday through Saturday from 11:00 A.M. to 6:00 P.M. (Thursday until 7:00 P.M.), and Sunday from noon to 5:00 P.M.

To round out your Kevin Smith pilgrimage, you can visit the following Red Bank places that showed up in *Chasing Amy*: Red Bank Catholic High School (10 Peters Place), The Galleria (2 Bridge Avenue), Take a Shot Billiards Club (6 Bridge Avenue), and House of Coffee (10 Bridge Avenue).

home furnishings, books, toys, tools, and much more. It's open Monday through Saturday from 10:00 A.M. to 9:00 P.M., and Sunday from 11:00 A.M. to 7:00 P.M.

Monmouth Mall
N.J. Highways 35 and 36, Eatontown
(732) 542–0333
www.monmouthmallonline.com
One of Monmouth's earliest, this well-established mall houses 150 stores including Macy's, Lord & Taylor, and Boscov's. There's a 15-screen Sony Theater; outside the movie area is a large food court. The mall is open Monday through Saturday from 10:00 A.M. to 9:30 P.M., and Sunday from 11:00 A.M. to 6:00 P.M. (Macy's and Lord & Taylor are open until 7:00 P.M. on Sunday.)

Auctions

Auctions, like sidewalk sales, are fun ways to shop for things you don't really need. (Well, all right, once in a while you do go home with an item that's actually useful.) Anyway, we have bought lots of stuff at William Barron Auctioneers, 504 Main Street, Asbury Park (732–988–7711). Another Shore perennial is Colonel Bob Randolph, 500 N.J. Highway 71, Spring Lake Heights (732–974–0640). Peter Costanzo (732–531–6799) also runs some good estate auctions; these generally take place on-site. If you love auctions, check the *Asbury Park Press* classified section regularly. In the summer, you're likely to see a couple listed every week.

This and That

Fameabilia
42 Monmouth Street, Red Bank
(732) 450–8411
www.fameabilia.com

Sports memorabilia, historical documents, autographs, music and movie memorabilia—you'll find all this and much more at Fameabilia. Sometimes a real, live sports hero—Rocky Graziano, for instance—shows up to sign stuff. The shop is open Monday through Thursday from 10:00 A.M. to 6:00 P.M., Friday and Saturday from 10:00 A.M. to 9:00 P.M., and Sunday from 11:00 A.M. to 5:00 P.M.

Fly-Away Kites, Inc
1108 Main Street, Belmar
(732) 280–8084, (888) 29–KITES
www.flyawaykites.com

We think there's nothing more sublime than flying a kite on the beach. Lots of folks must agree, for on a balmy day you'll find kite flyers here and there from Sandy Hook to points south. This store—the largest in the United States devoted exclusively to kites—features such eye-catchers as the Hughes Airplane and the Opie Dragon. The store also offers lessons in making and flying kites. Fly-Away Kites has sponsored the Great Belmar Kite Festival. The hours vary according to season. The store is open from 10:00 A.M. to 5:00 P.M. Tuesday through Saturday, and from noon to 5:00 P.M. Sunday.

Galleria Shops
Bridge Avenue and West Front Street, Red Bank
(732) 530–7300

Located in the heart of Red Bank's antiques district, these converted commercial buildings are a thriving city's answer to a mall. In this historic setting, you can dine, enjoy an espresso, play a game of billiards, or have your hair done. There's also a nice seasonal farmers' market in the parking lot on Sunday. As for the shopping, you'll find household furnishings, a leather shop, a jewelry shop, and a consignment shop. Most of the shops are open from 10:00 A.M. to 6:00 P.M. during the week (some are closed on Monday), and from 10:00 A.M. to 5:00 P.M. on Saturday; some are open on Sunday from noon to 5:00 P.M.

Tuesday Morning
1610 N.J. Highway 35 South (Orchard Plaza),
Ocean Township
(732) 663–0600
www.tuesdaymorning.com

What you'll find at Tuesday Morning are all kinds of expensive items that you have coveted in upscale catalogs or department stores: Italian linens, fine luggage, high-end home accessories, crystal, toys, and more. All are heavily discounted, from 50 to 80 percent—more during special sales. The store is open Monday through Friday from 10:00 A.M. to 7:00 P.M., Saturday from 10:00 A.M. to 6:00 P.M., and Sunday from noon to 6:00 P.M. However, Tuesday Morning closes for weeks on end for restocking, so call ahead or check the Web site.

Ocean County

Accommodations
Restaurants
Nightlife
Shopping

The farther south you travel in Ocean County, the more seasonal it becomes. Towns that are beloved by summer residents—Ship Bottom, Beach Haven, Harvey Cedars, and the rest—get very quiet when the weather turns cold. Many inns and restaurants close; shops either close for a couple of months or operate on limited hours. But in the summer, there's a population explosion, and everything is open for business. Prices at hotels and inns rise during July and August; so do the prices for rental homes and apartments. Everyone, it seems, wants to be here in mid-summer.

Accommodations

As is the case in other Shore counties, there's a wide range of possible accommodations in Ocean County, from full-service resort hotels to elegant inns to budget motels. This chapter includes some of each.

If you're contemplating a cold-weather getaway, keep in mind that many, if not most, of the accommodations on Long Beach Island close at some point, so call ahead before you make plans. If you like quiet, we can heartily recommend going to LBI in September, when the weather is still lovely, the ocean is still warm, and the crowds have disappeared.

It bears repeating that during the busy summer season, many establishments have a two- or three-night minimum stay requirement, especially on weekends. During holiday weekends prices generally bump up beyond the normal high-season rate.

We also repeat the caution about cancellation policies; most places have them. Some will refund your deposit if the cancellation is done sufficiently far in advance, some will still charge you a penalty. It's best to find out up front what, if anything, you will forfeit by canceling a reservation.

Hotel Price Code

For one night in a standard double room in high season.

$	Under $125
$$	$125 to $200
$$$	$200 to $300
$$$$	Over $300

Hotels and Motels

Buccaneer Motel $
2600 North Bay Avenue, Spray Beach
(609) 492–4582
www.buccaneermotel.com

The Buccaneer is located two blocks from the ocean and a mile north of Beach Haven's amusement area. Rooms and suites have two double or two queen-size beds (units with queen-size beds also have microwaves), refrigerators, air-conditioning, cable television, and coffeemakers. The two-room suites have microwaves, whirlpool tubs, a second television, and a VCR.

The bayfront location and private dock mean you can bring your own boat or rent one (or a jet ski). The picnic area has gas grills for outdoor barbecuing, and the roof decks afford swell sunset views. In summer, you can enjoy a heated outdoor pool; during the colder months, use the indoor pool or the six-person whirlpool.

Engleside Inn $$
30 Engleside Avenue, Beach Haven
(800) 762–2214

This beachfront property is Long Beach Island's oldest family-run hotel. It has a pool and three restaurants, and guests can walk to the water-slide park, the amusement park, or the beach. You have a choice of accommodations here to suit your vacation needs: motel rooms that sleep two or four (with either two full beds, two queen-size beds, or one king), or efficiencies, which add a kitchenette with microwave, refrigerator, coffeemaker, toaster, and dishes and utensils; some have a stove as well. All are air-conditioned and equipped with a television and VCR. The suites have a separate living room with a variety of sleeping arrangements. Many rooms have balconies; the oceanfront suite has a whirlpool.

Historic Grenville Hotel & Restaurant $–$$
345 Main Avenue, Bay Head
(732) 892–3100
www.thegrenville.com

The award-winning Grenville dates back to 1890 and is one of the Shore's few remaining dowager hotels—a reminder of a time when a holiday at the beach was a grander, more elegant affair. The wraparound porch, with its graceful white wicker furniture, invites you to lounge and daydream.

As the hotel has undergone considerable renovation in recent years, the 29 rooms and four suites are all air-conditioned, with queen-size beds, private bathrooms, and television sets. The guest rooms are on three floors, but there is an elevator, so there are no stairs to climb. No two rooms are alike, an unusual feature in a hotel. Yours might be decorated in shades of rose, with delicate lace accents. Or it might have a white wicker nightstand, a white dresser, soft blue carpeting, and a floral printed bedspread. Some of the rooms have ocean views; the larger ones have loveseats and refrigerators. The Family Suite, which comfortably houses a family of four, offers some of the finest ocean views.

Perhaps the hotel's most stellar attraction is the romantic period dining room (a local favorite for wedding receptions). During the summer, breakfast and lunch are served here six days a week (brunch on Sunday), and dinner is served daily.

The Grenville is a block from the beach; your beach badges are complimentary, and you'll be supplied with beach towels. Twilight Lake, a very pretty spot to watch a sunset, is also a few minutes' walk from the hotel.

Hurley's at Holgate Motel $
4804 South Long Beach Boulevard, Beach Haven Inlet (LBI)
(609) 492–2266

This small, two-story motel offers simple but cheerful rooms. Each has air-conditioning, cable television, a refrigerator, and an outside deck with table and chairs. You'll get complimentary coffee and juice to get you started in the morning—and then you're off to the beach, which is just 75 feet away. Since there are tables and barbecues, you can grill some burgers and corn and feast for peanuts.

The Jolly Roger $$
5416 South Bay Boulevard, Beach Haven Inlet (LBI)
(609) 492–6931

This is one of LBI's younger motels, which is a good thing in terms of the freshness of furnishings and public areas. It's also located at the southern tip of the island (a noncommercial area), just 150 steps from the beach, which, in our opinion, is a very good thing. The rooms are spacious and airy; they have either two twin beds or one queen-size bed, ceiling fans and air-conditioning, refrigerators, microwaves, and cable television. Guests receive beach badges (deposit required). The motel has many decks, which afford views of the ocean or the Forsythe Wildlife area as well as provide shelter for a bird-watch. Room occupancy is limited to two people or a couple with an infant under two.

North Shore Inn $–$$
806 Central Avenue, Barnegat Light
(609) 494–5001
www.northshoreinn.com

The inn is at the northern end of LBI and near Old Barney (the lighthouse). It's a block from the Atlantic and near the Barnegat Light beach tram stop; the tram will take you to a guarded beach (badges provided). The clean and spacious rooms are standard motel fare. They have two queen-size beds, air-conditioning, and cable television; the efficiencies have fully equipped kitchens.

Sandpiper Motel $–$$
10th Street and Long Beach Boulevard, Ship Bottom
(609) 494–6909, (609) 492–1925

If you like the idea of playing in busy Beach Haven and sleeping in quiet Ship Bottom, this 20-room family-run motel might be a good lodging choice for you. Of course, the area has its own attractions, including the famous Ron Jon surf shop, miniature golf, restaurants, and nightspots. The motel is across the street from the Atlantic (complimentary beach badges are provided) and also has a pool. Rooms (with twin, double, or queen-size beds) are air-conditioned and have cable television and refrigerators; microwaves also are available.

Sea Spray Motel $–$$
2600 South Bay Avenue, Beach Haven Inlet
(609) 492–4944
www.seaspray-lbi.net

Located across from the Atlantic, the Sea Spray is one of the island's family-friendly getaway spots. It has a large heated pool surrounded by a deck and comfortable lounge chairs. The patio has picnic tables and barbecue grills, so families don't have to eat out every night. Rooms (with either one or two queen-size beds) are spacious and comfortable; they

have air-conditioning, cable television, refrigerators, and coffeemakers. Efficiencies have full kitchens, and for larger families, there are some two-bedroom units.

Surf City Hotel $–$$
Eighth Street and the Boulevard, Surf City
(609) 494–7281, (800) 353–3342

The hotel, which is a block from the beach (beach tags provided), is part of a complex that includes a restaurant, lounge, pub, clam bar, and a spirits store, so expect a bustle of activity in high season. The rooms have double beds, air-conditioning and cable television; some have mini-refrigerators.

White Sands Oceanfront Resort $$$–$$$$
1205 Ocean Avenue, Point Pleasant Beach
(732) 899–3370, (888) 558–5958
www.thewhitesands.com

The original White Sands oceanfront property consists of 74 motel-style rooms (14 with ocean views), a private beach, two outdoor pools, a kiddie pool, and a deck overlooking the Atlantic. The newer part of this complex is the hotel (which has 130 rooms and efficiency units, a penthouse, a presidential suite, and a bridal suite), the Heatwave restaurant, a full-service spa, a fitness center, the Lido Cafe (for informal dining at breakfast and lunch), and the Coral Reef bar.

Everything here is spiffy and new. The motel rooms are, well, motel modern, done in pastel seashore colors; 10 have

The White Sands Oceanfront Resort in Point Pleasant Beach is a total resort, complete with a spa and fine dining at the Heatwave at Windows. PHOTO: COURTESY OF THE WHITE SANDS

ocean views. The hotel rooms all have king-size beds; most have a sitting area with a sofa and coffee table; a few have ocean views.

Bed-and-Breakfast Inns

Amber Street Inn $$
118 Amber Street, Beach Haven
(609) 492–1611
www.amberstreetinn.com

The picture-postcard inn is one of LBI's original Victorian homes; it was renovated in 1991. It's just a half-block from the Atlantic. Guest rooms have comfy queen- or king-size beds, private baths, air-conditioning, and ceiling fans. In addition to the typical inn breakfast, guests enjoy afternoon refreshments on the verandah.

Conover's Bay Head Inn $$
646 Main Avenue, Bay Head
(732) 892–4664, (800) 956–9099
www.conovers.com

Conover's is a welcoming blend of elegance and informality. There are lots of eye-catching antiques, but there's also a nice level of comfort achieved by such wonderfully old-fashioned touches as line-dried and hand-ironed linens. On the other hand, the 12 rooms have such modern amenities as air-conditioning and television/VCRs. The garden-side rooms overlook the outdoor Jacuzzi spa; the others have views of the ocean, bay, yacht club, marina, or the inn's pretty English garden.

The rooms are dressed in shades of pink or turquoise, other pale colors, or vintage Laura Ashley. Some have queen-size beds, with headboards of mahogany or brass; others have king-size beds. Many are topped with featherbeds. All of the rooms have private baths. Some are newish; others have wonderful claw-foot tubs (with shower).

Your breakfast here will be hearty, and if you desire it, you'll be served a very nice tea in the afternoon. When you go to the beach, which is just a couple of blocks away, you'll get a complimentary beach badge and towels.

Green Gables Bed & Breakfast Inn and Restaurant $–$$
212 Centre Street, Beach Haven
(609) 492–3553

Here's an interesting combination: an inn with six charming rooms and one of New Jersey's finest restaurants (see "Restaurants" section), located just a block from the beach. Even better, it periodically offers getaway packages that include not only breakfast (which you will get whenever you stay here), but also an extraordinary dinner, all at a very attractive price. The inn also has a tearoom that serves lunch and snacks; on Sunday afternoons, you can get your tea leaves (or tarot cards) read.

The Island Guest House $–$$
207 Third Street, Beach Haven
(609) 492–2907
www.islandguesthouse.com

Staying at Island House is like renting a big old beach house just steps from the ocean. It has 16 air-conditioned guest rooms with either private or semi-private baths; some have patios, refrigerators, or microwaves; the suites have television. There's a choice of beds: two twins or a queen or king. There's also a self-contained cottage for rent. Guests get beach badges, and you may borrow chairs and boogie boards and even a bicycle built for two.

The J.D. Thompson Inn $
149 East Main Street, Tuckerton
(609) 294–1331

If you don't need to stay near the beach, here's an alternative in the heart of Tuckerton, within walking distance of the Tuckerton Seaport. The large, attractively furnished guest rooms have queen-size beds, private baths, and air-conditioning. There's also a separate two-bedroom suite with a living room and bath (if you have children under 14, they're welcome in this suite). Breakfast is served in the spacious dining room; it is a typical, hearty inn meal that includes freshly baked breads. You can take your morning coffee out to the spacious wraparound deck. Afternoon tea is also served. And if you're not out and about all day, you can spend some time relaxing in the outdoor spa.

Julia's of Savannah $$–$$$
209 Centre Street, Beach Haven (LBI)
(609) 492–5004

Long Beach Island is known for its inns, and this one, located steps from the beach, is one of the nicest. As they might in Savannah, the rooms in this Victorian inn have names like "Miss Felicia's" and "Miss Angela's." They are beautifully furnished and have king- or queen-size beds, private baths, and air-conditioning. Miss Lisa's, for example, is a romantic suite with a king-size bed, a private bath (with a two-person Jacuzzi), a private verandah, and a fireplace. Whichever room you stay in, you will find the atmosphere gracious and welcoming. You'll be served a delicious breakfast and complimentary afternoon tea, and when you go to the beach (badges complimentary), you may borrow chairs and a bike.

The Magnolia House $–$$$
215 Centre Street, Beach Haven
(609) 492–0398

Magnolia House is one of Long Beach Island's oldest original guest houses; it's a charming turn-of-the-century Gothic Revival with a wraparound verandah, white wicker furniture, and blessed air-conditioning. Rooms are furnished in period antiques and have private baths (supplied with bathrobes and toiletries). Your breakfast will be delicious (sticky buns are a specialty), as will your afternoon tea (featuring fruit tarts or homemade breads). Beach badges are available free of charge, along with umbrellas, chairs, and towels. The inn will also provide you with snacks and cool drinks to take to the beach, which is just a block away. Later, borrow a bike and explore the island.

Pierrot by the Sea $$
101 Centre Street, Beach Haven
(609) 492–4424

This charming late-19th-century inn has antiques-filled rooms that whisper of the past. Six of the nine have private baths; five have ocean views. The inn has an inviting verandah and a pretty garden, but after you've had your robust breakfast, you'll probably want to walk the few

steps to the beach. Guests are provided with badges and chairs, and later, if you want to explore, you may borrow a bike.

The Sand Castle $$–$$$$
710 Bayview Avenue, Barnegat Light
(609) 494–6555
www.sandcastlelbi.com

The Sand Castle is a rare bird: a new bed-and-breakfast inn built along traditional lines. As you pull up to the dramatic bayfront location, you know you're going to like it here. Among the amenities are a heated free-form pool, a whirlpool spa, a fitness center, a music room, and a library. In short, this is a mini-resort, where you also get a sumptuous breakfast and afternoon tea. The air-conditioned rooms (ceiling fans, too) are bayfront; the suites are poolside. They are furnished in either period or contemporary style, and each has a queen- or king-size bed, television/VCR, and a private bath. Your room might have panoramic windows that offer knockout views, an oversize shower, a Jacuzzi tub, or a gas fireplace. You'll get badges, chairs, and towels for your trips to the beach.

The White Whale Revisited $$
20 West Seventh Street, Barnegat Light
(609) 494–3020
www.whitewhalerevisited.com

If you like the idea of "a literary bed-and-breakfast," the White Whale is for you. The owners are academics, and the inn boasts an excellent library. Though originally designed as a small motel, the perky blue-and-white Whale is being run as an inn. It's located at the northern tip of LBI in the shadow of Old Barney. The air-conditioned rooms are small, but each is equipped with a refrigerator, cable television, and a private bath. You'll get a full inn breakfast, served either in the Bay Room or on an open deck overlooking the bay, and beach tags to speed you on your way to the beach.

Windward Manor Inn $$
Atlantic and Amber Streets, Beach Haven
(609) 492–4468
www.windwardmanorinn.com

Here's another steps-to-the-beach establishment offering a variety of accommodations with complimentary continental breakfast. Rooms are furnished simply; they have private baths, refrigerators, and cable television with HBO. You'll get beach towels and badges, and when you get back from a day on the sand, you'll be within easy walking distance of restaurants, miniature golf, and an ice-cream parlor.

Seasonal Rentals

In Ocean County, there really are rentals for just about any budget. The high (astronomical) end would include oceanfront homes in Bay Head, Mantoloking, and Loveladies. An eight-bedroom, eight-bath (including two half-baths) Loveladies contemporary home, for example, was recently offered at $8,000 to $10,000 a week (depending on the week). However, in Harvey Cedars, an entire two-family home (that could sleep two medium-size families) close to the beach was listed for $1,400 to $1,775 per week.

More examples: An oceanfront Bay Head home was rented for $35,000 a month, while a one-bedroom oceanside condominium cost $9,250 for the season. In nearby Point Pleasant Beach, an attractive four-bedroom, two-bath Cape Cod house, two blocks from the beach, was listed for $2,300 a week. In Seaside Park, the upper unit of a duplex (three bedrooms, one bath), just four houses from the beach, was available for between $500 and $1,195 a week (again, depending on the week).

There's another possibility for those seeking summer rentals. Many inns and motels have freestanding cottages or multi-bedroom apartments that are available by the week. For example, you can rent a two-bedroom apartment at the St. Rita Hotel at 127 Engleside Avenue in Beach Haven (609-492-9192). These units sleep four to six people, have air-conditioning and ceiling fans, and are priced between $700 and $915 per week.

Another option for family-style getaways on Long Beach Island are the 10 apartments in the complex known as Sea Village Apartments, at Fairview and Bay Avenues in Beach Haven (609-492-9283, seavillageapts.com). The apartments, furnished simply and with just the basics (no bed linens), are arranged around a private courtyard with picnic tables and gas grills. They can sleep up to six people; each has a private porch and cable television. Weekly rentals run about $900 in high season, and are considerably less before Memorial Day and after Labor Day.

The simplest way to search for a rental is to contact a real-estate agent in the area you desire; refer to our Relocation chapter. Another possibility is to regularly check the "Summer Rentals" listings in the papers, the *Asbury Park Press* and the *Ocean County Observer*. If you start looking early (say, in February), you will have a bigger choice; you will also get first crack at listings that come along only rarely—like small cottages or guest houses in desirable towns such as Bay Head. If you wait, however, you have a chance at getting reduced rents from landlords who have empty properties on their hands.

Restaurants

Seafood? You betcha. Reasonably priced old favorites like Red's Lobster Pot and Harvey Cedars Shellfish Company are always busy. You'll also find finny fare with designer attitude and prices to match (at Yellow Fin, for instance) and fresh fish served sushi style (at Osaka). In Ocean County, the world really is your oyster.

This is not to imply that your dining options are limited to seafood—far from it. Upscale dining has arrived in Long Beach Island and other beach communities in a big way, especially in recent years. You'll find a number of fine Italian restaurants like Raimondo's and Roberto's Dolce Vita, but many other types of cuisine as well.

A word of advice: Call ahead. Restaurants are extremely busy in the summer, and a reservation can often save you a very long wait. In the "winter," by which we Shore folk mean any time between Labor Day and Memorial Day, many area restaurants, like other businesses, may have limited hours or close entirely, especially on Long Beach Island and towns on the Barnegat Peninsula.

Restaurants Price Code

Ratings reflect the average price for two entrees, excluding drinks, appetizers, dessert, tax, and tip.

$	. . . . under $25
$$	. . . . $25 to $40
$$$	. . . . $40 to $55
$$$$	. . . . over $55

Atlantic Bar & Grill $$
24th and Central Avenues, South Seaside Park
(732) 854–1588

Situated right at the entrance to Island Beach State Park, the Atlantic Bar & Grill is a great place to stop for lunch or something cold on the weekends. It's open for lunch and dinner daily, and there is a piano player on Friday and Saturday nights.

Beignet's Pub & Restaurant $$$
618 Boulevard, Seaside Heights
(732) 830–1255

Beignet's brings a little taste of New Orleans to the Jersey Shore, complete with live jazz on Saturday nights. The continental menu features prime meats and fresh seafood, all prepared with a little bit of Cajun spice.

C'est la Vie $$$$
7807 Long Beach Boulevard, Beach Haven Crest (LBI)
(609) 494–5372

Classic French dishes such as rabbit and frog's legs are a delicious change of pace for Long Beach Island. The Parisian ambience does not include wine, however, so bring your own.

Charles' Seafood Garden & Steakhouse $$$
8611 Long Beach Boulevard, Beach Haven Crest (LBI)
(609) 492–8340

The name seems to say it all—steak, lobster, fish, clam chowder. It's busy in summer, so either go early or expect to wait. There's no bar, so bring your own beer or wine. Charles' is open daily for lunch and dinner.

Clarks Landing $$$
847 Arnold Avenue, Point Pleasant
(732) 899–1111

Get a window table and enjoy sunset over the Manasquan River with your meal, or just stop for drinks in the bar, one of the few in Point Pleasant that's more for the over-30 crowd. The American/continental menu prominently features seafood dishes like crab cakes and scallops with shrimp over pasta.

Crab's Claw $$
601 Central Avenue, Lavallette
(732) 793–4447

There are not a million places to go in Lavallette, and so the Crab's Claw maintains its popularity. It's favored by some of the area's older folks who can't quite get used to spending a month's rent on a meal, which is what some of trendy new places in the chic towns of Ocean County seem to charge. It's open daily for lunch and dinner (Sunday brunch).

Dennis Foy's $$$$
816 Arnold Avenue, Point Pleasant Beach
(732) 295–0466

The minimalist decor leaves some cold, as do the minimalist portions (here at the Shore diners expect to take home a "doggy bag"). But chef Dennis Foy's creative way with American fare soothes the grumbling, and bringing your own wine saves some money on the bar bill.

Dennis Foy's Bay Head $$$$
512 Main Avenue, Bay Head
(732) 714–1041

At this summer-only outpost, dining is outdoors. Expect the same high prices and exceptional, creative dishes as at Foy's in Point Pleasant Beach. Remember to bring your own wine.

Diamonds Oceanside $$$–$$$$
1900 Ocean Avenue, Ortley Beach
(732) 793–5555
www.diamondsrestaurant.com

This upscale Italian place is a seaside outpost of Diamonds Restaurant in Trenton, a longtime favorite. It's known for a high level of service and a hefty wine list as well as excellent Italian fare.

Dorcas of Bay Head $
58 Bridge Avenue, Bay Head
(732) 899–9365

This little cafe and soda fountain is a Bay Head institution, a place where you can get breakfast all day, or a wonderful light lunch. Dorcas's homemade soups, sandwiches, quiches, and salads are some of the perks of living in Bay Head. If you've been good, treat yourself to a gooey sundae or a homemade cake. From late June to Labor Day it's open daily from 11:00 A.M. to 3:00 P.M.

Europa South $$$
521 Arnold Avenue (N.J. Highway 35 South),
Point Pleasant Beach
(732) 295–1500

After a day spent sun-worshipping, the dark interior of this Portuguese standby may come as a welcome relief. Cool gazpacho is the perfect summer soup, while the king-crabmeat soup rules. Europa is also known for its lobster, served broiled or stuffed with crabmeat; the fish of the day cooked Portuguese style; and paella Valenciana, the saffron rice casserole crammed with chicken, chorizos (spicy Spanish sausages), and a medley of shellfish. Europa South serves lunch and dinner Tuesday through Saturday, and dinner only on Sunday.

Green Gables Restaurant & Inn $$$$
212 Centre Street, Beach Haven
(609) 492–3553
www.lbinet.com/greengables

Take a look at some of the huge houses that have sprung up on Long Beach Island, and you'll realize who has $75 to drop on a five-course, prix-fixe dinner. You may want to call and see what's cooking as there's no set menu; dinner will be whatever the very talented chef decides to cook that day. It's open daily for lunch and dinner. BYOB.

Grenville Hotel & Restaurant $$$$
345 Main Avenue (N.J. Highway 35),
Bay Head
(732) 892–3100
www.thegrenville.com

Dining at this superb restored Victorian mansion, with its graceful porch, is truly a night out. Excellent service complements the top-notch, traditional American cuisine. Sunday brunch is really an event: In addition to the groaning-board buffet, where you'll find breakfast and lunch dishes, you can order an entree—eggs if you feel more like breakfast, or something like chicken in puff pastry if you're ready to move on. Though there are no liquor licenses in Bay Head, the Grenville is able to offer a selection of wines from the Renault Winery, which is under the same ownership. At dinner you still may want to bring your own, but at brunch, get giddy on the blueberry champagne punch. The restaurant is open daily for lunch (brunch on Sunday) and dinner.

Harvey Cedars Shellfish Company $$–$$$
7904 Long Beach Boulevard, between 79th
and 80th Streets, Harvey Cedars
(609) 494–7112
506 Centre Street, Beach Haven
(609) 492–2459

For atmosphere, the picnic tables and paper plates may not be all that, but you can't beat the prices for super-fresh seafood. Many LBI veterans avoid the long waits by getting the food to go and enjoying the lobster, broiled fish, or mussels in garlic on the comfort of their own decks, where they don't even have to tip the waitress.

Heatwave at Windows $$$–$$$$
White Sands Oceanfront Resort
1205 Ocean Avenue, Point Pleasant Beach
(732) 714–2030
www.thewhitesands.com

This splendid room at the oceanfront White Sands kicks the dining experience up several notches from the original Heatwave, a small Bay Head eatery (see below). Entrees such as Chilean sea bass, and tuna tartare in ponzu sauce suit this sleek, upscale environment. It's a far cry from the many honky-tonk spots in Point Pleasant.

Heatwave Cafe $$$
513 Main Street, Bay Head
(732) 714–8881
www.heatwavecafe.com

Bay Head natives lament that the bennies have discovered the tiny Heatwave, their Main Street mecca for dressed-up American food. Menu favorites include rack of lamb, crab cakes with wasabi coleslaw and roasted pepper coulis, and grilled Chilean sea bass with olive-tomato relish and sun-dried-tomato mashed potatoes. Locals are hoping that the bring-your-own-liquor policy will encourage fun-seekers to try the new location in Point Pleasant Beach (see above). At this writing, the Heatwave Cafe was in the midst of a renovation, so call ahead.

Jack Baker's Lobster Shanty $$$
83 Channel Drive, Point Pleasant Beach
(732) 899–6700

This big waterfront seafooder is always busy, as is the more casual Jack Baker's Wharfside next door. The stuffed lobster is always good, but the menu choices here lag behind those at some of the more innovative restaurants that have come to the area recently. For dessert, the flaming bananas Foster is a high-calorie extravaganza. The restaurant is open daily for lunch and dinner. Sunday brunch is an event, with a piano player and a huge, sprawling buffet.

Jeffrey's $$$$
73 Main Street, Toms River
(732) 914–9544

What is chef Jeffrey Schneekloth doing in Toms River, you may ask, when his shrimp with macadamia nut crust and yellowfin tuna with wasabi mashed potatoes would wow 'em in the big city? It's bring your own wine, and you might want to bring both a red and a white to ensure that you'll have wine to complement whatever dish you order.

La Spiaggia $$$$
357 West Eighth Street, Ship Bottom
(609) 494–4343

While a golf shirt and khaki pants are just fine at most Shore restaurants, the valet parking should tip you off that this Italian restaurant proffers fine dining of the dress-up sort. Bring your own wine, and your credit cards, too; La Spiaggia is pricey, but worth it.

The Marlin $$$
2 South Bay Avenue, Beach Haven
(609) 492–7700

The Marlin is like Dr. Jekyll and Mr. Hyde. In the off-season, it's a great place to get a nice meal. In season, summer people come here to go fishing for dates, drink beer after beer, and listen to the bands.

The Owl Tree $$$
7908 Long Beach Boulevard, Harvey Cedars (LBI)
(609) 494–8191

This casual LBI hangout is busy all summer, with music and dancing in the bar downstairs, and a pleasant dining room upstairs. Locals like to come in winter, when the crowds have gone home, and enjoy the cozy fireplace.

Osaka at Docksider $$$
1919 Bay Boulevard, Ortley Beach (LBI)
(732) 830–4422

Forget the traffic—dock your boat right at Osaka and stroll inside to enjoy fresh fish, Japanese-style. Sushi, tempura, and teriyaki are the mainstays, but there are nightly specials as well. It's open for lunch and dinner daily.

Raimondo's $$$$
1101 Long Beach Boulevard, Ship Bottom
(609) 494–5391

This high-end Northern Italian eatery puts its own spin on traditional pasta and fish dishes, and the results are magnifico. On a summer evening, opt for dining alfresco—the porch is much quieter than inside. BYOB.

Red's Lobster Pot $$
Inlet Drive, Point Pleasant Beach
(732) 295–6622

This small waterfront restaurant is a longtime local favorite for its super-fresh seafood, perfectly prepared, as well as its reasonable prices. You save even more by bringing your own bottle.

Roberto's Dolce Vita $$$
12907 Long Beach Boulevard, Beach Haven
(609) 492–1001

The friendly service and uniformly good food make dining at Roberto's a pleasure in spite of the summer crowds. Try the specials, often a little twist on the traditional. Bring your own wine.

Romeo's $$$
100 North Pennsylvania Avenue, Beach Haven (LBI)
(609) 493–0025

Romeo's is a favorite spot on Long Beach Island for a hearty Sunday brunch and is well known for its crepes. The dinner menu features classic continental cuisine and some house specials such as flaming roast duck. If you're inclined to leave the beach early, take advantage of the early-bird specials (before 6:00 P.M.).

Woodies Drive-In $
503 Long Beach Boulevard, Ship Bottom
(609) 361–7300

Long Beach Island's surfers would love to load up their woodies with their boards inside, if they could only get their hands on those prized classic station wagons. They would surely stop at Woodies Drive-In for burgers and fries before heading for the waves.

Yellow Fin $$$$
104 North 24th Street at Long Beach Boulevard, Surf City
(609) 494–7001

As you might have guessed, Yellow Fin specializes in tuna and other designer seafood, served with Asian seasonings and just a little New York City restaurant attitude. It's open late, unusual for a place that does not serve liquor.

Coffeehouses and Ice-Cream Parlors

I scream, you scream, we all scream for ice cream, especially at the Shore in the summertime. It doesn't take a genius to figure out that you can get ice cream at the boardwalk, whether it's in Point Pleasant, Seaside Heights, or down south in Ocean City and Wildwood. But we thought we'd mention a few other places that are definitely worth a slurp. And don't forget Dorcas (see page 268), known for catering to the sweet tooths (sweet teeth?) of Bay Head for more than 35 years.

Cafe Vacio
1511 Long Beach Boulevard, Beach Haven
(609) 492–7702

You can stop in at Cafe Vacio for excellent coffee and cake anytime, but you can relive the days of summer camp on Wednesday night, which is "S'mores Night." The traditional mélange of chocolate, graham crackers, and marshmallows is served with a mini campfire to toast them on.

Coffeehouse at Guild
Chestnut Avenue, Island Heights
(732) 270–3111

On the first Friday of every month, there's a free poetry workshop, when aspiring writers gather to share a cup of joe along with their latest odes.

Cool Beans Coffeehouse
635 Bay Avenue, Dover Township
(732) 797–2326

There's something cooking practically

every night at Cool Beans. Some nights, it's live music—acoustic rock or blues, jazz, or even karaoke. Among the other kinds of fun events held here are massage night and psychic night.

Hoffman's
804 Richmond Avenue, Point Pleasant Beach
(732) 892–0270

Standing in line at Hoffman's can practically be a social event—everybody's here. They all wait because the ice cream is to die for, or at least worth breaking your diet for. Every single wacky flavor is homemade and delicious.

Ralph's Italian Water Ice
600 Grand Central Avenue, Lavallette
(732) 854–0800

Sometimes a slippery chocolate or lemon ice is the most refreshing thing you can have, especially after a big meal. It's like a palate-cleansing sorbet in a paper cup. Ralph's also has a big selection of ice cream and confections made thereof.

Show Place Ice Cream Parlor
202 Centre Street, Beach Haven
(609) 492–0018

When you emerge from the Surflight Theatre across the street, you can get an encore at the Show Place, where singing waiters and waitresses entertain diners with little skits and routines. You have to wait to be seated for each performance though. On rainy days, they add shows to accommodate demand.

Sweet Note Ice Cream Shop
Schooner's Wharf, near North Bay Avenue and 10th Street, Beach Haven
(609) 492–6827

Walk off with a cone or settle in for a Belgian waffle; this place certainly never hits a sour note.

Nightlife

Point Pleasant Beach and Seaside Heights are both known as Ocean County party towns, with a number of big, loud nightclubs with live music and dancing. Of

---

Insiders' Tip

Many clubs have no cover charge if you arrive early, usually before 9:00 or 10:00 P.M. Of course, you'll have that much more time to buy drinks, as the first warm-up band may not even be playing at that hour.

---

course, there are other hot spots sprinkled around. On Long Beach Island, where many summer folk settle in for the duration and try not to cross the causeway until Labor Day, local clubs cater to their late-night needs.

Of course, having a good time is not the sole province of the young and tanned; there are quite a few places where grown-ups can hear live jazz or oldies, the kind of music they know how to dance to. In fact, many fine area restaurants also feature live music—Beignet's, The Marlin, The Owl Tree, and Buckalew's, just to name a few. With the exception of Jenkinson's, Yakety Yak, and a few other big establishments, many clubs, especially on Long Beach Island, are seasonal, so call to check their schedules.

The cover charge at most local clubs is about $10—more if there's a really big band. If you arrive before 9:00 P.M., you'll generally get in without paying a cover, but you may not save much money if you keep buying drinks until the first warm-up band goes on (generally well past 9:00 P.M.). Bars in New Jersey close at 2:00 A.M.

Club XS
408 Boulevard, Seaside Heights
(732) 830–3037

XS as in extra small? Only if you're talking about the tank tops you'll see on some of the girls in here. We think the name is more like "excess," as in the party-to-excess scene that the clubs along Seaside's Boulevard are known for.

The Casino Pier in Seaside Heights is busy day and night. PHOTO: COURTESY OF OCEAN COUNTY PUBLIC AFFAIRS

Jenkinson's Night Club
300 Ocean Avenue, Point Pleasant Beach
(732) 899–0569
www.jenkinsons.com

When we go to Jenkinson's, we don't see any other women with flat hair in the whole place. Teasing is not just a style choice here, it's a way of life, and many guys as well as girls dress for maximum exposure. There is something going on pretty much every night at "Jenk's," as you'll often hear it called in fast-talking radio ads describing drink specials and upcoming acts.

Joey Harrison's Surf Club
1900 Ocean Avenue, Ortley Beach
(732) 793–6625

Joey Harrison's is an Ortley Beach institution, if that isn't too weighty a word for a bar where people go to have a good time. Every year folks who haven't seen each other since Labor Day meet up on the huge dance floor. In summer there's live entertainment every night of the week.

Martell's Sea Breeze
310 Boardwalk, Point Pleasant Beach
(732) 892–0131

This restaurant and tiki bar with its own beach club is like Jenkinson's, but not quite so huge. We do like the outside deck, hanging right over the ocean; even when it's busy, it's so much nicer than many dark and airless nightspots.

Point Pleasant Elks
820 Arnold Avenue, Point Pleasant Beach
(732) 774–0559

You don't have to be an Elk to hoof like one. We believe this is the only spot in Point where you can learn country-western line dancing; lessons are held here on Thursday nights.

Sea Shell Motel, Restaurant, and Beach Club
10 South Atlantic Avenue at Centre Street, Beach Haven
(609) 492–2121.
www.seashell-lbi.com

During happy hour, people are clumped

around the outdoor Shell Pool Bar like a raft of mussels. Things quiet down around dinnertime, as people go home to shower and change. But the action picks up again later in the evening when the music starts. The Sea Shell has a DJ and also hosts local bands as well as some famous- or near-famous-name acts.

Yakety Yak Cafe
406 Boulevard, Seaside Heights
(732) 830–1999

"Yakety yak. Don't talk back," goes the old 1950s novelty hit. Put on your old saddle shoes and dance to the oldies at this cafe, which is fun for all ages.

Shopping

In the Shore towns of Ocean County, you'll find plenty of shops that sell everything you need for the beach: swimsuits, beach chairs and umbrellas, hats, and of course, paperback books. This area is also a hotbed of surf shops, some of which also stock other types of sports equipment.

What may come as a surprise is the large concentration of antiques shops that you'll find in Point Pleasant and Barnegat (see the Close-up on page 276). While you may well find some bargains, it is surely the number of wealthy communities nearby—Bay Head, Mantoloking, Brielle, Sea Girt, and the like—that sustain this lucrative trade.

Antiques and Collectibles

Antique Emporium
Bay and Trenton Avenues, Point Pleasant Beach
(732) 892–2222, (800) 322–8002
www.antiqueemporium.baweb.com

Whatever you collect, you're likely to find it here: antique furniture, bronzes and silver, linens and rugs, china and glass, and vintage toys. With 125 dealers under one roof, there's enough merchandise to satisfy even the most avid antiquer. The Emporium is open every day from 11:00 A.M. to 5:00 P.M.

Cobwebs
Shoppers Wharf
70-72 Bridge Avenue, Bay Head
(732) 892–8005

Antiques, collectibles, and gifts blend nicely in this inviting Bay Head shop. So you'll be able to pick up some Byrdi's Lime Cooler Cookies while you browse through ruby glass, costume jewelry, china, and cottage furniture. The store is open daily from 10:30 A.M. to 5:00 P.M. (sometimes later).

Fables
410 Main Avenue, Bay Head
(732) 899–3633
www.fablesofbayhead.com

This is another of those shops that sells antiques and gifts. You'll find country furniture, antique quilts, and American folk art. In season there's an old-fashioned ice-cream parlor, an excellent inducement to linger. The shop is open from 10:00 A.M. to 5:00 P.M., later on summer evenings; it's closed on Monday.

Recycling the Past
381 North Main Street (U.S. Highway 9), Barnegat
(609) 660–9760

"Nothing Reusable is Refusable" is the credo of this shop, which sells doors, gingerbread molding, ornate mantels, newel posts, and all those wonderful details that make older homes so interesting. Not only do they help you find the missing bits and pieces you need, they're helping the environment, too. The store is open Wednesday through Sunday from 10:00 A.M. to 5:00 P.M.

Unshredded Nostalgia
323 South Main Street (U.S. Highway 9), Barnegat

(609) 660–2626
www.unshreddednostalgia.com

Remember all the stuff your mom threw out when she cleaned out the attic? Things you wish you had today? You'll find them here: movie posters, old sheet music, casino memorabilia, and postcards and photos from days gone by. If you have a taste for nostalgia, you can indulge it fully here. The store is open daily from 10:00 A.M. to 5:00 P.M.

Auctions

The auctioneers listed in our Monmouth County chapter also operate in Ocean County. In addition, you'll find Friday night auctions once a month at Point Pleasant Galleries, 626 Ocean Road, Point Pleasant (732–892–2217). Local estates are the specialty. When there's no auction on, you can browse the gallery for 19th- and 20th-century antiques and collectibles. Call for hours.

Books

Bent Pages
1957A N.J. Highway 35 North, Ortley Beach
(732) 793–7733

Why take new books to the beach when used ones will do just as well? You can have your choice here. In addition to used books, Bent Pages carries some new ones—and newspapers, too. It's a seasonal store, open daily in summer from 7:00 A.M. to 8:00 P.M.

Book Bin
725 Arnold Avenue, Point Pleasant
(732) 892–3456
www.bookbinnj.com

Good-quality rare and pre-owned books are what you'll see at the Book Bin—science fiction, history, and even some romance. The shop is open Sunday and Monday from noon to 3:00 P.M., and Tuesday through Saturday from 10:00 A.M. to 5:00 P.M.

Clothing and Accessories

Grandma's Angel
626 Arnold Avenue, Point Pleasant
(732) 295–2229

The name says it all. It's a place for Grandma to shop for everything from layettes to beachwear for new babies and toddlers. The store is open from 10:30 A.M. to 5:00 P.M. Monday through Friday, from 10:00 A.M. to 6:00 P.M. on Saturday, and from noon to 5:00 P.M. on Sunday.

Mark, Fore & Strike
68 Bridge Avenue, Bay Head
(732) 892–6721

No doubt you've heard the name before in other upscale resort communities. So you know that what's sold here is classic casual sportswear and accessories for men and women. The store is open Monday through Saturday from 9:00 A.M. to 5:00 P.M.; in summer until 5:30 P.M. and Sunday from 11:00 A.M. to 4:00 P.M.

Young Innocents
64 Bridge Avenue, Bay Head
(732) 892–7752

Good-quality children's clothing has been sold here since 1956, so if you need a party outfit or something practical for the beach, check the attractive stock here. The store is open Monday through Saturday from 9:00 A.M. to 5:00 P.M. (reduced hours in winter).

Consignment Shops

Bazaar Bizarre
2204 N.J. Highway 37 East, Toms River
(732) 506–0020

A little of this and a little of that is on offer here: toys, crafts, jewelry, household items, and some antiques and collectibles. The store is open Tuesday through Saturday from 10:00 A.M. to 4:00 P.M.

My Friend's Closet
3003 N.J. Highway 88, Point Pleasant
(732) 899–2626

Gently worn designer clothes (names like DKNY, Chanel, and Versace) can be a bargain the second time around. The store is open weekdays from 10:00 A.M. to 4:00 P.M. (until 6:00 P.M. on Thursday), and from 10:00 A.M. to 3:00 P.M. on Saturday.

Time After Time Consignment
117 N.J. Highway 37 East, Toms River
(732) 473–0906

New and pre-owned upscale fashions—clothing, accessories, and furs—are on sale here. There's a bridal section, too. The store is open from 10:00 A.M. to 7:00 P.M. weekdays, and from 10:00 A.M. to 5:00 P.M. on Saturday.

Delectable Edibles

For more treats, see the "Coffeehouses and Ice-Cream Parlors" section.

Mueller's Bakery
80 Bridge Avenue, Bay Head
(732) 892–0442
www.muellerbakery.com

People line up on weekends for the scrumptious crumb buns, and once you try them, you'll know why. The bakery opens early (6:30 or 7:00 A.M.) every day and closes at 5:00 P.M. In winter, it keeps a weekend-only schedule. Call ahead to check.

Normandy Market
534 N.J. Highway 35 North, Normandy Beach
(732) 793–8788

Whether you want to cook something wonderful or buy prepared foods to go, this market can oblige. They have an old-fashioned butcher, a deli department, a grocery department, and delightful baked goods. And if you want to throw a beach party, they have an extensive catering menu. The market is seasonal and closes in the winter. Call for hours.

Stutz Own Make
14th Street and Boulevard, Ship Bottom
(609) 494–5303

If you have a yen for James' saltwater taffy in the off-season, this is the only shop on LBI that can help. It also carries chocolates, gifts,

and cards. It's open daily from 10:00 A.M. to 6:00 P.M. year-round (until 9:00 P.M. in season).

Flea Markets

Route 70 Flea Market
N.J. Highway 70, Lakewood
(732) 370–1837

This flea market has about 500 dealers and operates year-round. It's open Friday from 8:00 A.M. to 2:00 P.M., and Saturday and Sunday from 7:00 A.M. to 4:00 P.M.

Home

Casa Nova Decorative Gifts
4300 Long Beach Boulevard, Brant Beach
(609) 361–7200

When you want interesting and unusual furnishings for your home, without spending "decorator" prices, check out this shop, which also carries an interesting and eclectic selection of affordably priced home accents and children's items.

Holly's Fabric Fair
611 Arnold Avenue, Point Pleasant
(732) 899–0299

We fell in love with Holly's years ago, when we picked up some terrific off-white linen-blend fabric to slipcover two beat-up sofas. Voila, we had a "shabby chic" look at a rock-bottom price. Holly's 54-inch fabrics start at $5.99 a yard; the fancier stuff is higher, but it's all at outlet prices. The store is open Monday through Saturday from 10:00 A.M. to 5:00 P.M. (5:30 P.M. on Saturday).

Sea Maiden Herbs
512 Bay Avenue, Point Pleasant
(732) 714–7100

Bubble, bubble, toil and trouble . . . whether your brew of choice is tea or some exotic herbal concoction, you'll find the ingredients in this unusual shop. In addition to teas, it carries herbs and spices, essential oils, loose botanicals, and kitchen wares. And it smells nice, too. The shop is open Tuesday through Friday from noon to 6:00 P.M., and Saturday and

More Ocean County Antiques Emporia

Rainy days are made for antiquing, so here are some more places to check out in Point Pleasant Beach and Barnegat.

Point Pleasant Beach

Ambiance Antiques
707 Arnold Avenue
(732) 295–9202

Antiques Etc.
1225 Bay Avenue
(732) 295–9888

Class Collectibles
633 Arnold Avenue
(732) 714–0957

Company Store
628 Bay Avenue
(732) 892–5353

Fond Memories Antiques and Gifts
628 Bay Avenue
(732) 892–1917

Point Pavilion Antique Center
608 Arnold Avenue
(732) 899–6300

Barnegat

Barnegat Antique Country
684 East Bay Avenue
(609) 698–8967

Heart of Antique Alley
U.S. Highway 9 and Bay Avenue
(609) 698–8967

Lavender Hall
289 South Main Street (U.S. Highway 9)
(609) 698–8126

Sneak Box Antiques & Decoys
273 South Main Street (U.S. Highway 9)
(609) 698–8222

West Bay Antiques
349 South Main Street (U.S. Highway 9)
(609) 698–3020

Sunday from noon to 5:00 P.M. in summer, with shorter hours in winter.

Malls

Bay Village & Schooner's Wharf
Ninth Street between Ocean and Bay
Avenues, Beach Haven
(609) 492–4400
www.lbinet.com/9thandbay

This historic open-air waterfront complex, with its little mom-and-pop stores, is like an anti-mall. It encompasses more

than 40 shops, half a dozen eateries, and a dance bar. You'll find clothing, jewelry, gifts, toys, crafts, and a dollar store. This is a seasonal complex, open daily in summer, weekends through Christmas, then closed until May.

Ocean County Mall
Hooper and Bay Avenues, Toms River
(732) 244–8200
www.shopsimon.com

This big mall is anchored by Macy's, JC Penney, and Sears, and includes 115 specialty stores such as Old Navy, Gap, The

Disney Store, Bath & Body Works, and Victoria's Secret. There are chain eateries like Applebee's, too.

The Shoppes at Silver Sun Mall
Third and Bay Avenues, Beach Haven
(609) 492–3331
Here you'll find 30 stores and a food court under one air-conditioned roof. It's open daily.

Outdoor Gear

Beach Nutz
1301 Long Beach Boulevard, Beach Haven
(609) 492–3070
www.beachnutz.com
Surfers and kayakers have been patronizing this shop for 15 years. In addition to selling equipment, it also rents kayaks, bikes, skateboards, scooters, in-line skates, pedal boats, wetsuits, and surfboards. Surfing lessons and kayak tours are available, too. Lazy folks who simply lounge can buy chairs, umbrellas, and beach toys here.

Right Coast Surf Shop
214 Central Avenue, Seaside Park
(732) 854–9300
www.rightcoastsurf.com
Attention surfers, body-boarders, skateboarders, and skaters—you'll find what you need at this shop. There are also cool accessories, like Rip Curl watches. In winter the store is open weekdays (except Tuesday) from 11:00 A.M. to 6:00 P.M., Saturday from 10:00 A.M. to 6:30 P.M., and Sunday from 10:00 A.M. to 5:30 P.M. Call for extended summer hours.

Ron Jon Surf Shop
201 Ninth Street, Ship Bottom
(609) 494–8844
This is the original Ron Jon's, which opened in 1959. Since then the name has become synonymous with surfing, and the shop has evolved into a four-level emporium filled with a huge selection of board-sports equipment, active-lifestyle clothing, and more. The shop even features one of the world's largest surfboards—over 24 feet in length. Ron Jon is open from 10:00 A.M. to 7:00 P.M. daily; in summer it opens at 8:00 or 9:00 A.M. and stays open until 11:00 P.M.

This and That

Jackson Outlet Village (formerly Six Flags Factory Outlets)
537 Monmouth Road, Jackson
(73) 833–0680
www.jacksonoutletvillage.com
We've listed this 70-store outlet center in both the Monmouth County and the Ocean County chapters because it's sort of on the border, just a mile from Six Flags Great Adventure. See the "Shopping" section of the Monmouth County chapter for details.

The Jolly Tar
56 Bridge Avenue, Bay Head
(732) 892–0223
www.jollytar.com
This Bay Head perennial has been around for decades; it sells accessories for the home, carved decoys and other nautical items, Christmas ornaments and decorations, Waterford crystal, paper goods, and more. It's open Monday through Saturday from 10:00 A.M. to 5:00 P.M., and Sunday from 10:00 A.M. to 3:00 P.M. (closed Tuesday in winter, longer hours in summer).

Atlantic and Cape May Counties

Atlantic City and Cape May—so close and yet so far. They're both about the same vintage, and are both tourist resorts, yet the two towns could hardly be more different. Neon lights adorn the towering casino hotels of A.C., while inside the slots machines ring and clang night and day. In contrast, little white lights adorn the facades of the painstakingly restored Victorian inns that line the quaint streets of Cape May. Inside, gourmet meals, perhaps accompanied by a solo musician, are served in intimate dining rooms, where attention is paid to every detail.

Which appeals to you? As luck would have it, you don't have to choose just one or the other. Stay anywhere you like—Ocean City, Avalon, Wildwood—and a night out at the casinos or a special dinner date in Cape May are both an easy drive away.

In this chapter you'll find a variety of places to stay, eat, party, and shop on the Southern Shore.

Accommodations

Whether your tastes run to the personal attentions of an intimate bed-and-breakfast inn or to the glitzy casinos in the middle of all the action, you'll find it here. Also look for the opening of a spectacular new casino in the Marina District, the Borgata.

Hotel Price Code

For one night in a standard double room in high season.

$	Under $125
$$	$125 to $200
$$$	$200 to $300
$$$$	Over $300

Atlantic City Casino Hotels

Most of the overnight visitors to Atlantic City stay at one of the 12 casino hotels listed here. The price rating we'd give to these is $ to $$ (see above for details), but of course that's only part of the story. Regular visitors to the casinos get coded cards, and those who gamble a lot are offered all kinds of perks to keep them happy and bring them back. Rooms and services are "comped" or upgraded for high rollers; the highest of rollers get lavish accommodations and just about every comfort and amenity—including tickets to the city's hottest shows—"on the house."

If you don't fall into the "high" or even "medium" roller category, and you want to stay in a casino hotel, book as early as you can. Though more visitors come in summer, the casino hotels don't really have an off-season; gamblers don't care if the temperature outside is 30 degrees or 90 degrees, as long as the drinks are cold and the cards are hot. Also, check online to see if there are any special offers, like the $99 rooms we've seen occasionally.

We're discussing these hotels as a group rather than individually because to us, one isn't that different from the other. Yes, they tend to have a theme—whether it's the Wild West, the Exotic East, or Ancient Rome—but the theme decor is limited to the public areas. The rooms can generally be described as contemporary-hotel-in-neutral-colors. Some rooms have ocean views and some are nonsmoking. If you're not a smoker, be sure to ask for one of these because in many instances, the cumulative odor of smoke lingers in the room long after the previous guest has left.

All the casino hotels have recreational options like swimming pools and fitness centers; Harrah's in the Marina District has mini golf, tennis courts, and shuffleboard. If you own a boat, you can access the Trump Marina quite easily by docking your craft at the Senator Frank S. Farley Marina, which is owned by the New Jersey Division of Parks and Forestry, but is managed by Trump Marina Associates.

If we had to pick some favorite features from the casino hotels, we might choose the beach at the Hilton, because it's nicely maintained and there are chairs and umbrellas for your comfort. We like the pool at Caesars, and we very much like the spa at Bally's. In fact, if you're traveling with a gambler but you don't want to put in any time at the slots or wheels, you could easily spend a delightful day in the spa. Other hotels have newer spas, but this one—with an area of 40,000 square feet—is almost a destination unto itself. At the center of the complex is an indoor pool surrounded by acres of glass with drop-dead views of sky and sea. There are mosaic-tiled whirlpools surrounded by tropical plants, saunas, a poolside inhalation room, a spacious sundeck, an aerobics center, a weight-resistance center, and a pro shop. And we haven't even mentioned the terrific treatments or the tasty spa lunch you can get here. Hotel guests pay a modest fee to use the spa; the fee is waived if you purchase a service.

All the casino hotels offer dining options that generally include at least one "fine dining" restaurant, an all-you-can-eat buffet, fast-fooderies that offer pizza or Chinese food, and a coffee shop. All have live entertainment, with big-name stars, as well as lesser lights who fill out the year's calendar. If you enjoy dining and dancing, you'll find that at all these establishments, too. And, of course, there's gambling (see the "Casinos" section of this chapter for details).

Atlantic City Hilton $-$$
Boardwalk at Boston Avenue
(609) 347-7111, (800) 257-8677
www.hiltonac.com

Bally's Park Place/The Wild West $-$$
Boardwalk at Park Place
(609) 340-2000, (800) 225-5977
www.ballysac.com

Caesars Atlantic City $-$$
2100 Pacific Avenue
(609) 348-4411, (800) 524-2867
www.caesarsac.com

Claridge Casino Hotel $-$$
Boardwalk at Indiana Avenue
(609) 340-3400, (800) 257-8585
www.claridge.com

The Claridge is Atlantic City's oldest and smallest casino hotel. PHOTO: COURTESY OF CLARIDGE CASINO AND HOTEL

Harrah's Atlantic City $–$$
777 Harrah's Boulevard
(609) 441–5000, (800) 242–7724
www.harrahs.com

Resorts Casino Hotel $–$$
1133 Boardwalk at North Carolina Avenue
(609) 344–6000, (800) 336–6378
www.resortsac.com

Sands Hotel and Casino $–$$
South Indiana Avenue and Brighton Park
(609) 441–4000, (800) AC–SANDS
www.acsands.com

Showboat Atlantic City $–$$
Boardwalk at Delaware Avenue
(609) 343–4000, (800) 621–0200
www.harrahs.com

Tropicana Casino and Resort $–$$
Boardwalk at Brighton Avenue
(609) 340–4000, (800) 843–8767
www.tropicana.net

Trump Marina Hotel and Casino $–$$
Huron Avenue and Brigantine Boulevard
(609) 441–2000, (800) 777–1177
www.trumpmarina.com

Trump Plaza $–$$
Boardwalk at Mississipi Avenue
(609) 441–6000, (800) 677–7378

Trump Taj Mahal Casino Resort $–$$
1000 Boardwalk at Virginia Avenue
(609) 449–1000, (800) 825–8786
www.trumptaj.com

Other Hotels and Motels

Ala Moana $
5300 Atlantic Avenue, Wildwood
(609) 729–7666
www.alamoanamotel.com

Just a block from the beach, the Ala Moana is one of those family-friendly Wildwood motels. Rooms have two double beds, fully equipped kitchens with full-size refrigerators, air-conditioning, television with free HBO, and balconies. Outside there are two sundecks, a large heated pool, a kiddie pool, picnic tables, barbecue grills, and a game room.

Aladdin Motel $
Seaview Avenue and Forget-Me-Not Road, Wildwood Crest
(609) 522–0333
www.aladdinmotel.com

Two blocks from Wildwood Crest's gorgeous free beaches, this motel offers spacious poolside efficiency units that sleep four to six people. The decor won't evoke Martha Stewart—it's motel modern, simple and basic, but rooms do have air-conditioning and cable television. The studio efficiency has a kitchen area and a seating area with a sofa. The two-room suite adds a sofa bed. In high season you can get a basic room (two people) for about $55 (about $80 for four). Weekly specials run between $350 and $525 for four people. In addition to the adult pool, there's a kiddie version. You can walk to the Boardwalk, clubs, shopping, and restaurants.

Atlas Inn $
1035 Beach Avenue, Cape May
(609) 884–7000, (888) 285–2746
www.atlasinn.com

The Atlas motor inn is one of Cape May's reasonably priced oceanfront family vacation spots. It has pleasantly furnished oceanfront rooms and suites with microwaves, cable television, and air-conditioning. Outside, there's a seaside pool where you can eat lunch or sip a tropical drink; other extras include a kiddie pool, a poolside sauna, an exercise room, and even barbecue grills. While having a meal at the inn's Yesterday's Heroes Ballpark Cafe, you can view one of the largest collections of Babe Ruth memorabilia on public display.

The Chalfonte $$
301 Howard Street, Cape May
(609) 884–8409
www.chalfonte.com

In an area rich in historic buildings, the Chalfonte stands out—and not just because it takes up almost an entire city block. The hotel is pretty to look at, with its Italianate cupola, wraparound verandah, striped awnings, and ornate gingerbread; understandably, it is said to be the "most photographed building in Cape May."

Located steps from the Cape May beaches and promenade, the hotel was built in 1876 by Colonel Henry Sawyer, a local Civil War hero. Originally a boarding-house, the Chalfonte has undergone various expansions and renovations over the years. Today it is run like an old-time resort, with a calendar of concerts, workshops, events, and exhibits to enhance the pleasures of a Cape May vacation.

Rooms are also old-fashioned: They're furnished with marble-topped dressers, washstands, and ceiling fans. There is no air-conditioning and no television, but guests don't seem to mind; many return year after year. An option for families is the cottage on the grounds; it has 3½ bedrooms (the small one has bunk beds), two bathrooms, a family room, and a wraparound porch. Cooling is accomplished with ceiling fans and Nature's breezes, but the cottage does have a TV/VCR, a refrigerator, and a microwave.

The hotel's dining room, the Magnolia Room, is known for its Southern-style cuisine (however, a fish entree and a vegeterian one are served every night).

Chateau Bleu Resort Motel $
911 Surf Avenue, North Wildwood
(609) 522–2822
www.njshoreguide.com/chateau

If your idea of romance is swimming in a heart-shaped pool, here's your chance—it's the only one in the Wildwoods. The Chateau Bleu is a short walk from the Boardwalk, a little out of the hubbub of Wildwood. Rooms are furnished with two double beds, air-conditioning, television, and refrigerators. The efficiency and family units have fully equipped kitchens.

Concord Suites $$–$$$
7800 Dune Drive, Avalon
(609) 368–7800, (800) 443–8202
www.concordsuites.com

The Concord is an all-suite hotel, which makes it another good family choice. Each comfortable air-conditioned suite has a bedroom with double beds, and a

The graceful Chalfonte is Cape May's most photographed Victorian hotel. PHOTO: COURTESY OF THE CHALFONTE HOTEL

Wildwood Motels: Bargains by the Sea

True to its roots as a workingman's paradise, Wildwood is still kind to family budgets. With motels lining the main thoroughfares, you have a choice of basic, clean rooms for under $60 or $70 a night. There are package deals for stays of a week or more, and in the shoulder season—when the weather is still very good—your choices get even better. It's true the rooms lack the charm and grandeur you'll find at some inns in Cape May, but if you're traveling with kids, you'll spend most of your time at the beaches and boardwalks anyway. For more information on Wildwood, call 800–WW–BY–SEA or go to www.wildwoodsnj.com.

separate living room with a sofa bed and a television. Guests may use the property's shared efficiency kitchen and laundry facilities. The hotel has two swimming pools and three large sundecks. It sometimes offers attractively priced packages, which bring the high-season rate down to the single $ rating.

Golden Inn $$$–$$$$
Oceanfront at 78th Street, Avalon
(609) 368–5155
www.goldeninn.com

Located on the barrier island of Avalon and Stone Harbor, this upscale oceanfront hotel gives visitors a taste of life in these posh communities. In addition to a gorgeous beach, beautifully manicured grounds, and views of the native dunes, there's also an inviting pool. If you'd like to explore the island, you can borrow a bike; if you want to play tennis, there are 11 courts next door. The 154 rooms are spacious and well appointed, with climate control, television, and a refrigerator. The efficiency units also have a microwave and sink. The oceanfront studios add a dinette and are good for a family holiday. (If you want to get away from the kids for a while, the hotel can arrange baby-sitting.)

The hotel restaurants will do their best to tempt you: The Fish Company Restaurant entices with soups and chowders and chilled clams or shrimp as well as heartier fare like seafood pescatore (shrimp, clams, and sea scallops over linguine). If dining

poolside is your pleasure, Bellyflops Grill serves soups and hot or cold appetizers, salads, sandwiches, burgers, and other light fare. Luigi's Pasta and Vino features Italian dishes in a casual setting. There's live entertainment from spring through fall, Big Band music for dancing most Friday and Saturday nights from October to May, and contemporary music from June through September.

Holiday Inn $
Boardwalk at Chelsea Avenue, Atlantic City
(800) 548–3030

The 220-room Holiday Inn is an alternative to the Atlantic City casino hotels, yet it's close enough (next door to the Tropicana, and steps from the Hilton) for you to partake of the gambling/entertainment scene. The rooms, kings or doubles, are roomy and neat. Since hotels like this are after the family trade, they offer some attractive promotions such as "Kids Stay Free" and "Kids Eat Free" (at the Scribbles Cafe, when accompanied by an adult). The cafe serves breakfast, lunch, and dinner. Holiday Inn also offers getaway packages that include casino coins, casino buffet dinners, and more.

Lotus Inn $
6900 Ocean Avenue, Wildwood Crest
(609) 522–6300, (800) 522–6306
www.lotusinn.com

This oceanfront property is directly across from the beach and the bike path.

The air-conditioned rooms, done in pastel blues and rose shades, are spacious and well-equipped. Each has either a king-size bed or two doubles, a refrigerator, a microwave, a coffeemaker, and a television with free Disney channel. Suites have double sofa beds and can sleep up to six. Oceanfront rooms have private balconies; other rooms have shared balconies. There's a heated pool, a kiddie pool, an oceanfront sundeck, a game room, an on-site coin laundry, and a barbecue. In season, the hotel runs free hot dog cookouts for guests. They also offer complimentary newspapers and continental breakfast. If you're looking for things to do, there is a program of activities. In short, you get a pretty good bang for your buck here; special packages make the prices even more appealing.

Royal Hawaiian Beachfront Resort $–$$
Orchid Road on the beach, Wildwood Crest
(609) 522–3414
www.royalhawaiianresort.com

For those who prefer not to be so close to the bustle of the commercial boardwalks, Wildwood Crest might be a good choice. The Royal Hawaiian looks more like an oceanfront resort than a motel. It has a heated pool, a hot tub, and a gazebo with barbecue grills. The hotel provides a perfect setting for the plastic palm trees so popular in Wildwood. The rooms are nicer than most of Wildwood's motel rooms; they have pale walls and pale furniture, balconies (ocean views from all suites), refrigerators, and microwaves. And there's a private entrance to the beach.

Seaview Marriott Resort $$$–$$$$
401 South New York Road (U.S. Highway 9), Absecon
(800) 932–8000

When you arrive at this Jazz Age luxury resort, you're treated like Gatsby himself. Atlantic City's casinos are just a 20-minute drive away, but quite removed from these 270 acres on tranquil Reeds Bay. Seaview has 297 luxurious guest rooms, indoor and outdoor pools, an Elizabeth Arden Red Door Spa, tennis courts, an elegant dining room, and a casual pub.

The posh Seaview Marriott Resort is a golfer's paradise, with two championship courses and the Nick Faldo Golf Institute. PHOTO: COURTESY OF SEAVIEW MARRIOTT RESORT

Seaview is a dream getaway for golfers, with two championship golf courses as well as the Faldo Golf Institute. (See our Golf chapter for more.) The Donald Ross–designed Bay Course hosts the ShopRite LPGA Classic every year in June. Nearby are such attractions as the Edwin B. Forsythe Wildlife Refuge, the Noyes Museum, and the Historic Towne of Smithville.

Sheraton Atlantic City Convention Center Hotel $$
2 Ocean Way, Atlantic City
(609) 344–3535, (800) 325–3535
www.sheraton.com

The 502-room Sheraton is Atlantic City's largest non-casino hotel and our personal favorite. It has a fully equipped fitness center, an indoor heated pool, and an outdoor whirlpool. It's next door to the new convention center and is connected to the exhibit hall level by an enclosed skywalk bridge. The guests here tend to be conventioneers and other business travelers, rather than gamblers, although a three-block walk will take you to the Boardwalk and other attractions.

In sharp contrast to the casino hotels, with their over-the-top decor, the Sheraton is elegantly restrained, with a neo–Art Deco style and a boutique property atmosphere. As the hotel is the new headquarters of the Miss America organization, you'll see pageant memorabilia throughout the public and guest rooms. At the Shoe Bar, for example, there's a display of shoes and photographs from the traditional Miss America parade. In front of the hotel is a bronze statue of Bert Parks holding a stainless-steel tiara, where beauty queen wannabes can take souvenir photos of their "crowning moments."

The Starlux Motel $$–$$$
305 East Rio Grande Avenue, Wildwood
(609) 522–7412

In a town teeming with motels, the Starlux is unique, for it's a new place (with lots of new comforts) done in the doo-wop style. Walk into the slick all-glass lobby lounge and you may exclaim, "Ooh, my aunt had those chairs!" Owner Jack

Morey (who also owns Boardwalk amusement piers) has had a strong hand in Wildwood's doo-wop revival, and in this motel, he creates an atmosphere as well as a place. It's very cool and pure fun. Inside, there's Jetsons-style furniture; outside, there's a kidney-shaped pool and a whirlpool, surrounded by kitschy plastic palm trees—and you're just a block from the beach.

The groovy style is carried throughout the guest rooms, which are furnished with nifty 1950s-style furniture and retro bath and lighting fixtures. Each room has either a queen-size bed or two doubles, an entertainment center, and a refrigerator. Suites have full kitchens, dinettes, and sofa beds in the living rooms. As of this writing, plans were in the works to install several chrome Airstream trailers in a lot next door, which will be restored and available for rent.

Bed-and-Breakfast Inns

Abbott House $
6056 Main Street, Mays Landing
(609) 625–4400

This Victorian mansion built by attorney Joseph E. P. Abbott is a gingerbread confection in blue and white overlooking historic Mays Landing. There are just four guest rooms, decorated individually with antique and wicker furniture and such nice touches as handmade quilts. All are air-conditioned and all have private baths (though one is outside the room). The Chelsi Room offers panoramic views from its large windows as well as a whirlpool tub.

Breakfast includes an array of fruits and baked goods and hearty entrees. In the afternoon you may take your English-style tea either near the fireplace (in cool weather) or on one of the verandahs.

Angel of the Sea $$$
5-7 Trenton Avenue, Cape May
(800) 848–3369
www.angelofthesea.com

This lovely turreted Victorian bed-and-breakfast has 27 guest rooms, all with private baths and TV/VCRs, and many with ocean views. All guests may use the splendid wraparound verandahs. Rates include full breakfast, afternoon tea, and evening wine and cheese as well as use of bicycles and beach gear. Packages are also available that include dinner at the Peter Shields Inn next door, one of Cape May's finest restaurants.

Carisbrooke Inn $$
105 South Little Rock Avenue, Ventnor
(609) 822–9710
www.carisbrookeinn.com

This pretty seashore house is just a few steps from the lovely Ventnor beach, away from the noise and bustle of Atlantic City, but close enough if you wanted to visit a casino. Named for a grand oceanfront hotel that was demolished almost a century ago, the Carisbrooke does have some elegant details, like high ceilings and ornate moldings. The parlor is sunny and cheerful, and it's here that you'll be served afternoon tea. (When winter rolls around, tea is served beside a warming fire.) There's an ocean-view front deck for sunning, and a quiet back patio for relaxing.

Rooms have either a king-size bed, a queen-size bed, or two double beds. They're air-conditioned (June through Labor Day) and have ceiling fans and cable television. All have private baths, though the bath for one room is across the hall. The rooms are decorated in pastels and florals.

Breakfast is a hearty affair, featuring juice, fresh fruits, baked goods, a selection of cereals, and an entree such as a fajita scramble or multigrain pancakes. For your beach excursions, you'll get a complimentary badge and towel. Kids are welcome here, but they must be at least three years old.

Jonathan Pitney House $$
57 Shore Road, Absecon
(609) 569–1799
www.pitneyhouse.com

Jonathan Pitney, known as the Father of Atlantic City, settled in these parts in 1819. He wore many hats: doctor, notary, postmaster, and developer. He spearheaded the construction of the East/West railroad that would bring thousands of visitors to the area. And he lobbied the federal government to build a lighthouse at the north end of Atlantic City (the Absecon Lighthouse). This house, built in 1799 by Samuel Reed and later expanded, was his home.

Listed on the National Register of Historic Places, the house is now a charming bed-and-breakfast inn. In addition to guest rooms, there are also "guest quarters"—four suites that have whirlpool baths and private verandahs or sitting areas. All the rooms, except the Absecon Room (which lacks a tub), have full en suite baths. The furnishings, many authentic antiques, are as interesting as the house itself, ranging from the primitive colonial style to High Victorian. The Physician's Quarters, for example, features an ornate fireplace and a striking Victorian bed.

Breakfast, a full buffet served in the Colonial Dining Room, features fresh juice, homemade breads and coffee cakes, and hearty entrees such as a cheese soufflé or French toast. If you'd like afternoon tea with savory sweets and pastries, simply request it. As you sip, you might ask to hear the story of the house and to see photos of its renovation.

Mayer's Inn & Marina $$
800 Bay Avenue, Somers Point
(609) 927-3100
www.mayersinn.com

When you come to a gorgeous waterfront mansion standing on the mainland side of Great Egg Harbor, you'll know you've reached Mayer's Inn. Though the inn allows "well-behaved children over the age of 12," it's really a place for grown-ups to get away from it all—and maybe share a little romance. The rooms are quite lovely, with views of the bay, antique furnishings, and private baths.

After a sumptuous breakfast in the Bay View Lounge, you might take a towel and stretch out on the beach adjoining the inn. Or you might stroll over to the marina and go sailing, jet-skiing, canoeing, or fishing. If you're up for Atlantic City at night, that's an easy drive. If not, you might simply linger over a gourmet dinner in the inn's award-winning Grand View Dining Room.

The Sealark Bed & Breakfast $
3018 First Avenue, Avalon
(609) 967-5647

With no particular claim to being "historic," the Sealark is less formal and fussy than many inns; it's just a large, comfortable seaside home. There's spacious living room where you can read or watch a video from the inn's collection. The rooms are nicely furnished and vary in amenities: Some have private baths, others share; two face the ocean; one room is air-conditioned. The Lighthouse Loft on the third floor has a bedroom (with queen-size bed) and a living-room area. On the walls are views of New Jersey's lighthouses. The loft has a (shared) deck where you can barbecue (gas grills are available). The buffet breakfast includes juice, fruit, cereals, homemade baked goods, and entrees such as eggs Florentine and shrimp and cheese soufflé.

The Southern Mansion $$$–$$$$
700 Washington Street, Cape May
(800) 381-3888
www.southernmansion.com

If Scarlett O'Hara summered at the Jersey Shore, as many wealthy Southerners did before the Civil War, she would probably have had a house like the Southern Mansion. This opulent inn, set amid one and a half acres of gardens, is furnished with original antique furniture and fixtures, including elaborate fireplaces, claw-foot bathtubs, and hand-painted shower tiles. Modern comforts like private baths, air-conditioning, and king-size beds are provided, too. Enjoy a full breakfast in the solarium, and afternoon refreshments in the ballroom, and you'll soon be saying, "Fiddle-dee-dee. I'll think about it tomorrow."

Seasonal Rentals

On the beautiful barrier island that encompasses Avalon and Stone Harbor, rentals are costly, especially if they're on or near the ocean. A comfortable oceanfront home with several bedrooms might run as much as $35,000 or $40,000 for the season, according to the professionals at American Eagle Realty in Avalon (609–967-7000). The middle range here is $15,000 to $20,000, and rock bottom would be $8,000 to $10,000, maybe for a guest house not near the ocean and without many amenities. A condominium with three bedrooms and two baths could run between $1,200 and $2,000 per week.

Summer rentals in posh Longport are equally expensive, but rentals in other towns like Margate, Ventnor, or Ocean City would be as much as 40 percent less. To find an available house that fits your budget, you can check the real-estate section in the *Press of Atlantic City*, or contact a local real-estate agent. You'll find a number of them listed in our Relocation chapter.

Another possibility we ran across in Stone Harbor is the Sun 'N Sand Motel & Apartments, 284 102nd Street, (609–368-2722), which offers two-bedroom efficiency apartments. These are about 2½ blocks from the beach, are air-conditioned, have television, and can accommodate six people. High-season rates start at $180 a night, less for extended stays.

Another option for those on a budget is camping. Perhaps it's the milder weather or the mellower climate, but camping is hugely popular "down South," and there are dozens of private and state-owned campgrounds here. You'll find a list to get you started in the Outdoor Activities chapter.

Restaurants

In real estate, the mantra is location, location, location. When dining out in South Jersey in the summer season, it's reservations, reservations, reservations. And you still may have to wait. On weekdays the crowds may be somewhat lighter, but many of the area's fine restaurants, especially in Cape May, are quite small, so don't just amble in and expect to be seated. One way to get around the waiting game is to dine early; you may also be able to take advantage of "twilight" dinner specials offered by many restaurants.

A word on prices: The fine dining that has become so abundant in Cape May County does not come cheap. But many restaurants, even some of the best, do not have liquor licenses, and you can save quite a bit when your bring your own wine. When dining out in the off-season, especially in the Cape May or Wildwood area, call ahead, as many restaurants close for the winter or take extended breaks.

In Atlantic City, the casinos are known for their mammoth all-you-can-eat buffets, and though some are reputed to be better than others, we can hardly distinguish among them and have not included them here; furthermore, we find the lines and the noise tough to take, even when the meal is "comped" (free). The casinos also have high-end restaurants; most have more than one. Many, unfortunately, are little more than a pretty face, posh rooms where the food is very average, but the prices are anything but; we've tried to note a few of the exceptions. In our listings, we've tried to give space to freestanding restaurants that you might not otherwise find out about, places that are part of the real Atlantic City, from classic seafooders like Dock's Oyster House and old school Italian joints like Angelo's. Most of the restaurants serve lunch and dinner; many are closed on Monday and/or Tuesday, so call to double-check.

Restaurants Price Code:

Ratings reflect the average price for two entrees excluding drinks, appetizers, dessert, tax, and tip.

$	under $25
$$	$25 to $40
$$$	$40 to $55
$$$$	over $55

Angelo's Fairmont Tavern $–$$
2300 Fairmount Avenue at Mississippi, Atlantic City
(609) 344-2349

Angelo's has been around forever, and the reasonable prices for good food and plenty of it keep folks coming back. The service is friendly, if bustling. Photos of old sports heroes cover the walls, alongside shots of the owner's grandson in his pee-wee hockey uniform. We understand that the house red is actually made in the cellar, but we chickened out and got a regular Chianti instead. The routing of one-way streets in this part of town makes Angelo's a bit hard to find, and so many people end up instead at Angeloni's, which is also good. If you have trouble, park across from the White House (see page 292) and walk west one block.

Bacchanal $$$$
Caesars Casino
2100 Pacific Avenue (Boardwalk at Arkansas), Atlantic City
(609) 348-4411

It's not just for the food that high rollers come to this restaurant named for the Roman god of wine and revelry; Bacchanal is a dining experience cum Roman orgy, where over-indulgence is encouraged. You are served a lavish five-course meal ($49.95) with wine, and you even get a neck and back massage during your meal. Of course, it'll cost you, and you should probably tip that slave girl, too.

Big Ernie's Fabulous '50s Diner $
3801 Atlantic Avenue, Wildwood
(609) 522–8288

The stainless-steel exterior and the black-and-white checkerboard motif should alert you to the fact that Big Ernie's is more than a diner, it's a Fabulous '50s Diner. Visitors and locals alike go to Big Ernie's not just for the bacon and eggs or burgers and fries, but for the total Wildwood doo-wop experience. Wear your poodle skirt and spin some 45s on the vintage jukebox. Forget your triglycerides and cool off with a malt or a cherry coke.

Blue Planet Diner $
841 Asbury Avenue, Ocean City
(609) 525–9999

The Blue Planet is new, but it is really an old-fashioned diner, serving huge blue plate specials (chicken croquettes, meat loaf, chicken-in-a-basket, and the like) and breakfast all day. The cinnamon buns and blueberry and corn muffins are housemade several times a day, as they tend to be consumed quickly. Remember, no beer is served, and you may not even bring your own, as Ocean City is completely dry. (For this reason, when folks are in the mood for fine dining, they tend to head off island.)

Chef Vola's $$$, no credit cards
111 South Albion Place at Pacific, Atlantic City
(609) 345–2022

You don't need a secret password to get into this basement Italian eatery, but you do need a reservation, and the phone number is unlisted. Those in the know come here for excellent Italian cooking and a warm atmosphere. Bring your own wine, and your bankroll.

Deauville Inn $$–$$$
201 Willard Road and the bay, Strathmere
(609) 263–2080

You can avoid all traffic hassles if you travel by boat to this casual seafood place at the northern end of Sea Isle. The fare is fine, especially the basic items like soft-shell crabs and burgers; the sunset from the deck, though, is four stars. The lively bar offers trivia games, several TVs, plus a giant screen for sporting events.

Dock's Oyster House $$$
2405 Atlantic Avenue, Atlantic City
(609) 345–0092

Since 1897, Dock's has been serving fresh seafood, beautifully prepared. Watch your oysters being shucked or enjoy a cocktail at the piano bar. For your entree, may we recommend the lobster or the pecan-encrusted salmon? For dessert, the cheese pie is not exactly a Food Channel innovation, it's just yummy.

East Bay Crab & Grille $$
6701 Black Horse Pike, on the Cardiff Circle, Egg Harbor Township
(609) 272–7721

This laid-back, kid-friendly restaurant serves steaks, fish, ribs, and yes, crabs. The prices are also pretty relaxed, especially if you're one to get your money's worth from the all-you-can-eat specials. If you like clams, try the steamers. There is also a free happy hour buffet, and the restaurant serves until 11:00 P.M.

Ebbitt Room $$$$
The Virginia Hotel
25 Jackson Street, Cape May
(609) 884–5700

This gracious Victorian hotel is the perfect setting for a romantic dinner for two, with a profusion of flowers and piano music providing the appropriate ambience. The excellent service just enhances your enjoyment of a memorable meal. The menu features continental fare.

Elaine's Victorian Inn $$$$
513 Lafayette Street, Cape May
(609) 884–4358

The food at Elaine's is seafood and classic American, but the place is best known for the dinner theater, featuring shows like *The Secret of the Sphinx*. There is also a theme restaurant that's popular with families, Elaine's Haunted Mansion Restaurant. Boo!

Southern (Shore) Fried Chicken

If you don't have the opportunity to dine at the Chalfonte hotel's Magnolia Room, here's a recipe for Dot's famous Southern Fried Chicken.

Soak three pounds of cut-up chicken in salted water (one tablespoon per quart of water) for one hour. Pat dry. In a bag, mix one cup flour, salt and pepper to taste, and two tablespoons of paprika. Take two pieces of chicken at a time, pop them into the bag, and shake them in the flour mixture, making sure you cover them well. Pour two cups of Crisco or corn oil into a large skillet. Heat to medium/medium high and fry chicken until tender, crisp, and brown, approximately 20 minutes. Turn after 10 minutes. Test for doneness with a fork.

Dot's Secret: Before you fry the chicken, throw some thickly sliced onion rings into the hot oil or shortening.

Flying Cloud Cafe $–$$
800 New Hampshire Avenue, Atlantic City
(609) 345–8222

The Flying Cloud overlooks Gardner's Basin; in fact, you can arrive by boat. If the weather is pleasant, sit on the deck; if not, head for the cool comfort inside. As you might imagine, seafood is the specialty, although you can't go wrong with the burger of the day. The fried soft-shell crab sandwich slides down nicely with a cold beer. Read your place mat to find out about the *Flying Cloud*, an 1851 ship that set a speed record that has never been broken by another sailing ship.

Gary's Little Rock Cafe $$$
5212 Atlantic Avenue, Ventnor
(609) 823–2233

When Gary's opened in this town south of Atlantic City, dishes like the tuna with wasabi had the red-sauce-sated natives swooning. The innovative American food is consistently excellent, keeping this little restaurant filled with happy diners. BYOB.

Girasole $$$
3108 Pacific Avenue (Ocean Club Condominium), Atlantic City
(609) 345–5554

At this nouvelle Italian place, the cooking centers on fresh ingredients, easy on the red sauce. Even if you're not a trend-surfer, you've gotta love the wood-burning pizza oven.

Karen & Rei's $$$, no credit cards
1882 U.S. Highway 9, Clermont
(609) 624–8205
www.karenandrei.com

Chef Karen Nelson presents food adventures for the bold and the timid, offering superb traditional dishes like rack of lamb and more exotic fare such as tandoori ostrich, a dish that might not work in less talented hands. It's Nelson's own version of fusion, a culinary melting pot that she likes to call "true American food." The restaurant has recently moved from Avalon, and though the room is more spacious, it still seats only about 40, so reservations are a must. The restaurant accepts reservations one month in advance, and gets booked up immediately, as in shortly after midnight on the first day of the month. BYOB.

Knife & Fork Inn $$$$
29 South Albany Avenue at Pacific, Atlantic City
(609) 344–1133

This landmark Tudor castle has been a familiar sight off the U.S. Highway 40/322 (Albany Avenue) circle since 1912. The continental cuisine is solid, leaning toward steak and seafood, with classic dishes like lobster thermidor.

Le Palais $$$$
Resorts Atlantic City
1133 Boardwalk at North Carolina, Atlantic City
(609) 340–6400
www.resortsac.com

When money is no object, Le Palais offers fine French food in a posh, romantic setting. The service is superior, and the total experience rates high with diners, even those that aren't comped.

Lobster Loft $$–$$$
318 42nd Place at the bay, Sea Isle City
(609) 263–3000

This low-key seafood house also has a nice variety of steak and pasta dishes, all of which go nicely with its wonderful water views.

Maureen $$$–$$$$
Atlantic Avenue at Schellenger, Wildwood
(609) 522–7747
www./restaurantmaureen.com

You can't miss the neon martini glass on Maureen's facade—it's a not-so-subtle hint to try one of the inventive cocktails. The chocolate martini has even teetotalers swooning. The food is no gimmick, though, starting with the crab fritters and moving on to entrees such as seafood risotto with white truffle oil, and Chilean sea bass Niçoise. The tuna napoleon is seared ahi layered with crispy wontons, avocado, ginger, and wasabi vinaigrette. Maureen is a snowbird, open from May through October.

Orsatti's $$$
22-24 South North Carolina Avenue, Atlantic City
(609) 347–7667

This old guard Southern Italian place seems to have changed little in 30-odd years. It specializes in local seafood as well as pasta and classic Italian favorites.

Peaches at Sunset $$$$
1 Sunset Boulevard, West Cape May
(609) 898–0100

In Baja Jersey, trendy Peaches pitches contemporary California-style nouvelle cuisine. Some find it a little too much, but for others, it's the best part of a trip to Cape May.

Martinis at Maureen in Wildwood offer an array of choices and flavors. PHOTO: LILLIAN AFRICANO

Pilot House $–$$
142 Decatur Street, Cape May
(609) 884–3449

When you get tired of fine wining and dining at the precious Victorian boîtes in Cape May, stroll into this nautical-themed pub, where they'll have the Phillies game on in the bar, and get yourself a cold brew. The food is pretty fair, especially if you stick to the basics—burgers, chicken, and the like. The fish is usually fresh, though preparation falls short of some of the gourmet spots in this town.

The Ram's Head Inn $$$$
9 White Horse Pike, Absecon
(609) 652–1700

Away from A.C.'s glitz, this classy country inn in Absecon, with its welcoming fireplaces, is a true retreat. Known for superb service as well as first-rate classic cuisine, the Ram's Head is a perennial favorite.

Renault Winery $$$$
72 North Bremen Avenue, Egg Harbor City
(609) 965–2111

The gourmet five-course meal and the romantic atmosphere at this 130-year-old winery make this the perfect place to bring a date. We love the blueberry champagne as an accompaniment to the outstanding Sunday brunch.

Sabatini's $$$
2210-2214 Pacific Avenue, Atlantic City
(609) 345–4816

Sabatini has been serving classic Italian food—veal francese, shrimp fra diavolo, steaks and chops—here for more than 30 years; he is also the man who defied the Donald. Trump wanted to raze the restaurant to expand the parking lot for the adjacent Trump Plaza, but Sabatini fought back and won. His restaurant is still open till all hours, serving bar food to the table-weary until 5:00 A.M.

Smithville Inn $$$
1 New York Road, Towne of Historic Smithville
(609) 652–7777

This traditional American restaurant is the place to unwind while visiting historic

Smithville's shops and attractions. To find out about the lore of the Smithville Inn, birthplace of the Jersey Devil, see the Close-up in the Attractions chapter.

Tre Figlio $$$$
500 West White Horse Pike, Egg Harbor City
(609) 965–3303

Tre Figlio may be a little off the beaten path, but diners who love fine Italian food have put this little ristorante on the map. So many dishes are excellent, including the huge veal chops, excellent seafood dishes, and lobster ravioli and other housemade pastas.

Washington Inn $$$$
801 Washington Street, Cape May
(609) 884–5697

Flower gardens surround this elegant 1840s plantation house, where the traditional American food and the service are both top-drawer. Select a bottle from the vast wine cellar; better yet, take a quick tour. Be sure to reserve.

Water's Edge $$$$
1317 Beach Drive, Cape May
(609) 884–1717

This beautiful waterfront locale has been called the hippest place to dine at the Shore. The cuisine is innovative American, leaning toward fusion, as seafood dishes may have an Oriental or even Caribbean accent. Gourmets say the food is worth the high prices.

The White House $, no credit cards
2301 Arctic Avenue at Mississippi, Atlantic City
(609) 345–1564

The White House attracts truckers and construction workers from hundreds of miles around, as well as movie stars and sports celebrities from all over the world, as evidenced by the hundreds of photos both recent and faded that cover the walls. The cheese-steak sandwich is what they come for: Smothered in mushrooms, onions, tomatoes, and hot peppers, it's well worth the agita. One of their flavor secrets is the freshly baked bread from several local bakeries, including Formica's across the street. Be warned: A whole sub is about a foot and a half long.

Nightlife

From smooth jazz to punk rock, stand-up comedy to all-night dance clubs, you'll find a good time to suit your taste in South Jersey. Atlantic City is of course known for the play at the casinos; we've covered those in a separate section. A.C. is also known for the large number of topless bars frequented by some of the gamblers who come to town; we have not included those, but they're not exactly hard to find.

In Cape May and elsewhere, you'll find some inns and restaurants may have jazz combos or acoustic guitar players to accompany dinner or nightcaps later on. The towns of Cape May County, including Ocean City and Wildwood, are very seasonal; if you're going in the off-season, call ahead to make sure places are open.

We've tried to include places in each of the towns along the Southern Shore, with the exception of Ocean City; thanks to its Methodist heritage, Ocean City is dry, and that legality seems to be quite an impediment in the nightclub business.

Beach Club Tavern Beachfront Bar
Hereford Inlet, North Wildwood
(609) 523–8886

With an outdoor deck and live music on weekends, the Beach Club Tavern is a wonderful spot to unwind and listen to the rhythm of the ocean waves.

Boardwalk Hall
2301 Boardwalk at Mississippi Avenue, Atlantic City
(609) 449–2000
www.accenter.com

Formerly known as Convention Hall (before the new convention center was built), this historic 1929 building has just undergone a $72-million renovation. It's now a 12,000-seat arena that hosts special events, like the Target Stars on Ice show. For event information, check local papers or the Web site listed above. This new arena will also be home to A.C.'s new minor league hockey team, the Boardwalk Bullies. For ticket information, call Ticketmaster (800) 736–1420 or (609) 348–PUCK, or go to www.boardwalkbullies.com.

Casba Comedy Club
Atlantic and Spicer Avenues, Wildwood
(609) 522–8444

Local stand-up comedians and the occasional national name keep 'em laughing at this club two blocks from Wildwood's Boardwalk.

Charlie's
800 Shore Road, Somers Point
(609) 653–9848

Famous for its chicken wings, Charlie's is located in an area of Somers Point known as the "Beer-muda Triangle," because of the high concentration of bars there.

Deja Vu
Boardwalk at New York Avenue, Atlantic City
(609) 348–4313

This fashionable dance club right on the Boardwalk is open all night.

Gene's Beach Bar
4410 Ocean Avenue at the beach, Brigantine
(609) 266–3555.

Gene's is a popular spot to unwind for locals and casino employees. (After a day at the tables, *they* have money in *their* pockets.)

Henny's Lounge Hangout
9628 Third Avenue, Stone Harbor
(609) 368–2929

In sedate Stone Harbor, Henny's caters to the over-30 crowd, featuring live oldies music on weekends.

Ike's Corner
Tennessee and Arctic Avenues, Atlantic City
(609) 345–7332.

Located in Midtown Atlantic City, Ike's Corner has live jazz on the weekends.

Longport Inn
31st Street and Atlantic Avenue, Longport
(609) 822–5435.

This restaurant/nightspot in upscale Longport has live music on weekends, mostly of the adult/contemporary variety.

Lighthouse Pointe Restaurant & Bar
5101 Shawcrest Road, Shawcrest Island, Wildwood
(609) 522–SHIP
www.522ship.com

Lighthouse Pointe is a full-service seafood restaurant that stays open late so folks can enjoy the water views (Sunset Lake) along with live music out on the deck.

McGuire's Erin Bar
42 South Tennessee Avenue, Atlantic City
(609) 345–9607

Open 24 hours, McGuire's is a true Irish bar, with Guinness and Harp on tap and performers from all over the world, including dear old Ireland.

The Oasis
3511 Pacific Avenue, Wildwood
(609) 729–2919

Parched from the summer's heat? Wet your whistle at the Oasis, a rock club that showcases local talent as well as acts that are nationally famous.

Pelican Club
Marquis de Lafayette Hotel
501 Beach Street, Cape May
(609) 884–3500
www.marquiscapemay.com

Enjoy splendid ocean views from this grand room at the top of the Marquis de Lafayette Hotel, along with live music nightly in season. On weekends, the sounds are provided by a swinging jazz trio.

Playpen Rock Club
Holly Beach Mall, Wildwood
(609) 729–0580

Check your local papers to see who's appearing at the Playpen. It hosts nationally known acts as well as local bands.

The Princeton
21st Street at Dune Drive, Avalon
(609) 967–3457

The Princeton is a huge dance club with several rooms; it features live rock as well as acoustic guitar.

Rock'n Chair Restaurant & Jazz Cafe
2409 Dune Drive, Avalon
(609) 967–3200

Promising "sophisticated entertainment for appreciative audiences," Rock'n Chair features music nightly—jazz, blues, R&B, reggae, calypso. The restaurant menu is equally diverse, offering Italian veal dishes, steaks and chops, Caribbean jerk chicken, and Asian-accented fish.

Springfield Inn
43rd Street and Pleasure Avenue, Sea Isle City
(609) 263-4951

If you want to recapture your youth, this is the place—it has its own outdoor carousel. There is live music in the bar on weekends.

The Stardust Rock Club
248 East Schellenger Avenue, Wildwood
(609) 522-8503

When you're in Wildwood for the weekend, and you want to get out and party, the Stardust is just one of the places to check out. It has live bands on the weekends.

Studio Six Video Dance Club
14 South Mount Vernon Avenue, Atlantic City
(609) 348-3310
www.studiosix.com

Opening at 10:00 P.M. and staying open until dawn or even later, Studio Six is Atlantic City's biggest after-hours dance club, with five bars and a fantastic sound system. Studio Six has grown from a neighborhood bar into a hugely popular gay hangout, one of the largest in the state. In fact, it's really a complete resort complex with a 50-room hotel, the Brass Rail tavern (open 24 hours), a grill, and a heated pool with a sundeck.

Tun Tavern Restaurant & Brewery
2 Ocean Way (Miss America Way), Atlantic City
(609) 347-7800
www.tuntavern.com

Located right across from the new Convention Center in the Sheraton Atlantic City Hotel, the Tun Tavern is A.C.'s first microbrewery. It serves up its own hand-crafted beers along with a full menu of steaks, shellfish, sandwiches, and bar snacks. It's a great place for casual hanging out and snacking.

Ugly Mug
426 Washington Street Mall, Cape May
(609) 884-3459

As you stroll Cape May's wonderful pedestrian mall, you may feel like stopping for a burger or a brew. This low-key hangout has live music on weekends.

Wildwood Nights
3400 Pacific Avenue, Wildwood
(609) 729-2296

If all of Wildwood's doo-wop architecture gets you in the mood to do the lindy, Wildwood Nights is the place. Show off your poodle skirt and your swing dance lessons to the tunes of the largest jukebox on the island. There's live music Wednesday through Saturday. And if things just aren't happening here, there are a number of other clubs nearby, right on Pacific Avenue, including Club H2O (877-996-2420) and Club Hill 16 (609-729-3900).

Casinos

Going to a show at a casino can be great fun, especially if you're able to secure tickets to see your favorite star, whether that might be Tony Bennett or Britney Spears. The atmosphere at a casino show is much more intimate than at a stadium or large theater, as the hall is usually set up with nightclub seating (with tables) in front and theater seating in the rear. You can order drinks, another plus, and many performers also enjoy the interaction with the smaller audience.

The variety of acts that appear on the casino stages never ceases to amaze, from Al Martino to Lynyrd Skynyrd to Earth, Wind, and Fire to Janet Jackson, not to mention the occasional boxing match. If you're planning a trip to A.C., check newspapers or Web sites ahead of time to see

At Bally's Wild, Wild West casino, gamblers try to rope the big one. PHOTO: COURTESY OF BALLY'S PARK PLACE CASINO RESORT

who's appearing. Don't wait until you get on the Atlantic City Causeway, where you'll see billboards advertising shows you may have just missed.

In addition to its main hall, each casino will have one or more small, more intimate lounge areas suitable for mood music, cabaret acts, or dancing.

Atlantic City Hilton
Boardwalk at Boston Avenue, Atlantic City
(609) 340–7160, (800) 843–4726
www.hiltonac.com

The Hilton Theater is the large hall for big-name acts, but you'll also find small combos playing live music in the Dizzy Dolphin.

Bally's Park Place
Boardwalk at Park Place, Atlantic City
(609) 340–2709, (800) 677–7469
www.ballysac.com

At the Park Cabaret, Bally's presents the long-running *Legends in Concert*, a show featuring a group of singers who look like and sing like big stars such as Liza Minnelli, Ray Charles, and of course, Elvis Presley. In keeping with the casino's theme, the Wild, Wild West Mountain Bar is this joint's saloon, where you might expect a player piano, but in fact, there is live music on weekends. There is also live music, often a harpist, for Sunday Brunch at Prime Place.

Caesars
2100 Pacific Avenue, Atlantic City
(609) 348–4411, (800) 677–SHOW
www.caesars.com

The Circus Maximus is Caesars venue for spectacles like Wayne Newton's Christmas Show. If you come to the Gladiator Sports Bar looking for Russell Crowe, you're sure to be disappointed; but you will find live music on Fridays and Saturdays here and at the Forum Lounge.

The Temple Lobby at Caesars greets guests in Roman splendor. PHOTO: COURTESY OF CAESARS ATLANTIC CITY

Claridge
Boardwalk at Indiana Avenue, Atlantic City
(609) 340–3700, (800) 752–7469
www.claridge.com

The Claridge is the oldest hotel on the Boardwalk, the only one that pre-dates the casino era, and so it is much smaller than the others, with only one hall, the Palace Theater.

Harrah's
777 Harrah's Boulevard, Atlantic City
(609) 441–5165, (800) 242–7724
www.harrahs.com

Headline shows fill the Broadway by the Bay Theatre. There is live music in the Atrium Lounge Thursday through Sunday, and a piano player at the Steak House restaurant.

Resorts
1133 Boardwalk at North Carolina Avenue, Atlantic City
(609) 340–6830, (888) 771–1786, (800) 322–SHOW
www.resortsac.com

At Resorts' Superstar Theater, you'll see super stars like Regis Philbin, and in the Near Canopy Lounge, you'll hear Pinky's Corner, a news/talk radio program broadcast from 4:00 to 6:00 P.M. weekdays.

Sands
South Indiana Avenue and Brighton Park, Atlantic City
(609) 441–4137, (800) AC–SANDS
www.acsands.com

At the Copa Room, you might catch a swing-era singer like Keely Smith, or you might see a pro wrestling show. At the Copa Lounge, there's live music Wednesday through Saturday, often a pianist.

Showboat
Boardwalk at Delaware Avenue, Atlantic City
(609) 343–4000, (800) 621–0200
www.harrahs.com

The New Orleans Square Bandstand is the Showboat's large entertainment venue. At Champagne Charlie's, there's live music on the weekends.

Tropicana
Boardwalk at Brighton Avenue, Atlantic City
(609) 340–4020, (800) 526–2935
www.tropicana.net
www.thecomedystop.com

You'll find headline entertainment at the Tropicana Showroom, live music every night at the Tiffany Lounge, and live music every night except Monday and Tuesday at Top of the Trop. The Green Room is a multiuse space that sometimes hosts art exhibits. The Comedy Stop has a show every night, two shows on Fridays and Saturdays, often nationally known talent. Check their Web site, above, for schedules.

Trump Marina
One Castle Boulevard, Atlantic City
(609) 441–8300, (877) 4R SHOWS, (800) 777–8477
www.trumpmarina.com

> ## Insiders' Tip
> As many tickets are given away to the casino's preferred customers (i.e. high rollers), big-name shows can get sold out quickly. However, a few tickets may become available shortly before show time, as some of these "comps" will be "no shows."

Trump Marina has two halls in which headline acts perform, the Shell Showroom and the Grand Cayman. The Wave Nightclub has a DJ on Saturday night.

Trump Plaza
Boardwalk at Mississippi Avenue, Atlantic City
(800) 759–8786
www.trumpplaza.com

With three casinos in Atlantic City, Trump does not need to duplicate facilities, and so Trump Plaza just has the low-key Terrace Lounge, where combos play on Saturday night.

Trump Taj Mahal
1000 Boardwalk at Virginia Avenue, Atlantic City
(609) 449–1000, (800) 736–1420
www.trumptaj.com

In addition to Xanadu, the Taj's big stage, you can go to the Casbah on Fridays and Saturdays, and to the Hard Rock Cafe (609-441-0007), which has live bands, both local and national, on Tuesdays.

Shopping

The hours of operation for stores, like the schedules for restaurants and hotels, vary according to the season in many towns on the Southern Shore. Many, if not most, of the shops in Stone Harbor and Avalon are extremely seasonal. As we discussed hours with store owners, we were frankly flummoxed at the prospect of conveying them to you. That's because, in essence, store hours in this area are weather-dependent. What we can offer are some generalities. During the summer months, stores generally are open seven days a week, from 10:00 A.M. until 10:00 or 11:00 P.M. They either close completely during the winter months (except for the Christmas holiday season) or operate on a limited schedule. The hours increase around the Easter season—or sooner if the weather has been unusually warm. Given these variations, it's always best to call ahead. We've noted the stores that are open year-round and have regular hours.

A similar situation applies to many boardwalk stores, except in Atlantic City, where a steady, year-round stream of customers keeps them open. As for Cape May, keep in mind that "seasonal" here generally means reduced hours after Labor Day, since there are visitors year-round. Again, it's best to call ahead.

Antiques and Art

If antiques and collectibles are your passion, plan to spend time exploring the many shops in the Cape May area. We've listed a few to get you started.

Acquisitions at Congress Hall
251 Beach Drive, Cape May
(609) 884–0006

At this charming emporium, which carries both American and European antiques, you'll find furniture, art, and garden sculpture reproductions.

Aleathea's Parlor Antiques and Things
Beach Drive and Ocean Street, Cape May
(609) 884–5555

Aleathea's is one of Cape May's many attractive dining spots, but even if you don't visit the restaurant, you might want to peek into the antiques shop and look at the cut glass and gift items. The shop is seasonal, open daily spring through October from 9:00 A.M. to 10:00 P.M.

Antique Doorknob
600 Park Boulevard, Cape May
(609) 884–6282

If you need a period doorknob for your Victorian home, or perhaps an old fireplace mantle, have a look here. They also carry original lighting fixtures. During the summer season, the shop is open six days a week (closed Wednesday) from 10:30 A.M. to 4:30 P.M.; in the off-season, it's open Thursday through Monday (same hours), and Sunday from 11:00 A.M. to 4:00 P.M.

Bayside Basin Antiques
800 North New Hampshire Avenue, Atlantic City
(609) 347–7143

This establishment is open by appointment only, which is not conducive to recreational browsing, but if you're in the market for American Indian artifacts, fine art, or Oriental rugs, make the call.

Belrose Galleries
1505 Boardwalk, Atlantic City
(609) 345–2279

Many Boardwalk shops sell cheap souvenir items, but not this one. Belrose Galleries specializes in fine art, bronze sculpture, European furniture, porcelains, and other collectibles. You'll also find a selection of jewelry, both contemporary and antique estate pieces. The galleries are open daily from 10:30 A.M. to 5:30 P.M., with slightly longer weekend hours in summer.

Cape Island
609 Jefferson Street, Cape May
(609) 884–6028

Do you need a Victorian bed? A marble-top table? Or perhaps some vintage glassware? Try this shop. During the off-season, it's open Saturday and Sunday from 10:00 A.M. to 5:00 P.M.; from Easter weekend through Labor Day, it's open Friday through Monday.

Princeton Antiques
2917 Atlantic Avenue, Atlantic City
(609) 344–1943, (800) 253–6863
www.princetonantiques.com

Shop Cape May

In Victorian Cape May, you don't have drive to a huge mall complex to window-shop, just rely on old-fashioned foot power. The Washington Street Mall is a pedestrian street lined with restaurants and stores, including a Christmas store, a toy shop, a gift shop, candy shops (see "Delectable Edibles" section), and ice-cream parlors, all important when you've got kids in tow. To give the kids a treat, turn them loose in the Toy Shop at 510 Washington Mall (609–884–0442). They'll be delighted with the wonderful array of possibilities: giant bubble wands, beach toys, science kits—and even the classics like jacks and kites.

Talk about eclectic! This Atlantic City institution—it's been around for four generations—has five shops full of antique everything: silver, pottery, Oriental rugs, bronzes, old and rare books, and on and on. But even if you're not in the market for anything, you will surely appreciate the vast collection of Atlantic City memorabilia, including more than 20,000 images of the old Steel Pier, the Diving Horse, the older boardwalks—just about everything your parents or grandparents might remember from their trips to A.C. Shop online if you prefer, or visit Monday through Friday from 8:30 A.M. to 5:00 P.M., and Saturday from 8:00 A.M. to 1:00 P.M.

Sea Life Galleries
2900 Dune Drive, Avalon
(609) 368–7300
www.wylandsealifegallery.com

If you've been to the Wildwood Boardwalk, you've probably seen the "Whaling Wall" mural painted by noted environmental artist, Wyland. If you liked the mural and would like to see more of his work, you'll find paintings as well as bronzes at this gallery.

Seascape Antiques/Cobweb Corner
Sixth Avenue and White Horse Pike, Absecon Highlands
(609) 748–2522

This estate liquidation warehouse is one of those "you never know what you'll find" places. Browse amid pieces of high-quality used furniture, interesting architectural artifacts, and Atlantic City memorabilia, and you might come across something you can't do without. The hours are from 10:00 A.M. to 5:00 P.M. Monday through Saturday, and from 11:00 A.M. to 5:00 P.M. on Sunday.

Tabby House
479 Perry Street, West Cape May
(609) 898–0908

This shop specializes in authentic 18th- and 19th-century country furniture and home accessories. It also has a garden shop featuring reproductions; you'll find sundials, water pumps, cast-iron tables and chairs, and whatever else you might need to make your garden inviting. Warm-weather hours are from 10:00 A.M. to 5:00 P.M. daily except Wednesday; winter hours are from 10:00 A.M. to 5:00 P.M. Friday through Monday.

Tallman House Gifts & Antiques
636 Shore Road, Somers Point
(609) 927–8130

Located in a picturesque Victorian home, this shop specializes in antiques, small reproduction furniture, paintings and framed prints, and gifts. It is open in September, December, and April only for warehouse sales that offer markdowns of 40 percent or more.

W.S. Antiques
405 Perry Street, West Cape May
(609) 898-3636

Located in the old Rocking Horse building, this establishment has goods from some 60 dealers on display, which makes it a good place to hunt for that elusive doodad or quirky gift. You'll see vintage toys, old trains, weather vanes, out-of-print books, collectible photographs, paintings—well, you get the idea. If you need even more inventory, check out the other two locations, one on Sunset Boulevard, the another on U.S. Highway 9. The hours are Monday through Friday from 10:00 A.M. to 4:00 P.M., and on weekends from 11:00 A.M. to 5:00 P.M.

Yesterday's Past Antique Co-op
6773 Harding Highway, U.S. Highway 40,
Mays Landing
(609) 625-9244

Imagine an old-time general store packed with collectibles and antiques, and you have a pretty good picture of Yesterday's Past, a co-op of more than 30 dealers. Among their wares: "shabby chic" stuff, casino memorabilia, vintage crockery, primitives, and furniture.

Books

Atlantic Books
261 96th Street, Stone Harbor
(609) 368-4393

If you enjoy rummaging through bargain books, this shop will oblige with a big selection of publisher overstocks and remainders. But if you want the latest best-sellers, they have those, too, both hardcover and paperback, along with books of local interest. The shop is open year-round, but is open only on weekends with limited hours during the winter, so call ahead.

The Bookateria Two
1052 Asbury Avenue, Ocean City
(609) 398-0121

Come in with 10 bucks and some unwanted paperbacks to trade, and you'll walk out with a summer's worth of reading. There are more than 25,000 paperbacks to choose from; you can buy them outright or get a percentage off with trades. If you require new paperbacks, you'll get a 15-percent discount. Books-on-tape are available, too. During the summer, the store is open Monday through Saturday from 9:00 A.M. to 8:00 P.M., and Sunday from 10:00 A.M. to 2:00 P.M. The rest of the year, it's open Tuesday through Saturday from 10:00 A.M. to 5:00 P.M.

Gravelly Run Antiquarians
5045 Mays Landing–Somers Point Road,
Mays Landing
(609) 476-4444

Used books—our favorite kind—are what you'll find here. At this full-service shop, you can search the inventory of 20,000 used, out-of-print, and rare volumes. There are first editions, books on New Jersey, nautical books, children's books, and antiquarian books. There's also a collection of prints, maps, and photographs. The store is open from 9:00 A.M. to 5:00 P.M. almost every day. Call ahead. P.S. The shop's name comes from a small creek that feeds the Great Egg Harbor River.

Clothing and Accessories

Barrie Shoes
9501 Third Avenue, Stone Harbor
(609) 368-2822

You'll find brand-name shoes, all first quality, for men, women, and children at outlet prices here. Labels include Rockport, Top Sider, Tretorn, Etienne Aigner, and Hush Puppies. They also carry hard-to-fit sizes. The store is open year-round, Monday through Saturday from 10:00 A.M. to 5:00 P.M., and Sunday from 11:00 A.M. to 4:00 P.M.

Blue Moon Surf Wear
3011 Dune Drive, Avalon
(609) 368-3452

If anyone in your family forgot to pack a bathing suit, find a spare here—for Mom, Dad, or the kids. The store is open Monday through Saturday from 10:00 A.M. to 5:00 P.M. (open longer hours and on Sunday in summer).

The Happy Hunt
9720 Third Avenue, Stone Harbor
(609) 368–5734

Stone Harbor isn't exactly hunt country, but if you like horsey themes, you'll find them here, in clothing and accessories and embroidered gifts. The shop is open daily from 10:00 A.M. to 5:00 P.M. (longer hours in summer). During the coldest winter months, the hours are 10:00 A.M. to 5:00 P.M. on weekends only.

The Irish Pavilion
9825 Third Avenue, Stone Harbor
(609) 368–1112

As the name implies, the shop carries imports from Ireland: hand-knit sweaters, crafts, jewelry, and even wedding bands. The store keeps typical Stone Harbor hours: from 10:00 A.M. to 10:00 P.M. during the summer, and during the winter, it may close for a while and then open on weekends, from 10:00 A.M. to 5:00 P.M. on Saturday and from 11:00 A.M. to 4:00 P.M. on Sunday.

Just For Kids
810 Asbury Avenue, Ocean City
(609) 399–8789)

Need a christening dress? Or just some casual duds that the kids can romp around in this summer? This shop has clothes for kids from the cradle to age 12. They also carry sample sizes up to 10-12, with prices that appeal. The store is open year-round, from 10:00 A.M. to 5:00 P.M.

Monday through Saturday, and from noon to 4:00 P.M. on Sunday. The hours are extended during the summer.

Lace Silhouettes Lingerie
9504 Third Avenue, Stone Harbor
(609) 368–1259

Since you can't spend the entire summer in a bathing suit, we thought we'd mention this place, which sells pretty sleepwear and lingerie. It's open from 10:00 A.M. to 10:00 P.M. in summer and closes in the coldest winter months.

Looie's
9405 Ventnor Avenue, Margate
(609) 823–6643

Look here for designer swimsuits bearing labels like Calvin Klein and Karla Coletto, as well as beach bags, hats, and other necessities.

Pappagallo
744 Asbury Avenue, Ocean City
(609) 398–4009
237 96th Street, Stone Harbor
(609) 368–6141

Get your designer fix without going to the mall; shop for clothing and shoes by Ralph Lauren, Calvin Klein, David Brooks, and other luminaries. The Ocean City store closes during the winter, but the Stone Harbor shop opens on winter weekends from 10:00 A.M. to 5:00 P.M.

Stubbs' Dress Shoppe
741 Asbury Avenue, Ocean City
(609) 399–1169

A family-owned shop that's been around since 1934, Stubbs' sells versatile sportswear, dresses, and formals for weddings and special occasions. The store is open from 10:00 A.M. to 5:00 P.M. Monday through Saturday.

Consignment Shops

Again . . . on Asbury
921 Asbury Avenue, Ocean City
(609) 398–0340

Consignment stores specializing in good home furnishings are rare, but here's a place where you could get lucky. The shop is chock-full of furniture and accessories—antique to modern—at affordable prices. The store is open daily from 10:00 A.M. to 5:00 P.M. and some evenings by appointment. Call ahead.

A Second Look Consignments
3848 Bayshore Road, North Cape May
(609) 889–1555
Brides on a budget could get lucky here; most gowns, after all, are worn only once, and the savings on an almost-new one can run into the hundreds.

Delectable Edibles

You'll notice that in this section, we delve deeply into the pleasures of the sweet tooth. Consider, after all, that these are all beachfront communities, many with boardwalks; and where you have boardwalks, you have kids; and where you have kids, you have candy.

Formica Bake Shop
2310 Arctic Avenue, Atlantic City
(609) 344–8723
Ask locals where to buy bread and they'll tell you: Formica's. This award-winning family-owned bakery has been around since 1916, and every single day the little shop turns out some 15,000 loaves and rolls. Many are purchased by the famous White House sub shop across the street for their delectable sandwiches (see "Restaurants" section). You can also get cookies, biscotti, and other Italian treats here. The bakery is open every day from 8:00 A.M. to 6:00 P.M.

Fralinger's Saltwater Taffy
Bally's Park Place, Atlantic City
(609) 344–0442
Tennessee Avenue and Boardwalk, Atlantic City
(609) 344–0758
11th Street and Boardwalk, Ocean City
(609) 399–2202
Washington Street Mall, Cape May
(609) 884–5695
In 1885 Joseph Fralinger set up shop on the Atlantic City Boardwalk; now his taffy

not only comes in many flavors, but it's also available chocolate-covered and with filled centers. The shops also sell all kinds of other boardwalk treats, including fudge, chocolates, and nuts. The Atlantic City stores open at 9:00 A.M.; during the summer season, they stay open till midnight, in winter, until 4:30 P.M. The Ocean City store opens daily and stays open late in summer; it closes for the winter. The Cape May shop is open from 9:00 A.M. to 10:00 or 11:00 P.M. in season, on Saturday and Sunday from 10:00 A.M. to 5:00 P.M. in winter. Call ahead. (For more on the history of saltwater taffy, see the Close-up in the Attractions chapter.)

James' Candy
1519 Boardwalk, Atlantic City
(609) 344–1519
255 96th Street, Stone Harbor
(609) 368–0505
340 Oak Avenue, Wildwood
(609) 729–3318
www.jamescandy.com
The James' Candy Company has been making all kinds of saltwater taffy since the 1880s; in addition to the traditional variety, you can get filled taffy and taffy pops, as well as fudge, chocolates, and macaroons. Call ahead for hours, as they vary according to season. James also has a second Atlantic City location, a stand inside the Tropicana. The Stone Harbor and Wildwood stores close for the winter, but you can shop online anytime.

Johnson's Popcorn
1360 Boardwalk, Ocean City
(609) 398–5404
660 Boardwalk, Ocean City
(609) 398–5444
828 Boardwalk, Ocean City
(609) 398–4484
www.johnsonspopcorn.com
We buy this addictive stuff at the supermarket when we can find it. But we swear it tastes better when you buy it fresh on the Boardwalk—or is it the fragrance of warm caramel poured over popcorn that draws us? Johnson's has been around these parts since 1940; now they have three shops, open year-round, seven days a week. Call for hours.

Kohler's Bakery
2709 Dune Drive, Avalon
(609) 967–3694
www.kohlersbakery.com

Philadelphia-style sticky buns have been the specialty here for half a century: sweet buns hand-rolled and swirled with sugar—and garnished with roasted cashews, if you please. Kohler's also does coconut macaroons, Irish soda bread, and traditional German stollen. The store is seasonal, but you can shop online.

Laura's Fudge
357 East Wildwood Avenue, Wildwood
(609) 729–1555
2006 Boardwalk, North Wildwood
(609) 522–1992
11th Street and Boardwalk, Ocean City
(609) 399–4434
34th and West Streets, Ocean City
(609) 398–5293
311 Washington Street, Cape May
(609) 884–1777
www.laurasfudgeshop.com

In addition to fudge and saltwater taffy, you can buy sugar-free and salt-free candy as well as such popular items as cordial cherries, almond butter crunch, and chocolate-covered pretzels. During the warmer months, the stores are open from 10:00 A.M. (9:00 A.M. in Wildwood) to midnight. The Wildwood store remains open year-round, except for a few weeks in January; winter hours are from 10:00 A.M. to 4:00 P.M. on weekends.

Mallon's Homemade Sticky Buns
2888 Dune Drive, Avalon
(609) 967–5400
5010 Landis Avenue, Sea Isle City
(609) 263–1280
1340 Bay Avenue, Ocean City
(609) 399–5531

What you will find here are sticky buns, those tasty pastries permeated with cinnamon and laden with raisins and nuts. They are the perfect breakfast or anytime treat, but only in season.

Springer's Homemade Ice Cream
9420 Third Avenue, Stone Harbor
(609) 368–4631

The folks at this family-run spot dip some of the best ice cream around: There are 65 homemade flavors, including a lovely mint chocolate chip. Though there are lines around the block on a balmy summer night, this, too, alas, is a seasonal spot, closing right after Labor Day.

Steel's Fudge
2719 Boardwalk, Atlantic City
(609) 345–4051
1633 Boardwalk, Atlantic City
(609) 449–1633
1000 Boardwalk, Ocean City
(609) 398–2383
www.steelsgourmet.com

Steel's Fudge is the oldest continuously family-operated and -owned fudge company in the world. In addition to delicious fudge, it's known for it's sugar-free goodies, the kind that diabetics and others on sugar-restricted diets have yearned to sample. You'll also find taffy, cookies, rich sauces, jams, pie fillings, and other delights. The stores are seasonal, so call ahead.

Tastykake Thrift Outlet
Cardiff Plaza
6701 Black Horse Pike, Egg Harbor
(609) 383–1637
www.tastykake.com

Penny-pinching sugar junkies, take heart. Here, you'll find Tastykake cupcakes, Krimpets, Kandykakes, and more at 40 to 75 percent off the regular prices. The outlet is open weekdays from 9:00 A.M. to 6:00 P.M., and Saturday from 9:00 A.M. to 5:00 P.M.

Home

Inspiration Gallery
231 96th Street, Stone Harbor
(609) 368–5399

If you can't get to Wheaton Village, drop into this satellite shop and admire the handcrafted glass and pottery. (It carries jewelry and clothing as well.) Warm-weather hours are from 10:00 A.M. to 10:00 P.M.; it's open weekends only during the winter (call ahead for hours).

Trendz Home
215 96th Street, Stone Harbor
(609) 368-4243

If you can't bear to sleep on department-store linens, if you demand those exquisite Frette sheets, this shop will oblige. You'll also find the softest, plushest towels for your bath. During the warmer months, the shop starts the day at 10:00 A.M. and stays open until fairly late (call ahead). During the winter, shop on Saturday and Sunday from 10:30 A.M. to 4:30 P.M. or by appointment.

Jewelry

Artisans Alcove Estate Jewelers
523 Lafayette Street, Cape May
(609) 898-0202
www.artisansalcove.com

Do you love estate jewelry? Beware, then, for you could easily spend hours ogling the vintage watches, cameos, rings, and Victorian treasures. The shop specializes in vintage engagement rings, so if there's a wedding in your future, find a ring here that you're not likely to see on anyone else. You can also buy hand-engraved Hawaiian heirloom jewelry and Australian opals. The store is open daily from 10:00 A.M. to 5:00 P.M. (closed three weeks in January).

OXOXO Gallery
9727 Third Avenue, Stone Harbor
(609) 368-2100

The jewelry displayed here is wearable art, contemporary and nontraditional. The sculpted objects to adorn your home are also extraordinary. The gallery is open May through September from 11:00 A.M. to 10:00 P.M.

Malls

Consumer Square Mall
2300 Wrangleboro Road, Mays Landing
(609) 645-8555

Target is one of the big attractions of this mall, along with B.J.'s discount club, Kohl's, and popular chains like Old Navy. Most of the mall stores are open from

Insiders' Tip

There are lots of specialty shops on Stone Harbor's 96th Street and the streets feeding into it. Most are open during the warmer months and again during the Christmas holiday season; some have limited hours beginning Easter weekend.

10:00 A.M. to 9:00 P.M. during the week, from 10:00 A.M. to 8:00 P.M. on Saturday, and from 11:00 A.M. to 5:00 P.M. on Sunday.

Hamilton Mall
4403 Black Horse Pike, Mays Landing
(609) 646-8326
www.shophamilton.com

This indoor mall is anchored by Macy's, JCPenney, and Sears; it also houses 140 specialty shops and several restaurants. It's open Monday through Saturday from 10:00 A.M. to 9:30 P.M., and Sunday from 11:00 A.M. to 6:00 P.M.

The Shops on Ocean One
1 Atlantic Ocean, Atlantic City
(609) 347-8082
www.oceanonemall.com

This Boardwalk mall looks like an ocean liner; it juts out into the Atlantic and is home to more than 100 shops. You'll find candy stores, a sports collectible store, clothiers, souvenir shops, and just about anything you might wish to buy when you're not playing the slot machines or enjoying the beach. During the summer, the mall opens early and closes late. During the off-season, it's best to call ahead, but in general the daily hours are from 11:00 A.M. to 7:00 or 8:00 P.M.

Shore Mall
Black Horse Pike and Tilton Road, Egg

Harbor Township
(609) 484–9500
www.shoremallshopping.com

This is a typical Shore mall, with more than 70 stores and specialty shops, including the popular Boscov's, Value City, and Circuit City. For après-shopping, you'll find restaurants and a 14-screen movie house. The mall is open Monday through Saturday from 10:00 A.M. to 9:30 P.M., and Sunday from 11:00 A.M. to 5:00 P.M.

The Great Outdoors

Heritage Surf Shops
744 West Avenue, Ocean City
(609) 398–6390
3700 Landis Avenue, Sea Isle City
(609) 263–3033
9223 Ventnor Avenue, Margate
(609) 823–3331
www.heritagesurf.com

The first Heritage Surf Shop (in Sea Isle) opened more than 35 years ago. With outstanding customer service, Heritage grew times three. All three stores sell and rent surfboards (snowboards, too) and all the necessary surf gear and apparel. In summer, they offer surfing lessons. The shops operate year-round. Ocean City is open from 10:00 A.M. to 8:00 P.M. Monday through Saturday, and from 10:00 A.M. to 6:00 P.M. on Sunday. The Sea Isle and Margate shops are open Monday through Thursday from 10:00 A.M. to 6:00 P.M., Friday and Saturday from 10:00 A.M. to 8:00 P.M., and Sunday from 10:00 A.M. to 5 P.M.

Seaview Marriott Golf Shop
Seaview Marriott Resort
401 South New York Road (U.S. Highway 9), Absecon
(609) 748–7680, (800) 932–8000
www.seaviewgolf.com

Year after year, Seaview Marriott wins awards for its pro shop, one of the best in the nation. In addition to a fine selection of men's and women's equipment, Seaview showcases extraordinary custom golf bags and Italian leather golf shoes so elegant (and expensive) you can hardly imagine wearing them into a sand trap. You can also select a fine cigar, a necktie, or just make a tee time. The shop is open from 8:00 A.M. to 6:00 P.M., with longer hours in the summer.

Wild Bird Crossing
U.S. Highway 9, Seaville
(609) 624–9444
www.avianyard.com

Birders on their way to Cape May can pick up anything they might need for the expedition (binoculars, bird books) or perhaps something for the backyard birds, such as fountains, feeders, birdhouses, or seed. The shop is open weekdays (except Tuesday) and Saturday from 10:00 A.M. to 6:00 P.M., and from 10:00 A.M. to 4:00 P.M. on Sunday.

This and That

Adele's Jeweled Treasures
1814 Bayshore Road, Lower Township
(609) 886–6563
www.jeweledtreasures.com

It's difficult to classify this unique shop because it sells so many different kinds of things, both old and new, from loose gemstones to estate jewelry to dolls to clocks. When you walk in, you don't know whether you'll walk out with a gently

> ### Insiders' Tip
> If you're a first-time Atlantic City visitor, you may not know about the shops in the casino hotels. They sell just about everything you'd need for a Shore getaway—sportswear, bathing gear, and so on—as well as a lot of luxury items (like high-end jewelry) to tempt the gambler who's been lucky.

worn gown or a diamond ring. Some of the goods are on consignment. If you have something you'd like to trade for an interesting piece of jewelry, bring it in. Call for hours.

Crabtree & Evelyn
9712 Third Avenue, Stone Harbor
(609) 368–6548

The stores in this chain smell so good, it's hard to leave without picking something up, whether it's a bath product, a fragrance, or a hostess gift for that nice someone who's putting you up for the weekend. We'll say it again; the hours are seasonal.

Hoy's 5 & 10
732 Asbury Avenue, Ocean City
(609) 398–HOYS
301 34th Street, Ocean City
(609) 398–6244
2808 Dune Drive, Avalon
(609) 967–7271
219 96th Street, Stone Harbor
(609) 368–4697

Old-fashioned five-and-dime stores like Hoy's are an endangered species, which is why we like to patronize them whenever possible. And it isn't simply an act of charity; they carry so many different kinds of things—from notions to toys to housewares—that you might actually save time shopping here. The stores are open daily from 9:00 A.M. to 5:00 P.M.; closing times are later during the summer.

Junke & Treasures
3248 Dune Drive, Avalon
(609) 967–4700

You have to love a store than includes both "junke" and "treasures" in its name. You'll find some of each among the antiques and collectibles and second-time-around clothes. Call for hours.

Paisley Christmas
9512 Third Avenue, Stone Harbor
(609) 368–7873

If you like to buy Christmas decorations as souvenirs, you'll find some here with a seashore flavor. When the snow is falling, they'll remind you of all the fun you had on your summer vacation.

Surf Sundries
1306 West Brigantine Avenue, Brigantine
(609) 266–1435

Whatever you forgot to bring on your Shore holiday, you can pick up here: an extra swimsuit, T-shirt, hat, sunglasses, a raft, and assorted toys.

Veronica's Kloset
3735 Ocean Drive, Avalon
(609) 967–5179

Here's an inviting shop for browsers; among other things, it carries interesting antiques, collectibles, and handcrafted dolls and toys. The store is open year-round Monday through Friday from 10:00 A.M. to 5:00 P.M.

The Village Green
Towne of Historic Smithville
U.S. Highway 9 and Moss Mill Road, Smithville
(609) 748–6160
www.smithvillenj.com

Home to the historic Smithville Inn, this restored colonial village is just 12 miles from Atlantic City, and it's a complete change of pace from the casino culture. Stroll along the cobblestone paths, check out the 21 specialty shops and restaurants, and shop for crafts, candles, all kinds of handmade items, wine, bakery goods, and dozens of other things you won't find in the chain stores. There's also a resale shop with small-town prices. When you're finished you can enjoy a bite to eat at the inn or ride the carousel. The Village Green shops are open every day from 11:00 A.M. to 6:00 P.M. For more on Smithville, see the Attractions chapter.

Relocation

It's official: the latest census shows New Jersey to be rich, smart, and diverse, with the highest per-capita income in the United States, moving up from third in 1990.

The estimated median income was $54,226; in other words, half of the state's households earned more and half earned less. It's estimated that New Jerseyans earn a combined $184.4 billion in a year. New Jersey ranks fifth among the states in terms of the number of adults who have a bachelor's degree or higher, with one out of three New Jerseyans holding a college degree.

What does all of this prosperity mean? Well, one thing it means is that rents and real estate prices are high: The estimated median rent is $763, third highest in the nation, and the median value of an owner-occupied home is $171,988, fourth highest in the nation. In the desirable Shore areas the figures are often considerably higher.

In Monmouth County, for example, even modest ranch homes in posh towns like Deal, Allenhurst, or Spring Lake can easily cost half a million dollars. As one might guess, prices for oceanfront property and houses close to the beach can be through the roof, so to speak.

Even as the stock market slid, home prices in Monmouth and Ocean shot up, by over 20 percent in 2001. Local agents attributed the rise to the steady demand and the diminished inventory. In these counties, undeveloped land in the desirable coastal areas is extremely scarce, and getting harder to find even farther inland, which pushes up prices for new homes. In Monmouth County, the median price for a new home is $348,916, and in Ocean, it's $229,334.

It shouldn't come as a surprise, then, that *Money* magazine recently rated the Shore, specifically Monmouth and Ocean Counties, number three (out of 300 communities) in its list of best places to live.

Monmouth County Profile

In 2000, the population of Monmouth County was 615,301 (the state's total population was 8,414,350), making it the Shore's most populous county. Monmouth's economic health earned it a Triple A rating from Moody's and Fitch. Growth in the previous 10 years was 11.2 percent, as compared with the state's growth of 8.6 percent. Home ownership is high here, 74.6 percent. Median household income is also high, $57,985.

With some towns settled as early as the 1600s, Monmouth County is steeped in history. It is also rich in natural resources, with miles of sandy beaches, a rolling countryside, and even deep forests; its parks encompass 11,340 acres of open space. It has a lively business community and, to the west, a thriving agricultural industry, as well as "horse country."

Its proximity to New York City (about 47 miles at the northern end) and the good rail, bus, and ferry connections make it a popular home for people who commute into Manhattan. Its location in the center of the state makes it a good choice for people who commute or travel frequently "up North" as well. Monmouth is also located on the Boston-to-Washington corridor.

As Monmouth encompasses 53 municipalities, the range in median home prices is broad, anywhere from $100,000 to $450,000. The property tax rate ranges from a low of $1.02 per hundred in Deal to a high of over $4.00 per hundred in Asbury Park and Highlands.

New Jersey has the 12th-highest median rent among the 50 states, and this, too, is reflected here. If you want a one-bedroom apartment in an oceanfront high-rise in Long Branch, you'll pay between $1,000 and $1,200 per month, and much more if you rent for the summer season only. Farther inland, you might find a one-bedroom for about $600 a month.

Ocean County Profile

According to the 2000 census, Ocean County's population is 510,916, up 17.9 percent from 1990, making it the fastest-growing Shore county, as it has been since the 1960s. The reason for this continued growth is that house and land prices here are generally lower than they are in Monmouth or Cape May Counties, with the exception of the upscale towns on the Barnegat Peninsula and on Long Beach Island, where spectacular oceanfront homes command spectacular prices.

Many of the new residents are senior citizens. Ocean County has the greatest concentration of retirement communities in the Northeast and one of the largest senior populations in the United States. Many of these adult communities are quite new, and more are being built every year. These developments help explain the county's home ownership rate of 83.2 percent, the Shore's highest.

Ocean County has much to recommend it: an eastern shore with some 40-odd miles of ocean beaches, and twice that on the bay shores. The coast intricacies provide plenty of nooks in which boats can be berthed, offering boaters and fishers recreational pleasures galore. On the mainland, you'll find the Pinelands, majestic and mysterious, dotted with lakes and marshes, teeming with wildlife, and crisscrossed with lagoons and streams.

Atlantic County Profile

In Atlantic County, the population in 2000 was 252,552, reflecting a growth of 12.6 percent from 1990. Home ownership here was 66.4 percent that year, with a median household income less than $38,124, lower than its neighbors to the north and south.

Home prices in Atlantic County run from under $100,000 well into the millions. You'll see splendid oceanfront homes costing $3 and $4 million in Longport, up to $2 million in Margate, and $1 million in Brigantine. And at the other end, you can buy a home in Atlantic City for well under $50,000. This reflects the fact that while the casino industry is the county's biggest employer, and while there has been rehabilitation of Atlantic City's neighborhoods and thoroughfares, much still needs to be done to make Atlantic City a vibrant, thriving city.

Cape May County Profile

Located at the very tip of New Jersey and bordered by the Atlantic Ocean and Delaware Bay, the Jersey Cape is a wonderful place to vacation and a somewhat quiet place to live during the winter months. But those who live here like it that way.

The county population in 2000 was 102,326, a rise of 7.6 percent from 1990 and less than the state average of 8.6. Of course, that's the year-round population. The summer population is estimated at 10 times that figure.

Home ownership is at 74.2 percent (compared with the statewide average of 65.6 percent). Cape May has the lowest minority population of the Shore counties; the white population is 91.6 percent, considerably higher than the statewide average of 72.6 percent.

The prices of homes for sale in the county vary significantly; you might find a

A typical Allenhurst home of white clapboard, with a spacious porch, a tidy lawn, and an American flag— if it were for sale, the price would be over $1 million. PHOTO: JACK CONOVER

small 1950s home in Cold Spring Harbor for under $100,000, while an impressive young contemporary in Cape May might sell in the neighborhood of $2 million. In the upscale town of Stone Harbor, listings range from the low $300s for a two-bedroom home to more than $3 to $5 million for larger homes facing the Atlantic. In Wildwood, two-bedroom homes can be found for under $100,000, while prices can climb to the million-dollar range for a 5,000-square-foot oceanfront house in North Wildwood.

Real Estate Agencies

A good Realtor can assist you in choosing not only a house or an apartment, but also a community. Most Realtors have at their fingertips information on tax rates, schools, and local services. In general, the most desirable and most expensive communities tend to have the lowest tax rates. This means that it can, in fact, be cheaper to carry a $350,000 home in one of these towns than it is to carry a $200,000 house in another town. The municipalities with the lowest tax rates tend to be small and almost exclusively residential, which keeps their budget expenditures low. They may, for example, share fire departments or schools with larger towns. Let your realtor know what the priorities on your "wish list" are, so that he or she can locate as many choices as possible.

Experienced Realtors will also have on hand information about the school district you're considering as well as lists of houses of worship. In general, we can tell you that there are literally hundreds of the latter, in every faith, throughout the Shore.

Here we've listed some of the active real estate agencies in the various counties. When the agencies have multiple offices, we've given the ones located in coastal Shore communities. Most of these brokers handle not only sales of homes and condominiums, but also seasonal rentals. You'll find many more in the county Yellow Pages.

Monmouth County

Avon Realty
310 Main Street, Avon
(732) 988–8900

Barry Associates
1907 N.J. Highway 35 North, Ocean Township
(732) 531–9001

Brokers 3 Realtors (several offices)
45 Monmouth Road, Ocean Township
(732) 229–2800

Bronson & Blair Agency
53 Main Avenue, Ocean Grove
(732) 774–2080

Burns Bradshaw, Inc.
1508 Main Street, Asbury Park
(732) 776–6844

Clayton & Clayton Realtors
512 Main Avenue, Bay Head
(732) 295–2222

Coldwell Banker Residential Brokerage (several offices)
1123 Third Avenue, Spring Lake
(732) 449–2777

This beautifully restored seashore home on Sunset Avenue in Asbury Park was priced at $625,000 in 2002. PHOTO: JACK CONOVER

Conover Agency (John C.)
300 Main Street, Allenhurst
(732) 531–2500

Diane Turton Agency (several offices)
1216 Third Avenue, Spring Lake
(732) 449–4441

Donaldson Real Estate
617 Seventh Avenue, Asbury Park
(732) 775–0655

Dot Schulze Agency
369 Monmouth Road, West Long Branch
(732) 229–2600

Gloria Nilson Realtors (many offices)
829 West Park Avenue, Ocean Township
(732) 695–0295

Landmark Realtors
290 Norwood Avenue, Deal
(732) 531–1122

Murphy Realty (several offices)
94 Maple Avenue, Red Bank
(732) 842–1978

Prudential New Jersey (multiple offices)
35 Broad Street, Red Bank
(732) 345–9680

Re/Max (several offices)
2517 N.J. Highway 35, Manasquan
(732) 223–6066

Resources Real Estate Company
1070 Ocean Avenue, Suite 2A, Sea Bright
(732) 212–0440

Sonya Grill Real Estate
110 Norwood Avenue, Deal
(732) 531–3322

Weichert Realtors (several offices)
2165 N.J. Highway 35, Sea Girt
(732) 974–1000

Ocean County

Appleby Real Estate
1208 East Central Avenue, Seaside Park
(732) 793–6074

B & K Real Estate
1130 Ocean Avenue, Mantoloking
(732) 899–6460
551 N.J. Highway 35 North, Normandy Beach
(732) 798–7800
217 Main Avenue, Bay Head
(732) 701–1366

Bayshore Agency
1120 Long Beach Boulevard, Ship Bottom
(609) 494–6622

Chadwick Sales & Rentals
133 Strickland Boulevard, Normandy Beach
(732) 830–4220

Chambers Real Estate
1008 Long Beach Boulevard, Surf City
(609) 494–7391

Charles J. Johnson Real Estate
P.O. Box 949, Barnegat
(609) 698–7884

Christopher A. Myers Realty
217 North Bay Avenue, Beach Haven
(609) 492–7000

Coldwell Banker/Riviera Realty
219 Bridge Avenue, Point Pleasant
(732) 295–1400

Coldwell Banker/Sand Dollar Real Estate
6332 Long Beach Boulevard, Harvey Cedars
(609) 494–1130

Fortees, Inc.
231 Ocean Avenue, Point Pleasant Beach
(732) 892–1415

Inman Realty
17th Street and Central Avenue, Barnegat
Light
(609) 494–2776

Island Realty
110 Long Beach Boulevard, Loveladies
(609) 494–8822

Kelley Agency
2200 South Bay Avenue, Beach Haven
(609) 492–9100

Lee Childers Real Estate
701 Grand Central Avenue, Lavallette
(732) 830–2700
N.J. Highway 35 and Sixth Avenue,
Normandy Beach
(732) 793–5500
N.J. Highway 35 and Second Avenue,
Ortley Beach
(732) 793–3800

Oceanside Realty
7700 Long Beach Boulevard, Harvey Cedars
(609) 494–2300

Atlantic County

Bay Harbor Realty
750 Shore Road, Somers Point
(609) 927–2906

Beachfront Realty
3101 Boardwalk, Atlantic City
(609) 345–3918

Blumberg Associates Real Estate
8009 Atlantic Avenue, Margate
(609) 487–8000

Brigantine Realty Group
3312 Brigantine Boulevard, Brigantine
(609) 266–2121

Century 21 O'Donnell
1106 West Brigantine Avenue, Brigantine
(609) 266–7202

Kevin Corcoran Real Estate
4311 Ventnor Avenue, Atlantic City
(609) 348–0077

Marina Realty, Inc.
644 Bay Avenue, Somers Point
(609) 926–9000

Prudential Fox & Roach
9218 Ventnor Avenue, Margate
(609) 822–4200

Re/Max Coastal Properties
1201 West Brigantine Avenue, Brigantine
(609) 266–5122

Valentino Realty
3540 Atlantic Avenue, Atlantic City
(609) 344–2580

Cape May

A. Lewis Purdy Real Estate, Inc.
29th and Dune Drive, Avalon
(609) 967-7800

American Eagle Realty Inc.
150 96th Street, Stone Harbor
(609) 368-3005

Avalon Real Estate
30th and Dune Drive, Avalon
(609) 967-3001

C. A. McCann & Sons, Inc.
4111 Landis Avenue, Sea Isle City
(609) 263-7422

Century 21 Alliance
9600 Third Avenue, Stone Harbor
(609) 368-1440

Chris Clemans & Co., Inc. Realtors
1159 Washington Street, Cape May
(609) 884-3332

Chris Henderson Realty
5201 Ocean Avenue, Wildwood
(609) 729-4888

Coastline Realty
1400 Texas Avenue, Cape May
(609) 884-5005

Dellas Agency
309 Decatur Street, Cape May
(609) 884-3488

E. M. Hanscomb
917 Madison Avenue, Cape May
(609) 884-3330

ERA Calloway Realty
7601 Pacific Avenue, Wildwood Crest
(609) 522-7777

French Real Estate
1 Atlantic Avenue, Ocean City
(609) 399-5454

Goldcoast Realty
1760 Asbury Avenue, Ocean City
(609) 399-2500

Once a beauty parlor, now a splendid loft space, this Asbury Park property was featured in The New York Times *"Style" section; it was on the market for $375,000 in 2002.*

PHOTO: JACK CONOVER

Holly Properties
424 Atlantic Avenue, Ocean City
(609) 399-4422

Marr Agency Real Estate
2121 Asbury Avenue, Ocean City
(609) 399-7036

Oceanside Realty
4500 Atlantic Avenue, Wildwood
(609) 522-3322

Re/Max of Ocean City
3301 Bay Avenue, Ocean City
(609) 398-7100

Senior Services

As New Jersey has a substantial senior population, we've provided some general information numbers below, listed by county. It's worth noting that since Ocean County has one of the largest senior populations in the entire country, it has many age-specific residential communities, assisted-living communities, nursing homes, home-care options, support groups relating to various illnesses, and much more. Call the numbers listed here to learn about the many resources available to seniors in the county.

Information on Medicare and Medicaid can be obtained from local Social Security offices. The Social Security Administration's toll-free number is (800) 772-1213. The Medicare hotline is (800) 638-6833. This office can help you locate your local Medicare Beneficiary Counseling Program and send you the free Medicare handbook. The Web site is www.medicare.gov.

Monmouth County Office on Aging
Hall of Records Annex
One East Main Street, Freehold
(800) 246–9292

Ocean County Office of Senior Services
P.O. Box 2191, Toms River
(800) 668–4899

Atlantic County Division of Intergenerational Services
Shoreview Building, Office 218
101 South Shore Road, Northfield
(888) 426–9243

Cape May County Department of Aging
Social Services Building
4005 U.S. Highway 9 South, Rio Grande
(609) 886–2784

Chambers of Commerce and Business Associations

As you contemplate relocation, area Chambers of Commerce can be a good resource for information about the towns you're considering. They can supply you not only with lists of local businesses, but also with a snapshot of life in general in the communities.

State, Regional, and County Offices

New Jersey State Chamber of Commerce
50 West State Street, Suite 1310, Trenton
(609) 989–7888
www.njchamber.com

Shore Region Tourism Council
P.O. Box 3467, Toms River
(732) 929–2138

Eastern Monmouth Area Chamber of Commerce
170 Broad Street, Red Bank
(732) 741–0055

Greater Ocean County Tourism Advisory Council
101 Hooper Avenue, Toms River
(732) 929–2138

Southern Ocean County Chamber of Commerce
265 West Ninth Street, Ship Bottom
(609) 494–7211, (800) 292–6372

Greater Atlantic City Chamber of Commerce
1125 Atlantic Avenue, Atlantic City
(609) 345–5600

Cape May County Chamber of Commerce
P.O. Box 74, Cape May Court House
(609) 465–7181

Ocean County—Local Associations

Barnegat Chamber of Commerce
P.O. Box 1112, Barnegat
(609) 698–8967

Bay Head Business Association
P.O. Box 135, Bay Head
(800) 4 BAYHED

Beach Haven Business Association
P.O. Box 1224, Beach Haven
(609) 492–5103

Lavallette Business Association
P.O. Box 335, Lavallette
(732) 793–0147

Point Pleasant Area Chamber of Commerce
517A Arnold Avenue, Point Pleasant Beach
(732) 899–2424

Point Pleasant Beach Business Association
P.O. Box 1750, Point Pleasant Beach
(732) 892–5200

Point Pleasant Borough Business Association
P.O. Box 797, Point Pleasant
(732) 892–8211

Seaside Business Association
P.O. Box 98, Seaside Heights
(732) 793–1510, (800) SEASHOR

Cape May County—Local Associations

Greater Ocean City Chamber of Commerce
P.O. Box 157, Ocean City
(609) 399–2629

Greater Wildwood Chamber of Commerce
Schellenger Avenue and the Boardwalk, Wildwood
(609) 729–4000

Hospitals

No matter where you decide to live at the Shore, you'll probably find hospitals within easy reach. If you belong to an HMO, it would be a good idea to get a list of facilities and physicians within your network so you can be certain you'll have acceptable choices here. This is a listing of medical centers at the Shore. There are, of course, thousands of physicians, representing every specialty, as well as facilities that offer holistic healing and alternative medicine.

Monmouth County

Bayshore Community Hospital
727 North Beers Street, Holmdel
(732) 739–5900

CentraState Healthcare System
901 West Main Street, Freehold
(732) 431–2000

Meridian Hospitals Corporation
Jersey Shore Medical Center Division
1945 N.J. Highway 33, Neptune
(732) 775–5500

Meridian Hospitals Corporation
Riverview Medical Center Division
One Riverview Plaza, Red Bank
(732) 741–2700

Monmouth Medical Center
300 Second Avenue, Long Branch
(732) 222–5200

Patterson Army Health Clinic
1075 Stephenson Street, Building 1075, Fort Monmouth
(732) 532–1266

Ocean County

Community Medical Center
99 N.J. Highway 37 West, Toms River
(732) 240–8000

HEALTHSOUTH Rehabilitation Hospital of Toms River
14 Hospital Drive, Toms River
(732) 244–3100

Kimball Medical Center
600 River Avenue, Lakewood
(732) 363–1900

Meridian Hospitals Corporation
Medical Center of Ocean County
425 Jack Martin Boulevard, Brick
(732) 840–2200

Saint Barnabas Behavioral Health Network
1691 U.S. Highway 9, Toms River
(732) 914–1688

Southern Ocean County Hospital
1140 N.J. Highway 72 West, Manahawkin
(609) 597–6011

Atlantic County

Ancora Psychiatric Hospital
202 Spring Garden Road, Ancora
(609) 561–1700

Atlantic City Medical Center
City Division
1925 Pacific Avenue, Atlantic City
(609) 344–4081

Atlantic City Medical Center
Mainland Division
Jimmie Leeds Road, Pomona
(609) 652–1000

Bacharach Institute for Rehabilitation
61 West Jimmie Leeds Road, Pomona
(609) 652–7000

Shore Memorial Hospital
One East New York Avenue, Somers Point
(609) 653–3500

William B. Kessler Memorial Hospital
600 South White Horse Pike, Hammonton
(609) 561–6700

Cape May County

Burdette Tomlin Memorial Hospital
2 Stone Harbor Boulevard, Cape May Court
House
(609) 463–2000

Motor Vehicle Information

If you're going to live at the Shore, you'll
need to register your car and get a New Jersey driver's license. You can't get phone
numbers for individual stations—the
Department of Motor Vehicles doesn't
want you distracting their busy employees—but the general information numbers
and the list of locations provided here will
help you start the process.

General Information
(609) 588–3540, (888) 486–3339 toll free in
New Jersey

Monmouth County DMV
(732) 308–3713

> Asbury Park
> 1010 Comstock Street

> Eatontown
> N.J. Highway 36, east of N.J. Highway 35

> Freehold
> Poets Square Shopping Plaza, Kozloski
>   Road

> Freehold
> 801 Okerson Road

> Matawan
> N.J. Highway 34 and Broad Street

Ocean County DMV
(732) 341–9700, ext. 7513 or 7514

> Lakewood
> 1195 N.J. Highway 70, Store 9

> Manahawkin
> Ocean County Resource Center,
>   Recovery Road

> Miller Air Park
> Highway 530, Berkeley Township

> Toms River
> Village Square Plaza, 1861 Hooper
>   Avenue

Atlantic County DMV
(609) 645–5945

> Cardiff
> Cardiff Fashion Center, 6702 Black
>   Horse Pike

> Mays Landing
> Hamilton Industrial Park, 1477 19th
>   Street

Cape May County DMV
(609) 465–9001, ext. 11 or 13

Cape May Court House
6 West Shellbay Avenue

Rio Grande
1500 N.J. Highway 47 South

Libraries

Whichever community you choose, your local and branch libraries will be valuable resources, not simply for books and audio and video tapes, but also for information about your new home. The libraries will have such helpful items as all New Jersey telephone books and guides to government agencies and online services in your area.

The library system is much larger than these listings; we've included only the major branches and libraries in or near the Shore towns covered in this book.

Monmouth County

Brielle Library
610 South Street, Brielle
(732) 528–9381

Eastern Branch
N.J. Highway 35, Shrewsbury
(732) 842–5995

Headquarters Library
125 Symmes Drive, Manalapan
(732) 431–7220

Interlaken Library
100 Grassmere Avenue, Interlaken
(732) 531–7405

Manasquan Library
55 Broad Street, Manasquan
(732) 223–1503

Monmouth Beach Library
18 Willow Avenue, Monmouth Beach
(732) 229–1187

Ocean Township Library
Monmouth and Deal Roads, Oakhurst
(732) 531–5092

Sea Bright Library
1097 Ocean Avenue, Sea Bright
(732) 758–9554

Sea Girt Library
Railroad Station at the Plaza, Sea Girt
(732) 449–1099

West Long Branch Library
95 Poplar Avenue, West Long Branch
(732) 222–5993

Ocean County

Barnegat Branch
112 Burr Street, Barnegat
(609) 698–3331

Bay Head Reading Center
136 Meadow Avenue, Bay Head
(732) 892–0662

Bishop Building (New Jersey Reference Collection)
Next to Toms River Branch, 101 Washington Street, Toms River
(732) 349–6200, ext. 859

Island Heights Branch
Summit and Central Avenues, Island Heights
(732) 270–6266

Little Egg Harbor Branch
290 Mathistown Road, Little Egg Harbor
(609) 294–1197

Long Beach Island Branch
217 South Central Avenue, Surf City
(609) 494–2480

Point Pleasant Beach Branch
710 McLean Avenue, Point Pleasant Beach
(732) 892–4575

Point Pleasant Boro Branch
834 Beaver Dam Road, Point Pleasant
(732) 295–1555

Toms River Branch
101 Washington Street, Toms River
(732) 349–6200

Upper Shores Branch
112 Jersey City Avenue, Lavallette
(732) 793–3996

Atlantic County

In addition to the branches listed below, the Atlantic County Library system has a bookmobile program and a Books-By-Mail service (609-646-8699), which is basically a free lending library brought right to your own mailbox. You don't even pay postage. Check the Web site at www.aclink.org/ACL/homepage.htm for information.

Brigantine Branch
201 15th Street South, Brigantine
(609) 266–0110

Egg Harbor Township Branch
1 Swift Avenue, Egg Harbor Township
(609) 927–8664

Galloway Township Branch
306 East Jimmie Leeds Road, Galloway
(609) 652–2352

Hammonton Branch
451 South Egg Harbor Road, Hammonton
(609) 561–2264

Longport Branch
2305 Atlantic Avenue, Longport
(609) 487–0272

Mays Landing Branch and Administrative Offices
40 Farragut Avenue, Mays Landing
(609) 625–2776

Pleasantville Branch
810 South Main Street, Pleasantville
(609) 641–1778

Somers Point Branch
801 Shore Road, Somers Point
(609) 927–7113

Ventnor Branch
6500 Atlantic Avenue, Ventnor City
(609) 823–4614

Cape May County

In addition to the libraries listed here, Cape May County has an active and extensive bookmobile program. Call the county library for information or check its Web site (see below).

Avalon Public Library
251 26th Street, Avalon
(609) 967–4010

Cape May City Public Library
Ocean and Hughes Avenues, Cape May
(609) 884–9568

Cape May County Library
30 West Mechanic Street, Cape May Court House
(609) 463–6350
www.cape-may.county.lib.nj.us

Lower Cape Branch
2600 Bayshore Road, Villas
(609) 886–8999

Sea Isle City Public Library
125 John F. Kennedy Boulevard, Sea Isle City
(609) 263–8485

Stone Harbor Public Library
9508 Second Avenue, Stone Harbor
(609) 368–6809

Upper Cape Branch
2050 Highway 631, Petersburg
(609) 628–2607

Wildwood Crest Public Library
6301 Ocean Avenue, Wildwood Crest
(609) 522–0564

Welcome Centers

When arriving at the Shore by car, as most visitors do, you can stop at one of these Welcome Centers to pick up maps, brochures, local newspapers, and other useful tourist information.

Atlantic County

Atlantic City
Atlantic City Expressway, Mile Marker 3.5,
Atlantic City
(609) 383–2727

Atlantic City Expressway, Mile Marker 21,
Hammonton
(609) 965–6316

Cape May County

Ocean View
Garden State Parkway South, Mile Marker 18.3
(609) 624–0918

Media

When it comes to television, radio stations, and newpapers, New Jersey is divided into two spheres of influence; the northern part of the state gets New York stations and New York newspapers, while the southern counties get Philadelphia stations and newspapers. This creates a cultural schism of sorts; while people in Monmouth County are split on the important questions of Mets vs. Yankees and Jets vs. Giants, walk into a pub down in the Atlantic City area and you'll find the place filled with avid Phillies and Eagles fans. "How can people with such differing views share a state?" you may well ask. Well, it's a big enough state, and Ocean County turns out to be sort of a buffer zone, where some people are more New York–oriented, some receive Philadelphia television stations, and most are not interested in either city in the least.

In Monmouth County, many people look to *The New York Times* for national news; many also read the *New York Post*, the *New York Daily News*, the *Newark Star-Ledger*, and the *Wall Street Journal*, which are widely distributed throughout the Shore area. In Atlantic and Cape May Counties, the *Philadelphia Inquirer* and the *Philadelphia Daily News* are widely read.

Daily Newspapers

Asbury Park Press
3601 N.J. Highway 66, Neptune
(732) 922–6000
www.app.com

The *Asbury Park Press,* now owned by Gannett, is the leading newspaper in Monmouth and Ocean Counties; it is also the second-largest paper in the state. It's a very good source of information on local news, cultural events, festivals, movies, and shopping. It has an extensive Sunday real estate section, with listings for rentals, both seasonal and year-round. It also has a very dedicated fishing columnist who keeps tabs on who caught what and where.

Ocean County Observer
8 Robbins Street, Toms River
(732) 349–3000

The *Ocean County Observer* focuses mainly on the happenings in Ocean County, covering local news, high school sports, and the like.

The Press of Atlantic City
1000 West Washington Avenue, Pleasantville
(609) 272–7266
www.pressofatlanticcity.com

The Press of Atlantic City is the biggest paper in South Jersey, and it's the place to look for information on movies, restaurants, real estate, and cultural events in Atlantic and Cape May Counties, including who's appearing at the casinos. Though it covers national news, local events tend to get top billing.

Weeklies

The Islander
3601 N.J. Highway 66, Neptune
(732) 922–6000
www.injersey.com/islander

This free weekly paper is put out by Gannett, which also publishes the *Asbury Park Press.* It is full of listings for music and comedy clubs in Monmouth and Ocean Counties, and also has articles on fishing, boating, and diverse Shore happenings.

The Asbury Park Press *moved out of Asbury Park some years ago. Its present headquarters are on Highway 66 in Neptune.* PHOTO: ANDREW HASSARD

The Two River Times
264 Broad Street, Red Bank
(732) 219–5788
www.tworivertimes.net

Though Geraldo Rivera no longer lives in the Middletown estate he shared with ex-wife, CeeCee, he still owns *The Two River Times* and expresses his worldview in weekly editorials. People buy it to read its extensive coverage of social events in the affluent towns of Rumson, Navesink, and Fair Haven.

triCity News
601 Bangs Avenue, Asbury Park
(732) 897–9779

On the other end of the social spectrum from *The Two River Times* is the *triCity News,* a homegrown paper that covers Asbury Park, Long Branch, and Red Bank.

With its haphazard grammar and spelling, this paper is a huge cheerleader for those three cities, extolling in particular the funky charms of Asbury Park. The paper skewers politicians, developers, and just about anyone who stands in the way of Asbury's revival. As for Red Bank, well, since that's already "Hip City," *triCity* badgers its powers that be about such issues as rising rents and parking needs.

More Weeklies

There are dozens of little papers that serve the communities along the Shore in a small-town way that the big daily newspapers do not. They may report stories considered too small by the major papers, following local issues very closely, and they generally have more of a hometown quality. They may carry coupons or special offers from local advertisers: restaurants, hairdressers, car washes, and the like. You'll find that these papers focus on the towns in which they're published and the areas nearby.

Monmouth County

Atlanticville and **The Hub**
659 Broadway, Long Branch
(732) 870–6070

The Coaster
1011 Main Street, Asbury Park
(732) 775–3010

The Coast Star
13 Broad Street, Manasquan
(732) 223–0076

The Courier
Bayshore Press Inc., Middletown
(732) 957–0070

Ocean Grove & Neptune Times
41 Pilgrim Pathway, Ocean Grove
(732) 775-0007

Ocean County

Advance News
2048 N.J. Highway 37 West, Lakehurst
(732) 657–8936

The Banner
Barnegat
(609) 978–5500

The Beachcomber, The Leader, and The Sandpaper
1816 Long Beach Boulevard, Surf City
(609) 494–5900

Currents (seasonal)
2101 Central Avenue, Ship Bottom
(609) 494–5556

Ocean County Journal
Waretown
(609) 660–1900

Ocean Star
421 River Avenue, Point Pleasant Beach
(732) 899–7606

Times Beacon Newspapers
345 East Bay Avenue, Manahawkin
(609) 978–4531
This company publishes the *Beach Haven*

Times, *The Beacon,* the *Lacey Beacon,* the *Summer Times Islander,* and the *Tuckerton Beacon.*

Atlantic and Cape May Counties

Cape May County Gazette
North Wildwood
(609) 522–3423
www.catamaranmedia.com

Cape May County Herald
1508 Highway 47 South, Rio Grande
(609) 886–8600
www.capemaycountyherald.com

Cape May Star and Wave
600 Park Boulevard, Unit 5, West Cape May
(609) 884–3466

Gazette/Sandpaper Newspapers
109 34th Street, Ocean City
(609) 398–7964

The Hammonton Gazette
Hammonton
(609) 704–1939
www.hammontongazette.com

Ocean City Sentinel
112 East Eighth Street, Ocean City
(609) 399-5411

Wildwood Leader
North Wildwood
(609) 522–3423
www.catamaranmedia.com

Special Interest Newspapers

Doo Wopolis Times
3501 Boardwalk, Wildwood
(609) 729–4000
www.doowopusa.org

Published by the Doo Wop Preservation League of Wildwood, the *Doo Wopolis Times* is devoted to the 1950s architecture so prevalent in that town.

Golfer's Tee Times
Northfield
(609) 645–3621
www.news.golfsurfer.com/gtt

Golfer's Tee Times is a free paper covering golf in South Jersey. Read it to find out about new courses, bargain rates, charity tournaments, and more. This fine publication also features the work of Nina Africano, one of the authors of this guide.

The Italian Newspaper
1100 Jackson Street, Philadelphia, PA
(215) 336–0657
italiannewspaper@hotmail.com

Although it's published in Philly, *The Italian Newspaper* is widely supported by and distributed in Italian restaurants in the Atlantic City area.

Whoot!
214 East Verona Boulevard, Pleasantville
(609) 646–4848
www.whoot.com

This free weekly paper has extensive listings of music clubs and other happenings in Atlantic and Cape May Counties, including who's appearing at the casinos. You can pick it up almost everywhere.

Magazines

The Jersey Golfer
Westfield
(908) 233–9998

The Jersey Golfer is a free quarterly golf magazine, available at local clubs, that covers new golf courses, tournaments, and other golf news in the Garden State. It features the work of Nina Africano, an author of this book.

JerseyStyle Magazine
819A Chestnut Avenue, Trenton
(877) NJ STYLE
www.jerseystyle.com

JerseyStyle is a free monthly magazine available in bar and restaurant waiting areas. It covers the music scene as well as other happenings in the worlds of the arts and theater throughout the state.

New Jersey Bride Magazine
55 Park Place, Morristown
(973) 539–8230
www.newjerseybride.com

If you're planning a Shore wedding, have a look at *New Jersey Bride*. The content is pretty typical of bridal magazines, but it will help you locate stores and services here in the Garden State.

New Jersey Life
287 South Main Street, Suite 9, Lambertville
(609) 397–6347
www.newjerseylife.com

New Jersey Life is also a lifestyle magazine, with articles on food, travel, weddings, and other issues of interest to residents.

New Jersey Monthly
55 Park Place, Morristown
(973) 539–8230
www.njmonthly.com

With its emphasis on real estate, restaurants, spas, and high-end consumer issues, *New Jersey Monthly* resembles a *New York Magazine* for the suburbs. The magazine frequently runs lists like "Great Getaways," "Best Doctors," and so on, which can be interesting and possibly helpful if you're new to the state.

New Jersey Reporter
36 West Lafayette Street, Trenton
(609) 392–2003
www.njreporter.org

New Jersey Reporter is a bimonthly magazine that provides independent research and analysis of issues like the budget, charter schools, and local elections.

New Jersey Savvy Living
Short Hills
(973) 379–7749
www.savvyliving.com

New Jersey Savvy Living is a free consumer/lifestyle magazine. It's mailed to selected households in 10 northern and central counties, with a focus on affluent communities like Rumson and Deal. If you'd like to receive the magazine, call and ask to be put on their mailing list. The content is less dense than *New Jersey Monthly*'s and heavy on advertising, but you may find articles of interest on food, wine, and home decor.

Night & Day
Spring Lake
(732) 974-0047
www.nightanddayonline.com

Night & Day is a free magazine printed on newspaper stock that covers the music and club scene in Monmouth County, with listings of who's appearing where. It's available in bars and restaurants and comes out weekly in the summer and monthly in the off-season (as far as we can tell).

Shorecast
Starfish Media/South Jersey Publishing Co.
1000 West Washington Avenue, Pleasantville
(609) 272–7900, (888) AC VISIT
www.shorecast.com

Shorecast is a free monthly magazine focusing on happenings in the Atlantic City area, especially in the casinos. It also carries ads and coupons for restaurants and other tourist attractions.

Weird N.J.
www.weirdnj.com

This online magazine specializes in ghosts and haunted places in the state and such local legends as the Jersey Devil.

Television

The northern Shore communities receive the New York City stations, while the southern Shore gets broadcasting from Philadelphia. Here are some local stations that might be new to you.

CN8 Comcast Cable Channel 8
Comcast Cablevision of Monmouth County, Inc.
403 South Street, Eatontown
(732) 542–8107

News12NJ Channel 12 on Cablevision, Channel 42 on Comcast
News 12 New Jersey Monmouth County Bureau
450 Raritan Center Parkway, Edison
(732) 417-9412

NJN New Jersey Public Television and Radio
WNJB-TV Channel 58, New Brunswick
WNJS-TV Channel 23, Camden
WNJM-TV Channel 50, Montclair
WNJT-TV Channel 52, Trenton
50 Stockton Street, Trenton
(609) 777–5000
www.njn.net

WMGM-TV Channel 40 (NBC affiliate)
1601 New Road, Linwood
(609) 927–4440

WNJU-TV Channel 47, Telemundo Spanish Television
47 Industrial Avenue, Teterboro
(201) 288–5550

WPVI-TV Channel 6 (ABC affiliate)
9701 Ventnor Avenue, Margate
(609) 823–1137, (609) 344–6661
www.wpvi.com

WWOR-TV Channel 9 (UPN affiliate)
9 Broadcast Plaza, Secaucus
(202) 348–0009

Cable TV Companies

While many homeowners may choose to install a satellite dish, for summer people the practical solution to television reception problems is clearly cable TV. Cable companies enjoy a mini-monopoly in the areas that they serve, so contact the provider in your area.

Cablevision of Hamilton
(609) 586–2288

Cablevision of Monmouth
(732) 681–8222

Comcast Atlantic County
(609) 272–1764

Comcast Cablevision of Monmouth County, Inc.
(732) 542–8107

Comcast Cablevision of Ocean County, Inc.
(732) 920–6643

Comcast Cape May County
(609) 522–9265

Shore Radio Stations

Adult Contemporary

WBBO 90.5

WBNJ 93.1 FM, Atlantic City

WCZT 94.3 FM "The Coast," Cape May Court House

WKOE 106.3 FM, Northfield

WOBM 92.7 FM, Toms River

WOBM 1160 AM, Howell

WTTH 96.1 FM, Margate

Classical

WWFM 89.1 FM, Trenton

WWNJ 91.1 FM, Dover Township

Country

WPUR 107.3 FM "Cat Country," Northfield

WWZY 107.1 FM, Long Branch

Jazz

WBGO 88.3 FM, Newark

WSAX 102.3 FM, Atlantic City

News, Talk, Sports

WCTC 1450 AM, New Brunswick

WFPG 1450 AM, Atlantic City

WKXW 101.5 FM, also 97.3 FM, Linwood

WOND 1400 AM, Linwood

WRAT sponsors many area music events, where they often give away prizes. Look for the Rat Van, seen here in front of the Rat's Belmar broadcast facility. PHOTO: ANDREW HASSARD

Oldies

WCMC 1230 AM, Wildwood

WJRZ 100.1 AM, Manahawkin

WKTU 98.3 FM "Kool 98," Linwood

WMID 1340 AM, Atlantic City

WMID 99.3 FM, Atlantic City

WPDQ 89.7 FM, Howell

WTRR 89.3 FM

Public and College Stations

WBJB 90.5 FM, Brookdale Community College, Lincroft

WMCX 88.9 FM, Monmouth University, West Long Branch

WNJM 89.9 FM, Manahawkin

WNJN 89.7 FM, Atlantic City

WNJZ 90.3 FM, Cape May Court House

Religious

WFNN 106.7 FM, Cape May Court House

WJNN 106.7 FM, Green Creek

WYRS 90.7 FM, Manahawkin

Rock

B985 98.5 FM, Manahawkin

WAYV 95.1 FM, Atlantic City

WFPG 1450 AM, Northfield

WFPG 96.9 FM, Northfield

WHTG 1410 AM, Asbury Park

WHTG 106.3 FM, Asbury Park

WJLK 94.3 FM, Point Pleasant

WJSE 102.7 FM, Somers Point

WMGM 103.7 FM "The Shark," Linwood

WRAT 95.9 FM "The Rat," South Belmar

WWZK 98.7 FM, Cape May

WZXL 100.7 FM, Wildwood

Index

About the Authors

Lillian Africano

For Proust it was madeleines. For Lillian Africano, it's boardwalk food: the mingled aromas of cotton candy, french fries, and sausage and peppers. Just one whiff evokes child-

hood memories of sultry summer evenings strolling the boards, riding the carousel, playing a game of chance—and hoping against hope that her number would win a painted doll or a stuffed teddy bear.

The Shore has changed since Lillian's childhood, but so much that is wonderful remains the same: the exhilarating briny smell of the sea; the ocean itself, cleaner now than it has been for years; the miles of sand, enhanced by the Army Corps of Engineers replenishment program; the pleasures of a morning run on an empty beach; the discovery of a perfect seashell.

During her long and productive career, Lillian Africano has traveled the four corners of the globe. She has written 16 books, including a guide to the Middle East, as well as several best-selling novels. She has penned hundreds of magazine articles on everything from how to find the cheapest airfare to exploring Antarctica. But though her love of travel has taken her to many exotic destinations, Lillian always comes back to her first love: the Jersey Shore.

In this book, Lillian shares her favorite places and things with you.

Nina Africano

Nina Africano has been a "benny" (summer resident) since the age of two, when her parents rented a house in Long Branch. Formative childhood years spent searching for

shells and sea glass proved to be perfect training for picking up trash in the Clean Ocean Action Committee's Beach Sweeps, which have helped restore the Shore to its true beauty.

Like most people who live at the Shore, Nina seems to spend less time at the beach now than she did when she just came down on weekends. But that's okay, since the best place to work on your tan is at Hominy Hill Golf Course. Nina's work has appeared in *Golf for Women, Golf Digest,* the *Asbury Park Press, The Jersey Golfer,* and *Golfer's Tee Times.* She has spent countless hours personally double-checking facts at Shore golf courses like Seaview Marriott and Blue Heron Pines. Some people might think living at the Shore is just one long day at the beach. It isn't. It's a day at the links.